Pakistan

Pakistan

A POLITICAL STUDY

BY

KEITH CALLARD

*Associate Professor of Political Science,
McGill University*

*Issued in co-operation with the
Institute of Pacific Relations*

NEW YORK
THE MACMILLAN COMPANY

All Rights Reserved

This book is copyright under the Berne Convention. Apart from any fair dealing for the purposes of private study, research, criticism or review, as permitted under the Copyright Act 1956, no portion may be reproduced by any process without written permission. Enquiry should be made to the publishers.

© George Allen & Unwin Ltd, 1957

PRINTED IN GREAT BRITAIN

INTRODUCTION

DURING the decade following the end of World War II, many countries which had previously been ruled by the nations of Western Europe obtained independence. They proceeded from a state of tutelage to full self-government in a matter of two or three years. There was no time for the slow growth of political institutions such as had occurred in Europe or America.

The political ideas of these countries are based largely on what they had learned from their colonial masters. These ideas were coloured for them by the experience gathered in the struggle for independence. They had learned to criticize the institutions of Western democracy and, in part, to manipulate those institutions with a view to the embarrassment of their rulers. But they had no alternative system of government to put in the place of parliamentary democracy. Consequently these states have formed their constitutions after the general pattern of Britain and Western Europe, and they are trying to operate a system that had its origins in a vastly different social and political environment.

Pakistan is one of those countries. It is of particular interest, because it was brought into being only indirectly as the result of the demand of an Asian people to terminate European domination. It became an independent state because the Muslims of India were not prepared to accept independence from British rule within the framework of a united India, where the Hindus would be in a majority. This factor adds a feature to the politics of Pakistan that is not present in the other newly freed Asian states.

The period from 1947 to 1957 has been one of change and uncertainty. There have been few fixed ideas and few institutions whose validity has not been open to question. In Pakistan political parties have waxed, waned and suffered eclipse. Political leaders have argued, intrigued and reduced each other to impotence. Men of religion have laid claim to complete authority and have achieved almost none. In the meanwhile the state has been run

Pakistan

largely by the Civil Service, backed by the Army, which has carried on much as it did before independence.

This is the study of a people in search of a national identity. Uncertainty and conflict have lain within the mind of each citizen, and this confusion has been reflected in the public life of the country. Pakistanis are a people united by a common will to be a nation, but they do not yet know what kind of a nation they want to be.

The method adopted in this book has been to discuss certain predominant themes in the brief history and present experience of Pakistan. Its principal concern lies within the boundaries of the country, in observing the efforts of a new state to establish itself and to define its forms and basic principles. No state can now afford to disregard its neighbours and the rest of the world. A brief account of Pakistan's view of international affairs has therefore been provided in Chapter X, though this relies more heavily on secondary sources than do other chapters of this book.

The author wishes to record his obligation to the Rockefeller Foundation and to McGill University, which made it possible for him to pay two prolonged visits to Pakistan. The courtesy, generous assistance and encouragement of many persons in Pakistan, England and North America have contributed beyond measure to any value that this study may possess. To each of them the author is deeply grateful.

Montreal
February 1957

A NOTE ON PAKISTANI NAMES

UNFORTUNATELY there is no generally accepted scheme of transliteration of Pakistani names into roman script. There are at least five common variants of the English spelling of Muhammad. The name of the same individual may be spelled in several different ways in different publications. All that the author has attempted is to choose one commonly used spelling of the name of each person and adhere to that version throughout. A comparable difficulty arises in the order in which the several names of an individual are placed, and in the choice of one or more of those names as 'key names,' corresponding to an English surname. Thus the Pirzada Abdus Sattar Abdur Rahman appears sometimes simply as Pirzada or Abdus Sattar Pirzada. There is no logic to be found in this and, within limits, an arbitrary choice has to be made. Apologies are therefore due to any individual who finds that his name is given in a manner that he himself does not approve.

The index has been compiled as though the key name (e.g. Pirzada) were, in fact, a surname. Where confusion seemed likely, a second index entry has been listed.

CONTENTS

INTRODUCTION *page* 5

I	The Political Background	11
II	The Decline of the Muslim League	34
III	The Constituent Assembly	77

    I *Origin and Composition*
    II *Constitutional Proposals, 1949–54*
    III *The Interim Constitution, 1947–56*
    IV *The Federal Legislature*
    V *The Second Constituent Assembly*

IV	Cabinet Government	124
V	The Federal Structure	155

    I *The Centre and the Units*
    II *The Special Case of East Pakistan*
    III *The Unification of West Pakistan*

VI	Islam and Politics	194
VII	The Minorities	232
VIII	The Citizen and the State	266
IX	The Public Services	284
X	Pakistan and the World	302
XI	Prospect	325

APPENDIX

I	The Constitution (Extracts and Summary)	330
II	Central and Provincial Governments	342
III	Select Bibliography	347

GLOSSARY

INDEX

CHAPTER I

The Political Background

PAKISTAN was created to be the state organization of the Muslim nation of the Indian sub-continent. It does not possess a history of national unity, it has no common language nor uniform culture, and it is neither a geographical nor an economic unit. The force behind its establishment was based very largely on a feeling of insecurity. As early as 1888 Sir Syed Ahmed had speculated on a possible struggle for power in the event of a transfer of sovereignty to Indian hands.

'Is it possible that under these circumstances two nations—the Mohammedan and Hindu—could sit on the same throne and remain equal in power? Most certainly not. It is necessary that one of them should conquer the other and thrust it down. To hope that both could remain equal is to desire the impossible and the inconceivable.'[1]

This question was largely academic at the time of its posing, but it contains within it the seeds of Pakistan. For Sir Syed made the major assertion that there were two nations in India based not upon geography but upon religion and all that flows from it. This is a claim that the Indian nationalist could never concede and the Western observer could scarcely understand. Yet it is the only essential point behind the movement that led to Pakistan.

In their own view, Muslims are those who have entered the service of God according to the path revealed by His Prophet, Muhammad. The service of God is the whole duty of man. Thus it is not wrong to talk of the separation of religion and politics, it is meaningless. Muhammad was prince as well as prophet and he commanded the faithful in the field and led them to victory over the idolaters. He was no tribal leader or the ruler of a single

[1] Cited in Richard Symonds, *The Making of Pakistan* (London, 3rd ed., 1951), p. 31.

city, for he had to make war on his own people, the Qureysh, and against his own city, Mecca. His authority was, and is yet, binding upon all who recognize the sovereignty of Allah. They are the people (*millat*) of God, of the Prophet and of the Quran. In ideal terms, there can be only one nation of true believers and it embraces all Muslims. Some Indian Muslims refused to espouse the cause of Pakistan because it represented less than this political unity based on faith. But the majority, while hoping for world Muslim unity, concentrated upon the fact that a united India, with three Hindus for every Muslim, would carry them much farther from an Islamic way of life.

When the 'two-nation theory' is accepted the rest of the argument for Pakistan follows easily. Since the Muslim nation is heavily outnumbered in the sub-continent, the introduction of democracy along Western lines must inevitably involve the establishment of Hindu *raj* for the whole country. A permanent minority enjoys rights only on sufferance of the majority and this was a condition the Muslims resolved never to accept. The Indian nationalist leaders, including some Muslims, might talk of secular equality, but the Muslim reply was that firstly, they distrusted the reality of secularism among the majority of the Hindus, and secondly, that they themselves had no wish for a secular state. Islam was their way of life in public affairs as in private, and they were not prepared to renounce it merely because some Hindus professed a willingness to make a like sacrifice.

Before 1940 Muslim opinion had not grasped the possibility that British rule was rapidly approaching its end. Political activity was therefore directed largely toward building defences against rising Hindu influence. Muslim leaders were opposed to the continuance of British rule, but before they would commit themselves to drastic action they wanted to know what would replace it. The result was a policy that was a double negative—against the Congress before being against the British—and its consequence was qualified support for the existing regime. To the nationalist, the events of 1937–47 revealed that the day of self-rule could not long be delayed; to the Muslim they showed that a crisis was at hand at which all might well be lost.

The Political Background

This was no period to argue about the form of the future state or the policies it would pursue. The history of the movement toward Pakistan from 1940-47 was one of increasing momentum toward a single, fixed goal. Unity was made easier to preserve, since fear spurred from behind and a glorious vision beckoned from ahead. No other loyalty to person or principle was to be allowed to stand in the way of Pakistan. Sir Firoz Khan Noon, who had in recent years been a member of the Viceroy's Executive Council and High Commissioner for India in London, said in April 1946:

> 'If the Hindus give us Pakistan and freedom, then the Hindus are our best friends. If the British give it to us then the British are our best friends. But if neither will give it to us, then Russia is our best friend.'[1]

Fiat Pakistan *ruat coelum!*

Sceptics and opponents of Pakistan might raise difficulties. They asked, What would be the territorial boundaries of the new state? A grouping of contiguous Muslim majority areas would surely produce a monstrosity from the viewpoint of defence and communications. What would be the fate of the minorities left on the 'wrong' sides of the border? What chance would Pakistan have of economic survival or hope of prosperity? Muslim partisans did not seriously attempt to answer these questions. They countered by simple assertions: We, the Muslims of India, are a nation and we must and will have our own state. Give us that state and we will show you that it will work.

In 1947 that state was created and Pakistanis had to turn to the almost impossible task of making it work. Pakistan was born in chaos. Before it came into existence, authority in undivided India was beginning to disintegrate. British forces and those under British command found that their control and influence diminished as independence approached. Law and order began to give way to murder, looting and arson. Millions of people over wide areas of the sub-continent began to fear for their lives.

[1] Cited in A. B. Rajput, *The Muslim League Yesterday and Today* (Lahore, 1948), p. 109.

Pakistan

Whole communities had to contemplate leaving the districts in which they had lived in peace for generations and migrating with all the possessions they could carry. In the weeks immediately following partition the situation deteriorated and over vast areas law and order were preserved only within range of the rifles of the armed forces. Endless streams of refugees choked the roads and overcrowded the trains, where they were ambushed and slaughtered. No one will ever know the full total of the dead but estimates of the number of refugees run as high as twelve million.[1]

The new India suffered in the transition but Pakistan was virtually shattered. India inherited a working federal capital with the majority of the cabinet and other public servants willing to continue at their posts. Pakistan had to create a new capital and a new government. India had large areas which were substantially untouched by partition; the Central Provinces, Madras, Mysore, Bombay and other large units were preserved from chaos. In Pakistan there were few such areas of relative tranquillity. Pakistan consisted of half of Bengal, without its capital and major city; half of the Punjab where the capital city was devastated by fire and riot. These were Muslim majority provinces but in neither was there at partition a pro-Pakistan provincial government anxious to do all in its power to establish the speedy and firm control of the new state. There were also the North-West Frontier Province, with a government hostile to Pakistan, and Sind where no government could ever be regarded as stable and whose commerce and industry were largely in the hands of non-Muslims. Somehow through those early months Pakistan survived, and it is impossible to deny that this simple fact was a major achievement.

There were those in India (and elsewhere) who had disbelieved the possibility of the survival of Pakistan even under favourable conditions. And actual conditions were far from favourable. Many nationalists had spent their political lives in the struggle for a strong, united and free India. They accepted Pakistan with reluctance because the alternative was civil war.

[1] Richard Symonds, *op. cit.*, p. 83.

The Political Background

And pro-Pakistanis had looked upon the Hindu majority in India as hostile to their religion and their aspirations. Thus even before partition, Pakistan and India had grounds for mutual suspicion and dislike. The events of the second half of 1947 transformed mistrust into bitter hatred founded on fear and deepened by blood and cruelty. Hundreds of thousands of Indians and Pakistanis learned that their friends, relatives and co-religionists on 'the other side' had been killed, abducted or tortured and totally stripped of their possessions. Millions of refugees crossed the new frontiers, bringing with them hysterical tales of unimaginable barbarity and a frenzied will for revenge. Under any circumstances it would have been too much to expect that initial relations between the two Dominions should have been inspired by goodwill and the desire for mutual co-operation. In fact relations degenerated to the point where war seemed perilously close.

Underlying all other political events in Pakistan in the early years has been the problem of relations with India. This has dominated foreign affairs, defence and economic policy and has lain behind many of the moves of internal politics.

In large measure Pakistani feeling toward India has been a continuation of the political struggle before partition. Leaders of the Pakistan movement had spent most of their political lives in fighting against the Congress party. After independence they saw their former political opponents holding power in a neighbouring country, but the habit of criticism could not be effaced by the drawing of a new boundary. The struggle for independence had been designed to convince the Congress politicians and the world outside of the validity of the two-nation theory which is the justification for partition. Ten years after independence Pakistan is still concerned with proving the fact of Muslim nationhood. For while Indian leaders have conceded the fact of Pakistan they have never admitted the validity of the two-nation theory. The Congress agreed to partition because this was preferable to the coercion of 90,000,000 Muslims and possible civil war, but this did not imply the abandonment of the belief that a large Muslim minority could live in peace and freedom in a politically secular united India.

Pakistan

It is because of this ideological conflict that Kashmir is of such passionate importance to both parties. Kashmir is a Muslim majority area and, if the two-nation theory is valid, can rightly belong only to Pakistan. For India the successful and voluntary integration of Kashmir offers the chance to demonstrate the powers of nationalist sentiment to overcome in the political sphere the separatist urge of religion.

The issue in Kashmir is not solely one of prestige and sentiment. The question of power is also involved, for the occupier of Kashmir has outflanked the already weak natural defences of West Pakistan. Further, Kashmir contains the headwaters or upper reaches of two of the rivers that serve to irrigate the Punjab. Above all, Pakistanis feel humiliated and outraged that, as they see it, India by a combination of force and legal sophistry has triumphed in Hyderabad and Junagadh[1] and Kashmir. It has become an article of faith in Pakistan that Kashmir is rightfully hers and that no other solution can be tolerated.

There have been three main areas of dispute with India and in each instance the issue is of relatively much greater importance to Pakistan than to India. The most bitter conflict, which at one time resulted in collision between the armies of the two countries, has been Kashmir. The second dispute is that over the control of the Punjab canal waters. India has the power to devastate large areas of the Punjab (Pakistan) by cutting off supplies of water that run through Indian territory. As a sign of her power, in 1948 India totally diverted for some weeks the water that would normally have flowed into a part of the Pakistan canal system. It is one of the many tragedies of partition that the Indus basin cannot now be developed to give anywhere near the maximum benefit to its inhabitants because of an arbitrary political frontier that has been drawn through the centre of the area.

Equally regrettable are the consequences of the division of the economic unity of the sub-continent. The great commercial and industrial centres of united India were Calcutta, Bombay and Madras, and none of these fell to Pakistan. There was one system

[1] A small princely state whose ruler tried to accede to Pakistan but which was occupied by Indian forces. See below, p. 305.

The Political Background

of transportation, of banking and currency. Overnight a new economic nation had to be created and made viable. This was the third field in which India and Pakistan found themselves in conflict. There was deadlock over the distribution of the assets of the two countries and the corresponding division of the burden of the national debt. When the pound was devalued in 1949 the Indian rupee followed, but the Pakistani rupee did not change until 1955. For many months the Indian government refused to recognize this decision and trade came virtually to a standstill.

Normal commercial relations between the two states are affected by the failure to reach an agreement concerning the disposition of evacuee property. The millions of refugees who crossed the borders of the new states left behind land and buildings and commercial and industrial property. Often a whole village or section of a town was abandoned and left unprotected. It was important for both sides that resources and essential services should not be left idle, so tenants were installed in the vacant property while title passed to the care of judicial custodians. In many instances the original owners died and documentary titles as well as records of loans and mortgages were incomplete or missing. In any event the law relating to land tenure has always presented to the courts issues of the greatest complexity. Both sides wanted to take possession of as much property as possible while admitting the smallest reciprocal liability. The individuals involved wanted only to get as much as possible of their valuables into the country of their new residence. This led to smuggling and subterfuges countered by each government taking ever more drastic action to control evacuee property and to curtail the transfer of assets to the other state. These regulations have caused much real hardship and injustice and have provoked continued wrangling between the two governments.

The idea that a country has a foreign 'enemy' is easy for the mass of the people to understand, and it also provides a powerful stimulus to national unity. For Pakistan, India has filled this role. Consequently the primary objective of Pakistan's foreign policy has been to strengthen her position *vis-à-vis* India. All other issues such as the agreement with the United States and membership

Pakistan

in the South-East Asia Treaty Organization and the Baghdad Pact have been regarded as subsidiary to this overriding aim. The principal secondary theme in foreign policy has been support for other Muslim countries, especially for Muslim colonial peoples seeking independence and for Arab countries against Israel. This policy, stressing the special bonds that unite Muslims, is a logical extension of the fundamental assertion of Muslim nationhood in India.

Foreign affairs occupied a substantial share of the attention of the government, the press and the public. But there was no lack of urgent domestic problems. In the first place the whole structure of government had to be improvised. Pakistan took over the provincial government of Sind and the North-West Frontier Province, but the non-Muslim civil servants were transferred to India. In any event these were small and relatively backward provinces. The Punjab was partitioned, and although its capital, Lahore, fell to Pakistan a large proportion of its administrators had been Hindus and Sikhs. And the city itself being less than 20 miles from the Indian border had to bear the full impact of the disruption that accompanied partition. East Bengal was even less well provided with an operating government. The provincial capital had been Calcutta and the main composition of its administration had been Hindu. The new provincial government had to operate at a distance of more than 1,000 miles from the federal capital. In addition to the creation or re-modelling of the provincial governments Pakistan had to produce in a few weeks a complete central government for a nation of 75,000,000 people.

Furthermore, this task had to be accomplished at a time of social and political disorder. The economic structure of the new state was almost totally disrupted. Normal lines of communication were severed. All the complex machinery of trade and commerce had to be divorced from its Indian connections and be re-established in conformity with new and arbitrary political boundaries. On the whole, Pakistan took over the poorer areas of the sub-continent, areas lacking in industry, with a population predominantly uneducated and unskilled. It was not self-sufficient in any important manufactured product, and resources of fuel

The Political Background

and power were pitifully inadequate. Consequently dependence upon imports was high. Imports required foreign exchange which could be earned by the export of primary products, notably jute and cotton. When crops were good and world prices high, Pakistan was prosperous; but when demand and prices fell the effect was catastrophic.

As an added and most severe burden upon the over-strained economy came the refugees. They came by the million, most of them with nothing but a few rags and a small bundle of personal possessions. They flowed toward the towns where temporary relief camps were established and where some kind of free accommodation and sustenance was available. And there many of them have stayed, hundreds of thousands of them huddled into squalid overcrowded huts without adequate water and with almost no sanitation. More than nine years after independence acres of these refugee colonies disfigured even the central areas of the federal capital. Each change of government, central or provincial, has brought a promise of vigorous action to resettle the refugees, but their number seemed never to diminish.

The tasks that faced the new state in its early years were truly gigantic. The people had hoped for a new era of social justice and Islamic brotherhood; instead they found that the achievement of Pakistan had thrown them into the beginning of a long hard struggle for survival. They were proud of their new state and they wanted it to be strong and vigorous and sure of itself. And they looked for guidance to their Great Leader, *Quaid-i-Azam* Mohammad Ali Jinnah. There was no one else, he *was* Pakistan; and wherever he went he was received by vast crowds with adulation amounting almost to worship.

He was by nature a commander and leader of men. He was not to be treated as a colleague or even *primus inter pares*, for he demanded lieutenants who would serve him rather than partners who would argue with him. In manner he was cold, brilliant and unyielding, a man to inspire either fury or devotion. He organized the campaign for Pakistan as though he were a commander-in-chief issuing orders of the day to encourage the troops and tactical directions to control the provincial com-

Pakistan

manders.[1] As President of the Muslim League he felt that he was the effective head of the Muslim nation. When Lord Wavell formed the Interim Government in 1946, Mr. Jinnah felt that it was not for him to enter as minister to a Viceroy or as the equal of Hindu councillors, so Liaquat Ali was instructed to head the Muslim group.

When Pakistan was formed the *Quaid-i-Azam* was recognized to be above the political battle, a figure to whom all might turn for authority and justice and protection. He became Governor-General and President of the Constituent Assembly; he was no longer a party leader or even the nation's spokesman, he was the personification of the state.

No constitutional ruler and few autocrats have possessed such a plenitude of power. He had full authority over the civil administration and the armed forces. By his own order he could amend the existing constitution and promulgate laws that would be beyond the effective power of review of any court. These were not powers which existed merely on paper and which in practice were limited by the conventions of constitutional responsibility. On the contrary, cabinet ministers understood clearly that they held office as the agents of the Governor-General, and the Assembly, with its powerless Opposition, was in no mood to challenge any action of its own President.

In the early months the predominant position of the *Quaid-i-Azam* was a source of strength to Pakistan. But it was obvious that his own strength was failing, and his death in September 1948 left a gap too big to be filled by any successor. At that time Liaquat Ali Khan was already Prime Minister and was widely respected as Jinnah's principal lieutenant, but he could never take the place of the *Quaid-i-Azam* in authority or in the esteem of the people.

To succeed to the office of Governor-General, Liaquat Ali recommended Khwaja Nazimuddin, until then the Chief Minis-

[1] Thus when, in 1941, the Viceroy appointed the Muslim provincial Chief Ministers as members of the National Defence Council, Jinnah required them to resign because the invitations had not come through him (Symonds, *op. cit.*, p. 64).

The Political Background

ter of East Bengal. Under Mr. Jinnah the Governor-General had controlled the cabinet; henceforward it was Liaquat's intention to have the cabinet control the Governor-General. This involved a transition to the more usual conventions of parliamentary government. The formal written powers of the Governor-General were not changed although certain transitional sections of the Indian Independence Act were allowed to expire. The office of President of the Constituent Assembly went by election to Tamizuddin Khan, who had been Deputy President under Mr. Jinnah. This dispersal of the power of the *Quaid-i-Azam* among the Governor-General, the Prime Minister and the President of the Assembly was to have important consequences in 1953 and 1954.

Most of the evidence goes to show that Liaquat Ali was at first in effective control of the government, the Muslim League and the Constituent Assembly. But in the three years following Mr. Jinnah's death he did not succeed in solving any of the five main problems of Kashmir, canal waters, evacuee property, the state of the economy and refugees. Neither was he able to procure agreement on the constitution. Inevitably a sense of frustration spread in the country, and it was no longer enough to have survived. Men began to ask for tangible benefits, or at least for relief from all too tangible distress. Political opposition to the Prime Minister was not very effective, but it was growing. Above all, the provinces were getting out of hand.

In October 1951 Liaquat Ali was assassinated at Rawalpindi by an Afghan named Said Akbar. The motive for the crime is obscure,[1] and investigations continued for some years after the event. Sensational rumours and suspicions abounded—that it was the result of religious fanaticism, of a foreign plot, or of the machinations of a high-placed political rival. Only one thing was certain, that Pakistan had lost in four years both its pre-eminent political leaders.

The vacancy was filled by Khwaja Nazimuddin, who stepped down from his high dignity to become the nation's second Prime

[1] Government of Pakistan, *The Assassination of Mr. Liaquat Ali Khan*, Report of the Commission of Enquiry (1952).

Pakistan

Minister. Ghulam Mohammad, the Finance Minister, took his place as Governor-General. Nazimuddin, as Governor-General, had been in a position to know the state of government business, but he was entering a cabinet several of whose members had had more detailed recent experience both of administration and of national politics. His authority over his colleagues and over the country had to depend not upon accumulated prestige but on current performance and force of personality. Nazimuddin was a man of piety and integrity who gave little evidence in appearance or words or decisions that he was capable of imposing his will upon men or circumstances.

The Nazimuddin administration made little headway with the problems that had confronted its predecessor. In addition it encountered three new dangers. There was a food crisis as the result of a partial crop failure. Secondly, with the approaching end of the Korean War the world prices of jute and cotton suffered a sharp decline, and this precipitated a balance of payments crisis of major proportions as well as budgetary difficulties. Finally, religious opposition, stemming partly from disappointment with the constitutional proposals produced under Liaquat in 1950, broadened into a major politico-religious upheaval which threatened governmental stability throughout West Pakistan.[1] By April 1953 the necessity for strong action had been amply demonstrated.

The action came, not from the Prime Minister but from the Governor-General. On April 17, 1953, he issued a statement which said:

'I have been driven to the conclusion that the cabinet of Khwaja Nazimuddin has proved entirely inadequate to grapple with the difficulties facing the country.

'In the emergency which has arisen I have felt it incumbent upon me to ask the cabinet to relinquish office so that a new cabinet better fitted to discharge its obligations towards Pakistan may be formed.'

---

[1] *Report of the Court of Inquiry into the Punjab Disturbances of 1953* (Lahore, 1954). This report is subsequently referred to as the *Munir Report*.

The Political Background

Ghulam Mohammad called upon the ambassador to the United States, Mohammed Ali, to become the new Prime Minister. The new cabinet drew six of its members from the outgoing ministry. (This forms a strange comment upon either cabinet or party solidarity as usually understood in the parliamentary system of government.) The abrupt dismissal of a Prime Minister whose government had been supported by the legislature until the week of its demise, met with general praise from the Press and the public. Only the displaced Prime Minister and his ousted colleagues seemed to feel unhappy. The Assembly, which had been hastily prorogued, was not permitted to meet to express its view until September, by which time the new government was well established in office.

When Liaquat Ali was Prime Minister and Khwaja Nazimuddin was Governor-General effective power lay with the former. Ghulam Mohammad was a man of immense will-power, and although he had been installed in office on the advice of Nazimuddin he was unwilling to interpret his own role as merely ornamental. Until the break with his Prime Minister, the Governor-General observed all the outward forms of the office of a constitutional figurehead but, the dramatic intervention having occurred, matters could not revert to their former course. What had happened once could be repeated and, while the constitution remained unchanged, the office of Governor-General was to cast a shadow over that of Prime Minister. This was the more apparent in that Mohammed Ali was personal choice of the Governor-General. He was not the leader of a party or even of a substantial *bloc* within the Muslim League. He had been abroad on diplomatic service for some years before his elevation, and he had not been much before the eye of the public or Parliament. Moreover, his coming to power had displaced, and presumably offended, some of the best known and most powerful political leaders in the country, Nazimuddin, Nishtar, Pirzada and Fazlur Rahman.

Mohammed Ali (Bogra) was a Bengali, as also were Nazimuddin and Fazlur Rahman. The Province of East Bengal filled more than half (forty-four out of seventy-six) the seats in the

Pakistan

Constituent Assembly. However, it felt that it had not received its fair share of government benefits since partition and feared that the new constitution would perpetuate this state of affairs. This feeling of indignation was expressed in the provincial election of March 1954 when the Muslim League was all but annihilated by a coalition called the United Front. The Bengal contingent in the Constituent Assembly thus found itself repudiated in its home province at the same time as its most prominent leaders had been ousted from federal office.

The situation called for desperate remedies. Strong action was taken by the Mohammed Ali cabinet which dismissed the two-month-old United Front provincial government and installed Major-General Iskandar Mirza, an army officer turned civil servant, as Governor of East Bengal with full powers. Thus whoever controlled the centre could control East Bengal. In order to control the centre it was necessary to remove the power of intervention from the hands of the Governor-General. This was done, or thought to be done, in September 1954 by an amendment to the Government of India Act precluding him from acting except upon the advice of his ministers and requiring the choice of new ministers to be made only from amongst members of the Assembly. It remained only to capture the cabinet, and this could be accomplished by a vote of no confidence in the Assembly.[1]

The Governor-General struck first. Hastily summoning the Prime Minister from Washington, he secured the 'advice' that he needed and dissolved both the Constituent Assembly and the cabinet. A new cabinet was formed with the Prime Minister and three other ministers (and two Ministers of State) continuing in office. Nine new ministers were appointed, none of them having a seat in the Assembly at the time of its dissolution. They included General Ayub Khan, the Army Commander-in-Chief; General

---

[1] Further details of the various actions leading up to the dissolution of the Constituent Assembly will be found in subsequent chapters.

It is difficult to produce documentary evidence for the 'conspiracy' theory set forth above, but it does serve to explain the facts and is based upon the personal observations and conversations of the author in Karachi from July 1954 until after the dissolution had taken place.

The Political Background

Mirza, recalled from East Bengal; M. A. H. Ispahani, the High Commissioner in London; H. I. Rahimtoola, the Governor of the Punjab; Colonel Abid Husain Shah and Sardar Mumtaz Ali Khan from the Punjab; and Mir Ghulam Ali Talpur from Sind. In addition there were two ministers who had been clearly in opposition to the Muslim League, Dr. Khan Sahib, who had been Chief Minister of the North-West Frontier Province until dismissed by Mr. Jinnah in 1947, and Mr. H. S. Suhrawardy, the last Chief Minister of undivided Bengal and national leader of the Awami League. The Prime Minister described his new government as 'a cabinet of talent' rather than a coalition of parties.

After more than seven years Pakistan had no constitution other than the patched-up remnants of the Government of India Act. Furthermore, the Constituent Assembly was no longer in existence, and no provision had been made for its replacement. At the national level it could be claimed that Pakistan had survived its first seven years, but it could not be said that politically it had prospered.

The course of provincial politics during the same period had been even more dismal. In many ways provincial and central politics cannot be separated. Apart from a brief spell in East Bengal, all cabinets in Pakistan before 1955 had been drawn from members of the Muslim League. The leading political figures participated at both levels of government. It was possible to combine membership of both federal and provincial legislatures, and many of the important provincial ministers participated actively in central affairs. In fact a small, well-defined group of men monopolized political office throughout the country and transferred from one field to another as occasion seemed to warrant.[1] The conclusion seems unavoidable that a group of

[1] The following list gives some examples of men who participated at more than one level of government.

Nazimuddin	(MCA)	Ch Min EB	G-G	P M
Noon	(MCA)	Gov EB	Ch Min Pb	Cabt
Nishtar	(MCA)	Cabt	Gov Pb	Cabt
Mamdot	(MCA)	Ch Min Pb	Gov Sd	
Pirzada	(MCA)	Cabt	Ch Min Sd	
Shahabuddin	(MCA)	Cabt	Gov NWFP	

[Continued overleaf]

Pakistan

about twenty individuals made all important political and governmental decisions at every level. In particular they controlled the posts of central cabinet ministers, provincial Governors and provincial Chief Ministers. The changes of 1953 and 1954 showed that differences within this group could no longer be assuaged by compromise.

Provincial political life was closely bound to the tensions existing at the centre. But internally there were many other causes of conflict. The result was either chronic instability or a government maintained in office by means that could not be described as democratic.

The North-West Frontier Province before 1947 was opposed to the partition of India. But in that year its people, by a referendum, decided that since Pakistan was to be created, they would have to join that Dominion rather than India. The provincial government, under Dr. Khan Sahib, maintained its Congress character and was dismissed by Mr. Jinnah immediately after independence. In its place a cabinet was installed under Khan Abdul Qaiyum Khan, who ruled with a firm hand until he joined the central cabinet in 1953. So tight was his reign that political opponents, several of whom found themselves in prison, complained that democracy had been extinguished. Qaiyum's successor, Abdur Rashid Khan, had been the Inspector-General of Police in the Frontier Province, and he had previously had neither experience nor interest in politics. In 1955 in the cause of the unification of West Pakistan the Rashid ministry was dismissed and its place was taken by a government under Sardar Bahadur Khan.

The Province of Sind achieved its separation from Bombay

Continuation of footnote]
Qaiyum	(MCA)	Ch Min NWFP	Cabt		
Gurmani	(MCA)	Cabt	Gov Pb-W Pak		
Rahimtoola		Gov Sd	Gov Pb	Cabt	
Mirza		Gov EB	Cabt		G-G-Pres
Chundrigar		Cabt	Gov NWFP	Gov Pb	Cabt

(MCA) indicates membership at some period of the first Constituent Assembly. Appointments as provincial ministers (other than Chief Ministers) and as diplomats or civil servants are not shown.

The Political Background

only ten years before the creation of Pakistan. Its history had been turbulent, and it had witnessed a succession of ministries each endangered by intrigue and conspiracy.[1] In 1947 Sir Ghulam Husain Hidayatullah, the former Chief Minister, was appointed Governor and Mohammad Ayub Khuhro was commissioned to form a cabinet. Mr. Khuhro, whether in or out of office, has been the chief figure in Sind politics since that time. He was bold enough to oppose both Mr. Jinnah and Liaquat Ali on the question of the separation of Karachi from the administrative control of Sind. He was widely accused of maladministration and corruption, and although these have become normal charges against Sind ministers, he was dismissed in April 1948 by the Governor acting on instructions from the Governor-General. A judicial inquiry was instituted into his conduct as a result of which he was disqualified from public office. His successor was Pir Ilahi Bakhsh, who soon encountered difficulties and within a year found himself deposed and disqualified as a result of the findings of an Election Tribunal which had investigated his part in the election of 1946. The next incumbent was Mr. Yusuf Haroon, who resigned from office after a short while. Then came Kazi Fazlullah, who gave way, under pressure, to Mr. Khuhro, who had succeeded in having his disqualification set aside on technical grounds. He was again removed by the Governor, again investigated and again disqualified along with Mr. Fazlullah. In December 1951, there being no likelihood of stable representative government, the Governor assumed emergency powers and the Assembly was dissolved preparatory to new elections.

It took some while to make electoral preparations, especially to try to instil some semblance of unity into the Muslim League. In April–May 1953 polling took place and it became necessary

[1] G. M. Sayed, *Struggle for a New Sind* (Karachi, 1949). The final deadlock in 1946 is perhaps unique in the history of Parliaments. The Assembly, with sixty members, met on the morning of September 5th to consider a motion of no-confidence. Pledged votes were 30 to 29 against the government. The Speaker resigned in order to vote for the ministry and the Deputy-Speaker resigned in order to vote against. No one being willing to accept the Chair, business could not proceed and the Assembly was prorogued and later dissolved (Sayed, *op. cit.*, p. 176).

to form a new ministry. Mr. Khuhro was still the favourite of the provincial League Council but he was unpopular with the centre, and in any case was still disqualified from office. After considerable pressure from above, Pirzada Abdus Sattar, recently deposed as central cabinet minister, was installed as Chief Minister. To nobody's surprise he experienced great difficulty in controlling the Assembly, which adjourned its budget session of 1954 somewhat abruptly. However, he began to rally an impressive amount of support by his vigorous defence of provincial rights and his opposition to the 'One Unit' proposals. The authorities at the centre decided that the One Unit scheme must succeed, and he was duly dismissed for the normally assigned reasons of maladministration and abuse of power, Mr. Khuhro, having once more secured release from the penalties of disqualification, assumed office for the third time and proclaimed his intention to clean up the mess left by his predecessor. Thus in a little over seven years Sind had enjoyed seven ministries and a lengthy period of Governor's rule.

The political history of the Punjab is composed of similar elements. The first Chief Minister was the Khan of Mamdot, who was dismissed in 1949 and subjected to a judicial inquiry. A period of Governor's rule followed until the first universal suffrage elections were held in 1951. Mian Mumtaz Khan Daultana then became Chief Minister. Politically he was a popular figure, and he appeared to be ambitious to rise to a position of greater political power. He attempted to exploit a mixture of public prejudice and religious fanaticism in a manner that greatly embarrassed the central government. The consequence was widespread rioting and the imposition of martial law in Lahore from March–May 1953. Before martial law was lifted, Daultana's resignation had been procured and the usual judicial inquiry into his administration had been set in motion. He was replaced by Malik Firoz Khan Noon who had been Governor of East Bengal. He quickly encountered difficulties in his party and in the Assembly. But the influence of the centre was on his side and, having been among the early supporters of a single unit for West Pakistan, his position appeared to be strengthened by the events of October–November

The Political Background

1954. But all was not well, and he fell foul of the central government and the provincial Governor (M. A. Gurmani) over the election of members to the second Constituent Assembly, and in his turn he was dismissed. His successor was H. K. Dasti.

Until 1954 the political situation in East Bengal was outwardly stable. When Khwaja Nazimuddin moved to Karachi to become Governor-General, his place as Chief Minister was taken by Nurul Amin. East Bengal felt that it was neglected by the centre, but since both Nazimuddin and Mohammed Ali (Bogra) were Bengali its case should not have gone unrepresented. Within the province the government suffered from the usual allegations of corruption and mismanagement, and one prominent cabinet minister was dismissed and disqualified. There was not, however, the challenge from within the government party that had plagued the Punjab and Sind.

The provincial government was clearly alarmed about rising opposition. By dating the commencement of the provincial legislature not from the last election (1946) but from the first meeting after partition, the five-year term of the Assembly was allowed to run until 1953. But even this was not enough, and the Constituent Assembly was asked to prolong the life of the East Pakistan legislature for one more year.[1] One important by-election resulted in a major defeat for the government candidate, and other vacancies were left unfilled until as many as 34 out of 171 seats were empty.[2] A matter of months before the elections were due A. K. Fazlul Huq left his position as Advocate-General and went over to lead the forces of the Opposition. Thus three former Chief Ministers of undivided Bengal were active in Pakistani politics. Nazimuddin was sitting deposed and disgruntled in Karachi and Fazlul Huq and H. S. Suhrawardy were working for the provincial opposition. The opponents of the Muslim League combined their forces in an electoral alliance called the United Front. This was a loose coalition composed of two major and several minor parties held together by a common

[1] *The East Bengal Legislative Assembly (Continuance) Act*, 1953.
[2] East Bengal Legislative Assembly, *Proceedings*, Vol. XI, No. 1.

Pakistan

desire for autonomy for East Bengal and a shared determination to defeat the League.

The results of the election left no doubt of the feelings of the electorate. The League was overwhelmed and the Governor had no choice but to call on Fazlul Huq, as the leader of the United Front, to form an administration. Even before the new cabinet took office there was a serious breakdown of law and order within the province. After two months the central government reached the conclusion that matters were beyond the control of the provincial administration. Accordingly at the end of May 1954 the cabinet was dismissed and the Assembly was not allowed to meet. Governor's rule was proclaimed and a new Governor, General Iskandar Mirza, was sent from Karachi to take charge. When General Mirza returned to Karachi as Minister of the Interior his place was taken first by Sir Thomas Ellis and then by Mr. Justice Shahabuddin.

By the end of 1954 the half of the people of Pakistan that lived in East Bengal was without self-government. The Constituent Assembly, the only organ at the centre which could claim any shadow of democratic origin, had been roughly disbanded. And in November the Prime Minister had announced that the provinces of West Pakistan were to be merged into one unit and consequently their Assemblies would, in a short while, be liquidated. The career of democracy in Pakistan had not begun in a promising fashion.

The legislative branch in Pakistan, both central and provincial, seemed to have failed and the executive to be in complete control. The judiciary had yet to make itself heard. Soon after the dismissal of the Constituent Assembly, proceedings were instituted to test in the courts the validity of the action of the Governor-General. The Chief Court of Sind declared that the dissolution was invalid but the government appealed to the Federal Court. In its first judgment the court upheld enough of the government's case to decide the immediate issue but did not rule directly on the validity of the dissolution or indicate a permissible means of escape from the constitutional impasse. The Governor-General then asked the court for an advisory opinion covering these

The Political Background

points. In general terms, the conclusion of the court was that a reserve power of control over a legislature lay with the representative of the Crown and that the dissolution of the Assembly was therefore justified. But this did not mean that in the absence of a legislature the Governor-General might proceed to enact constitutional provisions by order. Legitimacy could be restored only by convening a new Constituent Assembly formed on a basis similar to that of its predecessor.

The Governor-General then summoned a second Constituent Assembly whose members were to be elected by the members of the provincial Assemblies. This meant that the government, if it was to stay in power, had to win the favour of the provincial politicians. In West Pakistan a government-in-being has usually contrived to obtain a majority for any of its proposals. The situation in East Bengal was rather different. The legislature elected the previous year had not been permitted to meet, and political opinion was bitterly resentful of the abrupt dismissal of the only non-Muslim League ministry. It was true that Mr. Suhrawardy and a nominee of Mr. Fazlul Huq (Abu Hussain Sarkar) had entered the central cabinet, but this could not placate those who were deprived of provincial office. During the period of Governor's rule the United Front had split; the Awami League, whose national leader was H. S. Suhrawardy, having separated itself from the rest of the Front which was still led by Fazlul Huq. Each of these groups claimed to be in a position to form a government with majority support. It was up to the centre to choose which element should be given the chance to take office. In spite of the presence of Mr. Suhrawardy in the central cabinet, Abu Hussain Sarkar was appointed Chief Minister and cabinet government was restored in June 1955.

The way was thus cleared for holding elections to the Constituent Assembly. The first meeting of this body took place in July, and it became obvious that the emergency cabinet which had held office since October 1954 would have to be reorganized. The Muslim League Parliamentary Party dropped Mohammed Ali (Bogra) as its leader and chose Chaudhri Mohamad Ali, the former Finance Minister. Mr. Fazlul Huq entered the cabinet while Mr. Suhrawardy crossed the floor to lead the Opposition. Ghulam Mohammad, who had been ill for many months, was replaced as Governor-General by General Iskandar Mirza.

The new Constituent Assembly first proceeded to restore constitutional order in place of the chaos that had followed the dissolution of its predecessor and the subsequent actions of the court and the government. It then turned its attention to the unification of West Pakistan. The decision to integrate the provinces and states of the west wing had been taken by the emergency government in 1954, but it required the Assembly to pass the necessary law. This measure was pushed through, and the united Province of West Pakistan came into existence in October 1955. M. A. Gurmani became the first Governor and Dr. Khan Sahib the Chief Minister. In January 1956 the members of the Assemblies of the former provinces elected an interim legislature for West Pakistan.

The next business of the Assembly was the framing of the constitution. The government-sponsored draft was introduced in January, approved in February and was brought into operation in March 1956. On the twenty-third day of that month the country ceased to be a Dominion and was proclaimed as the Islamic Republic of Pakistan.

The country as a whole breathed a sigh of relief that this perplexing task had at last been accomplished. But the adoption of the constitution did not portend a period of political tranquillity. In West Pakistan the Muslim League soon tried to oust Dr. Khan Sahib and to replace him with a League Chief Minister. Khan Sahib countered by forming the Republican Party, which was able to command a narrow majority in the provincial Assembly.[1]

The formation of the Republican Party upset the balance of political forces at Karachi. Chaudhri Mohamad Ali remained the leader of the Muslim League, but many of his parliamentary supporters had switched to the Republicans. A crisis was also brewing in East Pakistan, where the Awami League had become strong enough to overthrow the United Front government of

[1] This majority evaporated in early 1957 and cabinet government was suspended on March 20th. (*Dawn*, March 21, 1957.)

The Political Background

Abu Hussain Sarkar. Both issues were resolved in September 1956 in favour of the Awami League. Mr. Suhrawardy became Prime Minister with the support of the Republicans. In East Bengal Mr. Ataur Rahman became Chief Minister of an Awami League ministry with some participation by minor parties. The Muslim League, which had enjoyed the monopoly of office until 1954, was excluded from all three governments. The continued fluctuations in the struggle for power had taken place almost entirely among a small group of political leaders. As Pakistan completed her first decade of independent existence, the prospect of nation-wide popular elections still seemed remote.

CHAPTER II

The Decline of the Muslim League

WHEN Mr. Jinnah returned from England in 1934 the Muslim League was moribund. The Indian National Congress had clearly taken the lead with its demand for Indian self-determination. By comparison with the Congress the League was a defensive organization composed of some wealthy *zamindars* and a few discontented intellectuals who wanted greater access to government employment. Many of its members were still within the Congress or, like Mr. Jinnah himself, ready to co-operate substantially with it.

There was no air of enthusiasm about the League of that period; it had no sense of mission. Many of its members looked back nostalgically to the glorious days of the Khilafat movement.[1] Those were the days when the cause of Indian freedom and the cause of Islam coincided. It was a campaign in which religion, nationalism and political adventure were combined into a brew that proved powerfully intoxicating to many a young Muslim. It gave a chance to suffer, though not to suffer too much, for the cause. Many of the 'old guard' of Pakistan's politics in 1947-56 looked back with pride on their arrest and imprisonment during the Khilafat movement. Intellectually perhaps the cause of the last of the Caliphs was not very convincing. But then Indian Muslims were not likely to have to live under the successors of Abdul Hamid. In emotional terms they were the symbol of the unity of the Muslim world and of the political independence of the adherents of Islam.

---

[1] The agitation to preserve the caliphate and as much as possible of the Turkish empire. See Richard Symonds, *The Making of Pakistan* (London, 3rd ed., 1951), pp. 46-7.

The Decline of the Muslim League

Political parties are often founded upon the shared recollection of powerful emotions. It is for this reason that the significance of the period from 1919 to 1922 is essential to an understanding of the Muslim League in Pakistan. During this time a number of elements was added to the ideology of Muslim politics in India that was to be of importance in the ensuing years. Firstly the use of the vocabulary and concepts of classical Islam was accentuated. The movement directed attention to the Islamic heritage of the series of caliphs stretching back ultimately to the rule of the Prophet himself. It invited the defence of ancient Islamic forms as such. It was admitted that the actual caliphate of the twentieth century had its faults, but their remedy was to be found, not by trying to build a new structure but by a return to the ideals of the purer epoch of the rightly guided Caliphs.

Secondly, by a process of reaction, the movement strengthened the tendency towards opposition to anything Occidental. For two centuries the West had succeeded in overturning one Muslim state after another. Soon the Muslims, as a result of a mixture of Western aggression and perfidy,[1] would become a people without a country, hewers of wood and drawers of water for alien and infidel masters. This opposition to the West went beyond a simple dislike of imperialism. It became necessary to attack the foundations of Western civilization, above all to disparage the public morals of advanced Western states. Western observers complain of purdah. Is this not better than sexual licence and crowded divorce courts? Muslims are said to be backward, illiterate and lacking in business enterprise. But is the West proud of crime comics and drunkenness and stomach ulcers and psychiatric disorders?

The third product of the Khilafat movement in the minds of Muslim politicians lies in the field of political organization and tactics. The first object of the Muslim League, as declared by its

[1] The Muslim's view of recent world history is apt to differ markedly from that of non-Muslim historians. Thus Mirza Ali Azhar, writing in the *Pakistan Standard* (August 14, 1954), begins one paragraph with the words: 'The British Foreign policy that resulted in the Balkan War, the Macedonian atrocities and the Tripolitan war of 1912. . . .'

Pakistan

founders in 1906, was 'To promote, among the Mussalmans of India, feelings of loyalty to the British Government and to remove any misconception that may arise as to the intention of Government with regard to any of its measures.'[1] But the movement of 1919 was designed to embarrass that government to the point where it would feel obliged to secure more favourable treatment for Turkey. The movement was destructive in purpose and authoritarian in method, and was far removed from the parliamentary approach through Legislative Assembly and Council.

The Khilafat movement was independent of the League, but no Muslim political organization could fail to be subjected to its influence. In later years many of its participants became 'nationalist Muslims' and opposed the Pakistan movement as a betrayal of the universal principles of the earlier struggle. But a substantial legacy of ideas and emotions was also inherited by the campaign for Pakistan, which unleashed a second wave of Muslim political enthusiasm.

The Muslim League did not adopt the demand for Pakistan until its meeting at Lahore in 1940. From that time all other aims were relegated to a position of secondary importance. They served as tactical manœuvres in the grand strategy. In 1937–38 Mr. Jinnah had consolidated his hold upon the League, and had begun to secure mass support for its activities. At first this was based upon resistance to Hindu 'oppression.' Wide publicity was given to allegations of anti-Muslim activities on the part of Congress provincial governments. When the latter resigned as a consequence of the outbreak of war, Mr. Jinnah declared a Day of National Deliverance.[2]

The adoption of Pakistan as the objective simplified the task of political agitation. The Muslim masses were able to resent evidence of Hindu domination that fell within their own experience. But it was not so easy to make a peasant in Sind or the Punjab feel angry because a Congress flag had been flown on a public

[1] A. B. Rajput, *The Muslim League Yesterday and Today* (Lahore, 1948), pp. 19–20.
[2] Jamil-ud-Din Ahmad (ed.), *Recent Speeches and Writings of Mr. Jinnah* (Lahore, 5th ed., 1952), Vol. I, p. 110.

The Decline of the Muslim League

building in Madras or because Muslim children in Bengal had been required to sing *Bande Mataram*. Arguments about quotas and ratios in legislatures and cabinets and public services might convince the urban intellectual but would be unintelligible to the cultivator. But Pakistan could include all these lesser points and much more besides. It was a positive aim, not a defensive screen. It was a vision capable of sustaining unlimited hope and enthusiasm. The attainment of Pakistan was presented as a panacea that would open the way to the transformation of the lives of the Muslims of India.

The League's tactics and the presentation of its case were simple. It asserted that the Muslims of India were a nation and that they must have their own state. Because they were in a minority they must be united in order to achieve their purpose. The Muslim League was the only organization entitled to speak for the nation; other organizations and other allegiances represented treason to the nation.[1] The League had to accept an almost military discipline to accomplish its purpose. 'Faith, Unity and Discipline' was the watchword given to the party by its *Quaid-i-Azam*. The Great Leader's commands had to be obeyed if the nation was to be led to victory.

The League was indeed fortunate to have Mr. Jinnah as its leader. The lower levels of Muslim League politics might be filled with intrigue and personal rivalry, but at the top he was supreme. He was above intrigue, for there was no one to challenge his power. He had no colleagues, only lieutenants, and they were content to obey his orders. He was very able and very sure of himself and of his purpose. He knew what must be done and what might never be conceded.

In 1947 the victory was accomplished, though not without bloodshed and sorrow. The *Quaid-i-Azam* and his people rejoiced. The new era had dawned.

This was the victory of the Muslim League. Political loyalty for the Muslims before 1947 could not be given to the state which

[1] Thus one of the causes of the breakdown of the Simla conference was Mr. Jinnah's refusal to accept the Congress insistence on nominating a nationalist Muslim to the interim government.

was alien and in some respects hostile. Loyalty was due to the *millat*,[1] its political organization the League, and its leader the *Quaid-i-Azam*. The League was older than Pakistan; the League had given Pakistan to the people. The League had triumphed over its adversaries, the Hindus, the British and the Muslim apostates. It was not to be thought of that the League should become an ordinary political party competing with others on equal terms for the favour of the electorate.

Seven years later, when the League was largely discredited, it still seemed impossible to the old Leaguers that anything could take its place. The *Quaid-i-Azam's* sister, Miss Fatima Jinnah, wrote:

'I say to you, support the Muslim League, because the League alone won Pakistan and can serve and consolidate Pakistan. The League may not be perfect but it is the only organized party of Muslims, while other bodies are of recent origin. Don't oppose the League but come into it and remove its defects. If you destroy the League you destroy Pakistan.'[2]

It was difficult for politicians, who for many years had placed service to the League before all other political or personal claims, now to adjust their loyalties to the new state and its Constituent Assembly. Surely no Prime Minister of a constitutional state has ever spoken as slightingly of Parliament as did Liaquat Ali.

'This House [Council of the Muslim League] now carries more weight than the Parliament and every word uttered here should be in consonance with its dignity and responsibility.

'I have always said, rather it has always been my firm belief that the existence of the League, not only the existence of the League, but its strength, is equal to the existence and the strength of Pakistan.

'So far as I am concerned, I had decided in the very beginning, and I reaffirm it today, that I have always considered myself as the Prime Minister of the League. I never regarded myself as the Prime Minister chosen by the members of the Constituent Assembly.

[1] The community of believers.
[2] *Pakistan Standard*, Independence Day Number, 1954 (August 14th).

The Decline of the Muslim League

'The day I will come to know that the League has no faith and confidence in me, that very day you will not find Liaquat Ali the Prime Minister of Pakistan.'[1]

The quotation above is from an address to the party organization. But League adherents were equally unmindful of parliamentary sovereignty even within the Assembly chamber. Thus Begum Shah Nawaz, herself a member of the League Working Committee and of the Parliamentary Board, tried to reassure those who feared arbitrary action by the government:

'Sir, I think that my honourable friends on the right are not aware that the Muslim League Government, whether in the Centre or in the Provinces, is under the direct control of the Central and Provincial Parliamentary Board . . . it is the Central Parliamentary Board which can at any time censure any government anywhere in Pakistan, if it does not protect the civil liberties of its citizens.'[2]

It was June 3, 1947, before the League could be certain that it had won Pakistan. The task then before the leaders was to establish a working state. The role of the party—that of producing a programme and mobilizing support behind it—fell into the background. Most of its prominent men were absorbed into positions of importance at the centre, in the provinces or representing their country abroad. Parties other than the League were defeated, fearful, disorganized and bewildered. Those early months of struggle for survival were no time for party politics. But there were some members of the League who were not called by government to accept important posts. And as the first intensity of crisis eased, they felt that the party had an important part to play in legislation and in framing the new constitution.

The pre-partition Muslim League was, of course, an All-India organization with branches in every province. The Council of the All-India Muslim League held its last meeting in Karachi in

[1] Extracts from a speech to the Pakistan Muslim League Council, reported in *Dawn*, October 9, 1950.
[2] Constituent Assembly (Legislature) *Debates*, 1949, Vol. II, January 4, 1950, p. 296.

Pakistan

December 1947 with Mr. Jinnah presiding. It was decided to establish a successor for each of the new Dominions.[1] The Council of the Pakistan Muslim League was initially to be composed of former members of the All-India Council resident in Pakistan and all League members of the Constituent Assembly. Mr. Liaquat Ali Khan was elected convener of the Pakistan League.

The Council of the new League met in Karachi in February 1948 and once more the *Quaid-i-Azam* presided. The main task was to approve the constitution.[2] The Pakistan Muslim League consists of the convention, the Council, the Working Committee, and Provincial, District and City Leagues. There is also a Central Parliamentary Board and Provincial Parliamentary Boards. Membership in a primary League is open to a Muslim Pakistani, over 18 years of age, who is in agreement with the aims and objects of the League and pays a triennial subscription of 2 annas.[3]

The convention is an assembly of the members of the Central and Provincial League Councils. No convention was held during the first nine years of Pakistan. A summons was issued for late October 1954. Besides those entitled by the constitution to attend, all persons who had at any time been influential in League affairs were invited, including those who were no longer members of the League. It was hoped to use this meeting as a grand reconciliation of rival factions that would open the way to a united election campaign under the new national constitution. Nine days before it was due to open and when some Bengal members were already at sea the convention was postponed.[4] Two days later the Constituent Assembly was dismissed.

The Council of the League is intended to be the main controlling and policy-forming organ. It consists of nearly four

[1] All-India Muslim League, Council meeting, Karachi, December 14 and 15, 1947, *Resolutions passed*, Resolution No. 3.

[2] This constitution was substantially amended in 1952 and 1956 (Pakistan Muslim League, Council meeting, October 11, 12 and 13, 1952, *Text of Resolutions*, Resolution No. 3, and *Dawn*, January 31, 1956). Unless otherwise indicated, references are to the constitution as amended.

[3] The low membership due has the advantage of permitting almost anyone who wished to obtain membership.   [4] *Dawn*, October 22, 1954.

hundred persons mostly elected every three years by the Provincial Councils,[1] but also including League members of the central Legislature, party office-bearers and some nominated persons. The Council is intended to meet at least twice a year, one of which meetings is to be held in East Bengal. In fact this article was not observed and the Council held seven meetings between 1948 and 1956, only one of which was in Dacca. Meetings are summoned by the President, though any seventy-five members are entitled by written request to demand a special session. The function of the Council is to elect the office-bearers and to pass resolutions in the name of the League. The constitution may be amended by such a resolution. The Council also has power 'to affiliate, suspend, dissolve or disaffiliate a Provincial Muslim League.' It is empowered to delegate any of its functions to the Working Committee or to the President.

The office-bearers elected for three-year terms by the Council are: the President, the Vice-President, the General Secretary, the Treasurer and two Joint Secretaries.[2] All these persons are *ex officio* members of the Working Committee, which also contains not more than twenty-two members of Council nominated by the President. This body has power 'to control, direct and regulate all the activities of the various Provincial Leagues in consonance with the aims, objects, rules and declared policy of the Pakistan Muslim League.' It can also take disciplinary action against any individual member or constituent organization, subject to a right of appeal to Council. The Working Committee may delegate any of its powers to a committee or to the President.

The last of the central organs of the League is the Central Parliamentary Board, elected every three years by the Council.

[1] The 1948 provision was for an elected membership of 440 with 260 from West Pakistan and 180 from East Bengal. In 1952 this was changed to a total of 654 equally divided between East and West. In 1956, after the unification of West Pakistan, each province was assigned 180 members.

[2] The Council meeting of January 1956 accepted the resignations of all office-bearers and authorized the President to nominate their successors. The constitution was also amended to give the President the right to reconstitute or reshuffle the Working Committee and to remove any member (*Dawn*, January 31, 1956).

Pakistan

It consists of twelve elected members (six from East and six from West Pakistan), and the League President as *ex officio* chairman. Its role, in consultation with Provincial Parliamentary Boards, is to select candidates for the central legislature and 'to exercise general control over the Muslim League Party in the Central Legislature.' Further, it is 'to supervise and control the activities of the Provincial Parliamentary Boards'; and 'to decide all disputes arising between a Provincial Parliamentary Board and a Muslim League Party in a Provincial Legislature.'

The Provincial Muslim Leagues have been modelled fairly closely after the central pattern. Thus the Sind Muslim League (before 1956) had its plenary session, council, working committee, Parliamentary Board, President and office-bearers.[1] It had under the supervision of the Pakistan League comparable powers over its subordinate organizations, the District, City, Taluka, Town and primary Muslim Leagues or Branches.

Attention has been drawn already to the tendency of Muslim Leaguers to place their party before Parliament and on a par with the state. It is not surprising that League constitutions speak in similar terms. Even the Sind Provincial League, in its section on 'Aims and Objections' [*sic*], affirmed its duty:

(*a*) To safeguard the sovereignity [*sic*] and integrity of Pakistan;

and

(*d*) To promote the cause of peace, freedom and justice throughout the world.

Similarly the parent body, in addition to the above, has the intention 'to establish and maintain friendly relations with other peace-loving nations of the world and specially to strengthen fraternal relations with other Muslim States.'

This habit of speaking in words that clothed the party in the robes of full sovereignty and adopted a tone that implied superiority to Parliament, was bound to give rise to difficulties. The Prime Minister had declared that he was primarily responsible to the League. Did this mean that real power lay with the

[1] Sind Provincial Muslim League, *Constitution and Rules* (Karachi, 1950).

party and not with the government or the Constituent Assembly? In the first few months the question could not arise. Mr. Jinnah was Governor-General, President of the Constituent Assembly and President of the Muslim League. However, the 1948 constitution took two steps to separate the party and the government. Firstly, it provided that no member would be eligible for party office if he were a member of either the central or provincial cabinets. Secondly, it debarred members of the Parliamentary Board from standing for election to the central or provincial legislatures. Thus ministers were to be compelled to keep their hands off the party machine, and the Parliamentary Board, which was to control legislatures, was to have its integrity safeguarded by a self-denying ordinance.

While Mr. Jinnah lived, this separation of party and government was not of much consequence. Choudhry Khaliquzzaman became at first organizer and then President of the League. After the death of the *Quaid-i-Azam* his position became one of considerable importance. He nominated the Prime Minister and representatives of provincial governments to his Working Committee. But this action in some ways accentuated the main difficulty. The Prime Minister was being asked to participate in discussions and resolutions in a body which was not under his control. Matters would certainly arise which were the subject of government action or on which the government had information it was unwilling to disclose. Was the Prime Minister to sit in the Working Committee and yet refuse to be bound by its decisions? Or was he to go to cabinet as a man who had received his orders from higher authority?

The position in the provinces was more serious. In the Punjab, Mian Mumtaz Mohammad Khan Daultana was elected President of the Provincial League by the small margin of 198 to 176 votes,[1] largely on the basis of his declared opposition to the Chief Minister, the Khan of Mamdot. The result was the breakdown of cabinet government and the imposition of Governor's rule. In Sind Mr. Khuhro, the deposed Chief Minister, was elected President in December 1948 by 72 votes against 35 for his nearest rival.[2]

[1] *Dawn*, November 29, 1948.   [2] *Ibid.*, December 6, 1948.

Pakistan

Three days later he offered his resignation pending a verdict in the courts.[1] (He was at that time facing criminal charges as well as disqualification proceedings.) The resignation, however, was not to be effective until the Council met once more to elect his successor, and accordingly Mr. Khuhro continued to act. Six weeks later the Working Committee called on the then Chief Minister to resign.[2] Pir Ilahi Bakhsh, apparently not sharing Liaquat Ali's respect for the party, required stronger measures (disqualification by Electoral Tribunal) to remove him from office. Mr. Khuhro's popularity with the Sind Muslim League increased, and in 1950 he was unanimously re-elected its President. At once he set to work to undermine another League cabinet, and the Working Committee established a nine-man supervisory committee to watch the activities of the government.[3]

The situation came up for review at the Council meeting in October 1950, and cabinet members were henceforth permitted to hold party office. Further, the members of the Parliamentary Board were no longer to be forbidden to run for the legislature. The barrier having been removed, Liaquat Ali forthwith became President and parallel action was later taken in the Provincial Leagues.

Possible friction between the government and the party was thus to be avoided by concentrating the power of both elements in the hands of a single man. The Prime Minister was in a position to control the Working Committee since he nominated a large majority of its members. He was also chairman of the Parliamentary Board. The Council with infrequent meetings and more than seven hundred members was unlikely to prove a source of serious embarrassment. And yet the relations between the party and the government were not completely satisfactory, for the party felt that it had been deprived of influence and denied a creative role. This issue is always a problem of the party in power in a parliamentary system. It was made worse in Pakistan by the absence of a strong Opposition and the consequent expectation of an almost indefinite tenure of office. In 1952 the Working Com-

[1] *Dawn*, December 9, 1948.   [2] *Ibid.*, January 31, 1949.
[3] *Ibid.*, October 18, 1950, editorial, 'Sind's Super-Government.'

mittee discussed the matter and set up a committee to examine the practice in Britain, the United States and other countries, and to make recommendations.[1]

When Liaquat Ali Khan was assassinated, Khwaja Nazimuddin succeeded him both as Prime Minister and President of the League. Eighteen months later Nazimuddin was dismissed as Prime Minister, and Mr. Mohammed Ali, then Ambassador to the United States, was appointed by the Governor-General to be his successor. There is no evidence that the Muslim League Party as such was consulted as to his acceptability, though certain League leaders showed their approval by entering the cabinet. Nazimuddin was still President of the League, and he showed his intention of continuing in that capacity by nominating new members to his Working Committee, including two deposed cabinet ministers.[2] After a period of reflection he appeared to accept the situation and his resignation as President was accepted by Council in October 1953. Mohammed Ali was chosen by a large majority to replace him.[3] Qazi Mohammad Isa was his opponent, urging the old reason that the League President ought not to be a member of government. This view gained strength in the ensuing months, and immediately before October 1954 it was being widely suggested that the coming League Convention should choose Miss Jinnah as the new President.[4]

In August 1955 the League Parliamentary Party changed its leader and the former Prime Minister, who was still President of the national Muslim League, was re-appointed as ambassador to Washington. Obviously he could not continue as the effective head of a political party. His successor as Prime Minister, Chaudhri Mohamad Ali, had been a civil servant until 1951 and had never presented himself as an active politician. At the next meeting of the Council Mr. Mohamad Ali himself proposed the name of

[1] Muslim League Working Committee, *Minutes*, meeting of May 18, 1952.
[2] *Dawn*, June 15, 1953.
[3] Pakistan Muslim League, Council meeting, October 17, 18, 19 and 20, 1953, *Text of Resolutions*. The vote was 258 to 36.
[4] Mr. Mohammed Ali was reported to have welcomed this proposal (*Dawn*, September 21, 1954).

Pakistan

Sardar Abdur Rab Nishtar as President of the League, explaining that 'recent experience' had shown the undesirability of combining the two offices.[1] On the following day the Council amended the constitution to restore the position of 1948 by which party office might not be held by central or provincial ministers.

Elements in the Council were never prepared to accept the idea that the role of the party, when in power, is to give wholehearted support to its own government. Council resolutions were thus often highly critical of the government. One example will suffice:

> 'This meeting of Pakistan Muslim League Council notes with great regret that in spite of six years of our independent existence and with Muslim League Government at the helm of affairs, no concrete steps have been taken to give practical shape to those promises made from time to time by Quaid-i-Azam and other responsible League Leaders from various League platforms for the introduction of complete reforms for Baluchistan.'[2]

League party politics before 1947 had been a matter of the application of tactics of harassment and obstruction in order to force concessions from government. Muslim Leaguers were the men who entered the legislatures to bring down the Unionist Ministry in the Punjab, to undermine that of Dr. Khan Sahib in the North-West Frontier Province or to wage dubious battles to sustain Sir Ghulam Hussain Hidayatullah in Sind. The Muslim League participated continuously in political life from 1937 to 1947, but it had no experience of sustaining a stable government backed by a loyal party with a working majority. When these men met together in the Muslim League Council they united to proclaim their disgruntlement with the British and the Congress and to proclaim their faith that some day all former things would be swept away and a new world would be created. This apocalyptic vision was inspiring, but it was poor preparation for the prosaic routine of constructive nation building.

[1] *Dawn*, January 30, 1956.
[2] Pakistan Muslim League Council meeting, *Text of Resolutions*, Resolution No. 20, October 20, 1953.

The Decline of the Muslim League

The machinery of the League seems to be designed to ensure party regularity and discipline. At its head is the President who chooses his own Working Committee. The Council is too big, too seldom in session and too disorganized to provide any continuing control or check upon the party leadership. The President, when he was Prime Minister, was also in control of government and its power and its patronage. He could reward adherents with cabinet posts or ambassadorships; and he could threaten his adversaries with dismissal or with prosecution under PRODA.[1]

There should have been no chance of trouble from the party members elected to the provincial legislatures. Candidates are selected by a process of application and competition. When an election is announced a notice appears in the press inviting applications for the Muslim League ticket. Sometimes a deposit is required which is to be returned provided the applicant, if disappointed, refrains from working against the adopted candidate.[2] Opportunity is given by the Parliamentary Board of the province concerned for applicants to state the superiority of their own claims over those of their rivals. This stage corresponds to the American primary except that the right of choice is exercised by a party committee rather than by the local voter. After the Provincial Board has announced its allocation, appeals may be carried to the Central Board which acts as a court of revision, frequently overruling the original choice. On occasion, when the central party is out of sympathy with the Provincial League,

---

[1] See below, pp. 102 ff.

[2] *Dawn*, October 3, 1951, carried the following announcement:

'The Central Parliamentary Board of the Pakistan Muslim League invites applications from persons wishing to seek election on the Muslim League ticket to the NWFP Legislative Assembly in the forthcoming general elections.

'Applications should reach the Honorary Secretary of the NWFP Provincial Muslim League, Peshawar, by October 15 at the latest.

'Each application should be accompanied by a sum of Rs. 500 as application fee.

'In the case of applicants who fail to obtain the Muslim League ticket, three-fourths of the application fee will be returned, provided they fulfil the terms of the pledge which each applicant shall be required to sign.'

Pakistan

the Central Board proceeds directly to the issue of party tickets.[1]

Yet in spite of all the powers provided to maintain party discipline there has been no period since 1947 when some cabinet, central or provincial, has not been in danger from the likelihood of a mutiny among its own supporters. The League convention was postponed and the Constituent Assembly was dismissed because the party could not be relied upon to support the leadership it had accepted. The situation in the provinces was equally unstable, and the central party took the extreme step of dissolving no less than four constituent Leagues.[2]

Why was it that in the formative years the Muslim League was a source of weakness and dissension rather than of strength? Any answer to this question must be complex and must refer in large measure to the larger political forces that were moulding Pakistan's destiny; forces of geography and economics. Often in the history of nations, out of ordeal comes unity. The Muslim League was unified when Pakistan was created and Pakistan was united throughout its first few fateful months. This was a period of striving for one objective: to be born and to survive. When the first crisis was over there were many problems and many conceivable solutions. Socialism, industrialization, war with India, central control, decentralization, land reform—each of these (and many more) had its advocates. Perhaps Mr. Jinnah could have made the task seem simple, urgent and inevitable. But he was ageing, sick and tired, and soon he was dead. And the party that he had built began to disintegrate.

The electorate of Pakistan is predominantly rural and overwhelmingly illiterate. The voter can therefore understand either a very general idea, such as Pakistan and the triumph of Islam, or a very particular idea, such as the curtailment of the power of this landlord or that policeman. But there is a great gap between and it is there that political parties usually function. The Labour Party, for example, has millions of loyal adherents who vote for

[1] As in the Punjab in 1950. *Dawn*, October 16, 1950.
[2] Karachi (Muslim League Working Committee, *Minutes*, April 3, 1952): Baluchistan, Punjab and Sind (*Dawn*, December 22, 1953).

it in every election because they believe they know what it stands for. But when Pakistan was won, what did the Muslim League stand for? At first it stood *behind* the *Quaid-i-Azam*. Then it was merely the party that had stood behind him. (And, be it noted that the major opposition group soon incorporated the word 'Jinnah' into the name of that organization.) Neither Liaquat Ali nor Nazimuddin, influential as was each of them, could convey a similar sense of purpose to millions of men and women. Then Mohammed Ali came in as the Governor-General's nominee, chosen in part because he was not deeply involved in the struggle for control of the party machinery. He was a Bengali who was young and amiable and had made a success both as a Bengal cabinet minister and as an ambassador. He had few enemies but no popular following, and he was incapable of achieving one. During his tenure there were constant doubts as to the reality of his leadership. Rumour served to indicate that real power lay with other members of the cabinet or with the Governor-General who had been responsible for his appointment.

After the death of Jinnah and more markedly after the assassination of Liaquat Ali, the Muslim League was unable to present to the public either a convincing programme or an inspiring leader. It had therefore to turn for support to the local politician and local issues. A politician in Pakistan does not need to pay much attention to the opinions of the ordinary voter. He must pay attention, however, to the party. The Parliamentary Board may deny him the party ticket, so that he must protect his standing with the party leaders. The favour of the government-in-office (which may differ from the Parliamentary Board) is also important. The influence of a Home Minister, a police official or a District Magistrate may well make the course of an election campaign much smoother.

For a politician who wants to survive, when the leaders change, loyalties change too. An observer who is not accustomed to Pakistani politics is apt to be surprised at the ease with which a leader can be assured of the undying loyalty of his supporters to find on the following day that his supplanter in office has been greeted with unanimous enthusiasm. Thus Nazimuddin was dismissed and the League elected Mohammed Ali without serious objection being raised. Similarly in Sind, four-fifths of the Muslim Members of the Legislative Assembly pledged their support to Pirzada and his campaign for the maintenance of Sind autonomy; two months later Mr. Khuhro secured almost unanimous backing for the extinction of the province.

A politician must also consider the men who control blocks of votes in local areas. There can be little doubt that *jagirdars* and *zamindars*, *pirs* and *mirs*, *makhdooms*, *khans* and *nawabs* retain vast political influence. A glance through the lists of members of legislative assemblies shows how many such hereditary leaders or their near relatives are active in political life. The politician's map of Pakistan, particularly West Pakistan, is dotted with the signs of entrenched areas of personal political power.

Ultimately a successful democratic system depends upon an informed public opinion capable of weighing men and issues and deciding in favour of a policy that can be made to work. Public opinion in Pakistan is to be found in the urban middle-classes, the land-owners and some of the religious leaders. This is a small and unstable base on which to found a durable and efficient state.

In view of the nature of the electorate it is not surprising that the methods of political action have not resembled those appeals to enlightened opinion envisioned by the more optimistic nineteenth-century liberals. There is a strong desire to be on the winning side. This 'band-wagon' approach is to be noticed in many democracies but, if the system is to flourish it must not be carried to the point where Opposition abdicates its responsibilities. A change of ministry is normally 'hailed with enthusiasm' by the press and politicians without regard to previous expressions of confidence or hostility or of major differences of principle. The value of continued consistent opposition is seldom recognized by politicians in Pakistan even when they are out of office. Their ideal seems to have been one party and one government cheered on to greater efforts by whole-hearted approval from all sides. Opposition was raised, not because it is essential to democracy but because would-be office holders claimed that party and national unity would be more likely under their leadership. In

The Decline of the Muslim League

this fashion, leaving the League and going into Opposition became a tactical manœuvre to enhance personal influence rather than a sign of the acceptance of new ideas or objectives. The Khan of Mamdot, having been dismissed as Chief Minister of the Punjab and having lost control of the Provincial League to Daultana, went into Opposition and successfully won election to the new Assembly as a Jinnah Awami League candidate. When Daultana was in turn deposed and replaced by Malik Firoz Khan Noon, Mamdot was ready to return to the fold. At a crucial moment[1] he brought fourteen of his personal followers in the Assembly (half the Opposition) with him to the aid of the Chief Minister. A few months later he was appointed Governor of Sind. By April 1956 he was ready to join the Republican Party and enter the cabinet of Dr. Khan Sahib.

Under these circumstances Opposition has tended to be sporadic, short-lived and destructive. Violent protest is raised against one particular decision of government or the conduct of a single minister and a trivial issue becomes the cause of the hour to the exclusion of more important long-term matters. Political feelings, especially when a religious element is added, have often run high on matters far beyond the control of the Pakistan government. It has proved much easier to attract an audience on the subject of the Arabs of Palestine, the fate of the Muslim Brotherhood or the independence of Algeria, than to direct attention to the need for land reform or a reduction in the cost of living.

A Pakistan audience likes its politics in colours of straight black and white. Villains there must be, and their ways are evil indeed. The tone of political controversy often descends to outright abuse. The following view of a Chief Minister by a former cabinet minister is by no means exceptional.

> 'So long as Mr. Pirzada continues to be the Madame de Pompadour of the Court of Pakistan, it should not at all be difficult for him to wring out of his victims any number, and any kind, of statements. The story, however, would be quite different if the

[1] A vote of censure was pending in the Muslim League Parliamentary Party which it was believed would be carried against the Chief Minister (*Dawn*, November 28 and 30, 1953).

Pakistan

Centre becomes honest enough and institutes a judicial enquiry into his doings.

'Remove him from his present place of vantage, and incapacitate him from corrupting and coercing the people and this grand ideological air-bag will have been at once deflated to its true proportions.'[1]

For the most part political activity has been confined to the very small group of active politicians based on the urban areas. The common man, especially in rural districts, has been unaware of or indifferent to the manœuvres that were taking place at the provincial or national capitals. Ordinary people have not become accustomed to regarding themselves as voters. In ten years there was only one set of general elections (to the provincial Assemblies), and those could not be regarded as a model of democratic procedure.[2] Where popular feeling is seriously aroused, as in the language issue in Bengal or the anti-Qadiani movement in the Punjab, it makes use of more primitive methods to express itself. It would be quite wrong to suggest that public life in Pakistan displays continuous violence or that it is perpetually on the verge of violence. However, the repeated and widespread use of provisions of the law which forbid the holding of political meetings or processions seems to indicate that the authorities are uncertain whether some local agitation will not abandon constitutional methods and resort to direct action.

Political techniques operate on the same general level. The accepted means of mass agitation is to take out a procession which goes to demonstrate in front of public buildings. It is harangued at intervals by orators who use the most impassioned language. They induce the crowd to chant slogans which have an hypnotic

[1] Extract from a Press statement issued by Pir Ali Mohammad Rashdi, MLA, Sind (*Dawn*, September 13, 1954).

[2] The Electoral Reforms Commission had this to say: 'It is a fact beyond dispute that the existing machinery for superintendence, direction and control of the preparation, publication and revision of the electoral rolls and the conduct of elections to the Legislatures is absolutely unsatisfactory, and that it has totally failed to achieve a true representation of the people.' Report, *Gazette of Pakistan Extraordinary*, April 24, 1956, p. 929.

The Decline of the Muslim League

effect. This is how one such episode appeared to the local Superintendent of Police:

'In spite of my persuasion and advice these three persons asked their followers to shout "Sir Zafrullah *murdabad*," "Mirza Bashir Ahmad *murdabad*" and "*Mirzaeeat murdabad*"[1] and all their followers shouted these slogans vociferously and some of them jumped and clapped. This procession was swollen by more and more men as it advanced and after passing through Block No. 9 and Bansanwala Bazar it came back to the Katchery Bazar where it was met by another big procession which was equally strong in numbers and the whole procession then marched to the Municipal Gardens ... Abdur Rashid Ashk addressed the processionists at Gol Chowk and advised them not to disperse and go fearlessly through their proposed route. The processionists shouted anti-Zafrullah Khan and anti-Mirzaeeat slogans with great noise and voice and at one time it seemed as if there was no law and order.'[2]

In the towns there are always elements spoiling for a riot. Local 'goondas' take part in the hope of violence and loot. The students of colleges and high schools come out 'on strike.' Of course the authorities retaliate and the tongue of the demagogue is countered by the *lathi* of the policeman. Casualties are inflicted and rumour exaggerates them into a massacre. The mob begins to demand a 'hartal' (a cessation of business) in protest, and merchants who refuse to close their shops are pillaged and stoned. The processions grow larger, louder and more lethal. In default of effective democracy this has been the participation of the common man in politics.

But to return to the Muslim League. Not merely did it start in Pakistan with these many inherent sources of weakness, but it had to take responsibility for everything that had, or seemed to have, got worse since partition, and to answer for all the hopes left unfulfilled. There were floods, corruption, inefficiency and poverty, and there was no kingdom of heaven on earth. And Government, as always, was to blame.

[1] 'Death to Sir Zafrullah,' 'Death to Mirza Bashir Ahmad,' 'Death to the Mirzais' (a Muslim minority of which Sir Zafrullah was a member and Mirza Bashir Ahmad the leader). See below, pp. 204-7.   [2] *Munir Report*, p. 41.

Pakistan

It is easy to see why the League lost popularity. But the opposition also had its difficulties. The largest party in undivided India was the Indian National Congress. It had tried to attract both Muslim and Hindu, but the large majority of its members was Hindu. It had, of course, opposed partition vehemently until 1947, and its final acceptance was made unwillingly and with some bitterness. In India the Congress became the government, and as such the representative of a country that Pakistan feared and mistrusted. The Pakistan National Congress, which severed its ties with the Indian body, was forced into the position of being the spokesman for a minority. The Muslim League had insisted that the Congress was a communal organization of the caste Hindus; in Pakistan the Congress had little option but to fulfil that role. Many of its leaders, including the first Pakistan Leader of the Opposition, Krishan Sankar Roy, migrated to India. In West Pakistan almost all the Hindu and Sikh population fled and the party virtually ceased to exist. A small contingent of Bengali Hindus in the Constituent Assembly could not hope to play more than a minor and defensive part.

The position of anti-League Muslims was even more difficult. In pro-Pakistan eyes, a Hindu was expected to be in favour of Hindu *raj*. But a Muslim who was against the League was against Pakistan, and hence a traitor to the nation. To continue to regard partition as wrong or to suggest that any of its provisions might be modified became a criminal offence punishable by up to ten years' imprisonment.[1] Even to be suspected of regretting the events of 1947 was tantamount to facing an accusation of disloyalty. Some, who had sided openly with the Congress, transferred their activities to India. Others, like Khan Abdul Ghaffar Khan, wished to stay with their own people and suffered imprisonment or harassment in consequence. Those who had been unable to accept the full claims of either Congress or League but

[1] *Pakistan Penal Code (Amendment) Act*, 1950. An offender under this Act is a person who, to the prejudice of the safety of Pakistan, 'shall by words, spoken or written, or by signs or visible representation, condemn the creation of Pakistan ... or advocate the curtailment or abolition of the sovereignty of Pakistan in respect of all or any of the territories lying within its borders ...'

had pleaded for communal harmony, found themselves discredited and without a spiritual home in either camp.

There was a number of minor parties existing in Pakistan from the beginning. Membership in any of twenty such organizations was declared by the League Working Committee to be incompatible with membership of the League.[1] These included the Congress, the Communists, the Red Shirts and a number of splinter groups that had broken away from the League.

The first chance for a display of Opposition strength came in

Party	% Muslim Votes	Seats
Muslim League	52·0	143 (+10 transfers from other parties or independents)
Jinnah Awami League	18·3	29
Jamaat-i-Islami	4·4	1
Azad Pakistan	2·0	1
Independents		5
Minorities (non-Muslim)		5
		194 (+3 by-elections pending due to election of 3 candidates by 2 constituencies each).

It was noteworthy that, of twelve seats in the city of Lahore, six were won by the Opposition.

the Punjab election of 1951. The main opponents of the League ran candidates under the banner of the Jinnah Awami Muslim League. This party was the product of an alliance between two groups. The Awami (People's) League was led by Mr. H. S. Suhrawardy and claimed to fill the role of an all-Pakistan Muslim Opposition. The second group, called the Jinnah Muslim League, was composed mainly of the adherents of the Khan of Mamdot, who had been deposed as Chief Minister in 1949. A number of

[1] Muslim League Working Committee, *Text of Resolutions*, December 25 and 27, 1949, Resolution No. 11.

Pakistan

lesser parties also entered candidates for the election. One of these was the Azad (Free) Pakistan Party under the leadership of Mian Iftikharuddin, a former provincial cabinet minister of mercurial temperament and Marxist ideas. The Communist Party, the *Jamaat-i-Islami* and the Islam League were also in the field.

The election results shown on p. 55 gave a substantial margin of victory to the Muslim League.[1]

The elections in the North-West Frontier Province showed a similar trend, and the Muslim League obtained 67 out of 85 seats with substantial additional support from independents. In Sind (1953) the situation was enlivened by the participation of three former League Chief Ministers, each of whom was at the time disqualified from public office. Pir Ilahi Bakhsh organized the Awami Front and Mr. Khuhro (who had not clearly severed his connection with the League) sponsored the Sind League. But the result was none the less a substantial victory for the Muslim League.

This pattern of electoral successes for the Muslim League was rudely broken by events in East Bengal. The provincial (Muslim League) government had shown clear signs of reluctance to face the electorate. After the sensational defeat of the government candidate in a by-election, further vacancies were allowed to accumulate until by August 1953 34 seats were vacant out of 171.[2] The government then decided that the five-year term of the Legislative Assembly would be held to run not from the previous election or the first meeting of the legislature of undivided Bengal but from March 1948 when the East Bengal section first assembled. March 1953, however, found the government still unprepared and the Constituent Assembly acted to extend the life of the Provincial Assembly until March 1954.[3]

Up to this point the main opposition to the League had come

[1] The figures of party standings are taken from *Dawn*, April 1 and 2, 1951. The details are to be approached with reserve, since party affiliations (especially of independents) often change immediately before or immediately after election day.
[2] East Bengal Legislative Assembly, *Proceedings*, Vol. XI, No. 1.
[3] *The East Bengal Legislative Assembly (Continuance) Act*, 1953.

The Decline of the Muslim League

from the Congress, inside the Assembly, and the Awami League from without. In 1953, when the preparations for the election were already beginning, Mr. A. K. Fazlul Huq, who had been Advocate-General for East Bengal, broke with the government and began to re-form his old political associates into the Krishak Sramik (Peasants and Workers) Party. This party stood for the achievement of the degree of provincial autonomy envisaged by the Lahore Resolution of 1940. It also announced a plan of co-operation with the Nizam-i-Islam Party[1] to develop Pakistan in accordance with Islamic doctrine. In December 1953 Fazlul Huq reached an agreement with the Awami League by which the main Opposition forces should present a combined list of candi-

Muslim Seats		Non-Muslim Seats	
United Front	223	Congress	24
Khilafat-i-Rabani	1	Scheduled Caste Fedn.	27
Muslim League	10	United Front	10
Independent	3	Ganatantri Dal	3
		Christian	1
		Buddhist	2
		Communist	4
		Independent	1
	237		72

dates, under the name of the United Front. Committees of the Front were set up in most constituencies and candidates were selected. Much subsequent confusion was to arise from this selection since it was often uncertain which section of the Front could claim the primary allegiance of the candidates.

The Muslim League did not appear to be worried by these signs of unity among its opponents. In January 1954 the Dacca correspondent of a Karachi newspaper was prepared to forecast that the League would win 75 to 80 per cent of the Muslim seats, and two weeks before polling began that same journal was still confident of a League victory.[2]

[1] This group represented orthodox Muslim opinion.
[2] *Dawn*, January 27, 1954, and March 4, 1954.

Pakistan

Sixteen parties were concerned in the election with 1,285 candidates for 309 seats. The results (given on p. 57) were almost beyond belief, both to the League and the United Front.[1]

Such a massive defeat in a province containing more than half the national population inevitably undermined the position of the central government. Central and Bengal politics became intertwined, and neither can be understood in isolation. In East Bengal the United Front formed a government which was dismissed by the centre after two months in office. Five months later the Constituent Assembly was dissolved. The central cabinet was then reconstructed and a number of persons were included who were not members of the Muslim League. Mr. Suhrawardy joined, as Minister of Law, in December 1954. He was followed shortly by Abu Hussain Sarkar, who described himself as a nominee of Fazlul Huq. But the negotiations which led up to these appointments revealed a sharp cleavage between the forces led by Mr. Suhrawardy and those of Mr. Fazlul Huq. This, of course, gave the central government the opportunity to play one faction against the other.

At this stage the party situation was highly confused. At the centre there was no legislature and the ministry was composed of Muslim Leaguers, anti-Leaguers and non-party men. It was not a coalition of parties but a collection of individuals whose political friends reserved the right to continue to wage political warfare as opportunity offered. Confusion was deepened by uncertainty concerning the cohesion and leadership of the United Front. At the time of his dismissal Fazlul Huq had been described by the Prime Minister as 'a self-confessed traitor to Pakistan.'[2] There were rumours that some kind of legal action might be taken against him. The tactical situation seemed to indicate a need for taking cover. Accordingly Mr. Fazlul Huq announced

[1] *Dawn*, April 5, 1954. As with most election returns in Pakistan the figures cited are to be approached with caution.

The Ganatantri Dal had aligned itself with the United Front during the campaign and some of its members had secured United Front nominations for Muslim seats. It seems probable that a few members of the Communist Party also secured United Front nominations although this was not publicly announced.

[2] Broadcast on June 1, 1954.

The Decline of the Muslim League

that, on account of his age, he was retiring from public life.' This gesture was not taken at face value by those who knew him, but did succeed in increasing the confusion about the effective leadership of the United Front. As the prospect of a return to representative government became brighter the struggle for control became more fierce. Some kind of climax was reached at a meeting of the United Front Parliamentary Party in February 1955.

'The much looked-forward-to meeting of the United Front took place at the Assembly refreshment room yesterday (Thursday) from 2.30 and ended indecisively at 8 p.m. At 8 p.m. the District Magistrate arrived on the scene and asked the members to disperse on the request of the leaders of the two groups of warring politicians, none of whom wanted to leave the field before their opponents.

'In fact, if there was no agreement about anything else, there was agreement at least on one point, that there should be simultaneous evacuation of the battlefield.

'At one stage two simultaneous meetings presided over by two different persons, with speakers addressing their respective Chairs, and the audience indulging in catcalls and boos and crossfire of witty sallies at the top of their voices were going on.'[2]

At about this time a group of some twenty members of the Awami League broke away from their leaders and pledged their support to the other segment of the United Front. The 'battle of numbers' was intensified, each side claiming that it had a clear majority in the Assembly.[3] Since there was no legislative session

[1] *The Times of Karachi*, July 24, 1954.
[2] *The Pakistan Observer*, February 18, 1955.
[3] The following estimates of strength within the Front were made by correspondents of Karachi newspapers:

	April 1954	April 1955
Awami League	142	98
Awami League (Splinter Group)	–	20
Krishak Sramik	48	69
Nizam-i-Islam	19	19
Ganatantri Dal	13	12
Other	–	1
	222	219

Dawn, October 20, 1954, and *The Times of Karachi*, April 2, 1955.

Pakistan

during this period the various claims could not be put to a conclusive test. In June 1955 the members were called upon to choose the new Constituent Assembly. Of first preference votes Fazlul Huq secured 104 and Suhrawardy 93.[1]

Earlier that same month representative government had been restored in East Bengal. Abu Hussain Sarkar (Krishak Sramik) had resigned from the central cabinet in order to head the new ministry. No members of the main Awami League were included and that party finally announced that it had severed its connection with the United Front.[2] It was clear that no parliamentary majority would be possible without substantial support from non-Muslim sources, as well as the continued adherence of the minor parties within the United Front. The Hindu and Scheduled Caste members found themselves treated with a respect that had not always been accorded in the past. The Congress Party decided to co-operate but it did not attempt to conceal its lack of enthusiasm. 'In these circumstances,' stated the leader of the party, 'we had to choose between the two alternative allies with their own characteristic leaders. For reasons better imagined than explicitly stated, we decided to work with the United Front. But we kept our minds open.'[3] Ministerial appointments were given to members of the Congress, the Scheduled Castes and the United Progressive Parliamentary Party. A coalition such as this could have no conceivable common policy, but it was in a position to maintain a government while political attention focused on Karachi and the framing of the new constitution. Each group hoped to incorporate its ideas into that document and was prepared to maintain a government in East Bengal in order that its own influence might be enhanced. But those who opposed an Islamic constitution and hoped for almost complete autonomy for East Bengal were disappointed by the draft constitution. Major disagreements on both local and national issues caused four of the minor parties to announce their withdrawal from the coalition—the Ganatantri Dal, the Congress, the

---

[1] *Dawn*, June 23, 1955.   [2] *Ibid.*, June 24, 1955.
[3] *The Pakistan National Congress: Its Present Policy*, a statement by Mr. Basanta Kumar Das, Karachi, September 5, 1955, p. 2.

The Decline of the Muslim League

Scheduled Castes Federation and the United Progressive Party.[1] By splitting the two last-named groups some minority representation was retained in the ministry. A few months later the Awami League splinter group (led by Abdus Salam Khan) also parted company with the Front.[2]

By this time it was clear that the United Front had disintegrated and that the Krishak Sramik ministry could not survive. At the end of August 1956 it submitted its resignation and was replaced by a cabinet under Ataur Rahman Khan (Awami League). Three non-Muslims and a member of the Ganatantri Dal were included in the new government. Some indication of voting strength in the Assembly at this time was given by the results of the by-election to fill two Muslim vacancies in the National Assembly. The Awami League candidate secured 143 votes to 85 for his principal rival (United Front).[3] That popular support was also behind the Awami League seemed to be indicated by the outcome of seven provincial by-elections held simultaneously in December 1956. Of the six Muslim seats, five were won by the Awami League and one by the Nizam-i-Islam with Krishak Sramik support. The Muslim League contested five seats and polled just under half the votes cast for the winning candidates. The KSP entered in only one contest and gained less than 1,000 votes out of 18,000.[4]

In West Pakistan before 1956 the Muslim League had enjoyed a position of overwhelming superiority. The obvious political instability had been due to the rivalry of conflicting factions within the ruling party. In January 1956 elections were held to choose the members of the new West Pakistan Assembly. Direct elections would have required considerable preparation and the government decided that the then existing provincial legislatures should act as electoral colleges. In the original draft of the One Unit Bill it was provided that each Assembly should choose its full quota by majority vote. Thus the Punjab's 197 MLAs would select 124 members of the new chamber. This was modified

[1] *Dawn*, January 4, 10, 12 and March 4, 1956.
[2] *Ibid.*, July 14, 1956.
[3] *Ibid.*, September 6, 1956.   [4] *Ibid.*, December 16, 1956.

Pakistan

during the passage of the Bill so that the MLAs from each district elected a group of members. Thus from Sialkot 15 MLAs were empowered to return 10 new members.[1] Ten seats were reserved for non-Muslims but the same electoral groups were to make the selection. Consequently any faction which controlled a majority in a district could ensure the return of its own supporters for all seats. The elections took place in January 1956 and the result was obviously a victory for the Muslim League. But whose Muslim League? In what had been the Punjab the followers of Daultana appeared to outnumber those of Gurmani by about three to one.[2] In Sind Mr. Khuhro complained bitterly that 'illegal and unconstitutional methods' had been employed to defeat certain of his followers.[3] But Khuhro himself as well as three other former Chief Ministers were returned.

The original government of West Pakistan had been formed by drawing on the existing provincial governments. The three former Chief Ministers, Dasti, Khuhro and Bahadur Khan, were included, along with Daultana. Since Gurmani had been appointed Governor it was desirable to find a non-Punjabi as Chief Minister. It was also desirable that he should not be associated with any of the factions within the League. The choice fell upon Dr. Khan Sahib who had been Congress Chief Minister of the Frontier Province until August 1947. This appointment had the additional advantage that tended to make the One Unit scheme more acceptable to the Pathans. Dr. Khan Sahib regarded himself at this time as a non-party man.

It was obvious that the balance of forces in the cabinet represented an uneasy compromise. Immediately after the elections signs of friction became manifest. The Muslim League Council passed a resolution criticizing the leadership for failing to allot League tickets according to the normal party procedure. At the same time the new President, Sardar Nishtar, instructed the West

[1] These provisions which form part of the Establishment of West Pakistan Act, 1955, were debated at length in the Constituent Assembly on September 26, 27 and 29, 1955.
[2] The results and an indication of their factional significance are given in *Dawn*, January 20 and 21, 1956.   [3] *Ibid.*, January 21, 1956.

The Decline of the Muslim League

Pakistan legislators to form a League Parliamentary Party without delay.[1] (Such a party would of course not have included Khan Sahib.) In March, at a meeting of fifty-seven members from the Frontier Province and its tribal areas, Dr. Khan Sahib was unanimously chosen as leader,[2] though there was no indication that this action was intended to create a new political party. A few days later the central Prime Minister confirmed his support for the provincial leader: 'Dr. Khan Sahib was and remains a non-party man whose services are considered invaluable for the solidarity of West Pakistan.'[3]

The continuance in office of Dr. Khan was not acceptable to the majority of members of the provincial Muslim League Assembly Party and a formal resolution to that effect was adopted, though not without dissent.[4] Sardar Bahadur Khan was chosen party leader, and although still a member of the provincial cabinet he addressed a peremptory demand to the Governor. 'Now that the Legislative Party, consisting of an overwhelming majority of the members of West Pakistan Legislature, has been formed and a Leader elected according to the Constitution and well-established convention, I am entitled to be called upon to form a government.'[5] Khan Sahib's reply was to drop Sardar Bahadur, Daultana and Khuhro from the cabinet and to strengthen his ministry by adding, among others, the following former Chief Ministers: Mamdot, Kazi Fazullah and Abdur Rashid. On April 23rd the provincial League announced a series of expulsions and Dr. Khan Sahib proclaimed the formation of the Republican Party.

The stage was now set for a trial of strength, and this took place when the provincial Assembly held its first meeting in May. The scene was one of considerable confusion and the issue was that of the election of a Speaker. Amid protest that certain members had been physically prevented from voting as they wished, the result was announced: for the Republican candidate,

[1] *Dawn*, January 31, 1956.   [2] *Ibid.*, March 19, 1956.
[3] *Ibid.*, March 30, 1956.   [4] *Ibid.*, April 4, 1956.
[5] An exchange of letters took place between the Governor, the Chief Minister and Sardar Bahadur. The texts were published, *Ibid.*, April 9, 1956.

148; for the League candidate, 148. The acting chairman gave his vote to the Republicans and the ministry was saved.[1] As has often been the case in Pakistan, a demonstration of strength led to an accession of strength. Abdus Sattar Pirzada who, on the first day of the session fought hard for the League, promptly changed sides and reappeared for the second day as a minister in the Republican cabinet.[2] For the remainder of the session the League was careful not to challenge a division. The single vote that occurred on the budget was a contrived division which yielded a result of 169 to 0 for the government.[3]

It has already been observed that there is a close connection between provincial and central politics. In the days of the League's hegemony the support of the centre was usually the vital factor in the maintenance of provincial office. But when League majorities in the provinces disappeared the centre had to search for alternative sources of support. The second Constituent Assembly had an initial party composition as follows:[4]

Muslim League	26
United Front	16
Awami League	13
Congress	4
Scheduled Caste Federation	3
United Progressive Party	2
Others	16
	80

[1] *Civil and Military Gazette*, May 21, 1956.
[2] *Pakistan Observer*, May 22, 1956.
[3] *Civil and Military Gazette*, May 28, 1956.
[4] The names and party affiliations of members are given in *Dawn*, June 22 and 23, 1955 (provinces), and July 30, 1955 (states and tribal areas). The category 'others' included a wide range of political opinion. There was Firoz Khan Noon with two adherents, Fazlur Rahman (Independent Muslim League), Khan Sahib, Mian Iftikharuddin (Azad Pakistan), Fazlul Karim (often described as a communist), three Muslim League Associates (Gibbon, Abdul Bari and Kirpaldas) and six state and tribal leaders. These last six might be expected to vote for the government provided that the authorities of West Pakistan and the centre were pulling in the same direction. Thus the Muslim League at the outset expected to be able to carry at least ten of the miscellaneous votes.

The Decline of the Muslim League

The first meeting of the Assembly found the United Front in office in Bengal with the Awami League in Opposition. But Mr. Suhrawardy was still a member of the central cabinet. Although the ministry was still regarded as a collection of individuals rather than a coalition of parties, it seemed for a while as though a Muslim League-Awami League coalition were about to be concluded. The first division found those two parties aligned against the United Front, the Congress, the Scheduled Castes and Noon.[1] A month later, after the League had replaced Mohammed Ali (Bogra) by Chaudhri Mohamad Ali, it appeared that Suhrawardy was to lead a government with the support of the Awami and Muslim Leagues.[2] The United Front countered with an offer of co-operation which permitted the Prime Ministership to stay with the Muslim League. Accordingly a government came into being which contained members of the League, the United Front, the Scheduled Castes and the United Progressives. Where matters were put to the vote between August 1955 and the end of the year the official side recorded a maximum strength of 53 and the opposition of 19.[3]

The formation of the Republican Party in West Pakistan obviously altered the balance of power at the centre. Many of the prominent M.P.s from that province joined the Republicans, and one of its supporters, a minister in the provincial government, claimed that the Republicans were the largest party with twenty-two members in the National Assembly.[4] The new party showed no desire to unseat the Prime Minister or the central government. Dr. Khan Sahib stated emphatically: 'I wish to make it clear that Mr. Mohamad Ali has my and my party's fullest support. He is the leader of the Coalition Party in the National Assembly, and the formation of the Republican Party has not made the slightest

---

[1] Constituent Assembly of Pakistan, *Debates*, Vol. I, p. 18, July 7, 1955. The vote was 40 to 26.

[2] *Dawn*, August 9-13, 1955.

[3] The Awami League was joined from time to time by Noon, Fazlur Rahman, Fazlul Karim, Iftikharuddin, Mahmood Ali (Ganatantri Dal) and Abdur Rashid and Jaffer Shah (from the Frontier Province).

[4] *Pakistan Times*, June 21, 1956, statement by Kazi Fazlullah.

change in his position as the Leader of the Coalition Party in the National Assembly.'[1] The Prime Minister did not seem perturbed by the rise of a new party. His endorsement of Dr. Khan Sahib has already been noted. When the Muslim League Committee attempted to force him to intervene in provincial politics on behalf of the party, he reacted sharply. 'Let me make it clear that in any action that I have to take as Prime Minister I cannot be bound by a resolution of any political party. I have to do what I consider to be right under the constitution, and for that I am responsible to the Cabinet and to the Parliament.'[2] The result of this mutual respect of Mr. Mohamad Ali and Dr. Khan Sahib was that the central government maintained the support of two parties that were feuding fiercely in another arena, while the Prime Minister, the nominal leader of one of those parties, chose to remain above the battle.

The Muslim League in Parliament was now crumbling fast. It felt, with some reason, that its own leader and Prime Minister was not prepared to take strong action to prevent its total disintegration. In particular, his support for Dr. Khan Sahib in West Pakistan was regarded as a betrayal of the party. Two ministers were reported to have resigned from the cabinet and two others from the League. On September 8, 1956, Mohamad Ali resigned as Prime Minister and from membership in the League, accusing his party of undermining his authority.[3]

When Mohamad Ali resigned as Prime Minister, the Muslim League–Republican understanding came to an end. A coalition of the Awami League and the Republican Party formed the new administration. The Muslim League and United Front moved into Opposition. It was not clear how many M.P.s had transferred from the Muslim League to the Republicans, nor how many owed allegiance to the rump of the United Front. This uncertainty led to a contest between I. I. Chundrigar (Muslim League) and

[1] *Civil and Military Gazette*, May 26, 1956.
[2] *Pakistan Observer*, May 15, 1956. This statement is in marked contrast to the attitude of Liaquat Ali (see above, p. 38).
[3] *Dawn*, August 28, September 7 and 9, 1956.

The Decline of the Muslim League

Hamidul Huq Chowdhury (United Front) for recognition as Leader of the Opposition.[1]

The system of political parties in Pakistan bears little resemblance to that of most other democratic countries. Politics has begun at the top. Pakistan has neither a two-party system, in which the political struggle is waged between fairly stable groups, one of which is in office and the other in Opposition, nor a multi-party system, in which clear differences of programme or ideology separate a variety of opponents. In Pakistan politics is made up of a large number of leading persons who, with their political dependents, form loose agreements to achieve power and to maintain it. Consequently rigid adherence to a policy or a measure is likely to make a politician less available for office. Those who lack fixed ideas but who control legislators, money or influence have tended to prosper in political life.

Political parties, with the possible exception to the Awami League in East Pakistan, have not turned their attention toward the primary voter. This has not been necessary. The national legislature has never been chosen by popular vote. In West Pakistan each province had one adult suffrage election, but as the Electoral Reforms Commission observed: 'It was widely and persistently complained that these elections were a farce, a mockery and a fraud upon the electorate.'[2] And in East Pakistan many MLAs had been returned because in the few months immediately preceding the election they had discovered a sudden faith in the powers of leadership of Mr. Fazlul Huq. The electorate is predominantly illiterate, and this is an obstacle to intelligent voting. But more important than this has been the feeling of many politicians that elections were so remote that they could safely be disregarded. As long as the politician is not forced to be aware that his inconsistencies and factional manœuvres will be punished at the polls he can afford to forget the voter in favour of the pursuit of office by any means. It has been largely this inability to trust the professional politician that has led to the elevation to political office of men such as Chaudhri Mohamad Ali and Sardar

[1] *Dawn*, October 12, 1956. Chundrigar was successful.
[2] *Gazette of Pakistan Extraordinary*, April 24, 1956, p. 922.

Pakistan

Abdur Rashid who first became ministers and afterwards, if at all, became politicians and leaders of parties.

A major obstacle to the growth of an effective party system was the failure to emerge of a substantial and stable Opposition. In the first Constituent Assembly the Muslim League controlled the votes of almost all the Muslim members and the main Opposition party, the Awami League, was unrepresented. In the Punjab, Sind and the Frontier Province the government's majority was similarly overwhelming. In Bengal the League was in a position to dominate until 1954 when it all but disappeared from the Assembly. It required the disintegration of the United Front to provide both the government and a strong Opposition.

It has been observed before that the real political struggle took place within the League. It was from among those members of the League who had quarrelled with the leadership that an avowed Opposition began to emerge in 1949–50. In the North-West Frontier Province the Pir of Manki Sharif, who had been prominent in the fight for Pakistan in 1947, was forced out of the League and moved into Opposition. In East Bengal, Maulana Bhashani, a former President of the Assam Muslim League, felt that the League was losing touch with the people and he began to criticize the government. In the Punjab the Khan of Mamdot had been dismissed as Chief Minister largely due to intrigues within the League and he began to prepare to contest the coming elections against his former party.

At about this time Mr. H. S. Suhrawardy decided to live permanently in Pakistan. Suhrawardy had been a leading member of the Muslim League in Bengal from 1936, and had been the last Chief Minister of the undivided province. But in 1947 he had tried to preserve a united Bengal based on Hindu–Muslim cooperation. In this he failed, but after partition he remained on the Indian side of the border working for communal harmony. However, he had been elected to the Constituent Assembly of Pakistan, and he visited Karachi to take his seat and to take part in the last session of the All-India Muslim League in December 1947.[1] He was present to register a protest when the Assembly

[1] Raghib Ahsan, *He is That Suhrawardy* (Karachi, 1951), p. 15.

The Decline of the Muslim League

established a rule which, by requiring residence in Pakistan as a condition of membership, deprived him of his seat.[1]

Some months after his permanent establishment in Pakistan Mr. Suhrawardy began to piece together the constituent parts of an Opposition party—the Awami League—designed to operate in both wings of the country. Its organization is similar to that of the Muslim League, with a Convention, Council, Working Committee and Convener and comparable organizations for the provinces and districts.

A Convention was held in Lahore in December 1952 and the party adopted its manifesto. This document declared that 'the constitution and laws of Pakistan, its moral, social, political and economic order, and the policies of the State must be founded on the eternal injunctions of Islam.'[2] In the matter of the constitution the Awami League had three principal suggestions.[3] First, the head of the State should be elected by the direct vote of the people. Second, provisions defining fundamental rights should be incorported in the constitution and made enforceable in the law courts. Third, the independence of the judiciary should be strengthened by the separation of the judiciary from the executive.

There is little that is surprising and little that is definite in the programme of the Awami League. As with most political pronouncements in Pakistan it is hard to relate to contemporary reality. Thus the proposals for economic policy seem to be the product of wishful thinking rather than an analysis of the facts.

> 'The State should be self-sufficient and even surplus in food and national requirements; it must be in a position to export finished products; the agriculturists must be assured a reasonable price for their produce, and the labourers a reasonable wage. The cost of living must be proportionate to the income.[4]

It is suggested that the country should proceed towards industrial

---
[1] Constituent Assembly of Pakistan, *Debates*, Vol. III, p. 31, May 18, 1948.
[2] *Manifesto of the Jinnah Awami Muslim League* (Lahore, n.d.), p. 7.
[3] *Ibid.*, p. 8.
[4] This and the following proposals are to be found, *Ibid.*, pp. 13-16.

self-sufficiency and the government should take the initiative in setting up necessary industries. 'Taxes should be reduced, and should be such as to promote the prosperity of the people.' If government income is insufficient, 'a levy on surplus property' may make up the balance. In spite of the large programme of government activity it is promised that 'there shall be as little State interference to trade and business as possible. . . .' Finally the party proposes the 'abolition of . . . the system of landlordism,' and intends to limit ownership of land to not more than 250 acres of irrigated land. The state is to take over 'the surplus property of the landlords' and is to pay such compensation as the economic condition of the country permits.

Mr. Suhrawardy made vigorous efforts to distinguish his party from the Muslim League.

> 'In the very first place we do not believe in identifying the State with the party, the Ministry and the administration, i.e. we believe in democracy as opposed to fascism. Next, we believe that an opposition party is necessary for the proper functioning of democracy, this is the only influence that can keep the rulers in check and at work, and can create public opinion. The Muslim League, on the other hand, labels opposition as disruption, demands that there shall be no parties other than itself, and all other parties must be crushed out of existence.[1]

He accused the government of coercion, corruption and maladministration and of acting with a complete disregard for public opinion. 'The elections' (in the Punjab) 'were a farce, intimidation and coercion, fraud and manipulation of ballot papers and ballot boxes were practised on an unprecedented scale.'[2] Mr. Suhrawardy called for the immediate dissolution of the Constituent Assembly and its replacement by a body elected directly by the people.

By 1953 the Awami League was organized in every province and was led by a man with a national reputation. But it was not

[1] H. S. Suhrawardy, *Address to the Nation*, delivered at Dacca, May 8, 1953 (Lahore), pp. 6–7.   [2] *Ibid.*, p. 33.

The Decline of the Muslim League

represented in the Constituent Assembly, and occupied very few seats in the provinces. Further, it was by no means clear that its national unity depended on anything more than shared opposition to the Muslim League. Many of its leaders had joined less from conviction than because they found themselves in temporary disagreement with the government. The instance of the Khan of Mamdot has already been noted. Other elements of the Awami League differed with the official leadership on matters of policy. The East Pakistan Council took the initiative in dropping the word 'Muslim' from the name of the party and in advocating a system of joint rather than separate electorates. This stand was then endorsed by the national Working Committee.[1] Such a decision had the effect of alienating the more rigid Muslim members who regarded it as a departure from the principles of the 1952 Manifesto. Fourteen prominent members of the party in West Pakistan announced the formation of a new Awami Muslim League, and claimed to be the upholders of the original creed of the party.[2] They were particularly critical of the decision of the East Pakistan Council to admit non-Muslim members. 'The admission of non-Muslims into the Party is tantamount to permitting Bharati [Indian] and other anti-Pakistan influences to permeate the body-politic of the Party.' The party's attitude toward non-Muslims was also one of the causes leading to the defection of the splinter group led by Abdus Salam Khan in the East Bengal Assembly. A further source of disagreement on policy lay in the attitude of the Awami League toward the unification of West Pakistan. The official attitude of the party was that it approved of the scheme but objected to the method employed to bring it into being. The Frontier Awami League continued to demand a plebiscite on the issue. The action of Mr. Suhrawardy seemed to show that the autocratic spirit of the Muslim League had its counterpart in his own organization.

[1] *Dawn*, December 2, 1955. For a discussion of the issue of joint or separate electorates, see below, pp. 240-54.
[2] The fourteen dissidents included the Pir of Zakori Sharif, one MCA, one MLA and a joint secretary of the central party organization. The statement issued by this group is published, *ibid.*, December 2, 1955.

Pakistan

'In view of the fact that the NWFP Awami League has not accepted the resolution of the Central Awami League regarding the One Unit for West Pakistan and is continuing to propagate the doctrine of plebiscite on this issue, I, as convener of the All-Pakistan Awami League, disaffiliate the NWFP Awami League and appoint Khan Ghulam Mohammad Khan Lundkhor to organize the NWFP Awami League.'[1]

The second major party to emerge in Pakistan since partition was the Krishak Sramik party. This group is composed almost entirely of the personal followers of Mr. A. K. Fazlul Huq. The octogenarian 'Lion of Bengal' had enjoyed a remarkable power to sway large masses of people. The special correspondent of *The Times* reported that '. . . tears come into the eyes of middle-aged lawyers when his name is mentioned, and the faces of young trade unionists glow with devotional fervour.'[2] He has been active in the public life of Bengal for more than fifty years. He has been in and out of the Muslim League since its foundation, and it was he who moved the famous Lahore Resolution in 1940. But in 1937 he had led his own Krishak Proja Party and had emerged as Chief Minister of a coalition government. He then rejoined the Muslim League but was expelled by Mr. Jinnah in 1941. After partition he became Advocate-General for East Bengal, but he broke with the provincial government and in the latter half of 1953 began to form his own party to contest the coming elections. His main demand was for the achievement of the degree of provincial autonomy envisaged by the Lahore Resolution.[3] The Krishak Sramik Party first entered into alliance with the Nizam-i-Islam Party. This organization represented conservative Muslim opinion and drew its limited support from religious groups. At the end of 1953 it was announced that the Awami League and the Krishak Sramik Party had formed a United Front to fight the election. A joint manifesto, the 21 Points, was issued as the basis for the campaign.[4] It was a document which contrived to promise something to everybody. The preamble demanded that no laws

[1] *Dawn*, January 25, 1956. [2] *The Times*, December 6, 1954.
[3] *Dawn*, July 30, 1953. [4] *Ibid.*, December 20, 1953.

The Decline of the Muslim League

should be passed which were repugnant to the Quran and Sunnah. Many of the points related to the economic life of Bengal, and it was proposed to abolish *zamindari* without compensation and distribute the land to the peasants. There was also a section on civil liberties, demanding the repeal of the Safety Acts, the release of security prisoners and the safeguarding of the rights of the press. The crucial item was point 19, the demand for provincial autonomy:

> 'Secure all subjects, including residuary powers, except Defence, Foreign Affairs and Currency, for East Bengal, which shall be fully autonomous and sovereign as envisaged in the historic Lahore Resolution, and establish Naval Headquarters and ordnance factory in East Bengal so as to make it militarily self-sufficient.'

It was when Fazlul Huq carried this line of argument further, after his appointment as Chief Minister, that the central government described him as a self-confessed traitor and dismissed him. But by August 1955 he was a minister in the central cabinet, and a few months later he became Governor of East Pakistan. It would seem, therefore, that his insistence on full provincial autonomy had been laid aside. Apart from this issue it is difficult to discern any clear-cut programme advocated by the Krishak Sramik Party.

In one sense both the Awami League and the Krishak Sramik Party can be described as radical, in that they envisage drastic changes in the social and political structure of Pakistan. But neither could be classed as predominantly left-wing in its outlook. Pakistan is a country which has never achieved a highly developed capitalist economy. Government intervention over a wide area of the economy has been generally regarded as inevitable. But a systematic socialist approach, whether Marxist or otherwise, has been confined to relatively small groups. The Communist Party, even before it was banned in 1954, had little overt success.[1] In

---

[1] It is not easy to discover accurate information regarding the activities of the Communist Party in Pakistan. However, the party is discussed in Dilshad Najmuddin, *Political Parties in Pakistan* (thesis presented to the University of the Panjab, dated October 1, 1955).

Pakistan

East Pakistan less than ten communists as such were returned to the Assembly, though one of these was able to secure election to the second Constituent Assembly. However, the Prime Minister, justifying his dismissal of the United Front, gave communist infiltration as one of his reasons.' . . . The communists, who, although they were not openly a part and parcel of the United Front, were very actively supporting the United Front. Some of the communists were masquerading under different party labels, including the Gnantari [sic] Dal.'[1] A leading newspaper of Lahore viewed the situation with greater alarm. 'The Province [East Bengal] swarms with communist cells, University students in particular are affected with the germs. About 80 members of the newly elected Legislature of 309 are believed to be communists or fellow travellers.'[2]

There are two other left-wing parties, the Ganatantri Dal (Democratic Party) and the Azad (Free) Pakistan Party. The former has operated in the east wing and the latter in the west. The two organizations, having similar policies, decided in 1955 to explore the possibility of setting up a combined steering committee to co-ordinate their activities in national affairs.[3] The Ganatantri Dal was formed at a convention held in Dacca in January 1953, attended by about one thousand delegates. It was the first party, apart from the Congress, to adopt a secular approach to politics and to admit non-Muslim members on equal terms. It co-operated with the United Front in the election and remained associated with it until January 1956.

The Azad Pakistan Party held its first convention in September 1952. It appointed a convening committee which drew up a constitution and a statement of policy. One of the sections of the statement gives a clue to its general outlook. 'The real producer of industrial wealth is the working class; the happiness and welfare of a nation's workers must have top priority in any scheme of social justice.'[4] The party, through its parliamentary leader, Mian

[1] Constituent Assembly (Legislature), *Debates*, 1954, Vol. I, p. 1361, June 28, 1954. [2] *Civil and Military Gazette*, July 1, 1954.
[3] *Dawn*, July 18, 1955.
[4] Quoted in Dilshad Najmuddin, *op. cit.*, p. 128.

The Decline of the Muslim League

Iftikharuddin, was sharply critical of the government's friendly attitude toward the Western powers. In 1954, 31 out of 72 members of the National Council resigned from the party on the grounds that it was communist controlled and undemocratic.[1]

One other political party deserves mention.[2] The circumstances in which the Republican Party was created have already been discussed. It came into being mainly because the factions of the Muslim League in West Pakistan could not agree upon the distribution of power and influence. The Punjabis were divided, and the other members wanted to avoid the possibility of Punjabi domination. The party was formed to give support to one man, Khan Sahib, and to keep out of office two other men, Daultana and Khuhro. This was a party that could not wait for popular support to return its members to the legislature. It had to be formed from among the existing MLAs. And its membership thus acquired provided little in the way of common outlook or policy. An attempt to provide a wider base for the party took the form of a Convention attended by some thousand delegates. The Convention met in Lahore in September 1956. Its composition was described by a hostile observer:

'The component part of the Convention are old Unionists, Congressites, renegades and big landlords who brought with them their tenants, servants and friends. Major parts of the province were not represented at all. There was no delegate from the Tribal Area, Baluchistan, northern parts of the former Punjab and some parts of the former Sind. Of the three Karachi Republican MLAs none has come. Similarly only about half a dozen National Assembly members attended the convention out of the total claim of thirty-one. Mr. Abdul Ali, M.P., was the sole delegate from East Pakistan who apparently looked disgusted with the way the deliberations of the convention were being conducted.'[3]

It would seem that the Convention did not succeed in establishing a firm foundation for future activity. In December of the

[1] *Political Parties in Pakistan*, p. 130.
[2] Those parties which were confined to the minority communities are discussed in Chapter VI.   [3] *Dawn*, September 30, 1956.

same year the general secretary of the party resigned, giving three reasons. The party, he said, was insolvent, its leaders were too busy with ministerial posts to have time to spend on party affairs, and the party had no fixed policy. 'We have already made fools of ourselves on the electorate issue and are now busy making confusion worse confounded in our foreign policy.'[1]

The Republican Party was able to maintain its control of the provincial Assembly from April 1956 to March 1957 by securing the support of the Pakistan National Party. This organization was formed by an alliance of six minor parties (including Azad Pakistan, the Redshirts and the Sind Awami Mahaz).[2] Their leaders consisted of G. M. Syed, Abdul Ghaffer Khan and Mian Iftikharuddin and their policy was radical opposition to One Unit and support of joint electorates. The National Party's support was withdrawn from Dr. Khan Sahib in March 1957.[3]

[1] *Dawn*, December 5, 1956 (Mir Abdul Qayyum).
[2] *Ibid.*, August 9, 1956.   [3] *Ibid.*, March 20, 1957.

CHAPTER III

The Constituent Assembly

SECTION I: ORIGIN AND COMPOSITION

THE Constituent Assembly of Pakistan was born without the formal blessing of law. Its conception lay in the Cabinet Mission Plan of May 1946 and the Viceroy's statement of June 3, 1947, which announced the agreement to partition the sub-continent. The 1946 Plan envisioned a single Constituent Assembly for undivided India. This was to be an assembly of representatives chosen by the elected members of the provincial Legislative Assemblies with the addition of delegates from the princely states.

Elections to the provincial legislatures had taken place in 1945-46, that is before either independence or partition had been conceded. The legislatures were not chosen therefore with a view to their future as electoral colleges for the Constituent Assemblies. However, they were dominated by the Indian National Congress and the Muslim League, each campaigning for independence after its own fashion. From the standpoint of Pakistan, it must not be forgotten that the results of these elections yielded a Unionist ministry in the Punjab (though the League overwhelmingly carried the Muslim seats), a pro-Congress regime in the Frontier Province and a coalition in Bengal, which, although led by a Muslim, could not be counted on as an unshakable supporter of the cause. Inevitably the fierce partisan played a more prominent role than the mature statesman.

The franchise for participation in provincial elections was narrow. The details varied from province to province, but the right to vote was based on education and property, and it is unlikely that anywhere more than 15 per cent of the total population was entitled to vote. A number of special constituencies existed for such categories as landowners, university voters, organ-

Pakistan

ized labour and women. More important were the provisions for communal separate electorates and reserved seats. Muslims (and in some cases Christians and others) were entered on separate rolls and voted for candidates of their own community. The Scheduled Castes, while not being placed on separate rolls, were provided with a number of seats reserved for members of that community. This allocation of seats by communities was arranged to over-emphasize the representation of communal minorities, but it gave no help to political minorities within a community. These factors worked heavily in favour of the Muslim League, which scored an immense victory, winning 446 out of 495 Muslim seats in the provincial Assemblies.[1]

The Constituent Assembly of undivided India came into being in 1946. Members were elected by communal groups in the provincial Assemblies, voting by proportional representation. The over-weighting of minority communities was corrected by allocating seats in the ratio of one seat for each one million persons of that community in the province. The Constituent Assembly began its deliberations on December 9, 1946, that is six months before the principle of partition was accepted. The Muslim League members, not being satisfied with the Congress interpretation of the 'grouping' provision of the Cabinet Mission plan, declined to take their seats. Thus the Assembly was almost entirely without Muslim representation.

In June 1947 the partition of the sub-continent was agreed, and in consequence it became necessary to constitute a separate Constituent Assembly for Pakistan. This was brought about under the agreement of June 3rd and the Indian Independence Act. The legislatures of Bengal and the Punjab met and voted for partition. Since the Constituent Assembly members had been chosen as a group to fill the quota for all the Muslims of those two provinces, it became necessary for West Punjab and East Bengal to select new representatives. It was thus that the members were chosen who met together in Karachi on August 10, 1947, for the first meeting of the Constituent Assembly of Pakistan.

The numerical ratio of one member to one million inhabitants

[1] Richard Symonds, *The Making of Pakistan* (London, 3rd ed., 1951), p. 67.

The Constituent Assembly

had been designed to give a workable organization of about four hundred and fifty members for the entire sub-continent, including the princely states. In Pakistan, however, it yielded an Assembly with a maximum strength of less than eighty. For various reasons the effective working strength of the Assembly was always substantially less than this figure.

At the time of its inauguration the total authorized membership of the Assembly was sixty-nine. However, this included a number of persons who, in the aftermath of partition, decided not to remain in Pakistan.[1] Several of these were non-Muslims whose constituents had also left the country in large numbers. The Assembly, by resolution, decided not to refill one General (Hindu) and two Sikh seats from the Punjab. (A later vacancy in a Punjab General seat was also left unfilled, leaving one non-Muslim member from that province, a seat held first by a Christian and then by a Parsi.)[2]

From time to time additions were made to the Assembly. To give representation to the vast numbers of refugees who had entered the country since partition, five extra Muslim seats were given to the Punjab and one to Sind. Additional places were created also for the princely states as they executed instruments of accession. In this manner one seat each was allotted to Bahawalpur, Khairpur, the Baluchistan States Union and the states of the North-West Frontier. At the end of its life the Assembly had a total of seventy-nine seats, although four non-Muslim seats had in fact been vacant for a period of years.

Had it been able to work at full strength, the Constituent Assembly would have been very small for its task. But at every sitting there were many empty places.

---

[1] *The Gazette of Pakistan*, March 26, 1948, reports eight resignations, six of whom were non-Muslims, including the leader of the Opposition, Kisan Sankar Roy. One of the two Muslims to resign was Maulana Kabul Alam Azad who had joined the Indian cabinet.

[2] *Ibid.*, January 11, 1952, election of Mr. P. D. Bhandara. See also Report of the Committee of Re-distribution of Seats, Constituent Assembly of Pakistan, *Debates*, Vol. IV, p. 21, January 3, 1949.

CONSTITUENT ASSEMBLY: SESSIONS AND ATTENDANCE[1]

CONSTITUENT ASSEMBLY				CONSTITUENT ASSEMBLY (LEGISLATURE)			
Year	Session	Days	Average Members Attending	Year	Session	Days	Average Members Attending
1947	I	4	55	—			
1948	II	3	42	1948	I	22	37
	III	3	39		II	10	40
	IV	5	39				
1949	V	5	40	1949	I	16	40
					II	15	43
1950	VI	4	45	1950	I	22	44
	VII	4	41		II	16	54
	VIII	8	48				
1951	IX	4	56	1951	I	22	52
	X	3	55		II	7	57
1952	XI	8	49	1952	I	27	48
	XII	4	53		II	11	48
1953	XIII	1	43	1953	I	22	45
	XIV	1	42		II	19	51
	XV	28	54				
1954	XVI	31	37	1954	I	35	46
		116				244	

Average sessional attendance ranged from 37 to 56, and the maximum number of members recorded as voting at a division was 53.

There were many reasons for the empty places, one of which

[1] The table is based largely upon the Constituent Assembly of Pakistan, *Summary of Work Done*, and Constituent Assembly (Legislature) *Summary of Work Done*, each issued irregularly. Several sessions began in one calendar year and continued into the next; in the table they have been treated as falling entirely into the year in which they began.

On some days the Assembly sat both as C.A.P. and as C.A.(L); thus to add the number of days in each category would give a slight exaggeration of the total sittings of the Assembly as a whole.

The Constituent Assembly

is revealed in the table. This was the habit of convening very short sessions. This meant that a member might be asked to make a round trip covering thousands of miles in order to spend a few hours in his seat in Karachi. It is true that members were paid daily and travelling allowances rather than a fixed salary, but this in no way lessened the inconvenience or the loss of alternative income.

Other members failed to attend for a variety of reasons. Khan Abdul Ghaffar Khan, the Red-shirt leader, spent six years in prison during the life of the Assembly, but as his detention was for political reasons his seat was not vacated. Mr. J. N. Mandal, who was the first Minister for Law and Labour, left Pakistan for India in 1950 without troubling to resign, and his name was still included in the list of members in October 1953. Other members accepted public offices which required their attendance elsewhere than Karachi.[1] Dr. Omar Hayat Malik spent more than five years as ambassador to various foreign countries but retained his seat to the end. Many who took such offices resigned their seats, though after a period that was sometimes prolonged. Both Nazimuddin (who was later re-elected) and Ghulam Mohammad resigned after becoming Governor-General. Similarly Mohammed Ali, Ghazanfar Ali Khan and M. A. H. Ispahani resigned after accepting diplomatic appointments. Khwaja Shahabuddin resigned when he accepted a provincial Governorship, but Firoz Khan Noon, Sardar Abdur Rab Nishtar and the Khan of Mamdot did not. Casual vacancies in the membership of the Assembly also occurred through the more normal cause of death of the sitting member and the highly abnormal operations of PRODA[2] which removed two members from the House.

When a casual vacancy occurred the provincial legislature concerned was usually called upon to provide a replacement

[1] The provision of S.26 of the Government of India Act, 1935, relating to the disqualification of members of the Central Legislature holding offices of profit under the Crown was deleted by *The Pakistan Provisional Constitution Order*, 1947, GGO 22/1947.

[2] See below, p. 102 ff. The members were M. A. Khuhro and Hamidul Huq Chowdhury.

Pakistan

drawn from the same community as the former member. When the time came to fill the seat vacated by the death of Mr. Jinnah and the five seats for refugees in the Punjab, the provincial Legislative Assembly was no longer in existence. Rather than wait for the new provincial elections, the Constituent Assembly proceeded to co-opt members who retained their seats until the provincial Assembly should re-convene.

The filling of a vacancy in the Constituent Assembly offered no opportunity for the expression of public opinion. Members did not represent territorial constituencies, and there could therefore be no question of direct popular election. Until 1954 the Muslim League controlled all the provincial legislatures and, for a Muslim seat, it was enough to secure the endorsement of the Central Parliamentary Board; election by the provincial Assembly was then virtually assured. Little or no attempt was made to secure the representation of groups in the country that had not previously obtained seats in proportion to their significance. The main purpose served by the occurrence of casual vacancies was to make it possible to obtain seats for new cabinet members. When Abdul Qaiyum Khan, after five years as Chief Minister of the North-West Frontier Province, entered the federal cabinet, a seat was found for him from East Bengal. Thus even the desirability of provincial representation was subordinated to the dictates of political expediency. While election to the Constituent Assembly was directed to be held by proportional representation, the fact that vacancies were invariably notified singly prevented this system from accomplishing any result. Not a single Opposition Muslim was returned as a result of a casual vacancy by the provincial legislatures.[1]

Members of the Constituent Assembly had been chosen originally by the provincial legislatures at a time when the duration of the Assembly and the extent of its labours were not evident. Since there was no ban on membership of two legislatures, the provincial members largely chose themselves to go to

[1] Sardar Asadullah Jan Khan was elected from the Frontier Province to replace Maulana Azad and in 1949 he was expelled from the Muslim League Party and for a time joined the Azad Pakistan Party.

Karachi. As a consequence many MCAs had legislative duties to perform in two places. Furthermore many of them were called upon to fill positions in the provincial cabinets. Although provincial Chief Ministers were changed frequently, three out of four of them were usually to be found as members of the Assembly[1] besides some lesser provincial ministers. Two other MCAs, the Jam Saheb of Las Bela and the Wali of Swat, were rulers during their tenure.

The Constituent Assembly found itself burdened with members who held offices (as ministers of provinces and states, Governors and ambassadors) not directly related to the work of the House. In addition, of course, the Assembly had to provide the members of the central ministry which involved some fourteen persons. Ministers were often required to be away from Karachi and the Foreign Minister in particular spent much of his time abroad. Undoubtedly one of the reasons for the weakness of the Constituent Assembly was that so high a proportion of its members found themselves with public interests which took precedence over their loyalty to and attendance at the House.

In its seven years' life the first Constituent Assembly saw many changes in membership, and this was an additional cause of weakness. Its general conformation, however, remained the same. The foremost group was composed of central and unit officeholders.[2] Behind them came the Muslim League back-benchers. Successive Prime Ministers searched hard to find political or administrative talent among the Muslim League Parliamentary Party, and those who showed signs of promise were usually rewarded with an appointment either inside or outside the Assembly. The residue that had failed to secure office sat on the government back-benches. With one or two honourable excep-

[1] Thus, while holding the position of Chief Minister the following were members of the Assembly: Nazimuddin, Nurul Amin, Fazlul Huq (East Bengal); Khuhro, Pirzada (Sind); Mamdot, Daultana, Noon (Punjab); Kizilbash (Khairpur); Mahmud Hassan (Bahawalpur).
[2] *The Pakistan Civil List*, No. 10, January–March 1953, shows as MCAs, twenty 'Honourables' (including the President of the Assembly), four 'His Excellencies' as well as two Chief Ministers of states.

tions it cannot be maintained that the standard of achievement of those members was high. After the *coup* of 1953 the character of the League non-official benches changed, but not in the direction of intelligent independent support of government measures. What should have been a constant source of informal but friendly criticism became a feverish attempt to back the winner in the office stakes.

The lack of vitality among private members of the League was the more serious in view of the weakness of the Opposition. On this side the principal group was the small and unhappy band of members of the Pakistan National Congress. Throughout most of its life the Assembly contained fifteen non-Muslim members, thirteen from East Bengal, and one each from Sind and the Punjab. The Punjab seat was designed (after 1949) to give representation to the non-Hindu minorities of West Pakistan[1] and was occupied successively by a Christian and a Parsi chosen by the Constituent Assembly itself. Not all the non-Muslims regarded themselves as members of the Opposition. Mr. J. N. Mandal (Scheduled Castes), until he left the country, was a cabinet minister. Three other non-Muslim members were described as Muslim League Associates. Two of them, A. K. Das and Dhananjoy Roy (Scheduled Castes) staged a separate walkout after the Congress Party, in protest against the Islamic provisions of the proposed constitution. On this occasion the third Associate, Mr. Bhandara (Parsi) remained in his place.[2]

The Congress Party in Pakistan was composed of Hindus and was therefore compelled to adopt the role of spokesman for a minority. It could never fulfil the true part of a parliamentary Opposition, that of offering an alternative government for the approval of the electors. The background of the party was Indian, and the past views of most of its members had been opposed to the idea of Pakistan. It had to be constantly on the alert to defend itself against allegations of disloyalty to the state and of sympathy with an alien power. Moreover, its members had to contend with

[1] Report of the Committe on Re-distribution of Seats, Constituent Assembly of Pakistan, *Debates*, Vol. IV, p. 21, January 3, 1949.
[2] *Dawn*, November 3, 1953.

The Constituent Assembly

a substantial degree of suspicion and hatred toward the religion they professed. A true Opposition seeks to take the offensive against the government; the Pakistan National Congress had to concern itself with the defence of interests that it might yet lose.

Also in Opposition were various Muslim dissidents. Mr. H. S. Suhrawardy was disqualified in 1948 on grounds of non-residence,[1] and Khan Abdul Ghaffar Khan was in gaol for the greater part of the duration of the Assembly. Mr. Fazlul Huq was a member but he did not move into open opposition until 1953 when he chose to carry on his activities in Bengal rather than Karachi. The only organized Muslim Opposition group in the Assembly was the Azad Pakistan Party, which attained a maximum strength of three, diminishing later to one.[2] Finally there were a few members, such as Begum Ikramullah, one of the two women in the House, who, at least for some sessions, styled themselves as 'independents.' However, when it came to a vote such members normally agreed with the government or abstained.

SECTION II: THE CONSTITUTIONAL PROPOSALS 1949-54

The principal task of the Constituent Assembly of Pakistan was to frame the constitution, but in addition, until that constitution went into effect it was empowered to act as the federal legislature under the Government of India Act. These two roles of the Assembly were fairly sharply distinguished. Its proceedings were published in two series under the headings of 'Constituent Assembly' and 'Constituent Assembly (Legislature)' respectively.[3] The same members and the same officers served in both capacities, but there were separate sets of Rules of Procedure. The constitution-making body clearly regarded itself as superior, working

[1] For Mr. Suhrawardy's protest against this ruling, see Constituent Assembly of Pakistan, *Debates*, Vol. III, p. 31, May 18, 1948.

[2] All three members had been expelled from the League. Sardar Shaukat Hyat later rejoined that party, Sardar Asadullah Jan became an independent and Mian Iftikharuddin remained as the champion of Azad Pakistan.

[3] These debates are cited below as Constituent Assembly of Pakistan, *Debates*, and Constituent Assembly (Legislature), *Debates*, respectively.

on the assumption, which was later to be challenged, that it possessed sovereign authority capable of abolishing or amending any other organ of state. It was summoned and prorogued, not by the Governor-General but by its own President. Its enactments were not presented to the Governor-General for his approval, but were declared to become law on being signed by the President and published under his authority in the *Gazette of Pakistan*.[1] It was also claimed that the Assembly could be dissolved only by vote of its own members.[2]

It was always maintained, in theory at least, that the government and the Opposition did not exist for the purposes of constitution-making. The Assembly was to be a gathering of equals owing loyalty only to the people and themselves. In practice the presence of ministers in the Assembly was never forgotten. A cabinet member spoke with the same tone of authority whether the subject before the House was legislative or constitutional, and the Opposition and the back-benchers had the same sensation of relative inferiority. Mr. A. K. Brohi was not a member of the Assembly or of its Basic Principles Committee until after the 1953 *coup*. He then became Law Minister and acquired the responsibility of piloting the Basic Principles Committee Report through its final stages. He had this job because he was a minister, and he behaved as would any minister in charge of an intricate piece of legislation.

While the pretence was made that government did not exist in the Constituent Assembly, no one attempted to conceal the presence of political parties. The League had an overwhelming majority, so that, when it had reached agreement, there was little possibility or purpose of an effective debate in the House. There was even less point in pushing matters to a vote since the League majority held firm and the largest 'Opposition' total at a division was fifteen.[3]

---

[1] Constituent Assembly, *Rules of Procedure* (1954), Rule 62.
[2] *Ibid.*, Rule 15.
[3] Constituent Assembly of Pakistan, *Debates*, October 4, 1950. The issue was the right to suspend *habeas corpus*; three Muslims joined the Hindus against 37 votes for the League.

The Constituent Assembly

In practice, decisions on major constitutional matters were reached through a familiar series of stages. First the central cabinet and the Chief Ministers of the provinces would reach a decision. This would be submitted to the Muslim League Parliamentary Party, where discussion was often vigorous and prolonged, especially if complete agreement among the ministers had not been secured. Then the decision would be conveyed perfunctorily to the House, whose non-League members would already be aware through gossip and press reports that they were to be confronted with a *fait accompli*. There would be a brief discussion in which the small Opposition would raise a few half-hearted objections. The League members, having already debated the matter in the party, would confine themselves to a few observations on the desirability of national unity and the virtues of Islam as a political system. After a few hours' debate the matter would be carried either with or without the formality of a division.

This cavalier attitude toward Parliament by the leaders of the League is well illustrated by the method of dealing with two of the most controversial issues that confronted the Assembly—representation and the language question. A newspaper report[1] describes how the Prime Minister interrupted a meeting of the Muslim League Parliamentary Party to call a press conference:

> 'Beaming with joy—his face flushed with excitement—Mr. Mohammed Ali said: "I am very glad to say that all the decisions have been arrived at unanimously without any opposition from a single member of the Party.
> ' "I am now in a position to announce to my countrymen that the deadlock which had so long held up the progress of constitution-making has been broken." '

The Prime Minister went on to discuss the outline of the 'Mohammed Ali formula' governing the distribution of seats.

The second example makes even more plain the inferior role assigned to the Constituent Assembly. There was no constitu-

[1] *Dawn*, October 6, 1953.

Pakistan

tional question that had aroused more heated discussion than that of the national language or languages. This was how the Constituent Assembly arrived at its final decision:

April 20, 1954, Mr. A. K. Brohi (Minister of Law):

> 'There are some important matters which are under the active consideration of the Party and, therefore, it is requested that proceedings be not taken in hand and the House be adjourned for that reason.'

No objection was raised; the day's proceedings cover half a page.

April 22, 1954, Mr. Ghyasuddin Pathan (Minister of Parliamentary Affairs):

> 'Sir, you are well aware that due to the language controversy the atmosphere is not at all congenial for the consideration of any serious matter, not to speak of consideration of the Basic Principles on which the future constitution is to be based.'

The House was adjourned without objection; the day's proceedings cover half a page.

April 26, 1954, the next meeting of the Assembly, there being no quorum, no business could be transacted.

May 7, 1954, 10 a.m., Mr. Mohammed Ali (Prime Minister). The Prime Minister asked for an adjournment for half an hour, explaining:

> 'It is for some urgent and important consultations concerning the business before the House.'

This motion was opposed, unsuccessfully, by the leader of the Opposition.

May 7, 1954, 11 a.m. Mr. Ghyasuddin Pathan:

> 'I am very sorry that I have got to make a further request to you for adjournment for about half an hour more, Sir.'

May 7, 1954, 11.45 a.m. A short notice amendment was introduced by the Prime Minister containing the result of the compromise on the language issue. The motion was adopted before lunch without a division. Such was the true nature of the unanimity of the party and of the Assembly.

The reader of the *Debates* of the first Constituent Assembly will look in vain for a series of informed discussions of the principles and forms of modern constitutional development as applied to the unique circumstances of Pakistan. And yet a draft constitution was produced[1] and very few issues of substance remained to be decided when the Assembly suffered its unexpected demise. The discussion and approval of the various clauses did not take place in detail on the floor of the House. The Muslim League may have taken the controversial decisions, but it was not responsible for the line by line writing of the documents. This task was performed almost entirely behind closed doors, the public and the majority of Assembly members being given occasional glimpses of what was being prepared for them.

The first main step in preparing the constitution was the Objectives Resolution, which was introduced by Liaquat Ali Khan and accepted by the Assembly in March 1949. It is written in Islamic terms, a feature which aroused the resentment of the Hindus who moved a series of amendments.[2] Among Muslims, the Objectives Resolution has been almost uniformly accepted as the corner-stone of the new constitution, and it represented the high-water mark of agreement on constitutional principles during the life of the first Assembly.

The Resolution begins:

In the name of Allah, the Beneficent, the Merciful;
'Whereas sovereignty over the entire Universe belongs to Allah Almighty alone, and the authority which He has delegated to the State of Pakistan through its people for being exercised within the limits prescribed by Him is a sacred trust';

[1] The Report of the Basic Principles Committee was finally adopted by the Constituent Assembly on September 21, 1954, and a Drafting Committee, with the assistance of Sir Ivor Jennings, had prepared a Draft Constitution for submission to the next session of the Assembly. This document was printed but never released to the public.

[2] Only one of these amendments was carried to a division and was lost by 10 to 21, Constituent Assembly of Pakistan, *Debates*, Vol. V, p. 98, March 12, 1949.

Pakistan

The purpose of the Resolution was to provide a declaration of national objectives but certain aspects of the form of the future state are outlined in its provisions. The state is to be democratic, with guarantees of fundamental rights and social justice to all. It is to give Muslims the opportunity of leading their lives in full accord with the teachings and requirements of their religion; but special protection is to be accorded to the religious, cultural and other legitimate interests of the minorities. Finally, the state is to be a federation of autonomous units.

The Constituent Assembly at this time had been in existence for nineteen months and was then in its fifth session. It was therefore desirable to begin work in earnest on the new constitution. Accordingly, on the day on which the Objectives Resolution was adopted the Assembly established the Basic Principles Committee. This body consisted of twenty-five members (or about one-third of the Assembly), and was empowered to co-opt not more than ten other persons who were not required to be members of the Assembly. There can be no doubt that it was intended to be a 'strong' committee. Its president was Tamizuddin Khan, the President of the Assembly, but the vice-president was Liaquat Ali Khan, the Prime Minister. In addition there were seven members of Liaquat's cabinet, three lesser ministers and one other member who was to join the cabinet later that year. Two of the members were shortly to become provincial Governors and one was an ambassador. The 'official' side was further strengthened by the co-option of the Chief Ministers of East Bengal, Sind,[1] and the North-West Frontier Province,[2] and Sir Abdur Rashid, the Chief Justice of Pakistan. Among those who did not hold office during the life of the committee were three non-Muslims and one anti-League Muslim. Attendance at meetings ranged from eleven to twenty-three, and the average was eighteen, of whom some seven or eight were normally central ministers.[3]

[1] Replaced by the Legal Remembrancer at the time of Governor's rule in that province.
[2] The Punjab had no Chief Minister at that time, but Nishtar soon became Governor, and Daultana, who was already a member of the committee, became Chief Minister in 1951.   [3] Basic Principles Committee, *Minutes*, 1949–52.

The Constituent Assembly

Following the death of Liaquat Ali (October 1951), it was some months before the new Prime Minister established himself in personal control of the operations of constitution-making. The Basic Principles Committee met five times in May 1952 with no major changes in its composition. Then, at the meetings of August 1952, four months before the committee finished its work, seven new names appear. These comprised the Prime Minister, three other central ministers, two provincial ministers and one backbench MCA.

The Basic Principles Committee as a whole was too large to consider in full session all aspects of the constitution and most of its members were too busy elsewhere to give the time and attention that such a method would have demanded. Accordingly three main sub-committees were set up, namely, the Sub-Committee on Federal and Provincial Constitutions and Distribution of Powers, the Sub-Committee on Franchise and the Sub-Committee on the Judiciary. In addition it was decided to set up a Board of *Talimaat-e-Islamia*[1] to advise the various committees on the religious implications of their work.

The sub-committees were modelled after the composition of the main body. That on Federal and Provincial Constitutions was the largest, containing twenty members (nine central ministers), the Franchise Committee had fifteen members (six ministers) and the Judiciary Committee had eight members (four ministers). The Federal and Provincial Committee reported its conclusions in July 1950, and after these had been amended and approved by the main committee, an Interim Report was presented to the Constituent Assembly in September 1950. This marked the end of the second stage of drafting the constitution.

The presentation of the Interim Report was the first opportunity given to the public or to the majority of MCAs to examine the outline of the constitution that was taking shape.[2] It was a

[1] Teachers of Islam. The decision to establish this Board was taken 'after a prolonged discussion' (*Minutes*, p. 3, April 14, 1949).

[2] The proceedings of the Basic Principles Committee and its sub-committees were classed as confidential, but occasional brief statements about current business were made to the press.

short document, covering thirty-four pages of the official *Debates*, and it made no attempt to cover all aspects of the constitutional structure. (Thus, since the Franchise Sub-Committee had not reported, no recommendation was made on the highly controversial issue of the distribution of seats in the lower House of the legislature.) But the main outline was visible, and it bore a marked resemblance to the Government of India Act of 1935. So much so that one member said in comment: 'So far as this Constitution is concerned, if Mr. Churchill had been the Leader of this House (which God forbid), he would have drawn up just such a constitution.'[1]

Few of the provisions bore any clearly defined Islamic character, and this came as a disappointment to many who had been pleased by the Objectives Resolution. Furthermore, the representatives of East Bengal had two reasons for alarm. Firstly, they inferred that the composition of the new legislature would transform Bengal's numerical majority of the population into a minority of seats. Secondly, the Report contained the flat announcement that Urdu was to be the national language. A Muslim League member expressed his fears on the floor of the House:

'Unfortunately, with the publication of the Interim Report of the Basic Principles Committee, there has been a great agitation and very hostile comments even against the Leader of Pakistan. Sir, in some quarters these principles enunciated in the Report, have been ascribed [sic] as most undemocratic, un-Islamic and most reactionary.

'Sir, in East Bengal there is a growing belief—I must say that it is a wrong impression—that there are principles in the Report which, if adopted, will reduce the majority of East Bengal into a minority and it will turn East Bengal into a colony of Pakistan.'[2]

Mr. Liaquat Ali, who had been hoping to make rapid progress, bowed before the storm of criticism and announced that time

[1] Constituent Assembly of Pakistan, *Debates*, Vol. VIII, p. 181, October 6, 1950, Sardar Shaukat Hyat.
[2] *Ibid.*, Vol. VIII, p. 183, November 21, 1950, Nur Ahmed.

The Constituent Assembly

would be allowed for members of the public to make suggestions to the Basic Principles Committee, which would give them serious consideration. The volume of suggestions was described by the committee itself as 'enormous,'[1] and a special sub-committee with Sardar Abdur Rab Nishtar as chairman, was established to deal with these proposals and to suggest appropriate amendments. It was the normal type of constitutional committee with fourteen members, five central ministers and four provincial Chief Ministers.

It is difficult to judge the representative character of the suggestions submitted. They came from individuals (including members of the Constituent Assembly) and organizations of various kinds, religious, political, educational and occupational.[2] Many of the ideas did not claim to be original; for example, three copies of the *Draft Constitution for Pakistan* by Maulana Abul Ala Maududi were sent. The general tenor of the suggestions was quite clear. It was plainly urged that the constitution should be made more patently Islamic. Thirteen contributors asked that a declaration be included to the effect that 'Pakistan will be an "Islamic Democratic State" based on Holy Quran and Sunnah.'[3] One individual demanded that 'The prayers in mosques should be made compulsory for all Muslims and those who fail to discharge this duty should be punished.'[4] In particular many proposals called for the definition of the office of Head of the State (*Amir* or *Khalifa*) in classical Islamic terms with very substantial powers. Several persons wanted a clause ensuring that 'Only the most pious person is to be elected Head of the State,'[5] and one felt that 'School teachers, professors and social workers should be considered as the best candidates.'[6] There was also a strong body of opinion that the Head of the State should be answerable to

---

[1] Basic Principles Committee, *Report*, p. 1.
[2] *Consolidated Statement of Suggestions Received from the Public on the Basic Principles Committee Report* (n.d., but undoubtedly 1951). This document contains only suggestions received up to January 31, 1951, relating to the Interim Report. Suggestions received later or relating to Fundamental Rights, Judiciary or Franchise, were compiled separately.   [3] *Ibid.*, p. 1.
[4] *Ibid.*, p. 5.   [5] *Ibid.*, p. 13.   [6] *Ibid.*, p. 15.

the courts, and no fewer than thirty-two submissions suggested some form of impeachment.[1] One citizen went so far as to ask that 'Everyone will have a right to criticize both his public and private life.' There was a substantial measure of agreement that the judiciary, especially the federal and provincial Chief Justices, should play a more prominent role in legislative and executive matters than that envisaged by the Interim Report.

Besides this principal theme of the suggestions there was a secondary though important group of issues. These were submissions from Bengal asking for far greater decentralization of executive and legislative power and for the recognition of Bengali as an official language side-by-side with Urdu.

The Suggestions Sub-Committee, recognizing that most of the submissions before it sprang from orthodox Muslim opinion, decided that the appropriate method of procedure would be to discuss the contentious items with the Board of *Talimaat-e-Islamia*. Therefore it co-opted the Chairman of the Board, Maulana Syed Sulaiman Nadvi, as a full member of the committee, and held a series of conferences with the rest of the Board and its secretary.

This series of discussions, judged by the glimpses afforded by the minutes of the committee,[2] must have been of very great interest. On the one side was the majority of members of the committee, politicians by profession, lawyers by training and accustomed to expressing their thoughts in terms of Western logic and precedent. On the other side were the members of the Board of *Talimaat-e-Islamia*, together with two '*maulanas*'[3] who were, as MCA's, already members of the committee. This did not mean that the lawyer-politicians were automatically opposed to the addition of Islamic features to the constitution; but it did mean considerable difficulty in establishing a meeting of minds.

[1] *Consolidated Statement of Suggestions Received from the Public on the Basic Principles Committee Report*, p. 34.
[2] *Report of the Sub-Committee to Examine the Suggestions Received on the Interim Report of the Basic Principles Committee* (1952), Appendix.
[3] They were Maulana Abdullah-el Baqui and Maulana Mohammed Akram Khan.

The Constituent Assembly

One group started from the Government of India Act, or something much like it, and tried to show that it was already, or could easily be brought, into conformity with the requirements of Islam. The other group began with the Quran and Sunnah and tried to extract from them the institutional necessities of an Islamic state.

In theory the committee was merely seeking the Board's advice, and it was known that the committee would meet later, without the ordinary members of the Board, in order to reach its final conclusions. But in practice it seems to have been an open debate with each side striving to make its meaning clear to the other, and to gain acceptance for its view. The politicians knew well that to have the majority of *ulama* brand the constitution as 'un-Islamic' would prove a serious setback. It is plain that both sides wanted to reach agreement and, if the committee accepted certain major Islamic provisions, the Board made a prolonged effort to understand the other point of view.[1] Indeed, there seem to have been occasions on which the members of the Board allowed themselves to be persuaded that certain recommendations were in accordance with their wishes when, in fact, there existed a marked divergence between the two. Thus the proposal for the executive side of government advanced by the Board was as follows:

> 'The responsibility for the administration of the State shall primarily vest in the Head of the State, although he may delegate any part of his power to any individual or body. Governance by the Head of the State shall not be autocratic but consultative (*shura*), i.e. he will discharge his duties in consultation with persons holding responsible positions in the Government and with the elected representatives of the people.'[2]

---

[1] Two typical extracts from the minutes will serve to indicate this aspect of the proceedings.

'With regard to this para., the relevant recommendations made in the Interim Report were explained to the Board of *Talimaat-e-Islamia*, and they agreed that they were sound and acceptable to them' (*Op. cit.* p. 30).

'After hearing the above explanation, the Members of the Board were satisfied that the recommendations were according to Shariat' (*Ibid.*, p. 35).

[2] *Ibid.*, pp. 44–5.

Pakistan

Somewhat disingenuously the committee decided that these proposals 'have already been incorporated in paragraph 7 of the Interim Report,' that is to say that they amount to cabinet government with the Head of the State acting on the advice of a ministry which is responsible to the legislature. The Board apparently accepted this contention.[1]

The Suggestions Sub-Committee finished its report in July 1952 (twenty-one months after the presentation of the Interim Report). The full Basic Principles Committee, which had held only one meeting (to select the Suggestions Committee) between August 1950 and May 1952, had by this time received the reports of the Franchise and Judiciary Sub-Committees and could proceed toward its final report. A draft was completed and signed in August 1952. A further series of meetings was held in November in order to consider a lengthy memorandum from Sir Robert Drayton, the Assembly's Chief Draftsman, and also to discuss certain 'notes' on the report submitted by the Board of *Talimaat-e-Islamia*. It was at this late stage that a number of important amendments was made. For example, the provision for the reservation of legislative seats for women was removed from the report,[2] and the articles covering the procedure to avoid repugnancy of legislation to Islamic law were re-worded and substantially modified. One final meeting was held in December 1952, and the Report, in the form in which it was to be presented to the Assembly, was signed.

For the second time the leaders of the Assembly hoped that rapid progress might be made. Three days after the committee had signed, the Report was introduced in the House (December 22, 1952). On the first day of the new year the Assembly adjourned for three weeks to give members an opportunity to study the new proposals.

Unfortunately the final Report did not receive a much better welcome than its predecessor. Now it was not the absence of

[1] *Report of the Sub-Committee to Examine the Suggestions Received on the Interim Report of the Basic Principles Committee*, p. 30.

[2] Basic Principles Committee, *Minutes*, pp. 118–23, November 20 and 22, 1952.

Islamic provisions but the awkwardness of their insertion into the constitution that aroused criticism. Of more consequence was the fact that the Bengal members continued to feel that they had not received their due, while the Punjabis held that too much had been conceded to the East Wing. (The language question, which the committee had left open, was a cause for mutual suspicion and hostility.) When the three weeks were over the Assembly adjourned once more and, although it met twice in March, the Report was not on the order of business.

In April the political flood swept away the last hope of a completed constitution in 1953. The new Prime Minister, Mr. Mohammed Ali, had been absent from Pakistan during the whole of the preceding constitutional discussions. Beside his need to take over the reins of the administration, it was necessary for him to spend some months in measuring the difficulties in the path of constitution-making and trying to find some way around them. The principal issue was stated by the Chief Minister of East Bengal:

> 'Sir, it is within the knowledge of everybody that on account of this difference of opinion between East Bengal and West Pakistan in the matter of composition of the Houses, the work on constitution-making was stopped. . . . The deadlock . . . is working as a dead-weight on the nation. The nation is going to lose confidence in the leaders, in those who are at the helm of the Administration.'[1]

The Prime Minister's patient manœuvres were rewarded, and a compromise, known as the 'Mohammed Ali formula,'[2] was reached. It was laid before the House with pride by the Prime Minister.

> 'The House will be pleased to learn that the formula has been unanimously accepted by my colleagues, by the Chief Ministers of East Bengal, the Punjab, Sind, the N-W.F.P. and Bahawalpur and by all members of the Muslim League Parliamentary Party. This

---

[1] Constituent Assembly of Pakistan, *Debates*, Vol. XV, p. 183, October 14, 1953, Nurul Amin. [2] See below, p. 180.

unanimity of opinion is in itself a remarkable feature. It serves to underline the basic unity and cohesion of the country—a unity which transcends all provincial boundaries.'[1]

This episode illustrates only too well the nature of the process by which important decisions were taken. As Mr. Nurul Amin had said it had been, 'within the knowledge of everybody,' that the deadlock involved a clash between the East and West Wings. And yet no clear public presentation was made of the issues involved, and certainly no public vote in the Assembly was taken to demonstrate how the opposing forces stood. The general public, on a matter of the most vital importance for the future of the nation, was left to guess at what was going on, on the basis of unofficial accounts of party meetings and cryptically worded threats and warnings from some of the leading participants. The debate was behind closed doors, and the public and non-League members of the Assembly had to wait until the official ranks had been dragooned into line. Such unanimity was indeed 'a remarkable feature,' and it is not surprising that it bred bitter resentment and that its duration was precarious in the extreme.

The conclusion is unavoidable that, on major constitutional issues, the place of decision was transferred from the Assembly to the Muslim League Parliamentary Party. But issues became contentious precisely because the League was divided. Without doubt lengthy and at times heated discussions took place in the party, and certain issues were decided by free vote. But where East was aligned against West the matter was not so simple. Since the Bengalis normally had a majority, this meant that the West Pakistanis were not prepared to accept the consequences of being outvoted by a process of counting heads. And, running across this fundamental East–West cleavage, was a complex network of personal alliances and hostilities.

In such areas decision-making was therefore withdrawn from the Parliamentary Party.

[1] Constituent Assembly of Pakistan, *Debates*, Vol. XV, p. 14, October 7, 1953.

The Constituent Assembly

'Yesterday the Muslim League Parliamentary Party was again unable to take up the consideration of the Constitution because the "leaders" had made no progress in their attempt to resolve the controversy over representation.'[1]

The same issue of the newspaper cited above reports the sixth in a series of meetings of central ministers and provincial Chief Ministers, a meeting which lasted until the small hours of the morning. There can be little doubt that some such body as this was the true location of final authority in constitutional as well as administrative matters.

This was the level of high and sometimes ruthless politics. Chief Ministers could be dismissed by the Centre, cabinet ministers could be changed, and it was to be remembered that an entire cabinet might be overthrown. Constitutional issues were intricately involved in the manœuvring for political power, the maintenance of control of a province or of influence within the federal cabinet. Each decision was one of a series of hard-fought compromises. Each new issue and each fluctuation of real political power, altered the balance of the whole and opened the way for fresh manœuvres. At no stage did the leaders of the League make up their minds to endorse an entire scheme of government, and to demand its acceptance or rejection as a whole. Each issue was resolved after hard bargaining, accepted 'unanimously' by the Muslim League Parliamentary Party, and presented as a *fait accompli* to the Assembly. Debate in the chamber was feeble, for the Hindus knew that they had no real power and little influence, and large sections of the Muslims were sitting in unhappy and embarrassed silence, aware of an unfortunate contradiction between their votes and their conscience.[2]

---

[1] *Dawn*, October 2, 1953.
[2] Thus in April 1952 a motion appeared in the name of Mr. Nur Ahmed (East Bengal, Muslim League) urging the adoption of Bengali as an official language. There had recently been riots in Bengal on this issue and the Chief Minister in person had introduced in the provincial legislature a motion urging the Centre to adopt Bengali. But in the Constituent Assembly the Bengal members sat silent. The mover proposed his motion but declined to speak to it. The case for Bengali had to be urged entirely by the Hindus. 'Sir,' said Mr.

Pakistan

In such fashion was the proposed constitution prepared. The Report of the Basic Principles Committee was discussed, amended and adopted by the Constituent Assembly on September 21, 1954. The Report of the Committee on Fundamental Rights of Citizens of Pakistan and on Matters Relating to Minorities was approved on September 7th. A drafting committee was established, and it prepared a Draft Constitution which was ready to be presented to the next meeting of the Assembly. The Prime Minister declared his hope and belief that the new constitution would be proclaimed on December 25th, the birthday of the *Quaid-i-Azam*.[1] But one month after the approval of the Basic Principles Report the Assembly had been dismissed, and General Mirza, the new Minister of the Interior, was talking of his desire to begin 'with a clean slate' in planning the new constitution.

It would have been unrealistic to the point of fantasy to expect that the writing of the constitution would have been uninfluenced by current politics. And the fact that the Constituent Assembly and the Federal Legislature were one and the same body, emphasized the political nature of the task. It is no cause for surprise, or even for condemnation, that each group of politicians wanted to shape the future state in such a way as to yield maximum benefit to itself and to the local and provincial interests which it represented.

If criticism is to be brought to bear, it must lie upon the shoulders of the political leaders. The Muslim League was fashioned as an instrument to secure united action, and under Mr. Jinnah it was successful. In constitutional matters, effective leadership appears to have ceased from the time the Interim Report came under attack (late 1950). From that date it is impossible to say just what were the main principles of constitutional structure that successive Prime Ministers (Liaquat Ali,

---

D. N. Dutta, 'it is most regrettable that silence has been imposed upon my friends who come from East Bengal' (Constituent Assembly of Pakistan, *Debates*, Vol. XI, p. 37, April 10, 1952). The League ultimately voted solidly for the postponement of a decision, which resulted in uncertainty and suspicion for the next two years.   [1] *Dawn*, September 23, 1954.

The Constituent Assembly

Nazimuddin, Mohammed Ali) wished and thought possible to see enacted. Constitution-making became little more than an attempt to gather support for any compromise that stood a chance of acceptance. In a country where radical divisions exist, compromise is essential if a constitution is to be made to work. But the result of these particular compromises was, at least in the opinion of the Governor-General and the Prime Minister, the breakdown of the constitution-making machinery.

The real criticism to be levelled is that the government tried too much to control and too little to lead. And this was because, either as individuals or as a group, the men who controlled the destinies of Pakistan never resolved their own minds as to what they wanted.

SECTION III: THE INTERIM CONSTITUTION
1947–56

In its capacity as a constituent body the Assembly's main task was to write the new constitution. It was empowered also to amend the interim constitution, which was to bridge the gap between independence and the proclamation of the Islamic Republic. In this capacity forty-four Acts were passed between March 1948 and September 1954, each amending or supplementing the Government of India Act or the Indian Independence Act. Some of these measures were small and non-controversial; for example, the Indian Independence (Amendment) Act, 1950, substituted the title 'the Punjab' for 'West Punjab.' Others were of substantial importance, such as the Delimitation of Constituencies (Adult Franchise) Act, 1951, and the Privy Council (Abolition of Jurisdiction) Act, 1950.

Since such Acts were passed by the Assembly as a constitution-making body, they were not submitted for the assent of the Governor-General, and they were accepted as law on being published under the authority of the President of the Constituent Assembly. Thus the interim constitution could be amended by a process that was even more simple than the passing of a normal

Act of legislative character. There was one chamber, seldom attended by as many as sixty members, so that thirty votes in a single day could be sufficient to alter the whole structure of the state.

Most of the forty-four Acts in this category were intended to adapt the provisions of the Government of India Act to changing circumstances, and few of them introduced new principles or institutions. However, the most publicized of them added a new word to the language and a new institution to the machinery of government. This was the Public and Representative Offices (Disqualification) Act, 1949, usually called PRODA. It provided a form of impeachment and was sub-titled 'An Act to provide for the debarring from public life for a suitable period of persons judicially found guilty of misconduct in any public office or representative capacity or in any matter relating thereto.'

The procedure established contained a mixture of judicial and executive elements. The Governor-General or the Governor of a province was empowered to refer to the courts or to a special judicial tribunal any charges of misconduct in public office. If the report of the court or tribunal proved to be adverse, the Governor-General (but not a Governor) might, by order, impose a penalty of disqualification from public office for a period of not more than ten years. In making any such order the Governor-General or Governor was to act in his discretion, that is, he was not required to act upon the advice of his ministers. It was further provided by rules issued under the Act[1] that charges might originate with the Governor-General or Governor, or be brought by any five persons. Such persons were required to make a deposit of Rs. 5,000 and to give full particulars of their allegations. The Governor or Governor-General would then order a preliminary inquiry before referring the matter to a court or tribunal. This method offered a magnificent opportunity for politicians who could afford Rs. 5,000 to harass the ministers of the day. As Mr. M. H. Gazder described the situation, 'Epidemics of these petitions cropped up in Sind, and it made the life of

---

[1] *Gazette of Pakistan*, July 9, 1949, and *Extraordinary*, July 4, 1950.

people in Sind very miserable.'[1] Accordingly penalties were provided in case of false and malicious allegations.[2]

The main sufferers under PRODA were politicians who had incurred the displeasure of the central government. Disqualification was imposed on four provincial ex-ministers,[3] while an adverse finding on minor charges drew no penalty.[4] There was one case in which the tribunal could not agree,[5] and one in which proceedings were never concluded.[6] The result of nearly five years of PRODA was that seven cases (in which four former Chief Ministers of provinces were involved), were referred for judicial inquiry. The series of investigations had been prolonged and expensive, and involved elaborate searches of government records, as well as testimony by civil servants against former (and possibly future) ministers. The real objection to PRODA was the possibility of its use as a political weapon. A provincial Governor had to maintain a ministry (unless he was willing to assume personal power under Section 92A). A charge against a politically popular Chief Minister could be brought only when an alternative was available. The very vagueness of the charges—'nepotism,' 'wilful maladministration'—meant that few ministers could be quite certain that they would emerge unscathed from a searching inquiry. In any event, the necessity of offering a public defence of day-to-day administrative decisions was likely to embarrass most office-holders. It could also prove exceedingly expensive. A provincial politician who lost office because of central intervention or by a revolt within his own party was likely to find himself

---

[1] Constituent Assembly (Legislature), *Debates*, 1952, Vol. I, p. 1455, April 17, 1952. At one stage there was only one Sind cabinet minister who was *not* the subject of a PRODA petition (*Dawn*, November 30, 1951).

[2] *Criminal Law (Amendment) Act*, 1952 (Act XXXII of 1952). Under this Act the Governor of Sind ordered the prosecution of six persons who had brought charges against Pirzada Abdus Sattar, then Chief Minister. The Rs. 5,000 was declared forfeit and Rs. 2,000 given to Pirzada (*Dawn*, September 7, 1954).

[3] M. A. Khuhro (Sind), Kazi Fazlullah (Sind), Aga Ghulam Nabi Khan Pathan (Sind) and Hamidul Huq Chowdhury (East Bengal).

[4] Mir Ghulam Ali Khan Talpur (Sind).

[5] The Khan of Mamdot (Punjab).

[6] Mian Mumtaz Mohammed Khan Daultana (Punjab).

fighting for his political life. Those who had supplanted him would be in a position to search official files for evidence of his 'misconduct in office.' And the provision that the Governor-General or Governor should act in his discretion, far from meaning that such inquiries should be removed from politics, in fact confronted the Governor-General with the necessity for taking a highly political decision. Incidentally it also provided him with a potent weapon with which, if desired, he might coerce a recalcitrant office-holder.

In 1951 Mr. M. H. Gazder, then a private member from Sind, had introduced a Bill for the repeal of PRODA, but it was not taken up by the Assembly until September 1954. The reason for the delay and for the decision to take up the measure at all at that late day was never authoritatively explained. But rumour, mentioned in the Press and in the repeal debate,[1] suggested that certain Bengal MCAs had reason to believe that the new Section 92A Governor of that province (General Mirza) was preparing a substantial number of charges against former office-holders.

Mr. Gazder's Bill was passed, although some amendments were added. The government took no public stand in the matter and no central minister spoke in the debate. The Chief Minister of Sind, Pirzada Abdus Sattar, successfully moved two amendments. One of them provided that:

'This repeal shall not affect any penalty, forfeiture, disqualification or punishment already incurred or awarded under the said Act or any reference pending before any Court or Tribunal on or before September 1, 1954.'[2]

The first part of this amendment maintained the disqualification of three former Sind ministers (Pirzada's rivals), and the second part permitted proceedings to continue against Mr. Daultana.

The only vote during the passage of the Bill came on an amendment by a Hindu member seeking to abrogate all previous

[1] Constituent Assembly of Pakistan, *Debates*, Vol. XVI, September 20, 1954.
[2] This amendment became the *Public and Representative Offices (Disqualification) (Repeal) Act*, 1954, S.4.

The Constituent Assembly

penalties awarded under the Act. The voting was 26 to 9 against the amendment. Although the Bill had not been introduced by a member of the government it had been approved by a meeting of the Muslim League, and party discipline was applied. Opposition within the League, which was considerable, manifested itself in abstention rather than an attempt to defeat the measure.

This was not the end of the PRODA story. The final chapter was written by the Governor-General and formed a stinging rebuke to the Assembly. In a proclamation he noted that the orders of disqualification had been allowed to remain. Since these had been imposed by the Governor-General in his discretion they could be amended similarly, and he announced the termination of disqualification in all cases and the dropping of proceedings against Daultana. He noted that PRODA had been repealed because the Assembly thought it had been misused. He said, 'I myself do not agree with this contention, but I must take note of the fact that the contention was seriously advanced and accepted by the constituent Assembly.'[1] If it had been misused, then there could be no justification for the continuance of penalties. 'I do take note of the fact that public opinion in the country has strongly denounced the repealing Act, and particularly its discriminatory character to which I have just referred.'

This episode of the repeal of PRODA is, of course, one of the events of the political crisis of late 1954. Another major event also concerned the role of the Constituent Assembly amending the interim constitution, and took place the day following the repeal of PRODA. This was the move to make the government completely dependent upon the Assembly and to prevent the repetition of the exercise of the Governor-General's power of intervention. The title of the Act was outwardly inocuous—The Government of India (Fifth Amendment) Act, 1954. It contained four main provisions. Firstly, the Prime Minister, at the time of his appointment by the Governor-General, was required to be a member of the Assembly. (Had such a provision been in force in 1953 Mr. Mohammed Ali could not have been appointed.)

[1] *Gazette of Pakistan Extraordinary*, October 20, 1954.

Pakistan

Furthermore, other ministers, to be appointed on the advice of the Prime Minister, were also required to be members of the existing Assembly. (Previously a minister who was not an MCA had been allowed a period of ten months to find a seat.)

Secondly, it was declared that the cabinet was to be collectively responsible to the Assembly and should 'cease to hold office on the expression of want of confidence in any one of them [ministers] by the Federal Legislature.' (This superseded the merely conventional basis of collective responsibility. However, it goes further, since in most parliamentary systems the government, faced by a vote of no confidence, has the option of resigning or of dissolving the legislature.) Thirdly, the Prime Minister was given the right to force the resignation of any minister. Fourthly, the following new clause was inserted into the Government of India Act:

> 'Wherein in this Act the Governor-General is required to perform any function or exercise any power, he shall until [sic] the context otherwise provides be deemed to perform this function and exercise these powers in accordance with the advice of the Ministers.'

The apparent effect of this Act was to deprive the Governor-General of all independent power, and to confine the tenure of federal ministerial office to the existing members of the Assembly, or rather to the fifty-seven members of the Muslim League in the Assembly. It is this Act and the manner of its passage that form the focus of the theory that explains the downfall of the Assembly as a result of a conspiracy to achieve power by a certain group of members.

The Bill came before the Assembly in an extraordinary manner. It was introduced by Mr. M. H. Gazder, then Deputy-President of the Assembly. It was a piece of legislation affecting the current powers of the Prime Minister and the Governor-General, but it was moved by an officer of the House rather than by a member of the government. The powers that it affected would, in any event, have ceased to exist when the new constitution was enacted, and this event was generally expected to take place by the end

The Constituent Assembly

of the year. The period of validity of the amending Act was therefore presumably to be a mere three months from September until December 1954.

Under the rules of procedure of the Assembly there were two methods of introducing a Bill. Either fifteen days' notice must be given and a motion then moved for leave to introduce the Bill, or the President might order the publication of a Bill, in which case no motion for leave was required.[1] The printed copies of the Bill were to be in the hands of members for at least three days before the measure came up for consideration by the Assembly unless no member objected to a shorter period or the President suspended the rule.[2] In this instance the President having ordered the Bill to be printed, copies were circulated to the members during the evening of September 20th. The Bill was introduced the following morning and was finally passed within an hour. All that remained for it to become law under the current procedure was to publish the Act in the official *Gazette*. This was done the same day. The Bill was accompanied by a Statement of Objects and Reasons, which is given below in its entirety:

> 'The Bill is designed with a view to give legislative sanction to certain accepted principles and conventions connected with the formation and working of Government in Parliamentary system of Government. Therefore it is necessary to amend sections 9, 10, 10A, 10B and 17 of the Government of India Act, 1953, in certain respects. The principles underlying the Bill have already been accepted by the Constituent Assembly for being incorporated in future Constitution of Pakistan. Certain drafting changes have also been proposed in the Bill.'

This is the subsequent course of events as described by an admittedly hostile observer.[3]

[1] Constituent Assembly of Pakistan, *Rules of Procedure* (1954), Rules 43, 44.
[2] *Ibid.*, Rule 47.
[3] Pir Ali Muhammad Rashdi, at that time an ex-minister of Sind and an open enemy of the Pirzada ministry in that province. After Pirzada's downfall Rashdi was to return to office.
The quotation is from an article headed 'From Democracy to Absolute Fascism,' *The Times of Karachi*, September 27, 1954.

Pakistan

'This is how this constitutional fraud had been perpetrated. At 4 p.m. on September 20th, Mr. Gazder gives notice of this Bill. Two hours later, meets the so-called Stearing [sic] Committee which hurriedly alters the original order of Business and takes up, and adopts, this Bill by giving it precedence over all items already on the agenda, including the consideration of the Basic Principles Committee Report, of which the Committee as well as the Assembly was actually already seized. An hour later comes out, under the orders of the President, a Gazette Extraordinary, publishing this Bill. In the evening, as the Assembly session is ending, the President announces that there would be another brief session of the Constituent Assembly early next morning at 9 a.m. At midnight are shoved into the letter-boxes of the sleeping members, covers containing the Bill. Next Morning (September 21st) at 9 a.m. there takes place a thinly-attended session of the Constituent Assembly. Till then, many members had not even opened their covers containing the Bill; many of them were actually in their beds thinking that the House, as originally scheduled, would be meeting only at 10 o'clock and that too, as Legislature and not as Constituent Assembly; many of them who had not heard the previous evening's verbal eleventh-hour announcement by the President, did not even know that there was going to be a sitting at 9 a.m. And thus, in that 9 o'clock-morning meeting, and in less than 10 minutes, is moved, and finally passed this Bill.

One or two matters in Mr. Rashdi's account call for comment. The 'notice' given at 4 p.m. on September 20th was presumably addressed to the President and the office of the Assembly. The formal introduction of the Bill did not take place until the 9 a.m. meeting the following morning. The announcement that the Assembly was to meet at 9 a.m. does not seem to have drawn the attention of all members to the fact that a change of plan was involved. Between 11 p.m. and midnight, after a day in which the House had sat three times, the President announced, as though it were a matter of routine, 'The House stands adjourned till 9 a.m. tomorrow.'[1]

---

[1] Constituent Assembly of Pakistan, *Debates*, Vol. XVI, p. 493, September 20, 1954.

The Constituent Assembly

Mr. Rashdi says that the passage of the Bill required ten minutes. Certainly it cannot have taken very long. The relevant proceedings cover four pages.[1] Mr. Gazder's opening speech occupies eighteen lines, mostly devoted to an outline of the measure but ending with the claim that 'This will revitalize our political life and re-establish our reputation of being a democratic country.' Six relatively minor amendments were moved and adopted without debate. They were sponsored by Mr. Pirzada and by two back-bench members from Bengal. Finally, the Bill as amended was accepted by the House. No division or vote of any kind took place and no member raised any objection either substantive or procedural. The only contribution made by a central minister was as follows: 'The Honourable Dr. Ishtiaq Husain Qureshi (East Bengal: Muslim): On a point of order. Has clause 1 been put?'

When the Constituent Assembly reached Legislative business it found itself confronted with an interesting pendant to the earlier proceedings. This was an amendment to the Pakistan Federal Legislature (Deputy President's Salary) Act, 1948. It provided that the person concerned (Mr. M. H. Gazder), in addition to the salary he was already drawing, should be entitled to certain allowances including a rent-free house or house allowance. The Bill was moved by a minister, Mr. Ghyasuddin Pathan (East Bengal). Two amendments were moved successfully by Mr. Abdul Monem Khan (East Bengal), each having the effect of raising the amount due to Mr. Gazder, including the back-dating of the allowances to the date of Mr. Gazder's election eighteen months previously.

September 20th and 21st were the last sitting days of the Constituent Assembly. They had proved to be eventful. It could not be doubted that some devious political manœuvres had been executed, largely out of sight of the general public. But it remains to be asked whether in fact there was a conspiracy, and, if so, what were its aims and who were its members. The 'conspiracy hypothesis' can be stated quite simply. The arbitrary action of the Governor-General in dismissing the Nazimuddin ministry had

[1] *Debates*, pp. 499–502, September 21, 1954.

Pakistan

been neither forgotten nor forgiven. Two of the more prominent of the dismissed ministers (Mr. Nazimuddin himself and Mr. Fazlur Rahman) were from Bengal and their influence, combined with that of Mr. Nurul Amin the late Chief Minister, far exceeded that of Mr. Mohammed Ali (a Bengali) with the MCAs from that province. Many of Bengal MCAs had been defeated in their attempts to secure election to the East Bengal Legislative Assembly, and one lesson that they had drawn from their defeat was that it had become necessary to stand up more strongly for Bengal rights against Karachi (especially Punjabi) domination. It seems relevant to observe here that the President of the Assembly, Moulvi Tamizuddin Khan, was a Bengali, and was reputed to be on terms of personal friendship with Khwaja Nazimuddin.

By themselves the Bengal dissidents could not control a clear majority in either the Assembly or the League Parliamentary Party. Of forty-four Bengal seats, thirteen were held by Hindus, four by members of the government, and three by non-Bengalis, and not all of the remaining twenty-four votes could be regarded as secured. But there were allies at hand: Pirzada, the Chief Minister of Sind, had also been dismissed from the central cabinet in April 1953, and it seems clear that his fellow Sindhi, M. H. Gazder, was also willing to collaborate. It was strongly suggested that at least one member of Mr. Mohammed Ali's cabinet was not unfavourable to a change in the office of Prime Minister. And there were others, such as Abdul Ghaffar Khan or Mian Iftikharuddin, who, while probably not well disposed to the Bengali cause, had no reason to reward the government with their support. And there were thirteen Hindu Bengali votes which might very well be attracted by a promise of a new deal for the East Wing. In sum, it seems possible that the dissidents might have mustered twenty-five to thirty votes inside the League and thirty-five to forty votes in the Assembly, and in neither case would the government have been able to win.

The rebel tactics were quite simple. Firstly, they wanted to make sure that the Governor-General could not hamper them by a spate of PRODA prosecutions. So PRODA was repealed. Secondly, they wanted to deprive the Governor-General of any

The Constituent Assembly

independent power. Thirdly, they wanted to be sure of bringing down the government by a hostile vote. Fourthly, they wanted to confine the future ministry solely to the then members of the Assembly, and to ensure the cabinet's continuing dependence upon the legislature. The last three purposes were believed to have been accomplished by the Fifth Amendment.

The preceding paragraphs have given an account of the conspiracy hypothesis. A leading Karachi newspaper had no doubt that the conspiracy was real and that its direction lay predominantly in the hands of one man.

> 'Mr. Fazlur Rahman is not merely a member of the Muslim League Parliamentary Party which sustains the Government, but he has, during recent months, emerged as its leading light. His powers are indeed amazing. It is he who is the real author of the constitution which will soon overtake the country. It is he who trounced the Punjabi stalwarts (with what sinister pleasure!) and put his foot down on the one-unit proposal as well as that of zonal federation. It is he who contrived the repeal of PRODA—Mr. Gazder only acted as a stooge to earn a reward which he has duly received—simply because he wanted to protect his friends who were in danger of being proceeded against....
>
> 'Mr. Fazlur Rahman has indeed succeeded in compassing the entire sovereignty of the Constituent Assembly into the few votes of the coterie that he controls.'[1]

Before the conspiracy theory is accepted in its entirety, one or two questions require to be answered. If the Bengali group had a clear majority, why was it necessary to proceed with such frantic haste on September 20th and 21st? Perhaps the answer is that the Governor-General or his agent, General Mirza, was about to proceed under PRODA against several prominent Bengalis. But then, having declared war on the Governor-

---

[1] *The Times of Karachi*, September 27, 1954, editorial headed 'The Boss Speaks.'

In December 1954 Mr. Fazlur Rahman was confined to the province of East Bengal by a government order under S.3 of the Security of Pakistan Act (*Dawn*, December 11, 1954).

Pakistan

General, why did the Assembly consent to adjourn itself without bringing about the fall of the cabinet? If there had been no intention of a vote of no confidence, then the Fifth Amendment would have had the sole effect of bolstering Mohammed Ali's position from September until December 25th. This is highly improbable. Pakistani politicians have had much experience in the making and unmaking of majorities, and they could hardly have assumed that the Bengalis were so strong that they could destroy the ministry whenever they chose, having given ample warning to all concerned. There remains the possibility that they felt that they were acting mainly to protect themselves. It is true that the new constitution was expected to come into force at the end of three months. But it would be far longer before a new Parliament and a new President could be elected. In the meanwhile an interim President would have to be chosen by the Assembly. It was rumoured that pressure was already being exerted upon the members to choose Ghulam Mohammad; with this in view, the conspiracy can be regarded as a means of countering this pressure.

The major outstanding question is this: why did the government take no open stand on either PRODA repeal or on the amendment of the Government of India Act? It is known that the Muslim League Parliamentary Party held a prolonged and heated discussion on the repeal of PRODA, and that the decision was taken by a narrow majority. It may well be that the government here realized for the first time how strong were the forces arrayed against it. It is not clear exactly how many people knew that the Fifth Amendment Bill was to be introduced. Printed copies were not available until the late evening of September 20th. And the Assembly was in almost continuous session on that day. Yet *Dawn* carried the following announcement on September 21st: 'The Muslim League Parliamentary Party yesterday approved the Bill to amend sections 9 and 10 of the Government of India Act, 1935, it is learned.' Some League MCAs denied having received a summons to such a meeting, but most sources seem to agree that a meeting was held and that discussion took place.

The government itself was divided and rather than stand and

The Constituent Assembly

fight it chose to capitulate. Many of the Assembly members did not know what was going on, but were accustomed to being presented with *faits accomplis* and duly refrained from asking awkward questions. (This factor does not account for the silence of the Hindu members.) If the government had fallen the Governor-General would have a more cogent reason for attempting the dissolution of the Assembly than in fact he could allege in October. But the Prime Minister and his colleagues stood in silence while the basis of their power was undermined and they gave no indication of their approval or disapproval. The Prime Minister was about to leave for the United States to seek aid for his country and no doubt felt that a government crisis would weaken Pakistan's prospects. But the real weakness arose from five years of vacillation and faction.

SECTION IV: THE FEDERAL LEGISLATURE

The principal task of the Constituent Assembly of Pakistan was to frame the new constitution. But the Indian Independence Act also provided that it should act during the interim period as the central legislature of the new Dominion. In this latter capacity its duty was to sustain and control the government, to consider and pass legislation and to grant supplies. This in itself would have been no mean task for a legislature of a maximum of seventy-six persons, acting on behalf of a nation of 76,000,000 and responsible for building and strengthening a new state.

In practice the Legislature, being the lesser aspect of the Constituent Assembly, played an almost insignificant role. It is ironic that the real struggle for political power, which has just been described, was carried on in the constitution-making body and not in the Legislature. For, in theory, government and Opposition did not exist in the Constituent Assembly; it was in the Legislature that the cabinet was to be held responsible to the representatives of the people.

The Legislature never became an arena in which a real challenge could be brought against the government, though it did provide the only public means of exposing the shortcomings of the administration. The real opposition lay within the Muslim League, and party discipline and a general preference for secret diplomacy prevented its expression on the floor of the House. The Legislature had no real Opposition. The Assembly had been elected to bring Pakistan into being; the Opposition members were the unhappy dissenters who had been left on the wrong side of the border. The first leader of the (Pakistan) Congress Party moved to India; his successor, Mr. S. C. Chattopadhyaya, was a man of seventy-five in 1947 who had hoped to spend one or two years giving sage advice on the framing of a constitution. The rising Muslim Opposition—notably the Jinnah Awami League—was denied a voice in the Legislature because it had not existed in 1947. The government gave no opportunity for the Opposition to find places for its most able spokesmen.[1]

The Legislature was never in a position to forget that it was an interim body chosen primarily to fulfil another task. From year to year it expected that its life would soon be over and that its successor, the first real Parliament of Pakistan, would be in a better position to represent the people. Consequently the Legislature's approach to legislation was tentative and piecemeal, for the new constitution might give the opportunity for a bold and comprehensive programme that was beyond the scope of an interim body. In any event the leading members of the Legislature had too many other problems to be able to consider a major programme of new legislation. The Legislature was small enough, and apathetic enough, to enable most legislation to be passed quickly and carried through all its stages in the floor of the House.

[1] The disqualification of Mr. H. S. Suhrawardy has been noted above, p. 85.

Since casual vacancies were filled by election by provincial Assemblies by proportional representation, the simultaneous filling of a group of vacancies might have resulted in the return of Opposition candidates. But when three vacancies arose in the same session of the East Bengal Assembly, they were filled by elections on three separate days, thus defeating the working of proportional representation. (See Mr. Suhrawardy's complaint, *Dawn*, September 4, 1953.) The existence, by the end of its life, of some thirty-four vacancies in the East Bengal Assembly also worked to prevent the Opposition from having any chance of returning anti-League members to Karachi.

A few complex measures were referred to select committees, but this was the exception rather than the normal procedure. Divisions were rare, and the size of the government's majority robbed them of any interest.

The most important and wide-ranging of the annual debates came on the government's proposals for expenditure and taxation. In March of each year the Finance Minister presented his budget and made a lengthy speech on the economic position of the government and the country. This was followed by a general debate on the Budget Resolution which lasted two or three days. A time limit of fifteen or twenty minutes was placed on the duration of speeches. The House then proceeded to examine the Demands for Grants put forward by the government. In some years, in response to pressure by the Opposition and back-benchers, selected demands were taken first to allow greater debate on matters of controversy or importance. But this practice did not establish itself firmly, and the 1954 Demands, which enjoyed the longest period of discussion, were treated *seriatim* in the order presented in the government's printed schedule. Five days were spent in this discussion with a normal limit of one and a half hours for each Demand and ten minutes for each speech. On occasion selected demands received a longer period, and fifteen minutes were allowed to a speaker. The total was in no year sufficient to permit the consideration of more than a small fraction of the Demands and, at the close, the remaining grants were voted together without discussion. In 1954 Demands 16 to 86 inclusive were thus submitted for the 'approval' of the Legislature.[1] The final steps of financial procedure were the taxation proposals embodied in the Finance Bill. This permitted an even more general debate on government policy, but it was allotted no more than three days.

Legislative control over taxation and expenditure was not very

[1] Constituent Assembly (Legislature), *Debates*, 1954, Vol. I, March 26, 1954, p. 656.
In view of the relatively small number of sitting days (see table, p. 80), the government could hardly plead pressure of other business as an excuse for this limitation of debate.

effective in advance of the activities proposed. Unfortunately it was no more successful in exercising a check after the money had been spent. A committee on Public Accounts was established in 1948, containing seven members with the Minister of Finance as chairman.[1] It was to be expected that the accounts for the partition period would be in a state of near chaos, and it might have been found desirable to disregard the 1947-48 accounts and to proceed to a thorough examination of those for 1948-49. However, the Auditor-General persisted with the earlier figures and, as result, the committee held no meeting before September 1952 when the accounts for 1947-48 and 1948-49 were placed before it. In spite of the government majority on the committee, the report struck a somewhat plaintive note.

'We had a general feeling that some of the Ministries did not attach the same importance to the deliberations of the Committee as should have been done by virtue of its being a Committee of the Legislature.'[2]

And again:

'Expenditure not provided for in the budget should not be incurred as far as possible. It is not in order for the executive to take the approval of the Legislature for granted in the matter of the provision of funds.'[3]

That this latter warning was no small affair can be judged from the fact that, when the committee met in August 1953 to consider the accounts for 1949-50, they found that excess (unvoted) expenditure had been incurred on twenty-one items, including one amount of Rs. 150,000,000 (on Defence Services) and another of Rs. 20,000,000 (on State Trading).[4]

The Legislature possessed a series of Standing Advisory Com-

[1] *Gazette of Pakistan Extraordinary*, May 8, 1948.
[2] Constituent Assembly (Legislature), *Report of the Public Accounts Committee for 1947-48*, p. 1.   [3] *Ibid.*, p. 10.
[4] Constituent Assembly (Legislature), *Report of the Public Accounts Committee for 1949-50*.

The Constituent Assembly

mittees, one of which was assigned to each of the principal Ministries.[1] They contained three to five members with the appropriate Minister as chairman. They were intended to hold not less than two meetings a year to consider proposed legislation, reports of special committees, general policy, annual reports and other matters.[2] In practice, either these committees did not meet or, if they did, transacted no business of consequence. One member said that they were not standing committees but 'sleeping committees,' and added: 'Sir, I am sorry to say that the Economic Affairs Committee did not hold any meeting in spite of my repeated expostulations.'[3]

The sole Parliamentary device that was used with real effect to exert a check on the ministry was the Parliamentary Question. A handful of assiduous back-benchers maintained a constant barrage of requests for information. But sessions were short, and there was a limit to the number of questions that might be asked. And it must be admitted that members' use of supplementary questions was not very skilful in anticipating ministerial evasion. None the less many grievances were aired and many points of view expressed at Question Time that would otherwise have gone unheard. Other members, notably Mian Iftikharuddin, made frequent attempts to move the adjournment of the House in order to discuss a definite matter of urgent public importance. This device, partly because the attempts were often improper[4] and partly because the House was seldom in sympathy with the mover, failed to prove effective.

Above all, what was lacking in the Assembly was a 'sense of the House,' a feeling that it is Parliament that sets the standards of public life, and that ministers are to be measured by the House and not the House by ministers. This is the essence of responsible

---

[1] *Gazette of Pakistan*, February 27, 1948.
[2] Constituent Assembly (Legislature), *Debates*, 1948, Vol. I, p. 360, March 8, 1948, J. N. Mandal.
[3] *Ibid.*, 1953, Vol. I, p. 630, March 24, 1953, Shaikh Sadiq Hasan.
[4] Such adjournment motions, modelled after similar procedure of the United Kingdom House of Commons, have to fulfil exactly a number of conditions before they can be accepted.

parliamentary government, and it was not present in Pakistan's Constituent Assembly.

Perhaps it is worth summing up the reasons for the Assembly's general and undoubted failure. It was too small to function as a national legislature, and too many of its members had official duties to perform, leaving far too few active back-benchers to advise and control. It was not adequately representative of the country, and as time went on this defect became more and more important. The Opposition was a negligible force, the spokesmen for a permanent minority which could not hope to become an alternative government. The government habitually treated the House with disdain, and it was never permitted to have much self-esteem. Its sessions and business were chopped and changed to meet the convenience of those who had power. Governments were made and unmade but not by the Assembly. All that the House could do was to counter arbitrary action on the part of its masters, by conspiracy and intrigue behind closed doors. Consequently it failed to educate the public on matters of general concern and was unable to win the confidence of the ordinary citizen. The Constituent Assembly of Pakistan led an unhappy and deteriorating existence for over seven years, and then, in the words of a leading newspaper, it 'was wiped off the country's political map like one wipes spilt milk from a table.'[1]

SECTION V: THE SECOND CONSTITUENT ASSEMBLY

The first Constituent Assembly held its last meeting in September 1954 and was dissolved in October. In May the following year the Governor-General issued an order providing for the formation of a successor.[2] The new Assembly was to have eighty members divided equally between East and West Pakistan. Of these seventy-two were to be chosen by the provincial Assemblies and electoral colleges for Karachi and Baluchistan. The method of selecting the representatives from the states and tribal areas was to be decided by the Assembly itself. The elections in the

[1] *Dawn*, October 27, 1954, editorial.
[2] *The Constituent Assembly Order*, 1955 (G.G.O. 12/1955).

provincial Assemblies were to be by the single transferable vote system, though eleven seats were required to be filled by non-Muslims. The main elections were held in June 1955, and the Assembly held its first meeting in July. There were substantial changes between the membership of the first and second Assemblies. Only fourteen persons who were members of the first Assembly at dissolution were returned. Not surprisingly the greatest changes were in the delegation from Bengal. Fazlul Huq, Fazlur Rahman and Mohammed Ali (Bogra) were familiar faces, and H. S. Suhrawardy was able to return to the seat which had been taken from him some years before. Although there were substantial changes in the West Pakistan representation most of the leading figures were present: Daultana, Gurmani, Mamdot, Mohamad Ali, Noon and Khuhro. Among the new members were Iskandar Mirza and Khan Sahib.

The United Front had decided that those holding provincial cabinet posts should not be candidates from the Assembly. (Though this did not prevent those who became MCAs from accepting provincial office.) This rule was not applied by the other parties and the Assembly, when it held its first meeting, contained two Governors,[1] seven central ministers, nine provincial ministers, two rulers of states and one minister of a state government. The central cabinet was soon reorganized to include more MCAs, but this was partially offset by the consolidation of the ministries of West Pakistan. Since the Constituent Assembly had been chosen by the members of the provincial Assemblies usually from among their own members, many individuals were members of two legislatures.[2] Thus the second Assembly found itself working under many of the handicaps that had beset its forerunner.

In general the second Constituent Assembly functioned in

[1] Under the Constitution (Art. 70(5)) a Governor is ineligible for a seat in the Assembly. Accordingly the seats held by Fazlul Huq and Gurmani became vacant in March 1956.

[2] Art. 79(1) of the constitution bars a member of the National Assembly from occupying a seat in the provincial Assembly, but this prohibition did not apply in the interim before the first general election (Art. 225(4)).

Pakistan

much the same manner as its predecessor. The distinction was maintained between constitutional sessions and those for ordinary legislative business.[1] This involved the continuation of the fiction that the government as such was not concerned with constitutional matters.[2] The early discussions concerned the representation of states and tribal areas, the validation of laws and the unification of West Pakistan. This business consumed the first forty-nine sittings of the House. Debate was prolonged, rambling and often highly contentious. The Speaker's frequent attempts to induce some respect for the rule of relevance were almost completely fruitless. It was noticeable that the larger share of the speeches came from the Opposition. These speakers, many of whom had had recent experience in central or provincial office, were in a position to be much more effective than the Opposition members in the first Assembly.

When the second Assembly held its first meeting, it was by no means clear whether it held any substantial Opposition. Mr. Suhrawardy, leader of the Awami League, was still in the cabinet, and the United Front minister, A. H. Sarkar, had recently moved with cabinet approval to head the government of East Bengal. The two Bengali groups were conducting a bitter quarrel in that province, and this made it difficult for them to vote on the same side in the Constituent Assembly. The first division revealed a combination of the United Front, the Congress, the Scheduled Castes and Firoz Khan Noon, to give twenty-six votes against forty for the government (composed of Muslim League, Awami League and Independents).[3]

In August the Muslim League–United Front coalition was

---

[1] A constitutional sitting included not only one devoted to writing the new constitution but also one in which amendments to the Government of India Act or the Indian Independence Act were being considered.

[2] The true extent of government responsibility was always implicit in the conduct of business. Thus, for example, on occasion the Speaker announced that he had conferred with 'the Leader of the House and the Leader of the Opposition' in order to agree on a limitation of debate (Constituent Assembly of Pakistan, *Debates*, Vol. I, p. 901, September 19, 1955).

[3] Constituent Assembly of Pakistan, *Debates*, Vol. I, p. 18, July 7, 1955.

The Constituent Assembly

formed and the Awami League moved into Opposition. The representatives of the non-Muslims varied their attitude according to the issue at stake. The highest 'Opposition' vote at this period came on the decision to adopt the title of 'Islamic Republic.' Two non-Muslim ministers voted with the Awami League and others to give a recorded division of forty-seven to twenty-two.[1] The fact that members of the government were permitted to vote against the majority indicates that, on an issue of conscience, cabinet discipline was not applied on constitutional matters.

The government resolved to profit by the lessons of the previous attempts to reach agreement on the constitution, and the new Assembly was not asked to set up machinery to prepare a draft. Instead the government prepared its own draft, which was published in January 1956. On the day after publication the Law Minister rose to introduce 'A Bill to provide a Constitution for the Islamic Republic of Pakistan.' After the minister's speech the House adjourned for a week, so that the members might have an opportunity to study the provisions of the Bill. After general discussion had taken place on twelve days, the Assembly proceeded to consider the Bill in detail. This required a further seventeen sittings, during which the closure was frequently invoked. On one occasion the Opposition was so unwise as to leave the chamber in protest against a ruling of the Chair; this enabled the government to secure approval of many clauses without discussion.[2]

The final debate and approval of the constitution took place on February 29th. The proceedings were marked by the expression of considerable bitterness by those who were not members of the governing coalition. Mr. Suhrawardy appealed to the government to summon a round table conference to discuss the contentious issues. When this suggestion was ignored he, followed by his party, left the chamber. The Congress party then stated its opposition and left the chamber. Their example was then followed by Mian Iftikharuddin (Azad Pakistan), Mahmud Ali

[1] *Dawn*, February 22, 1956.
[2] On this day some fifty clauses of the constitution were adopted (Constituent Assembly of Pakistan, *Debates*, Vol. I, February 7, 1956).

Pakistan

(Ganatantri Dal), S. K. Sen (United Progressive), and Rasa Raj Mandal and Gour Chandra Bala (Scheduled Castes).

The general framework of the constitution forms a logical continuation of the provisions of the Government of India Act. In form the constitution follows the lines of a statute. Some other countries have chosen to write their constitutions in simple language whose meaning can be understood by any educated man. But this constitution is long (234 articles and 6 schedules) and couched in the language of lawyers.[1] This is, in one sense, a serious defect. It is hard for the layman to feel that the constitution is a living reality which he can understand, respect and defend against encroachment or wrongful interpretation. A legal document is apt to be left to the care of the courts rather than protected by strong public sentiment. However, once the statutory form is admitted, the document is, in outline, relatively simple and straightforward. In order that the constitution shall contain some general indication of the hopes and purposes of the people the document contains one feature not normally found in a statute. This is Part III, entitled 'Directive Principles of State Policy,' and its provisions are not enforceable in any court.

The general scheme is that of government by a cabinet of ministers responsible to an elected National Assembly.[2] The nominal head of the state is called the President, who is elected by the combined votes of the central and provincial Assemblies. He is expected to act on the advice of the cabinet except when choosing a Prime Minister or in matters relating to the Election and Delimitation Commissions. The cabinet is responsible to the legislature, which is composed of a single chamber called the National Assembly. This contains 310 members equally distributed between East and West Pakistan. Each of the two pro-

[1] It is doubtful whether generations of schoolboys will learn by heart a clause such as the following: 'Any property which has no rightful owner, or which but for the enactment of the Constitution, would have accrued to Her Majesty by escheat or lapse, or as *bona vacantia* for want of a rightful owner, shall, if it is property situate in a Province, vest in the Provincial Government, and shall, in any other case, vest in the Federal Government.'

[2] Various aspects of the new constitution are discussed in more detail in subsequent chapters.

The Constituent Assembly

vinces has a similar form of government. The Governor is appointed by the centre, but the real power is supposed to lie with the provincial ministry which is responsible to a provincial Assembly also of 310 members.

Until general elections could be held under the new constitution the existing Constituent and provincial Assemblies were to be transformed into the corresponding national and provincial Assemblies. As such they were directed to function as nearly as possible under the provisions of the constitution. The interim President was to be chosen by the Constituent Assembly, and he was to hold office only until the permanent machinery of constitutional government had been brought into operation. All other office-holders were to continue in their posts. Thus on March 23, 1956, the transition from the Government of India Act to the provisions of the constitution took place smoothly and without any disruption of the normal process of government.

CHAPTER IV

Cabinet Government

CONSTITUTIONAL government has normally come into being as the result of pressure by the people, or those who lead them, upon the holders of power. A democratic constitution asserts that there shall be no arbitrary power, and that, in the last resort, the rulers shall be judged by those who are ruled. A system of responsible government implies that the power of the executive shall be subject to limitations, which will be enforced at the behest of organized public opinion. In particular, the history of cabinet government is the long story of the transformation of an autocratic monarch and his circle of personal advisers into the group of leaders of a political party who derive their authority through Parliament from the electorate.

This is the English system, and its roots lie deep in the history of that country. The system has been transplanted with considerable success to such countries as Canada, Australia and New Zealand, which form logical offshoots of the 'old country.' In part the adaptation has been successful because the people who made it work had known its conventions and outlook before moving to their new homelands. But cabinet government also developed its own roots and traditions in the new soil. The actions of self-willed Governors and a meddling Colonial Office had to be curbed and made responsible to local opinion. In the course of this struggle the people of these former colonies came to know for themselves what were the essential features of responsible government that must be fought for and defended. In recent years cabinet government has been introduced into countries whose people and political tradition are quite different from those of England or the English-speaking Dominions. Amongst these countries Pakistan has been, in some ways, the least prepared by history and by circumstances to bring such a system into successful operation.

Cabinet Government

The need for a strong executive authority was paramount in the early years of the new state. In August 1947 the area that is now Pakistan was verging on chaos. National existence depended upon the strength of will of a handful of individuals. Order was established and the government was able to feel that its writ would run throughout the country. But the situation was still precarious. East and West Pakistan were separated by 1,000 air miles and 2,000 miles of sea; communication by land was out of the question. Refugees by the million had to be assembled, fed, clothed and doctored. New governments had to be created and the army had to be reformed and consolidated. The economy had to be strictly controlled in order that scarce resources might be applied to the most urgent tasks.

In the midst of such an upheaval some of the elements of which remain to the present day, no one could expect to question and restrain and control the actions of the executive. Public opinion, even in the most mature and long-established democracies, has to reserve its judgment when the life of the community is in danger. Pakistan, as a democracy, was neither mature nor long-established. Public opinion was largely ill-educated, and was totally unused to the careful weighing of small issues that is required if the power of government is to be kept within due bounds. In a democracy this kind of public opinion is usually organized by political parties. In the early years in Pakistan there was only one such party, the Muslim League, which was in power, and therefore unwilling to arouse popular feeling against the administration of its own leaders.

The force of circumstances compelled the government to keep a tight rein. But there was little in the history of the Muslims of India to prepare them for the conduct of government limited by public opinion and freely expressed opposition. In a later chapter it is shown that the tradition of Islam has not encouraged systematic opposition. The vision of good government possessed by many Muslims is that of a people united under a strong leader and confident in the possession of certain truth. If any limit is to be placed on the authority of the rulers it must be found in the law, which governs all things.

Pakistan

The Muslim League operated before independence according to an autocratic pattern. It demanded the unity of the Muslim nation and conceded no right to an Indian Muslim to differ from its essential position. And in the pursuit of its aim the party freely accepted complete subordination to the will of the Great Leader. Mr. Jinnah gave his followers this watchword: Unity, Faith and Discipline.

The people of Pakistan were not likely to learn the concept of the limitation of government power from their religion or from the course of the struggle that led them to independence. Nor would they derive such a lesson from the system of government which prevailed in undivided India before partition. The generation of 1947 had lived under the Viceregal system of autocracy which was sometimes benevolent and sometimes repressive. Successive constitutional measures had provided a forum for the expression of political opinion, and the Act of 1935 had transferred a substantial element of power in the provinces to ministers responsible to elected legislatures. These provisions were fully effective only from 1937 until the outbreak of war. And even while they lasted, the central government was still the final authority whose power had not been made accountable to Indian opinion.

Power in India proceeded downward from the King-Emperor, not upward from the people. The British Parliament, through the Secretary of State and the Viceroy, possessed ultimate power. As an act of grace it chose to delegate some of its authority, within certain limits and under certain safeguards, to the ministers and legislatures of the Indian provinces. It was the intention of the Parliament of the United Kingdom that this delegation should be carried progressively farther; in particular, that it should be applied in substantial measure to the central government of India. The right to determine the rate of progress, or even to decide on a change of direction, remained firmly in British hands. In the light of Commonwealth history it was to be presumed that, at some future stage, the balance of power would tilt and final effective authority would have come to rest with the Indians themselves. But this had not occurred by

Cabinet Government

1946–47, and there was no time for the slow accumulation of the traditions of self-government. The transfer of power, unlike that in the older Dominions, took place abruptly and in an atmosphere of violence, and not as the recognition of a state of affairs that had long existed in fact.

The transfer of power took place at the summit. In the older Dominions the Governor-General had gradually been transformed into a figurehead, and his powers had atrophied rather than been abolished. In India the Viceroy was far from being a mere figurehead, and it was his final authority (and that of the Secretary of State) that was to be handed over.

Until 1947 the Viceroy had functioned in part under the Act of 1935, but since its provisions regarding the central government had not come into force he continued to act substantially under the Act of 1919. He had an executive council to aid and advise him, but he was clearly its superior and could over-rule its decisions or recommendations. Attention was focused on one individual whose name and face were known to millions of Indians who would not have been able to repeat the name of a single member of his council. He represented the King-Emperor. This was a status that could easily be grasped by the uneducated. There was in India a direct chain of authority descending from the King-Emperor, through the Viceroy and the provincial Governor to the District Officer. Each of these was an identifiable person to whom appeal might be made and from whom redress might be obtained. The idea of independence was simple, but the scheme of responsible government through Indian ministers, though intelligible to the Western-educated middle-class, was much harder to the understanding of the cultivator.

There is an outward respect for power in Pakistan that stands in the way of democracy, though it can be used to further the cause of stable government. Any act of political strength is likely to be welcomed. The Governor-General received hundreds of addresses of congratulation and support when he dismissed Nazimuddin in spite of the latter's undoubted strength in the Constituent Assembly. No serious public attack was made on the Governor-General's action, and no real discussion of the issues took place with a view to defining and limiting his powers. The action was presented as a *fait accompli*, and passed unchallenged because Ghulam Mohammad was *in* and Nazimuddin was *out*. A similar reaction prevailed when the Assembly was dismissed and a kind of central Governor's rule was introduced. The courts took action, the organs of public opinion did not. When a new Assembly was convened it made no effort to consider the political defensibility of the Governor-General's action; the leaders of almost all political groups having entered his cabinet it would have been difficult for any party to take a stand on constitutional principle.

One of the consequences of this respect for power is that a politician who appears successful is certain to have a large following, but, should his fortunes appear to decline, his supporters will soon disappear. This may be said to be true of politics everywhere, but the extent of its operation in Pakistan has made a mockery of political loyalty. Within the same party and in the life of the same Assembly a series of leaders can be imposed from outside: Nazimuddin gave way to Mohammed Ali; Khuhro to Pirzada to Khuhro; Daultana to Noon to Dasti; Qaiyum to Rashid to Sardar Bahadur. These leaders were successively picked by higher levels of political authority and imposed on their Assemblies; yet none of them was defeated in the Assembly, and most of them experienced no serious difficulty in keeping a majority.

It is not unusual in democratic communities to find that popular attention is focused upon one man rather than upon a party or a policy. In Pakistan attention has concentrated upon individuals virtually to the exclusion of any consideration of policies or regard for party discipline. In each province there has usually been one man in power and one or more prominent individuals trying to supplant him. Each of these leaders has behaved as a local chieftain with his private army of political clansmen. Each enters into alliances, both offensive and defensive, with other princelings or with the central government, which has reserved to itself the role of overlord. The result has been that, while the machinery of cabinet and Assembly has been preserved (with long intervals of bureaucratic rule), the essence of responsible cabinet government cannot be said to have come into existence.

In the light of history and of circumstances, neither the informed public nor the man in the field has any very strong prejudice in favour of government through ministers and Assemblies. What they wanted was efficient government, honest government and, as far as possible, cheap government. After taking a close look at the activities of some of the elected politicians, there was often a sense of relief at the prospect that the Governor or Governor-General might take over the reins. 'The cause for which Hampden had died on the field and Sidney on the scaffold' means little to a Pakistani. His political battle was for independence from British and Hindu rule, and not for the restraint of executive power.

At midnight on August 14, 1947, Pakistan became an independent Dominion within the Commonwealth. It was governed by certain specific legal provisions, notably the Government of India Act (as modified by the Pakistan Provisional Constitution Order), and the Indian Independence Act. But it had also acquired a status shared by the other autonomous nations of the Commonwealth, and Pakistan might be presumed to have inherited certain conventions that normally guide the working of the system of cabinet government. These conventions provide the essence of responsible government, which does not appear on the surface of the constitutional documents of the Commonwealth. Throughout the Dominions executive power rests with a cabinet which is responsible to an elected legislature. If the government of the day is unable to command a majority it must either resign or appeal to the electorate for support.

The Governor-General, who represents the Queen, is appointed in accordance with the wishes of the cabinet of the Dominion concerned. It is generally accepted that if the Governor-General proves unacceptable to the ministry, his appointment may be terminated and a more suitable successor nominated. In this respect a Governor-General is not the counterpart of the Queen since his appointment is in any event limited and may be shortened still further if he displeases his masters. In all matters of public

Pakistan

policy convention requires that he accept the advice of his ministers. There remains with the Crown (in the person of the Governor-General) a certain reserve power, the limits of which are not precisely defined. It might be used to control a ministry or a legislature which was violating the constitution, indulging in acts of wanton irresponsibility or flagrantly damaging the larger public interest. But the benefit of any doubt must be accorded to the responsible ministers, and the reserve power retains its significance precisely because it is in reserve and not a regular means of political action. An exercise of this reserve power would be expected to take the form, not of the assumption of personal rule by the Crown's representative, but of an appeal to the people or its representatives against those who seemed to be betraying its interests. Thus a cabinet which unreasonably refused to summon Parliament might be dismissed, but it would be necessary immediately to summon Parliament to approve the formation of a new ministry. Or a legislature which endeavoured to perpetuate its own existence might be dissolved and an appeal carried to the electorate.

In order that Pakistan should begin life as an independent and democratic state, it was necessary, between June and August 1947, to amend the previous constitutional provisions. It would have been inappropriate for the United Kingdom Parliament or a British Viceroy to assume responsibility for the introduction of a major constitutional scheme. In the first place there was insufficient time and, secondly, it would have anticipated the right of the new state freely to decide how it was to be governed. There were, however, many modifications that were essential before the day of independence. Among other matters the responsibilities of the Secretary of State for India and of the Governor-General as his agent had to be terminated. These changes were accomplished by the Indian Independence Act and in greater detail by an order under that Act, the Pakistan Provisional Constitution Order, 1947, promulgated by the Viceroy on August 14, 1947.[1]

Section 3(2) of this order provided that the Governor-General

[1] G.G.O. 22/1947.

and the provincial Governors should lose their powers of acting independently of their ministers. The 1935 Act had conferred many powers on the Governor-General or a Governor to be used 'in his discretion,' or 'exercising his individual judgment.' These phrases were now to be omitted wherever they occurred throughout the constitution. It seems that the intention was to provide a status for the Governor-General of Pakistan equivalent to that enjoyed by his counterpart in Canada or Australia. Other sections of the Indian Independence Act which appeared to confer extensive powers upon the Governor-General were not, therefore, to be taken at face value. When it was written that 'The Governor-General shall by order make such provision as appears to him to be necessary or expedient . . .,' it must be understood to mean that when the cabinet considered it to be necessary or expedient, the Governor-General should, on its advice, issue such an order.

The new Dominion of India was in a comparable position. The former Viceroy, Lord Mountbatten, agreed to remain as the first Governor-General of independent India. This continuity with British rule was a source of both strength and weakness. Lord Mountbatten had been a Viceroy and had been accustomed to personal authority. He was bound to be more than a mere distinguished figurehead. He had played a major part in bringing about the transfer of power, and he could not stand aloof from the consequences of his own efforts. In addition he was both admired and trusted by 'his' ministers. But he was not an Indian, and could never claim to represent the people against the government. And the most powerful political figure in India, Pandit Nehru, was Prime Minister, conscious of the fact that it was he who appointed and dismissed Governors-General.

Affairs were quite otherwise in Pakistan. Mr. Jinnah towered over all other political leaders so that they were reduced to relative insignificance. And Mr. Jinnah chose to become Governor-General. As a consequence of this decision the normal conventions of cabinet government had no chance to develop. The *Quaid-i-Azam* could have held any position or none; he would still have retained ultimate authority in his own person. The members of his council of ministers felt themselves to be his lieutenants. They were prepared to execute his orders or to be overruled by him on any point, either individually or as a group. The possibility of instructions proceeding from the cabinet to the Governor-General did not arise; it was, in fact, unthinkable. From the beginning it was assumed that the normal conventions of the office of Governor-General could never apply to Mr. Jinnah.

> 'Whatever the constitutional powers of the Governor-General of a Dominion may nominally be, in Quaid-i-Azam's case no legal or formal limitations can apply. His people will not be content to have him as merely the titular head of the government, they would wish him to be their friend, philosopher, guide and ruler, irrespective of what the constitution of a Dominion of the British Commonwealth may contain.'[1]

The circumstances prevailing during Pakistan's first few months of independent existence called for strong executive action. The Constituent Assembly did not meet as Legislature until February 1948, and it showed little disposition to question the actions of the *Quaid-i-Azam*, who was also its own President. Its attitude had been indicated during the brief constitutional session in 1947 when a resolution was adopted requiring the use of the term *Quaid-i-Azam* (Great Leader), for all official purposes.[2] During the two brief sessions of the legislature that took place during Mr. Jinnah's lifetime the only overt criticism of the acts of the executive, identified with the Governor-General in person, occurred over the decision to separate the area of the federal capital from the province of Sind. This criticism was regarded at the time to amount to *lèse majesté*.[3]

With the death of Mr. Jinnah in September 1948, the political situation came to resemble cabinet government. Liaquat Ali Khan was clearly the leading statesman of the country, but he did not

[1] *Dawn*, July 13, 1947.
[2] Constituent Assembly of Pakistan, *Debates*, Vol. I, p. 47, August 12, 1947.
[3] *Ibid.*, Vol. III, May 22, 1948.

Cabinet Government

dominate his colleagues in the manner of the founder of Pakistan. He chose to remain as Prime Minister, and Khwaja Nazimuddin was installed as Governor-General. At the time of his appointment, Nazimuddin was an active politician, the Chief Minister of East Bengal. But he accepted the status of his exalted rank and played the role of a constitutional Governor-General with considerable distinction. Liaquat Ali had been the chief lieutenant of the *Quaid-i-Azam*, and was clearly expected to be his successor by the politicians and by the public. He had been Prime Minister for thirteen months while Nazimuddin was still in East Bengal. Thus within the central government Nazimuddin could not possess the detailed knowledge of men and issues that was at the disposal of the Prime Minister.

This state of affairs lasted for twenty-five months. In October 1951 Liaquat Ali was assassinated. This was an emergency situation in which the reserve powers of the Governor-General might be expected to operate. Nazimuddin summoned the remaining members of the central cabinet to consider the problem of succession. There was no heir apparent, and the decision cannot have been easy. Nazimuddin had had great political experience, having served as Chief Minister of undivided Bengal as well as of the largest province of Pakistan. It was also considered proper that a Bengali should succeed to the position of real authority. It was therefore decided that he should become Prime Minister and that Ghulam Mohammad should be the new Governor-General.

The decision that Nazimuddin should step down to head the government did nothing to establish the tradition that the Governor-General should hold himself aloof from everyday political life. Nor did the choice of Ghulam Mohammad. In other Commonwealth countries the position of Governor-General has been filled by men expected to be personally unconcerned with the struggle for power—elder statesmen, junior members of the royal family, distinguished soldiers. But Ghulam Mohammad was one of the stronger members of the cabinet. As Finance Minister he had exerted substantial control over most aspects of domestic policy. As a former civil servant he was intimately acquainted with the working of the administration. His strength and influence lay within the central government and not with the country at large. He had not been a leader in the struggle for Pakistan. While Jinnah, Liaquat Ali and Nazimuddin had been engaged in politics, Ghulam Mohammad had been Finance Minister in the state of Hyderabad. The public had heard him praised for his control of the nation's finances, but apart from respect for his skill with money, there was little knowledge of the personal nature of the man or his political position. He had made few public speeches and done little to attract to himself a nation-wide following.

It is possible that Ghulam Mohammad was appointed in order that a strong Punjabi should be in a position to balance a Bengali Prime Minister. The position of Governor-General had been regarded as one of considerable political importance, and it was widely insisted that if one of the two top offices went to East Pakistan the other should be given to the West.[1] An alternative explanation is that those who opposed Punjabi influence felt that Ghulam Mohammad would enjoy less real power as Governor-General than as the strongest member of Nazimuddin's cabinet. A third and quite reasonable theory is that Ghulam Mohammad's failing health made it difficult for him to carry a heavy administrative burden but not impossible for him to perform ceremonial functions.

The transfer took place and Nazimuddin entered the cabinet and Ghulam Mohammad left it. The new Prime Minister was not surrounded by men of his own choosing. The cabinet, Liaquat Ali's cabinet, was already in existence, and it would have been difficult to carry out a large-scale reconstruction. Chaudhri Mohamad Ali, the Secretary-General to the government (and a principal collaborator of Ghulam Mohammad as Finance Minis-

[1] Such a provision was proposed in the original 'Mohammed Ali formula' for incorporation in the constitution though it was not adopted by the Assembly. The east-west division prevailed in practice when Nazimuddin and Mohammed Ali (Bogra) were Prime Minister. The departure from this emerging convention when Iskandar Mirza and Chaudhri Mohamad Ali were Governor-General and Prime Minister, drew a sharp protest from Mr. Suhrawardy (*Dawn*, August 13, 1955).

Cabinet Government

ter), was promoted to fill the vacancy in the Ministry of Finance. Nazimuddin gradually began to assert his authority in the administration, in the party and in the country. The new Governor-General made no attempt to exceed his proper function. He kept himself informed of all that was taking place, and developed a considerable interest in the armed forces.

In the spring of 1953 it was obvious that the country was facing a crisis in several spheres at once. The Governor-General and his friends looked with increasing alarm at what they considered to be the incapacity of the government to take firm action. On April 17th the Governor-General issued a Press communique, which said (in part):

> 'I have been driven to the conclusion that the cabinet of Khwaja Nazimuddin has proved entirely inadequate to grapple with the difficulties facing the country. In the emergency which has arisen I have felt it incumbent upon me to ask the cabinet to relinquish office so that a new cabinet better fitted to discharge its obligations toward Pakistan may be formed.'

The Governor-General had taken an action that was clearly political and beyond the normal scope of a constitutional head of state.

It cannot be denied that the administration had failed to surmount all the many obstacles that lay in its path. After eighteen months in office it had not provided a constitution (but neither had Liaquat Ali after thirty-eight months as Prime Minister); it had encountered a food crisis and was experiencing the consequences of the disastrous decline in the value of Pakistan's exports following the end of the fighting in Korea. But perhaps foremost in the mind of an old servant of the government of India was the weakness shown in standing up to the politico-religious agitation that had plunged the Punjab into civil violence. A government that is incapable of maintaining law and order does not deserve to retain office. But was this a fair charge to bring against the Nazimuddin ministry? The government had finally, after exhausting every possibility of compromise, stood firm

Pakistan

against the politico-religious agitators who led the anti-Ahmadiya movement. Martial law had been proclaimed in Lahore, and the Punjab was rapidly returning to order. Nazimuddin had gone to Lahore and brought about the replacement of Daultana by Noon. The country had visibly been on the verge of disruption in late February and early March, but that particular corner had been turned. The dismissal of the Prime Minister was the outcome of a disbelief in the strength of his personal character, and because of signs of a general lack of competence in the top levels of the administration.

The Governor-General's action was not a personal seizure of power. A new cabinet was immediately installed, and it must be presumed to have accepted full responsibility for the dismissal of its predecessor. No less than half the members of the former cabinet joined the new administration.[1] The Governor-General must have been aware that his proposed action had the backing of several ministers. It would therefore have been possible for the cabinet to have discussed any areas of policy in which the government's actions had been felt to be lacking in firmness. If the dissident ministers had felt strongly they might have resigned, thus provoking a major cabinet crisis, which, unless resolved by the Prime Minister, would have given considerable justification for intervention by the Governor-General. But if such a crisis had occurred, Nazimuddin would have appealed to the Muslim League Parliamentary Party or to the Constituent Assembly. And, as far as can be told, he would have had a majority.

The Governor-General's action was in effect directed as much against the Assembly as against the Prime Minister. A Governor-General who dismisses a ministry must normally find another which possesses a majority in Parliament or which is prepared to face an election in defence of the Governor's action. The Assembly was sitting until thirteen days before the dismissal. It had accepted the budget and thereby approved the government's economic and general administrative policies. It had been given a chance to

[1] Ministers not reappointed: Nazimuddin, Nishtar, Fazlur Rahman, Pirzada, Mahmud Husain. Reappointed: Zafrullah, Sardar Bahadur, Chaudhri Mohamad Ali, A. M. Malik, Gurmani and I. H. Qureshi.

debate the Punjab disturbances and the removal of Daultana, but no threat to the government had materialized.[1] When the new ministry was formed it showed itself by no means anxious to meet the Assembly, which was not summoned to meet again until September 23, 1953. In April Nazimuddin was in command of the Muslim League both nationally and in Parliament. He was unwilling to fight even for control of the party, perhaps motivated by considerations of public and private tranquillity. He acquiesced in the transfer of his authority over the party to the man who had supplanted him as Prime Minister. By the time the Assembly met the change of ministry was ancient history, and was not considered worthy of a debate.

The Governor-General had taken a great risk. If Nazimuddin had learned what was being prepared, he could have requested the Queen to revoke Ghulam Mohammad's commission.[2] The final decision may have been that of the Governor-General, but he must have taken political soundings to assure himself of the chances of success. Alternatively, Nazimuddin might have chosen to fight the issue either in the party or the Assembly.[3]

The price of the Governor-General's *coup* was high. Three major conventions of cabinet government had been destroyed or gravely weakened. First, the tradition of the impartiality of the Governor-General had been demolished. Second, the convention of cabinet and party solidarity had been disregarded. Third, the role of the Legislature as the maker and sustainer of governments had been impugned. Ghulam Mohammad was left with an awkward political situation on his hands. There was no visible machinery for the replacement of the Assembly. Consequently

[1] Constituent Assembly (Legislature), *Debates*, 1953, Vol. I, March 19 and 28, 1953.

[2] There was a rumour current in Karachi that Nazimuddin, on hearing of his dismissal, had attempted to telephone to the Queen, but that his telephone had been disconnected.

[3] It will be remembered that as a constitution-making body the Assembly could be summoned by its President. While a vote of no confidence could not have been moved under those circumstances, the Assembly could have amended the constitution in a manner indicating its distrust of the Governor-General. This was the course it adopted in September 1954.

Pakistan

it was up to the then existing House to sustain the government and to complete the new constitution in spite of the fact that many of its leading members had been bitterly antagonized by the Governor-General and his chosen Prime Minister. For all this the Governor-General had to take the greater part of the responsibility. He had stepped out of the role as formal head of the state. It was not possible for Parliament or the public to believe that he could step back into dignified and benign impotence.

Between April 1953 and October 1954 Ghulam Mohammad did not attempt to intervene in the day-to-day administration of the various departments of government. But he was personally responsible for the installation of the cabinet and, in particular, of its Prime Minister. Mohammed Ali had been an original member of the Constituent Assembly and had held previous ministerial office in Bengal, though not at the centre. From 1948 he had represented his country successively in Burma, Canada and the United States, and he had relinquished his seat in the Assembly. He had been out of daily contact with the details of political manœuvre for nearly five years. He was then asked to assume the Prime Ministership at a time of extreme tension and under circumstances that demanded the exercise of immense political skill. He had no personal following, and he had never been regarded as a very senior member of the Muslim League hierarchy. However, he was fresh from the United States, where he had enjoyed great success as ambassador; this made him the right man to redirect the foreign policy of Pakistan into close military and economic alliance with that country. Moreover, he was a Bengali, and the government desperately needed evidence that it represented Bengal. Further, he was a Bengali who was acceptable to the Governor-General and to the stronger members of the new ministry—Chaudhri Mohamad Ali (Punjab) and M. A. Gurmani (Punjab).

Mohammed Ali found that his cabinet had been chosen for him. Six ministers came from the outgoing administration; the three additional members are reported to have entered the cabinet at the invitation of the Governor-General rather than that of the

Prime Minister.[1] The new Prime Minister began his tenure of office as 'the man brought in by the Governor-General,' but it is doubtful whether close personal ties ever linked the two men. For obvious reasons of location he had not been close to Ghulam Mohammad; his past career had been in Bengal and abroad. Other members of the cabinet had been much more intimately associated with the Governor-General. They were Punjabis and were believed to be opposed to some of the aspirations of the more vigorous representatives of Bengal. They were bound together by long association, personal friendship and substantial agreement on matters of policy. The impression is not surprising (though it is not easy to prove) that many decisions of government were effectively taken by a group that included the Governor-General and these influential ministers. The cabinet functioned in a normal manner, and issues of policy came up for full and free discussion. But the suspicion remained that, on certain important matters, the stronger personalities of the cabinet had reached agreement in advance. There is nothing new or improper about an 'inner cabinet.' What was unusual was that it appeared to centre on the Governor-General rather than the Prime Minister.

Under these circumstances the government continued until it was confronted with the crisis of September–October 1954. The parliamentary aspects of this conflict have been discussed in an earlier chapter (Chapter III). Shortly before the onset of the crisis the government began to realize that the Assembly was getting out of hand. The idea of an interim constitution was then discussed. This would have adopted the agreed clauses of the Basic Principles Committee Report but left the controversial items undecided. The Assembly would have been dissolved and direct elections held to choose its successor. This would have avoided the charge that an unrepresentative Assembly was prepared to impose an unsatisfactory constitution on an unwilling country. But it would also have extended the tenure of the Governor-General and the cabinet at least until the results of the elections became known. The Bengal members, who had recently been

[1] The new ministers were: A. K. Brohi (Sind), Abdul Qaiyum (North-West Frontier Province) and Shuaib Qureshi (Punjab).

repudiated in their own province, had much to lose in an election and were unfavourable to any extension of the term of the Governor-General. The proposal therefore failed to achieve the necessary support. The anti-government members of the Muslim League then proceeded to move against the administration by repealing PRODA and by limiting the powers of the Governor-General and the cabinet.

During September the government made no visible attempt to combat its opponents. Cabinet ministers sat in silence while private members undermined their authority, and it was a minister who rewarded Mr. Gazder for his part in this action by moving an increase in his pay and allowances. The Governor-General was touring in the North-West Frontier; his lieutenants seemed either unaware of what was being attempted or too feeble to do anything about it. But the dissidents did not press home their superiority. They allowed the legislature to adjourn without moving a vote of want of confidence in the government. The Governor-General returned from the north and the Prime Minister departed for London and Washington.

From this point events began to move with melodramatic suddenness and intensity.[1] The Governor-General began to hold consultations with prominent individuals. General Ayub Khan proceeded to Washington as previously planned, to assist the Prime Minister in arranging for military aid from the United States. General Iskandar Mirza took leave from his post as Governor of East Bengal, and after a stay in Karachi flew to London. The Prime Minister had arranged to visit Ottawa after his stay in the United States, but after receiving a message from the Governor-General he cancelled this plan and crossed the Atlantic, accompanied by General Ayub. They were met in London by General Mirza and M. A. H. Ispahani, then High

[1] The account which follows is based on reports in *Dawn* and *The Times of Karachi* for October 21st to 25th, supplemented by accounts in *Time* magazine dated November 1st, *The Times* and the *New York Times* and on the author's personal observations and conversations in Karachi during that period. The account given is the least sensational of the many variants that were in current circulation.

Commissioner in the United Kingdom. There were reports that they spent several hours together at London Airport while arrangements for a special aircraft were first made and then cancelled. The four men and Begum Mohammed Ali returned together to Karachi, where they arrived late at night on October 23rd, in an atmosphere of intense crisis. Leaving his wife at the airport the Prime Minister and the two generals drove straight to Government House. The conference with the Governor-General lasted until after 2 a.m. when the Prime Minister returned home. Reports in the foreign Press said that he wept and was passionately resentful of the position that had been forced upon him.

At 1 p.m. a Proclamation issued from the Governor-General:

'The Governor-General having considered the political crisis with which the country is faced has, with deep regret, come to the conclusion that the constitutional machinery has broken down. He, therefore, has decided to declare a State of Emergency throughout Pakistan. The Constituent Assembly as at present constituted has lost the confidence of the people and can no longer function.

'The ultimate authority vests in the people who will decide all issues including constitutional issues through their representatives to be elected afresh. Elections will be held as early as possible.

'Until such time as elections are held, the administration of the country will be carried on by a reconstituted Cabinet. He has called upon the Prime Minister to reform the Cabinet with a view to giving the country a vigorous and stable administration. The invitation has been accepted.

'The security and stability of the country are of paramount importance. All personal, sectional and provincial interests must be subordinated to the supreme national interest.'

The new cabinet was sworn later that same evening. It included four members of the old cabinet and four newcomers: General Ayub, a soldier; General Mirza, a civil servant with an army background; M. A. H. Ispahani, a business man and diplomat; and Mir Ghulam Ali Talpur, a landowner and politician from Sind. Six other members were added during the next ten weeks, including representatives from both sections of the United Front and Dr. Khan Sahib.[1] Such a cabinet might be regarded as a government of national unity, representing the major political groups, the business community, the armed forces and the civil service.

The Prime Minister described the new cabinet as a 'Ministry of Talent'[2] and the level of individual competence was undoubtedly high. But it was not a normal responsible government, and it had no basis for unity of outlook except a common desire to overcome the immediate crisis. The Prime Minister stressed the government's dedication to democratic principles: 'We are all directly responsible to the people in the absence of the legislature.'[3] General Mirza, reputed to be the 'strong man' of the cabinet, was making statements on the same day that had a markedly different flavour.

'The masses of this country are overwhelmingly illiterate. They are not interested in politics. They are bound to act foolishly sometimes, as they did in East Pakistan and again their elected leaders did in the Constituent Assembly. It was thus necessary, in fact essential, that there should be somebody to rectify their blunders. . . .
'Then the General went on to say. People of this country need controlled democracy for some time to come. He emphasized that by this he did not mean dictatorship.'[4]

Those who agreed with the action of the Governor-General were left with no remedy other than an appeal to the courts. The first stage was to apply to the Sind Chief Court for writs declaring that the government had no right to prevent the Assembly from continuing to function. The Sind Court upheld this plea and the

[1] The fact that seven former ministers were omitted from the cabinet cannot be taken to indicate disagreement with the action of the Governor-General. Zafrullah had already accepted election to the World Court, Gurmani became Governor of the Punjab, Sardar Bahadur became Chief Commissioner of Baluchistan and Shuaib Qureshi returned to a diplomatic post.
[2] *Dawn*, October 31, 1954.   [3] *Ibid*.
[4] *Ibid*. It should be noted that both the above quotations are indirect, though the speaker's words seem to emerge quite clearly.

Cabinet Government

government appealed to the Federal Court whose decision was made known on March 26, 1955. Its effect was to support the Governor-General in his dismissal of the Assembly. But the issue was not faced squarely, being reached on the ground that the procedure for challenging the dismissal had not been validly enacted by the Constituent Assembly. This line of argument had the result of invalidating also forty-three other Acts of the Assembly as well as hundreds of Acts and orders of provincial governments and orders issued under the authority of the invalid central Acts. The consequence seemed to be a state of legal chaos. The government was constrained to take immediate action, and a state of emergency was proclaimed on the following day. Under cover of this proclamation the Emergency Powers Ordinance was issued. This declared that most of the impugned laws were to be deemed to operate as though they had been properly enacted from the beginning. However, the Ordinance went much farther than the rectification of the consequences of the Court's decision. It provided that the Governor-General might, by order, constitute the province of West Pakistan.[1] And then, as a final section, the Ordinance assumed the whole power of constitution-making:

> '10. Provision for future Constitution.—The Governor-General shall by order make such provision as appears to him to be necessary or expedient for the purpose of making provision as to the constitution of Pakistan and for purposes connected therewith, and any such order may contain such incidental and consequential provisions as the Governor-General may deem necessary or expedient.'

The Emergency Powers Ordinance represented the high-water mark of the assertion of complete authority by the executive. Indeed, it is difficult to see how it could have been carried farther. There was no central legislature, nor any provision for bringing one into being. The legislature of East Bengal had not been permitted to meet, and the Governor-General was now to terminate the existence of the legislatures of West Pakistan by amalgamating the provinces into one unit.

[1] Ordinance IX, 1955, S.3.

Pakistan

The Federal Court had not yet finished its contribution. Within three weeks it had told the Governor-General firmly that he had no power to make constitutional provisions. *A propos* of the claim to validate the impugned laws by ordinance, the Chief Justice remarked: 'If you ride roughshod you will bring disaster to this country. You do not have a validating machinery nor [do] you intend to create one.'[1]

The government accepted this ruling and moved toward the creation of a new Constituent Assembly or Convention. Its first idea was that the Convention should be confined to making constitutional provisions; that is, it should not be in a position to unseat the government by a vote of no confidence. The Convention was to continue for six months 'unless sooner dissolved by the Governor-General.'[2] The Law Minister (Suhrawardy) warned the country of the consequences of failing to accept this scheme.

> 'Now if the people do not co-operate in setting up this Constituent Convention and in legalizing the laws through that Convention [at] as early a date as possible, then, in view of the fact that the Federal Court have held that in the written law the Governor-General has no power to validate these laws retrospectively, one or other of the following measures outside the written laws will be necessary to resolve the situation: (*a*) A revolution after which we start afresh and legalize such laws as the new revolutionary party may wish to legalize; (*b*) A civil dictatorship with military support; and (*c*) Martial law.'[3]

The government obviously had some doubt whether this step had effectively brought it within the compass of the law. Accordingly, the Governor-General referred the whole matter of the dissolution and its consequences to the Court for its advisory opinion. In the course of the hearings in the Chief Court of Sind and the three cases in the Federal Court the whole field of the

---

[1] *Dawn*, April 13, 1955.
[2] *The Constituent Convention Order*, 1955 (G.G.O. 8/1955), dated April 15, 1955. [3] *Dawn*, April 24, 1955.

constitution of Pakistan was widely discussed.[1] The four hearings form a logically connected whole, and their significance has to be considered jointly.

The first and fundamental question to be decided was whether the Constituent Assembly was, of itself, a sovereign body; secondly, it had to be determined whether the Governor-General was a necessary part of the law-making process. The Chief Justice, speaking for the majority, dealt directly with these issues. 'In my opinion it is a mistake to suppose that sovereignty in its larger sense was conferred upon the Constituent Assembly, or that it could function outside the limits of the Indian Independence Act. The only power given to that Assembly was the power to make laws, constitutional or federal. . . . Apart from these powers, it had no other power, and it lived in a fool's paradise if it was ever seized with the notion that it was the sovereign body in the State. It had, of course, legislative sovereignty as the legislature of the Dominion, but then the Governor-General was a constituent part of the Legislature. Every Act passed by it required the Governor-General's assent. . . .'[2] Mr. Justice Cornelius, in a vigorous and closely reasoned dissent, held a different view of the nature of the Assembly. It was distinguished from the normal legislature of a Dominion by the fact that it was, 'as a body, not a creation of the British Parliament. It is, in my opinion, to be regarded as a body created by a supra-legal power to discharge the supra-legal function of preparing a Constitution for Pakistan. Its powers in this respect belong to itself inherently, by virtue of its being a body representative of the will of the people in relation to their future mode of Government.'[3]

[1] The judgment and a summary of the pleadings and arguments before the Sind Chief Court are given in Abbas H. Farooqi, *Unique Trial* (Abridged edition) (Karachi, 1955). Two of the Federal Court cases were printed as separate volumes by the Government Printing Office, Punjab. They are Federal Court of Pakistan, *Judgment in the case of Federation of Pakistan and Others versus Moulvi Tamizuddin Khan* (Lahore, 1955) (referred to as Tamizuddin's Case), and Federal Court of Pakistan, *Report on the Special Reference made by His Excellency the Governor-General of Pakistan* (Lahore, 1955) (referred to as Reference Case). The third case is Usif Patel's Case, reported in *All-Pakistan Legal Decisions*, 1955, F.C. 387. [2] *Tamizuddin's Case*, p. 72. [3] *Ibid.*, p. 150.

Pakistan

The Court decided that the Governor-General was a necessary part of the law-making process, but this was not the same as establishing the right of dissolution. The power to dissolve the Federal Legislature had been deleted from the Government of India Act by the Pakistan Provisional Constitution Order, and no specific power to dissolve the Constituent Assembly had been conferred by the Indian Independence Act. If such a power existed it had to be found in the common law prerogative of the Crown, which had been transferred in general terms by the Independence Act. The Court held that the prerogative of dissolution must continue to exist since it had not been expressly removed by the terms of the Act. However, the Act required that the Assembly must be given a chance to fulfil its function, and the prerogative was, to that extent, limited. According to the Governor-General, the Assembly had delayed unreasonably the framing of the constitution, had become unrepresentative and had sought to acquire unlawful powers. Consequently, said the Chief Justice, 'it seems to me that the Constituent Assembly never functioned as it was intended to function, with the result that the prerogative to dissolve all along remained with the Governor-General.'[1]

The Constituent Assembly having been dissolved and its powers not being exercisable by the Governor-General, it was necessary to establish a new Assembly. The Court advised that this might be done in conformity with the explicit requirements of the Independence Act. But this still left a substantial measure of discretion with the Governor-General. 'It is obvious that in setting up the new Constituent Assembly the Governor-General is not only entitled but is bound to take cognizance of the altered conditions, the new issues, the views of the different political parties and the measure of agreement among them.'[2]

Finally, the Court dealt with the question of the validation of laws. The Governor-General could not assume full legislative powers, but he might take action to meet the requirements of an emergency situation. This power was derived from 'the common law of civil or state necessity.' 'On this part of the case,' writes

[1] *Reference Case*, p. 40.   [2] *Ibid.*, p. 43.

the Chief Justice, 'Mr. Diplock [counsel for the government] has addressed us an eager and anxious argument claiming for the Governor-General, as representative of the King or as Head of the State, certain powers which entitle him in the interests of the State temporarily to act outside the limits of the written constitution. He has relied in this connection on the maxim cited by Bracton . . . "*Id quod alias non est licitum, necessitas licitum facit,*" . . . and the maxim(s) *salus populi suprema lex.* . . .'[1] This argument was accepted by the Court (Cornelius and Muhammad Sharif JJ. dissenting), at least to the extent that the validity of the impugned laws was accepted in the interim until the Assembly should pass upon them.

The Court had had its say and it is now for the constitutional lawyers to decide upon the merits of its judgment. It is worth noting that the Chief Justice was quick to point out the true nature of the task confronting the judiciary. We have come to the brink of a chasm with only three alternatives before us: (1) to turn back the way we came by; (2) to cross the gap by a legal bridge; (3) to hurtle into the chasm beyond any hope of rescue.'[2] So the Chief Justice built his bridge.

A constitution is as much a matter of politics as of law and the political aspects of the Governor-General's powers deserve some attention. The Act of 1947 had operated primarily to create the independent states of India and Pakistan. Each was to have a Constituent Assembly to frame the future constitution. The Assembly was to have full power to enact that constitution without any ratification by the provinces or the people. The Governor-General was installed to ensure continuity of administration under the Act of 1935 until the new constitution should take effect. If there should be a conflict between the two, was the voice of one appointed man to prevail, or the voice of seventy-six men who had been chosen by some method of election? The theory of cabinet government seems to indicate that the Legislature controls the cabinet, which in turn controls the Governor-General, though in exceptional cases the Governor-General may appeal from the legislature to the electorate. But in this instance

[1] *Reference Case*, pp. 49–50.   [2] *Ibid.*, p. 2.

Pakistan

the Governor-General was certain that he and his ministers knew the interests of the people better than the members of the Assembly, and the executive assumed the powers of both branches of government. It is obvious that there should be some safeguard against a legislature which refuses to vacate office after a reasonable term. But was this the case in Pakistan? Until the day before the dissolution the Prime Minister had been proclaiming with pride that the Assembly would complete the constitution before the end of the year. The final draft constitution was ready for presentation to the Assembly at the time the Governor-General acted. And one of the reasons for the delay in framing the constitution had been the unfortunate consequences of the Governor-General's action in dismissing Nazimuddin. It is possible to make a strong case against the Assembly and in favour of the Governor-General, but such a case must inevitably depart from the basic assumptions of Parliamentary and cabinet government.

Official exponents of the interim constitution and of the Basic Principles Committee Reports always maintained that a system of cabinet government was intended to prevail. Mr. A. K. Brohi, then Law Minister, explained the provisions of the 1954 draft constitution to the House. 'I shall plead here that we ought to have a strong Central Government to be able to deal adequately with the problems which are peculiar to Pakistan.'[1] But the strength of the government was not to lie in the hands of the future President. '... it is a misnomer to call him the Head of the State. He is only there for *"Nam ke waste"*! He is there for ceremonial purposes.... His position is that of a figurehead, as much and as little as that of the King in England. He has no power at all.'[2]

The constitution of 1956 forms a logical continuation of the scheme of government under the Government of India Act. Many of its terms and even whole clauses have been transferred from one document to the other. Both in politics and in law it must be expected that the established practice of the former constitution will continue, except where the new document

[1] Constituent Assembly of Pakistan, *Debates*, Vol. XV, p. 349, October 23, 1953.   [2] *Ibid.*, p. 369 (*Nam ke waste*—for the name's sake).

Cabinet Government

requires a change to be made. The relationship of the President to the cabinet and of both to Parliament has to be understood, not merely by looking at the words of the constitution, but also by scrutinizing the relationships of the precursors of those authorities before March 1956.

Under the constitution the President is to be elected by an electoral college consisting of the members of the National and Provincial Assemblies. If no candidate obtains a majority of the votes cast, the weakest candidate is to be dropped and a new poll held. To qualify for election a candidate must be a Muslim and at least forty years of age. The President may be removed from office by impeachment provided that such a motion is approved by not less than three-quarters of the members of the National Assembly. The term of office of the President is five years and no one may serve more than two terms. If the office becomes vacant or the President is unable to fulfil his duties, the Speaker of the National Assembly is to act in his stead until the President resumes his duties or a new President is elected.

In providing for the cabinet, the constitution has attempted to put in writing what in other countries is left to convention. The President is to appoint a Prime Minister who must be a member of the Assembly and who seems 'most likely to command the confidence of the majority of members of the National Assembly.' Other ministers are to be appointed by the President on the advice of the Prime Minister. The cabinet is to be collectively responsible to the National Assembly. The Prime Minister is to hold office 'during the pleasure of the President,' but he is to be dismissed by the President only if the latter is satisfied that 'the Prime Minister does not command the confidence of the majority of the members of the National Assembly' (Article 37(6)). Whenever a new Prime Minister is appointed, the Assembly, unless already dissolved, must be summoned within two months (Article 50(2)).

The key provision regarding the independent power of the President is Article 37(7), which reads: 'In the exercise of his functions, the President shall act in accordance with the advice of the Cabinet or the appropriate Minister . . . except in cases

Pakistan

where he is empowered by the Constitution to act in his discretion, and except as respects the exercise of his powers under clause (6).' [Clause (6) deals with the dismissal of the Prime Minister.] This seems clearly to mean that the President has no power of independent action except where discretionary authority is explicitly conferred. There are four articles which give power to the President to act in his discretion. They relate to the appointment of the Prime Minister, the Election Commission, the Delimitation Commission and the Public Service Commission. The powers of appointment of the three last-named bodies are designed to take out of politics the control of electoral procedure and of the public services.

Is it, therefore, safe to assume that the role of the President has been reduced to that of a figurehead? In the first place, the President may choose a Prime Minister. If the party position in the Assembly is clear and the major party is solidly united behind its leader, then the element of discretion disappears. But in Pakistan the party situation is often fluid and party loyalties are often weak. And it has been shown that, once appointed, a Prime Minister tends to acquire the majority that he may have lacked before his appointment. A similar reasoning applies to the dismissal of a cabinet. The President is to dismiss only when he considers the ministry to have forfeited the confidence of the Assembly. But dismissal and forfeiture (as shown by subsequent acceptance of a successor) went hand-in-hand in the case of Nazimuddin. Might the President dismiss his Prime Minister and then dissolve the Assembly? Article 50(2) reads: 'Whenever a Prime Minister is appointed, the National Assembly, *if at the time of the appointment*, it is not sitting and does not stand dissolved, shall be summoned so as to meet within two months thereafter.' The implication would seem to be that an incoming ministry cannot advise a dissolution until after it has met the Legislature. But it is possible that the President should dismiss the cabinet, dissolve the Assembly on his own initiative and then appoint new ministers. The President is bound to accept the advice of his cabinet; but if there is no cabinet the constitution does not say that he is precluded from taking any action except that of

Cabinet Government

appointing a new Prime Minister. It must always be remembered that the maxim *salus populi suprema lex* has been held to justify action outside the limits of the written constitution. There is no reason to suppose that the maxim lost its force with the adoption of the new constitution. This, at least, appears to be the line of argument canvassed by the Law Minister in a broadcast on the subject of the new constitution.

> 'A dissolution need not necessarily follow a dismissal. But what, for instance, would be the President's powers in a supposed case where a dissolution was advisable in the country's interest and the Government refused to advise a dissolution? The powers available might depend on the degree of advisability of the dissolution. It might amount to urgency. It would all be a question of judgment. Some would answer that the President is bound by the provisions relating to advice, and that in such a case he could neither dissolve nor dismiss. Others would point to the President's oath and assert the responsibility and the power to decide upon both in a case of the gravest national emergency.'[1]

There is a specific article (42) in the constitution dealing with the relations between the Prime Minister and the President.

> 'It shall be the duty of the Prime Minister—
> (a) to communicate to the President all decisions of the Cabinet relating to the administration of the affairs of the Federation and proposals for legislation;
> (b) to furnish such information relating to the administration of the Federation and proposals for legislation as the President may call for; and
> (c) if the President so requires, to submit, for the consideration of the Cabinet, any matter on which a decision has been taken by a Minister but which has not been considered by the Cabinet.'

It seems impossible to reconcile this article with the theory of a purely ceremonial role for the President. If he were merely the agent of the cabinet, the Prime Minister might well decide what information he might properly have and what might be kept

[1] Text given in *Dawn*, July 24, 1956.

Pakistan

from him. And the President's power to 'require' cabinet consideration does not sound as though this were a function to be performed on advice.

It must be borne in mind that the President is in office for a fixed term. While he is there the party composition of his cabinet may well change. The situation is likely to arise at some stage, that the President will disapprove of the policies of his government. His access to information as well as his power of dismissal may then assume major political significance. A Governor-General could be removed by a simple telegram to London; a President is in office for five years provided one-quarter of the members of the Assembly refuses to vote his impeachment. All these potentially dangerous considerations would lose much of their force if a tradition were to be established that the President should be a man above considerations of politics or personal ambition. The first incumbent, however, was General Iskandar Mirza, who had been Minister of the Interior and whose views on the need for 'controlled democracy' have already been noted.

The position of the Governor of a province is analogous. Most of the clauses relating to the powers of the President are reproduced, *mutatis mutandis*, in the chapters relating to the administration of the provinces. There is one important issue where tradition and common sense would indicate that the Governor is to act in his discretion even though those words are not employed in the constitution. This relates to the emergency powers under Article 193. The President, 'on receipt of a report from the Governor of a Province,' may issue a proclamation of a provincial emergency. Does this mean 'the Governor on ministerial advice'? If so it would mean that the provincial government would be voluntarily asking the central government to take over. The history of Section 92A indicates that this is unlikely. Secondly, the President, under such a proclamation, may 'direct the Governor of the Province to assume on behalf of the President, all or any of the functions of the Government of the Province.' In this instance it is clear that the Governor in person becomes an agent of the central government.

The first Governors to hold office under the new constitution

Cabinet Government

gave little promise that their duties could be regarded as occupying a sphere beyond the influence of politics. In East Pakistan the incumbent was Fazlul Huq, who continued to be the head of the Krishak Sramik Party; in West Pakistan it was M. A. Gurmani who had been a major participant in the political controversies of the first and second Constituent Assemblies.

It remains to consider the relationship of the government to the Legislature. It has already been noted that the Assembly is to be summoned within two months of the appointment of a new Prime Minister. The power of dissolution has also been discussed. The government has no discretion in the conduct of elections which is entrusted to the Election Commission. Not more than six months may elapse between a dissolution and a general election. It is also provided that two sessions of a legislature shall be held each year and that not more than six months shall elapse between the sessions.

While the Assembly is not in session the government may make ordinances having the force of law. Such an ordinance has the same validity as an Act of Parliament, but it must be laid before the Assembly and ceases to operate six weeks after the Assembly has convened, or sooner if disapproved by resolution.

A Bill when passed by the Assembly is presented to the President. Within ninety days he has to assent to the Bill, declare that he withholds assent, or return the Bill to the Assembly requesting reconsideration. If the President withholds assent, the Bill may be passed again by the Assembly, and if approved by two-thirds of the members present and voting the President is required to assent. If the Bill has been returned for reconsideration it will become law if repassed by a simple majority. With a single chamber Legislature the need for a power of veto is not immediately apparent. If the government has a majority it should be able to secure the rejection of any Bill that it opposes. However, it is possible that a government might be faced with a sudden current of political extremism in the legislature which it felt unwise to combat. There would then be an interval of ninety days in which public opinion might cool, or the members of the Assembly persuaded to change their minds.

Pakistan

There is one aspect of the veto power that arises only in the case of the provincial Legislatures. In addition to giving or refusing assent or returning for reconsideration, the Governor may 'reserve the Bill for the consideration of the President.' It is not clear whether the Governor here is to act on the advice of his ministers or as the agent of the central government. There are certain subjects on which provincial legislation does not become valid unless it has received the approval of the President; a law under the Concurrent List amending an Act of Parliament is an example. It could be that the power of reservation is intended to apply only to such instances. Alternatively this provision could be designed to give the central government a veto over the legislative power of a province.

The effect of the emergency powers is to enlarge the authority of the central government mainly at the expense of the provinces. Under Article 191 the central government may take over the functions of the provincial government and Parliament may legislate in place of the provincial Assembly.[1] The fundamental rights enumerated in Part II of the constitution may be suspended while a proclamation of emergency is in operation. Such a proclamation is to be laid before the National Assembly 'as soon as conditions make it practicable for the President to summon that Assembly.' The constitution makes no provision for suspending the operation of the National Assembly.

The executive powers under the constitution are undoubtedly very strong. But there is nothing that would impede the working of normal cabinet government if the various interests concerned are prepared to make the system function according to its spirit as well as its letter. The fundamental reason for the failure to establish genuine responsible government under the Government of India Act was the failure of the political parties to provide a stable basis for the formation of effective ministries.

[1] The emergency powers of Article 191 are in addition to those under Article 193 discussed at p. 162. Article 191 relates to a national emergency, 193 to a provincial.

CHAPTER V

The Federal Structure

SECTION I: THE CENTRE AND THE UNITS

BEFORE West Pakistan was consolidated into a single political and administrative entity, Pakistan consisted of a complex array of units of government. In the east, East Bengal formed a single province. The position in the west was more complicated; there were three Governors' provinces, the (West) Punjab, Sind and the North-West Frontier Province, as well as (British) Baluchistan, the Baluchistan States (Khalat, Las Bela, Makran and Kharan which were grouped together as the Baluchistan States Union), the North-West Frontier States (Dir, Amb, Swat and Chitral), the frontier tribal areas, the federal capital area of Karachi and the princely states of Khairpur and Bahawalpur.[1]

It may well be imagined that these units varied widely in population, resources and experience and capacity for self-government. (See Table, p. 156.)

The Governors' provinces were ruled before 1956 under the provisions of Part III of the Government of India Act (as amended), and they were equipped with a developed system of democratic government. The princely states varied from almost complete autocracy to a close approach to the position of Governors' provinces. Baluchistan, Karachi and the tribal areas have come under the direct authority of the central government.

One fact that the table does not reveal is the geographical separation of the two wings of Pakistan. Nearly 1,000 miles of Indian territory lie between the two halves of the country. And the intervening area has had to be regarded as hostile or potentially hostile. Most of the border was sealed for many years, and it was not until 1955 that direct rail traffic was restored

---

[1] Pakistan also laid claim to the states of Junagadh and Kashmir, but of these only a sparsely populated portion of Kashmir was under actual Pakistan control.

Pakistan

POPULATION AND RESOURCES[1]

	Population '000	Per cent Total	Ann. Rev. Rs. mil.	Rev. per cap. Rs.
Punjab	18,815	24·9	246·2	12·0
Sind	4,606	6·1	97·0	21·1
N.-W.F.P.	3,223	4·3	65·0	20·1
Bahawalpur	1,822	2·4	50·5	27·7
Khairpur	319	0·4	12·0	37·6
B.S.U.	552	0·7	5·8	10·5
Baluchistan	602	0·8		
Karachi	1,123	1·5		
N.-W.F. Agencies	2,642	3·5		
Total W. Pakistan	33,704	44·6		
East Bengal	41,932	55·4	234·5	5·6
Total	75,636	100·0		

between the major centres of the two countries. Persons wishing to travel between one wing of Pakistan and the other had to proceed by air, which was expensive, by sea, which was time-consuming, or by submitting to two sets of passport and customs controls and numerous changes of conveyance.

This factor of distance has, by itself, proved a major obstacle to the attainment of effective unity of Pakistan. East Bengal has been increasingly dissatisfied with its status as a constituent part of the federation. The province contains 56 per cent of the population of the country, and yet it is clearly a less advanced area than

[1] Sources: *Census of Pakistan*, 1951, Table 6, and *Explanatory Memorandum on the Budget of the Central Government for 1955–56*, p. 142. (Governors' provinces only.)

Revenue figures for states are derived from newspapers and other sources. Comparable items for centrally administered areas are not available.

All revenue figures relate to estimates for 1954–55. Population figures are for Pakistan nationals only.

The Federal Structure

West Pakistan in matters of industry, trade and urban development. The inhabitants of East Bengal can rightly complain that for many decades their area has been backward and neglected. This has been particularly true of the Muslim population which found itself subordinated to the Hindu community, which showed itself more ready to acquire modern commercial and administrative skills.

The Muslims of the eastern districts of Bengal had grievances against the Hindus and against the power exercised by Calcutta, but they had no desire to exchange the domination of that city for that of Karachi. The inhabitants of East Pakistan[1] are, for the most part, Muslim Bengalis. As Muslims they hold themselves the equal of any of their brethren in the Punjab or Sind. But as Bengalis they have a culture and a tradition of which they are very proud. This forms a link with the Bengali Hindus, and especially with the city of Calcutta. While the ties between the two halves of the Punjab were totally severed by partition, those between East and West Bengal were not, and many patriotic East Bengalis still treasure friendly relations with other Bengalis across the border. There can be no doubt that this feeling of cultural and social separateness hinders the creation of sentiments of common nationality and patriotism.

> 'Pakistan is a unique country having two wings which are separated by a distance of more than a thousand miles. . . . These two wings differ in all matters, excepting two things, namely, that they have a common religion, barring a section of the people in East Pakistan, and that we achieved our independence by a common struggle. These are the only two points which are common to both the wings of Pakistan. With the exception of these two things, all other factors, *viz.* the language, the tradition, the culture, the costume, the custom, the dietary, the calendar, the standard time,

[1] The name of the province was East Bengal until 1956. When West Pakistan was united it was proposed to change the name of the eastern province but the protests of the Bengal members of the Assembly caused this to be left out of the Act (Constituent Assembly of Pakistan, *Debates*, Vol. I, September 19, 20, 21, 22, 1955). However, a few months later, in the new constitution, the terms East and West Pakistan were adopted.

practically everything, is different. There is, in fact, nothing common in the two wings, particularly in respect of those which are the *sine qua non* to form a nation.'[1]

East Bengal was strongly in favour of Pakistan even at the cost of partition, although some of its leaders, notably Mr. H. S. Suhrawardy, hoped to preserve a united Bengal. But the Pakistan desired by the Bengalis was a state that would have left them with substantial autonomy for their own province. The famous Lahore Resolution of 1940, in which the League had first explicitly demanded the creation of Pakistan, was moved by a Bengali (Fazlul Huq). The resolution demanded 'that the areas in which the Muslims are numerically in a majority, as in the north-western and eastern zones of India, should be grouped to constitute "Independent States" in which the constituent units shall be autonomous and sovereign.'[2] The wording of the resolution seems to leave no doubt that it was intended to establish two 'Pakistans,' each of which was to contain autonomous units. It was clear, however, that a united effort would be necessary to obtain Muslim independence. The claim to Pakistan was being made by one organization on behalf of one nation and put forward by one leader.

The Lahore Resolution had envisaged East Pakistan as comprising the whole of Bengal and Assam, which would have had a population of over 60,000,000 and large economic resources. The partition of Bengal separated the eastern districts from the major industrial and commercial centres, and virtually eliminated the possibility of independence. The circumstances of partition and its aftermath demanded strong central action to establish effective government control over the new state. East Bengal could not find amongst its own inhabitants sufficient members of the armed forces or civil servants to constitute an autonomous East Bengal governed by Bengalis. And the *Quaid-i-Azam* was in supreme command at Karachi, and Pakistanis from Bengal were

[1] Constituent Assembly of Pakistan, *Debates*, Vol. I, p. 1816, January 16, 1956, Abul Mansur Ahmad.

[2] Quoted in A. B. Rajput, *Muslim League Yesterday and Today* (Lahore, 1948), p. 79.

quite prepared to follow his directions for strengthening their newly-won independence.

When the stress of the first phase of the emergency diminished, the desire for provincial autonomy re-emerged in both East and West Pakistan. The intention to introduce a genuine federal system was reaffirmed in the Objectives Resolution adopted by the Constituent Assembly. It was declared that the territories of Pakistan 'shall form a Federation wherein the Units will be autonomous with such boundaries and limitations on their powers and authority as may be prescribed.'

If autonomy, within limits, were the objective, it might have been expected that a substantial transfer or delegation of power from the centre to the provinces might have taken place as soon as order was assured and the economy in working order. Under the Government of India Act the provinces had been assigned a definite area within which they could work without interference from above. Ultimate central authority was maintained since it was necessary to preserve final British authority concerning the security of the country as a whole. But when the system was working well the centre (and its agents the provincial Governors) refrained from exercising its special authority.

The war years and the political situation immediately afterward had necessitated a much greater degree of centralization, both because self-government had broken down in the majority of provinces and because of defence requirements. The two years following the war had been filled with political unrest and crisis and provincial government had to take second place in the struggle for national self-rule.

Provincial leaders hoped that this trend would be reversed after independence, but in fact the degree of central control was increased. Its most spectacular application was in the political sphere. Powers existed under Section 93 of the Government of India Act for a provincial Governor, on behalf of the centre, to take over the administration of a province if the normal constitutional machinery had broken down. This power, with its undemocratic implications, was removed by the Pakistan Provisional Constitution Order. However, Mr. Jinnah, acting under the

Pakistan

extraordinary powers of the Independence Act, inserted a new section (92A) into the Act.[1] This section gave to the Governor-General in case of emergency, power to 'direct the Governor of a Province to assume on behalf of the Governor-General all or any of the powers vested in or exercisable by any Provincial body or authority' (excluding a High Court).

The original Section 93 had been widely used and strongly resented during the war, but it was clearly an exceptional measure designed to deal with cases where a provincial ministry was unwilling to accept the implications of British rule. Section 92A, on the other hand, became a normal part of the working of federal political relations between the centre and the provinces. It was brought into operation in the Punjab from January 1949 until April 1951 and in Sind from December 1951 until May 1953. In both instances the Chief Minister had been dismissed and, with the existing provincial Assembly, it seemed impossible to find a ministry which could obtain a vote of confidence. The length of the period of Governor's rule was ascribed to the need to prepare for the first experience of adult franchise elections, but it also provided a period of political manœuvre in which to influence the composition of the future legislature.

The third major use[2] of Governor's rule occurred in East Bengal from May 1954 until June 1955. The United Front ministry had been in office for less than two months and the new legislature had not had a chance to meet. The central government decided that the ministry was endangering the maintenance of good government, and orders were issued for its dismissal. A new 'strong' Governor (General Mirza) was immediately despatched to Dacca. Politically this employment of Section 92A had much more serious implications than on the two previous occasions.

[1] G.G.O. 13/1948. This section remained in force until a few months before the adoption of the new constitution. In view of the hostility of the second Constitutional Assembly, a modified version of these powers was then inserted as S.93 by the *Government of India (Amendment) Act*, 1955.

[2] Governor's rule was proclaimed in East Bengal for a two-week period in March 1954. This was because the legal term of the old legislature had expired and also to cover the period of the elections and the installation of a new government. It was not used for the purposes of political pressure.

The Federal Structure

The United Front had just routed the Muslim League at the polls, and thus indicated that the League had lost the confidence of half the nation's population. The election had been fought to a substantial extent on the desire of Bengal to achieve greater freedom from supervision by Karachi. This was the first opportunity to show that democracy in Pakistan was strong enough to allow different parties to control central and provincial governments without disrupting the state.

The Prime Minister, broadcasting a statement on the crisis in Bengal, announced that 92A would 'remain in force for the minimum time necessary to restore law and order and public confidence so that Parliamentary Government can function successfully.'[1] The central government, of course, was to be the judge of the minimum time required. Six months later the then Minister of the Interior seemed to be in no hurry to restore self-government.

> 'One thing is certain—the Centre will never allow this province to again incur the danger of disintegration. The well-being and happiness of the masses, as always, will be the paramount consideration. There are many schemes to be completed and I am convinced that the 92A Administration can still do more solid work for the people and further tone up the basic administration.'[2]

In the course of time the United Front split in two. The promise of the centre to restore self-government as a gift to one faction or the other was undoubtedly used as a powerful bargaining counter in the confused political situation of the summer of 1955.

Section 92A was used for political purposes on three occasions, but its influence was constantly at work. No provincial politician could fail to be aware that the centre possessed and was willing to use power to govern without provincial legislative or ministerial assistance. In most federal systems provincial governments are in law or by political convention irremovable by the national authorities. But in Pakistan the possibility of the indefinite

[1] Broadcast, May 30, 1954. [2] *Dawn*, November 18, 1954.

suspension of parliamentary government constantly influenced the attitudes of both central and provincial cabinets.

It is not surprising that there should have been a substantial demand that the constitution should contain nothing as drastic as Section 92A. The corresponding article (193) provides that the President, if he is satisfied that 'the government of the Province cannot be carried on in accordance with the provisions of the Constitution,' may proclaim a state of emergency. Under such a proclamation he may 'assume to himself, or direct the Governor of the Province to assume on behalf of the President, all or any of the functions of the Government of the Province.' Further, he may 'declare that the powers of the Provincial Legislature shall be exercisable by, or under the authority of, Parliament.' In turn, Parliament may then confer on the President the power of the provincial legislature to make laws. A proclamation under this article may remain valid for not more than two months unless extended by the National Assembly for a further period of not more than four months. Thus provincial self-government may be suspended for two months by the central government alone and for six months after discussion and approval in the National Assembly. But these are very considerable powers and could be used to enforce central superiority in the event of a conflict between the two levels of government. In the light of the use of emergency powers from 1947–55 it remains to be seen whether this article will be put to serve political ends.[1]

In addition to dismissals of provincial ministries under the emergency provisions, the central government also had power to depose a cabinet by means of the prerogative power of the Governor. In nine years there were many abrupt changes of

[1] Article 193 was employed for the first time in May 1956. The Speaker of the East Pakistan Assembly had ruled on procedural grounds that the provincial budget might not be presented. An emergency was therefore proclaimed, the central government provided an interim budget for two months and, after a week, the ministry was restored (*Pakistan Observer*, May 23, 27 and June 2, 1956). It was used again from August 31 to September 6, 1956, after the Sarkar ministry had resigned (*Dawn*, September 1, 7, 1956) and in West Pakistan, for political reasons, from March 1957 (*Dawn*, March 21 and April 17, 1957).

ministry in the provinces. On one occasion only was this the result of the vote of the electorate,[1] and no provincial government was voted out of office by its Assembly. Discretionary power was also used to remove Chief Ministers (and hence bring down the ministry) when the Governor or Governor-General sanctioned PRODA proceedings against a person holding that office. In cases when the centre had brought about the downfall of a ministry it often sought to impose its own candidate as successor. Persons who were not members of the provincial Assembly and who were not engaged in any form of political life were appointed in this fashion. Thus Firoz Khan Noon was brought back from his post as Governor of East Bengal to become Chief Minister of the Punjab and Sardar Abdur Rashid was translated from Inspector-General of Police to Chief Minister in the Frontier Province.

One final form of central political control deserves mention. This was the party organization of the Muslim League. Liaquat Ali, Nazimuddin and Mohammed Ali (Bogra) were successively President of the Muslim League. In this capacity each had major powers of supervision and regulation of provincial party affairs. This extended as far as the dissolution and reconstitution of provincial Leagues and to the expulsion and disqualification of provincial office-holders.

Even had it not possessed these drastic powers, the centre was well equipped to exercise substantial control over the provincial governments. The Government of India Act divided legislative powers into three lists, Federal, Provincial and Concurrent.[2] The Federal legislature had exclusive authority over List I, the provincial legislatures over List II, and each might pass laws under List III, but, in the event of conflict, the federal law was to prevail. The matters over which the provinces were given exclusive jurisdiction were not extensive. In the main they were public order, land and agriculture (including water supplies and forests), and

[1] The resignation of the Sarkar ministry was due to the impossibility of obtaining a vote of confidence in the Assembly.
[2] References to the distribution of powers under the Government of India Act are to the Act as it stood immediately before the new constitution came into force.

Pakistan

local government (including public health and poor relief). Under the Concurrent List provincial authority extended to criminal law, certain aspects of commercial law (but excluding banking and insurance), and certain economic matters such as factories, labour and electricity. But by contrast the federal list was extensive, and phrased in such a manner as to permit the widest possible interpretation. Thus item 34 read: 'Development of industries where development under Federal control is declared by Federal law to be expedient in the public interest.'

The balance of the federal structure provided by the Government of India Act was heavily weighted in favour of the centre if that government decided to utilize its authority to the full. But if the centre so wished it could allow the provinces a substantial measure of autonomy. Of course it must not be forgotten that from 1947 to 1956 the centre could alter the interim constitution whenever it chose. Until 1949 this could be done by an order of the Governor-General and subsequently by an Act of the Constituent Assembly. The modifications made to the Act after independence showed the decision of the centre to enlarge rather than to limit its powers. Thus provision was made for the establishment of a central police establishment to deal with 'certain offences committed in connection with matters concerning the Central and Provincial Governments.'[1] Similarly the central powers concerning preventive detention were extended,[2] and the central legislature assumed exclusive control over labour exchanges and training establishments.[3]

In the eight or nine years before the adoption of the constitution virtually no steps had been taken to expand the degree of autonomy of the provinces. It was not, therefore, to be expected that the central authorities would be willing to permit a drastic revision of the distribution of powers to begin in 1956. However,

[1] List III, new Section 1 (*b*) added by the *Government of India Act (Seventh Schedule) (Amendment) Order*, 1948. This was an anti-corruption measure but one of its effects was to permit a centrally controlled police force to investigate the acts of provincial authorities.
[2] List III, 1A inserted by the *Government of India (Second Amendment) Act*, 1952.
[3] List I, 12A inserted by the *Constitution (Amendment) Act*, 1953.

The Federal Structure

it was necessary to pay some attention to the widespread demands of provincial spokesmen. The number of items allotted to the provinces is consequently much greater than before.[1] To a limited extent there has been a real transfer of authority. As under the former Act, federal powers under its own list take priority over provincial powers, and federal law prevails over provincial under the Concurrent List. The following major items appear in the Provincial List: railways (though provincial control is not to begin unless and until the national Parliament makes the transfer); industries, factories, mines and mineral development and regulation of professions. The provinces retain the control that they formerly enjoyed over land and agriculture and local government functions including education and health. These powers operate subject to the right of the federal Parliament under the Concurrent List to legislate regarding labour relations, price control, economic and social planning, iron, steel, coal and mineral products, and banking, insurance and corporations. In addition the federal Legislature has exclusive power over mineral oil and natural gas, over industries which are owned wholly or partially by the federation or a corporation set up by the federation, and over corporations doing business in more than one province. Finally, it should be noted that, if anything has been overlooked in the 143 enumerated items, the residual power rests with the provinces.

Even within the limited field of provincial control the provinces have been hampered by lack of financial resources. The original scheme of the Act of 1935 had given the major sources of revenue to the centre but had provided that the proceeds of certain taxes should be shared between the centre and the pro-

[1] The following entries appear in the *Government of India Act* (amended to 1956) and the new constitution:

	Government of India Act	Constitution
Federal List	61	30
Provincial List	55	94
Concurrent List	37	19

One reason for the sudden increase in the size of the Provincial List is that, while nine federal tax sources are grouped as one item, twenty provincial taxes are listed separately.

vinces. With the establishment of Pakistan, the central government's need for funds was so great that the policy of sharing the proceeds of the income tax was abandoned. In 1948 the administration of the sales tax was taken over by the centre, although a proportion of the receipts was transferred to the units.[1] Further, the centre appropriated the right to levy succession and estate duties on agricultural land. In 1952, in view of the substantial surplus of revenue over expenditure in the central accounts, it was decided to give the provinces a share in the proceeds of certain central taxes. Sir Jeremy Raisman was invited to inquire into the financial position and his proposals were accepted by the government.[2] The constitution allowed the financial provisions of the 1935 Act to continue in operation, except that estate and succession duties on agricultural land were returned to the provinces and all stamp duties were transferred to them.

The position in 1956 was that the provinces possessed severely limited revenues independent of the central government.[3] These resources were either inflexible or subject to arbitrary fluctuation with natural factors (such as crop yields). These sources provided a comparatively small share of provincial revenue; in 1954–55 the North-West Frontier Province derived about 15 per cent of its revenue from provincial taxation, the Punjab 21 per cent and East Bengal 43 per cent. Sizeable additional funds were obtained from other sources under provincial control, such as revenue from irrigation schemes, government lands and forests and commercial

[1] The sales tax was taken over on a temporary basis for two years in 1948. This was extended for another two years in 1950 and made permanent in 1952. [*Government of India (Amendment) Act*, 1948, *Government of India (Fourth Amendment) Act*, 1950, *Government of India (Amendment) Act*, 1952.]

[2] *Report of the Financial Enquiry Regarding Allocation of Revenues between the Central and Provincial Governments* (Karachi, 1952).

[3] The principal independent sources of revenue under the constitution are: taxes on agricultural income and the capital value of agricultural land; estate and succession duties on agricultural land; taxes on land and buildings; stamp duty; excise on alcohol and drugs; electricity tax; taxes on vehicles, advertisements, animals, boats, professions and trades, luxuries; capitation taxes; tolls, terminal taxes and taxes on goods and passengers carried by road or inland waterways.

The Federal Structure

undertakings.[1] Thus in 1953-54 Sind received more than one-quarter of its income from the net profit on its irrigation schemes.

The remainder of provincial revenue came from central grants and shared taxes. Half the proceeds of the income tax was divided among East and West Pakistan in the ratio 45 : 55. The same principle of division applied to the central excise duties on tea and tobacco. Each province retains half the net proceeds collected from its area through the sales tax; in addition West Pakistan receives 47 per cent of the collections in the federal capital area. Finally, East Pakistan obtains about 20 per cent of its revenue from the share it receives ($62\frac{1}{2}$ per cent) of the export duty on jute. One province (North-West Frontier Province) received an annual unrestricted grant of Rs. 12,500,000. Other grants were made in case of emergency, such as grants for flood, famine or earthquake relief. In addition there were special funds set up from central sources to assist the provinces in road development, 'social uplift,' higher education and refugee rehabilitation. The Province of Sind received special compensation for the transfer of the city of Karachi from provincial to federal jurisdiction. Apart from the subsidy to the Frontier Province the grants-in-aid were given at the annual discretion of the central government, and could not be claimed as a right by the provinces.

Without doubt the major sources of income have been assigned to the centre. But for purposes other than defence, the provinces administer larger expenditures than does the federal government.[2] The provinces, however, had little control over the size of their income, and they have to plan their expenditure in the light of what they expect to receive from the centre. This was also the case in the field of capital expenditure for development purposes. Each province wished to undertake large-scale projects of industrialization and construction. This could not be done out of

[1] The constitution allotted the manufacture and sale of salt and opium, which had previously been with the centre, to the provinces.
[2] The Revised Estimates for 1955-56 show federal expenditure (less defence services and contributions to provinces) as Rs. 485,000,000 while provincial budget estimates for the same period showed expenditure of Rs. 736,000,000. (*Explanatory Memorandum on the Budget of the Government of Pakistan for 1956-57*, pp. 143, 144.)

Pakistan

taxation and the financial structure of the country restricted the possibilities of raising loans on the open market. Consequently, the provinces had to borrow heavily from the centre, and in eight years some Rs. 1,000,000,000 was provided in this manner.[1] In this matter also the provinces were in the position of having to come to the central government to ask for assistance which might be denied at the pleasure of the federal authorities.

The constitution substantially continues the previous scheme. However, the President is to constitute, at intervals of not more than five years, a National Finance Commission. This is to contain the ministers of finance of the central and provincial governments and 'such other persons as may be appointed by the President after consultation with the Governors of the Provinces.' The Commission is to make recommendations regarding the sharing of taxes and the making of grants-in-aid, and the President is to make an order giving effect to such recommendations. This means that at least the financial relations between the two levels of government must be discussed by their respective governments. But the composition of the Commission is, in the last resort, in the hands of the centre, and its recommendations are not likely to be unacceptable to that government.

Two other provisions of the constitution may prove to have an important bearing on relations between the central and provincial governments. Article 199 provides for the establishment of a National Economic Council, composed of five central and six provincial ministers with the Prime Minister as chairman. The Council is to survey the state of the economy and to prepare plans for financial, commercial and economic policy. In formulating such plans, 'the Council shall aim at ensuring that uniform standards are attained in the economic development of all parts of the country.' The administration of these plans shall be decentralized by 'setting up in each province, necessary administrative machinery to provide the maximum convenience to the people, and expeditious disposal of Government business and public requirements.'

[1] *Explanatory Memorandum on the Budget of the Government of Pakistan for 1956-57*, Table VII, Development loans, p. 151.

The Federal Structure

The second of these interesting provisions is that governing disputes arising between the centre and a province or the two provinces, other than disputes within the jurisdiction of the Supreme Court. Such a dispute is to be referred to a tribunal appointed by the Chief Justice and its report is to be forwarded to the President so that he shall make an order giving effect to its provisions.

It has been shown that with the distribution of legislative power and financial resources, the central government has been in a position to dominate the provinces. This domination is made more effective by the nature of the administrative system.[1] It is quite clear that the constitution, following the Government of India Act, envisions a degree of administrative control of the provinces by the centre. The federal government is required to protect each province against 'internal disturbance,' and to ensure 'that the Government of every Province is carried on in accordance with the provisions of the Constitution' (Art. 125). Further, the government of a province must ensure compliance with all Acts of Parliament and shall use its own authority so 'as not to impede or prejudice the exercise of the executive authority of the Federation.' For the purpose of obtaining compliance with these provisions the federal government may issue directions to the provincial administration. Provincial action may also be controlled by the centre in any question involving 'any grave menace to the peace or tranquillity or economic life of Pakistan, or any part thereof' (Art. 126). A more explicit power of giving directions occurs in the provisions governing the proclamation of a state of financial emergency. This may be proclaimed by the President, after consultation with the Governors, if it seems that 'the financial stability or credit of Pakistan, or any part thereof, is threatened.' Such a proclamation empowers the central government to give orders on economic matters to the provincial authorities (Art. 194).

The government of Pakistan (and of India also) is remarkable in that, in a nominally federal structure, a single higher civil service is common to all levels of government. Thus the principal

[1] See also Chapter IX, *passim*.

civil servants at the provincial capitals and those in charge of districts are predominantly members of the Civil Service of Pakistan. This service is recruited and controlled by the central government, and its members are normally transferred at intervals between Karachi and the provinces or from one province to the other. The members of the C.S.P. (and of other all-Pakistan services) are given special protection under the constitution which would prevent disciplinary action against them being taken by a provincial government (Art. 181). Thus a provincial government, if it becomes involved in a dispute with the centre, may feel that it is not fully master in its own house. It might also reflect that, if the dispute goes too far the civil servants may soon be governing the province under the authority of President's rule.

It is in the light of all the foregoing factors that the place of the provincial Governor must be considered. The 1947 modification of the Government of India Act removed the Governor's special responsibilities and his discretionary powers. He was appointed by the central government, but he was expected to rely on the advice of his ministers. There were three main areas in which he was not to act on advice. The first concerned the appointment and dismissal of ministers. 'In the exercise of his functions under this section with respect to the choosing and summoning and the dismissal of ministers, the Governor shall be under the general control of, and comply with such particular directions, if any, as may from time to time be given to him by the Governor-General.'[1] The second instance could occur when a Governor, in his discretion, initiated proceedings against one or more of his own ministers under PRODA. The third occasion for acting without advice was when a Governor had assumed powers of direct rule under Section 92A.

It has been characteristic of constitutions on the British model that powers which appear strong on paper may in practice remain unused. It would have been possible for the role of the Governor to be transformed into that of a constitutional figurehead. Clearly this did not take place in Pakistan from 1947 to 1957. The lengthy

[1] *Government of India Act*, 1935, S.51(5) substituted by G.G.O. 22/1947 for the original S.51(5).

The Federal Structure

periods of Governor's rule and the appointment of strong Governors, such as General Iskandar Mirza, testified to the reality of the power of the Governor. Many of the persons appointed were leading politicians and it was clear that their active participation in public life was not finished. Nishtar, Chundrigar and Shahabuddin had previously been cabinet ministers; Hidayatullah and Mamdot had been Chief Ministers; Fazlul Huq had held both offices. Noon and Gurmani continued to take an active part in the proceedings of the Constituent Assembly while holding office as Governor. It was not to be expected that such men should willingly accept a purely formal role, and it was noticeable that, when matters of political importance were at stake, the provincial Governors as well as their Chief Ministers would be summoned for consultation.

Immediately before the adoption of the constitution it was clear that the Governor was a figure of great political importance, and that he was used as an instrument of central control of provincial affairs. The constitution appears to weaken both aspects of this position. The Governor is appointed by the centre, and holds office during the pleasure of the President. But there is no provision that he shall act under central direction. He is to have limited discretion in choosing a Chief Minister, but he must pick a member of the Assembly who is likely to command a majority. And the only legitimate ground for dismissal is that the Chief Minister no longer commands a majority. In other matters the Governor is to act in accordance with the advice of his ministers. The Governor is precluded from being a member of either the provincial or national Assembly.

It would be premature to conclude that the Governor has been deprived of personal power or has ceased to be an agent of the centre. The first two Governors to hold office under the constitution were M. A. Gurmani in West Pakistan and A. K. Fazlul Huq in East Pakistan. Mr. Gurmani had been for a long time a member of the central cabinet, and he was most active in the campaign to unite the units of West Pakistan. Mr. Fazlul Huq had been Chief Minister of East Bengal, and even while Governor continued to be the titular head of a major political party. It is

Pakistan

impossible to regard either of these gentlemen as an impartial referee standing above the turmoil of the political arena.

A Governor may be dismissed at will by the centre. It follows that the centre can, if it wishes, procure a Governor who will be willing to take instructions. It has been observed that central and provincial politics have been closely linked, and that it has been very difficult for a provincial ministry to survive if it is opposed by the central government. In view of the chronic uncertainty of political alignments in Pakistan it would frequently be possible to reach the conclusion that a provincial cabinet could no longer be assured of a majority. The fact that the Governor so declared might well make sure that the majority would indeed disappear. Until evidence to the contrary is produced it would seem prudent to assume that the role of the Governor remains much as before.[1]

SECTION II: THE SPECIAL CASE OF EAST PAKISTAN

Until 1955 the lower level of government in Pakistan contained four provinces and several lesser units. Any discussion of federalism had to deal with two distinct problems; there was one set of conditions that governed West Pakistan and a quite different set to be applied to East Bengal. What was appropriate for Sind or Khairpur might be totally unsuited to Bengal.

For many Bengalis the real issue was not to secure provincial autonomy, important though that might be, but to obtain fair recognition, in theory and practice, of the claim of the east wing to equality with the west. There was always a desire for Bengali autonomy, but this was greatly enhanced, and made more bitter, by the feeling that the national government was fundamentally hostile to all things Bengali.

'Sir, I actually started yesterday and said that the attitude of the Muslim League coterie here was of contempt towards East Bengal, towards its culture, its language, its literature and everything concerning East Bengal. . . . In fact, Sir, I tell you that far from con-

[1] For a further discussion of certain aspects of the position of the Governor, see above, pp. 152–153.

The Federal Structure

sidering East Bengal as an equal partner, the leaders of the Muslim League thought that we were a subject race and they belonged to the race of conquerors.'[1]

It was no answer to this kind of charge to point out that a majority of seats in the first Constituent Assembly and one-half of those in the second had been assigned to East Bengal. Whether through Bengali ineffectiveness or the machiavellian wiles of their opponents Bengali influence had never been decisive. Nazimuddin had been Governor-General, but the real power lay with Liaquat Ali. Nazimuddin became Prime Minister, but lacked force of will, and was ultimately dismissed by the (Punjabi) Governor-General. Mohammed Ali (Bogra) was brought in as Prime Minister but, although a Bengali, he remained the captive of the West Pakistan group that provided the main strength of his government. The Bengali members attempted to use their majority to diminish the powers of the Governor-General, but as a result they found themselves out of their own jobs. The electorate of East Bengal had repudiated the Muslim League, but the outcome was rule for more than a year by West Pakistan bureaucrats. The armed forces were West Pakistani, the national civil service was predominantly West Pakistani, and trade and industry were largely in the hands of non-Bengalis. It is in some such terms as these that most Bengalis view the history of the first ten years of Pakistan. In consequence, despairing of equality on a national basis, they turned increasingly to proposals for home rule for their own province.

In the early years of independence, and while the *Quaid-i-Azam* was still in supreme command, the centre assumed control of most aspects of government in order to establish the new state and to confront the many emergencies that arose. It laid hold of the principal sources of revenue and assumed wide authority to control social and economic life. Its activities were centred at Karachi, within fairly easy reach of Sind and the Punjab but remote from East Bengal.

[1] Constituent Assembly of Pakistan, *Debates*, Vol. I, p. 530, September 7, 1955, Ataur Rahman Khan.

Pakistan

The sense of neglect among Bengalis arose almost immediately. 'It seems, Sir,' said one Bengali Muslim Leaguer in March 1948, 'that in the present scheme of things East Bengal is really very much neglected.'[1] The Chief Minister of East Bengal presented a list of demands on behalf of his province. 'First and foremost, among these is that as far as Eastern Pakistan is concerned, we must have a fair and proper share in the Armed Forces of Pakistan.'[2]

The government countered these complaints with the argument that was to be used against all demands for greater provincial autonomy or for greater concessions to Bengal. 'Today in Pakistan there is no difference between the Central Government and a Provincial Government. The Central Government is composed of the representatives of the Provinces. . . . We must kill this provincialism for all times.'[3]

The sense of grievance was, as might be expected, expressed much more strongly in the provincial Assembly. The debate on the provincial budget of 1949 was largely devoted to attacks upon central policies. Muslim League members did not hesitate to denounce their own national leaders. This tone was initiated by the Finance Minister (Hamidul Huq Chowdhury, who was soon to be proceeded against and disqualified under PRODA). Private members carried the matter farther.

> 'I would respectfully submit that it is a disgrace that our Provincial Ministers could not impress upon the Central Government regarding our needs and demands. They could not push through their demands to the Centre and they could not make their grievances felt even by His Excellency the Governor-General [Nazimuddin] to see that the Members of his Cabinet did not care to meet the legitimate demands to carry out the orders of this Government. It is not only a disgrace for these Provincial Ministers;

[1] Constituent Assembly (Legislature), *Debates*, Vol. I, p. 82, March 1, 1948, Azizuddin Ahmad.

[2] *Ibid.*, p. 127, March 2, 1948, Nazimuddin. The constitution includes a Directive Principle to the effect that a fair distribution should be maintained in the armed forces and the civil employment of the federal government (Art. 31).

[3] *Ibid.*, pp. 140–1, Liaquat Ali Khan.

it is a disgrace for us also, because, Sir, we have sent there such incapable Members to represent us. (Applause.)'[1]

The provincial Chief Minister made no effort to defend the central government.

'... I should mention another point, that is, the anxiety on the part of the Central Government to encroach on every field of provincial activities.

'... After achievement of freedom there has been a race for centralization of power both in India and in the Central Government of Pakistan. I consider this to be the most unsound and short-sighted policy. The provinces must be allowed to enjoy the full autonomous position, must be as free from the Central Government as it is thought practical. But particularly this province of East Bengal which is so far flung from the capital of the Central Government must enjoy the fullest autonomy. (Cries of hear, hear.)'[2]

The quotations given, and they could be multiplied many times, are sufficient to show that, within two years of independence serious discontent prevailed in East Bengal. This discontent was almost universal, and certainly was shared by the provincial government and the provincial representatives in Karachi. At that stage it was hoped that the new constitution might soon be adopted and that under its provisions relations between East Pakistan and the rest of the country might be adjusted with more regard to the justice of Bengal's claims. But the years went by, and there was no constitution and no readjustment of federal relations.

An increasing source of Bengali complaint arose from the distribution of available financial resources. Beyond all doubt East Bengal is afflicted with much greater poverty than large areas of West Pakistan. This is reflected in the annual revenue of the provincial governments. Income from all sources amounted in East Bengal to Rs. $5\frac{1}{2}$ per head compared to more than twice that

[1] East Bengal Legislative Assembly, *Proceedings*, Vol. III, pp. 164–5, March 16, 1949, Shamsuddin Ahmad Khondkar.
[2] *Ibid.*, p. 265, March 18, 1949, Nurul Amin.

Pakistan

sum in the Punjab and almost seven times in Khairpur. Of this very small amount more than 40 per cent was provided from the share of central taxes (including the jute tax), while the Punjab received only 16 per cent of its revenue from this source, and Sind less than 9 per cent. It is the claim of many Bengalis that the chronic poverty of East Bengal should be a primary concern of national policy; that federal resources should be allocated to bring the standards of the east into line with those of the west as quickly as possible. The central answer to this is that their first task must be to raise the national income by spending federal resources wherever they will bring the greatest return.

The complaints of the Bengalis are numerous and have been put forward on many occasions. One difficulty in assessing their true significance lies in the uncertainty of some of the statistical evidence put forward. A major grievance is that very little of the expenditure of the central government takes place in East Pakistan.

'I shall show, Sir, from statistics published by our Government that the share of East Pakistan to the Federal revenues from 1947–48 to 1954–55 has been 168 crores and 14 lakhs [1,681,000,000]. During this period West Pakistan contributed 553 crores and 53 lakhs [5,535,000,000] to the Federal Revenues. These figures may make our West Pakistani brothers, like Mr. Gurmani, boast and say: "Look! East Pakistan is contributing only 18 per cent, West Pakistan contributes more than treble." But, Sir, look at the expenditure side. This is the expenditure. The Central Government has spent during these nine years 42 crores and 66 lakhs [427,000,000] in East Pakistan as compared to 790 crores and 67 lakhs [7,907,000,000] spent in West Pakistan. Therefore, Sir, we have got back much less than what we have contributed.'[1]

Even if Mr. Abul Mansur Ahmad's figures for the allocation of expenditure are not accepted without question, it is still apparent that by far the greater part of federal money has been spent in West Pakistan. The armed forces, which consume about 60 per cent of the annual revenue (and a substantial share of capital

[1] Constituent Assembly of Pakistan, *Debates*, Vol. I, pp. 1818–19, January 16, 1956, Abul Mansur Ahmad.

The Federal Structure

outlay as well), are located predominantly in the west, and, of course, a large part of national expenditure takes place in Karachi.

In the field of shared taxes East Bengal occupies a more favourable position, having received in eight years Rs. 730,000,000 out of a total of 1,300,000,000.[1] However, no less than 425,000,000 of this came from the share of the jute duty. Since this is raised entirely from the produce of Bengal, there have been many suggestions that the whole proceeds of this tax should be assigned to that province. The division of federal grants-in-aid and development loans has provided East Bengal with substantially less than its ratio of population would indicate but probably more than its relative wealth and contribution to central revenues would require.[2]

During the life of the first Constituent Assembly the members from Bengal were trying to shape the constitutional drafts in conformity with their desires, but they enjoyed very little success. The committees that were set up to do the major work in preparing the draft were heavily weighted with central ministers. The Basic Principles Committee did not contain a majority of Bengali members, and neither did its sub-committees.[3] Thus the sub-committee on Federal and Provincial Constitutions and Distribution of Powers contained nine Bengalis out of twenty members. It was this committee which laid down the basic pattern for the federal aspects of the proposed constitution. Its minutes record several dissents by the Chief Ministers of East Bengal and the Frontier Province in protest against undue central predominance.

Mr. Nurul Amin used the meetings of the sub-committee on Suggestions[4] to re-open the issue of the federal balance. He pro-

---

[1] *Pakistan 1954–1955* (Karachi, 1955), pp. 32–3.

[2] Grants-in-aid: (8 years) East Bengal Rs. 180,000,000; total 676,000,000. Development loans: (6 years) East Bengal 147,000,000; total 561,000,000.

[3] A distinction must be drawn between Bengali members and members sitting for Bengal seats. Thus Ishtiaq Husain Qureshi and Mahmud Husain who were original members of the B.P.C., sat for East Bengal seats but their province of origin was the United Provinces. They were both central ministers and most Bengalis did not regard them as adequate champions of Bengali interests. [4] See above, p. 93 ff.

Pakistan

posed that residuary powers be assigned to the provinces; this was defeated by seven votes to five. He asked for provincial control of the administration of customs collection and for consultation in determining the tariffs; the committee refused. He suggested that the provinces should control the railways; the committee divided 4 : 4 and the amendment was lost. He proposed that all but sixteen of the proposed items of the Concurrent List should be transferred to the Provincial List; the committee conceded that the licensing of motion pictures should become a provincial subject.[1] The final outcome in the adopted report of the Basic Principles Committee was to leave the distribution of powers roughly where it rested at that time.

The fight for provincial autonomy in the committees of the Assembly was conducted behind closed doors. The general public saw merely the final reports, although rumours of disagreement between the provincial and central leaders were in constant circulation. Two crucial issues aroused concentrated popular interest, and both of them had the effect of widening the gap between east and west. They were the decision on representation in the future federal legislature and the language issue. An account has been given already of the method in which decisions were reached on these two problems,[2] and it is sufficient here to point out that in neither case were the arguments openly debated, and the result determined by a free vote which would have revealed to the nation exactly where stood the contending groups.

The allocation of seats in the central legislature was certain to involve major difficulty. It is a normal principle of a federal system that no one unit should possess a clear majority in the national legislature, and it is usual for the larger units to accept some diminution of the share of representation that would be accorded on a population basis. In Pakistan, East Bengal has 56 per cent of the population, and in view of its strong feeling of separate identity it would be unreasonable to expect that it would receive less than half the total legislative places. The first official proposal on this subject was made by the Franchise sub-

[1] Suggestions sub-committee, *Minutes*, pp. 55–71, November 25, 29, 30 and December 1, 1951.   [2] See above, pp. 87–89.

The Federal Structure

committee which recommended equality of seats for east and west in each of two Houses.[1] This involved the sacrifice by East Bengal of about 10 per cent of the seats it would have received according to population. The Punjab was also to accept a sacrifice in relation to the smaller units of West Pakistan. This recommendation was modified before it was accepted by the Basic Principles Committee, although the principle of parity in both Houses between east and west was maintained. The relative shares of the Punjab and Sind were reduced and the smaller units

[1] For comparative purposes the successive proposals on representation are given below:

Unit	Lower House (1)	(2)	(3)	(4)	Upper House (1)	(2)	(3)
East Bengal	200	200	165	155	60	60	10
Punjab	100	90	75		33	27	10
Bahawalpur		13	7			4	4
Sind	34	30	19		10	8	9
Khairpur		4	1			2	1
N.-W.F.P.	39	25	13		11	6	10*
Tribal		17	11*			5	
Baluchistan	8	5	3		3	2	3
BSU		5	2			2	
Karachi	10	11	4		3	4	3
Total West Pakistan	200	200	135	155	60	60	10
Total	400	400	300	310	120	120	50

Col. (1) Franchise sub-committee, *Report*, pp. 1, 4.
Col. (2) Basic Principles Committee, *Report* (1952).
Col. (3) Basic Principles Committee, *Report* (as adopted, 1954).
Col. (4) Constitution. (No Upper House.)
* Including Frontier States.

Pakistan

gained further. This form of parity was unsatisfactory to Bengal because it seemed to make it possible for West Pakistan, with the aid of one or two Bengalis, to impose its will upon that province despite its numerical majority. East Bengal could resist such coercion only if Muslim and Hindu members formed a common front, and at least in the eyes of the Muslim League this appeared to be undesirable.

The next attempt at a solution was the 'Mohammed Ali formula.' This was designed to strengthen the negative power of each wing. East Bengal was given a majority in the lower House but a minority in the upper. Parity was to be maintained when the two Houses were added together in joint session. This would mean that any proposal which was solidly opposed by either wing could be defeated in one House. In case of disagreement between the Houses and for other major decisions such as votes of confidence or the election of a President, the issue was to be decided at a joint session. But in such instances the motion would require the support of at least 30 per cent of the members present and voting from each of the two wings.[1] Such a scheme gave rise to the possibility of complete deadlock and to the probability that the frequent use of joint sessions would convert the Legislature into a single chamber with two rigid committees.

Before the constitution was passed, the units of West Pakistan had been consolidated into a single province. This destroyed the basis of the 'Mohammed Ali formula' and the second Constituent Assembly adopted a single chamber scheme, with equality of representation for each province. Most matters are to be decided by a simple majority. The exceptions are the impeachment of the President and the amendment of the constitution. The former requires the votes of three-fourths of the total membership, and the latter the consent of a majority of the total and two-thirds of those present and voting. In addition certain articles (including that relating to the distribution of legislative power) can be amended only with the consent of the provinces.

The second crucial issue involving antagonism between east and west involved that status of the Bengali language. The

[1] Basic Principles Committee, *Report*, paras. 15, 65, 66.

The Federal Structure

languages spoken in Pakistan and the proportion of people speaking them are as follows:[1]

	Percentage
Bengali	54·6
Punjabi	28·4
Urdu	7·2
Sindhi	5·8
Pushto	7·1
English	1·8

Bengali employs a script that is derived from Sanskrit while Urdu and Punjabi use the Persian script. The principal language of Muslim India before 1947 was Urdu which, in its spoken form, shares a large common content with Hindi.[2] Urdu is thus understood over a great part of the sub-continent, whereas Bengali is confined to a single province. Hostility to Bengali also arises from the fact that it forms a link with West Bengal. Bengali culture has been largely centred in Calcutta, whose influence is still felt in East Bengal. The preservation and promotion of Bengali in East Pakistan therefore might serve to weaken the ties with West Pakistan and strengthen those with Indian and Hindu Bengal. Some of the advocates of the superior merits of Urdu managed to convey the impression that the defence of Bengali was both un-Islamic and opposed to the interests of national unity.[3]

It cannot be denied that a serious issue was at stake. There are disadvantages in any country in the establishment of two or more official languages. In Pakistan, where so many other factors divide east and west, the failure to be able to communicate freely

[1] *Census of Pakistan*, 1951, Vol. I, statement 4B, p. 71. The total exceeds 100 per cent since some persons speak more than one language.
It should be observed that Punjabi and Urdu are fairly closely allied.

[2] The Hindi language uses many terms from classical Hindu literature; Urdu borrows heavily from Arabic and Persian. Thus, long before Pakistan came into being, the struggle between Urdu and Hindi was an important cause of Hindu–Muslim rivalry.

[3] Mr. Ataur Rahman ascribed this view to Liaquat Ali and to Punjabi leaders (Constituent Assembly of Pakistan, *Debates*, Vol. I, p. 518, September 6, 1955).

Pakistan

would tend to add to the lack of mutual understanding. And yet to make Urdu the only national language and to relegate Bengali to a lesser status would impose an additional burden upon an already handicapped province. Since English is still in use for higher education and government purposes, a young Bengali would have to master three languages in order to play a part in national affairs.

This single issue aroused more heated feelings than any other, and it arose sharply at the very beginning. In February 1948 a Hindu Bengali moved an amendment to the Assembly rules to permit Bengali to be used in the House along with Urdu and English. The Prime Minister replied:

> 'Pakistan is a Muslim State and it must have as its *lingua franca* the language of the Muslim nation. . . . [The mover] should realize that Pakistan has been created because of the demand of a hundred million Muslims in this sub-continent and the language of a hundred million Muslims is Urdu. . . . It is necessary for a nation to have one language and that language can only be Urdu and no other language.'[1]

A month later Mr. Jinnah's authority was used to put the same proposition before an audience in the capital of East Bengal.

> 'Let me tell you in the clearest language that there is no truth that your normal life is going to be touched or disturbed so far as your Bengali language is concerned. But ultimately it is for you, the people of this province, to decide what shall be the language of your province. But let me make it very clear to you that the State Language of Pakistan is going to be URDU and no other language. Anyone who tries to mislead you is really the enemy of Pakistan. Without one State Language, no nation can remain tied up solidly together and function.'[2]

Liaquat Ali was strong enough to carry this uncompromising attitude into the Interim Report of the Basic Principles Committee, which stated flatly: 'Urdu should be the national language

[1] Constituent Assembly of Pakistan, *Debates*, Vol. II, February 25, 1948. Motion moved by D. N. Dutta, p. 15, reply by Liaquat Ali Khan, p. 17.
[2] *Quaid-i-Azam Speaks* (Karachi, n.d.), p. 133.

The Federal Structure

of the State' (para. 120). But when the Report ran into criticism, this item was among those to be challenged. In February 1952, after Nazimuddin had spoken on behalf of Urdu, the students of Dacca University engaged in violent demonstrations, demanding the full recognition of Bengali; the police opened fire and fatal casualties occurred. Within twenty-four hours the Chief Minister of the province successfully carried a motion in the provincial Assembly calling on the centre to adopt Bengali as one of the state languages.[1] Later that year, when the final report of the Basic Principles Committee was published, it contained no mention of the state language.

The struggle continued in uncertainty and bitterness for two years more, before a compromise was reached in May 1954. This recognized Urdu and Bengali, but expressed the pious hope that 'the State should take all measures for the development and growth of a common language.'[2] The constitution omits all hope for a common language, recognizes Urdu and Bengali, but provides that English shall continue to be used for official purposes for twenty years. A commission is to be established after ten years to make recommendations for the replacement of English.

Constitutional recognition is thus accorded to the equal status of Bengali. But most Bengalis cannot forget the immense difficulty they experienced in obtaining that recognition, and they are still convinced that full equality of status in practice has not been achieved. The language question has been merely the most flagrant example of a series of issues on which Bengalis feel that they have had to fight desperately to secure satisfaction that should have been theirs without argument, as a matter of simple justice.[3]

SECTION III: THE UNIFICATION OF WEST PAKISTAN

The division of Pakistan into east and west is a fact of geography whose consequences cannot be abolished, but only

[1] *Dawn*, February 23, 1952.
[2] Basic Principles Committee, *Report* (as adopted), para. 276.
[3] That feeling still runs high is shown by the passage in the East Pakistan Assembly of a resolution demanding 'Full regional autonomy' (*Dawn*, April 4, 1957).

diminished or accentuated by political or constitutional provisions. But within West Pakistan the unit boundaries were the product of history and administrative convenience. Sind had enjoyed only ten years of autonomy when Pakistan came into being, and the Frontier Province less than fifty. This is not to say that the units were purely artificial creations denoting no real difference between people and traditions. The Pathan of the Frontier has little in common with the peasant of Sind or the shopkeeper of the urban Punjab. There are marked distinctions of physical feature, language and social structure and custom. Without doubt the Punjab represented the most advanced component of the new state. The Punjabi middle-class was the only group that could fill the gap left by the departing Hindu and Sikh urban communities. Consequently the Punjabis tended to occupy the best positions, not only in their own province but at the centre, and they began to spread into other provinces as well. This led to considerable resentment by those who found that 'strangers' were coming to dominate the entire machinery of government and commerce. The threat of 'Punjabi domination' has been a major theme in the political struggle at the national and provincial levels.

However strong the feelings of local separatism might be, the prevailing division of the country in 1947–55 was highly unsatisfactory. The 1954 draft constitution would have permitted nine units to continue their individual existence in West Pakistan.[1] All of these form part of the Indus river basin, and all depend upon a single port—Karachi. Several of the nine were too poor to maintain adequate machinery of government and to undertake large-scale programmes of development. The Baluchistan States had an annual revenue of less than Rs. 6,000,000 and could never expect to operate a full scheme of provincial self-government. And Sir Jeremy Raisman remarked that he 'was particularly impressed with the inelasticity of the [North-West Frontier Province]

[1] Punjab, Sind, North-West Frontier Province, Baluchistan, Baluchistan States Union, Bahawalpur, Khairpur, Karachi and the states of the North-West Frontier. It is possible that Baluchistan and the Baluchistan States Union might have merged, and the status of the North-West Frontier states was not clearly defined.

The Federal Structure

Provincial revenues and their inadequacy to finance even modest schemes of social improvement.'[1] By way of contrast, it was noticeable that both Bahawalpur and Khairpur were able to amass substantial annual surpluses on revenue account.[2] No doubt this factor offered an added incentive for the merger of those states with less wealthy areas.

In the first few years after independence most of the accusations of provincialism were levelled against Bengal. But friction also arose within West Pakistan. In the Frontier Province the Chief Minister consolidated his own power to the point where he was largely beyond the reach of central intervention. In Sind the provincial government found itself involved in quarrels with the centre over the absorption of refugees and the establishment of Karachi as a federal district. The Chief Minister complained openly on the floor of the Constituent Assembly about the degree of centralization of power in the hands of the central government.[3] This kind of protest drew a violent response, especially from Punjab members.

> 'Sir, this provincialism really is going to lead to dictatorship, because of the unreasonableness of certain members and their petty-mindedness and I tell you that today dictatorship is not a bad thing for Pakistan. Every time I would prefer benevolent dictatorship to inefficient and corrupt democracy which has existed in the Province [Sind]. (Loud cheers.)[4]

Mutual dissatisfaction with the working of the federal system was thus in evidence within West Pakistan from the very beginning. The next few years were to show the operations of provincial self-rule in a most unfavourable light. The existence of

---
[1] *Raisman Report*, p. 6.
[2] Khairpur, by far the richest unit in per capita revenue, budgeted in 1953–54 for a surplus of Rs. 5.3 million out of a total of Rs. 13.3 million.
[3] Constituent Assembly (Legislature), *Debates*, Vol. I, p. 123, March 2, 1948, M. A. Khuhro.
[4] Constituent Assembly of Pakistan, *Debates*, Vol. III, p. 87, May 22, 1948, Firoz Khan Noon.

separate provincial ministries and legislatures gave opportunity for local politicians to engage in intrigue, chicanery and outright coercion. Democracy was reduced to a mere pretence carried on in the interests of a handful of self-seeking political bosses. The central government depended for its existence on maintaining the support of groups of such men. It might throw over one group in favour of another, or even impose central rule for a while, but it could not depend on a direct appeal over the heads of the local politicians to the electorate. And if Bengal were not to dominate completely the first Constituent Assembly, some basis of unity among the western leaders had to be maintained. (When that unity broke down the end of the Assembly's life was the consequence.)

It would be unfair to suggest that the only interest at stake in provincial autonomy was that of the politicians. There was a general and deep-seated fear in all other units that unification would mean control of West Pakistan by the Punjab. An administration located in Peshawar or Hyderabad could be expected to understand and to promote the interests of the Frontier or Sind. A government in Lahore may well speak a different language, literally and figuratively. It may be that the benefits of unification will be felt throughout West Pakistan in cheaper and more effective administration, but the initial cost is likely to be felt by the people of the smaller units who find that a remote and alien government has replaced a local and indigenous regime. And it remains to be seen whether the addition of Sind's talents for corruption and intrigue to those of the Punjab will result in a higher degree of united purity.

While the first Constituent Assembly was alive the 'One Unit' proposal made little headway. The suggestion was made from time to time, but it was not seriously considered until 1954. The event that caused the plan to be put forward as a matter of urgency was the victory of the United Front in East Bengal. It was necessary to consider granting a substantial measure of autonomy to East Pakistan and to find some comparable organization in the west to receive similar powers. The first suggestion was that of a zonal federation; this would have involved a three-tier

The Federal Structure

system of government, central, zonal and provincial.[1] This scheme was laid aside when the United Front government was dismissed. Further discussion of integration took place before the dissolution of the Assembly but without firm agreement being reached. The Chief Minister of Sind voiced firm opposition to such a scheme. He expressed surprise that such an important proposal had been brought up at that late stage. 'At no time, as has been rightly said, was this one-unit question or the Zonal Federation question raised throughout all these six or seven years that we have worked on this Constitution.'[2] Pirzada Abdus Sattar said further that the proposal had come before the Muslim League Parliamentary Party 'just a few days ago' and that, when it came to a vote, the resolution in favour of one unit was defeated by 32 to 2.[3]

When the Assembly was dismissed the government had less need to worry about political opposition. A conference of central and provincial leaders was held in Karachi, and on November 22, 1954, the Prime Minister announced in a broadcast that the units of West Pakistan were to be merged into a single province. Immediately machinery was set in motion to secure the formal approval of the scheme by the legislatures of the provinces. Within a month the three Assemblies had met and voted their approval with only the faintest flicker of overt opposition. In the Frontier Province, where unanimous agreement was not to be expected, the Opposition did not attend the session and the only speeches were made by the Chief Minister and his cabinet colleagues. A few days later the Punjab Assembly voted a similar resolution, also without opposition. In Sind it was known that the Chief Minister, Pirzada Abdus Sattar, was opposed to the

[1] An account of the genesis of the One Unit plan is to be found in a speech by Sardar Abdur Rashid, Constituent Assembly of Pakistan, *Debates*, Vol. I, pp. 488 ff., September 5, 6, 1955.

[2] Constituent Assembly of Pakistan, *Debates*, Vol. XVI, p. 371, September 15, 1954.

[3] *Ibid.*, p. 372, Pirzada Abdus Sattar observed that the negative vote, with more than half the League members, included himself, a Baluchi and some Punjabis. Other sources indicate that the larger part of the opponents was composed of Bengalis.

One Unit scheme, and he had been supported in a signed statement of 74 of the 110 members of the Sind Assembly.[1] On November 8th he was dismissed from office and replaced by Mr. Khuhro. Pirzada issued a Press statement:

> 'The dismissal of my ministry has not come unexpected. My firm stand against the "One Unit" issue for West Pakistan in the Constituent Assembly and outside has been so uncompromising that today's step was no surprise to me. . . .
>
> 'It seems that this action has been precipitated because of my proposal to summon the session of the Sind Legislative Assembly on the 15th instant. A notice of resolution against "One Unit" had already been received, and I am certain this resolution would have been carried in the Assembly. It was therefore imperative to take action as quickly as possible.
>
> 'It seems Mr. Khuhro, who has been called upon to form the Ministry, has accepted "One Unit" and taken upon himself the responsibility of making the Members of the Assembly and the people of Sind to accept this move.'[2]

Mr. Khuhro's methods of persuasion were so effective that the Assembly approved the One Unit resolution by 100 votes to 4.[3]
In this fashion the approval of the peoples' representatives having been recorded with near unanimity, the government was in a position to proceed. In December the Governor-General issued an order establishing a Council for the Administration of West Pakistan, which was to make recommendations concerning the administration of the new province.[4] It began to meet on the day after its establishment and presented its report in February 1955. In March the Emergency Powers Ordinance sought to amend the Government of India Act to the effect that:

> '(3) The Governor-General may by order make such provision as appears to him to be necessary or expedient—
> (a) for constituting the Province of West Pakistan';[5]

[1] *Dawn*, October 24, 1954.   [2] *Ibid.*, November 9, 1954.
[3] *Ibid.*, December 12, 1954, Pirzada was one of five members not attending.
[4] G.G.O. 8/1954, dated December 17, 1954.
[5] Ordinance IX/1955, March 27, 1955.

The Federal Structure

Under cover of this ordinance, an order (G.G.O. 4/1955) was issued on the same day. Its title was the West Pakistan (Establishment) Order, and it authorized the Council for the Administration of West Pakistan 'to take such steps as it may deem necessary or expedient for the purpose of enabling the Province of West Pakistan to be constituted on the appointed day....' A week later Mr. Gurmani was named as Governor-designate of the new province and Dr. Khan Sahib as prospective Chief Minister.

At this stage the Federal Court intervened to inform the Governor-General that his powers did not include the amalgamation of provinces. The enactment of the scheme had therefore to await the session of the second Constituent Assembly.

It might have been thought proper to leave the unification scheme to form part of the constitution, especially as there was every need to complete the constitution in the shortest possible time. But the government was determined to establish West Pakistan before starting to bargain about the shape of the larger aspects of the future body politic. The Establishment of West Pakistan Act was the first major piece of legislation to be adopted by the Assembly. Debate occupied thirty days of the Assembly's time and was frequently heated and bitter. The Bill was attacked on two main grounds: that its real motive was to diminish the power of Bengal, and that in its origin and content the Bill was arbitrary and undemocratic.

Fazlur Rahman, who had succeeded in blocking the scheme in the first Constituent Assembly, pointed out that its effect would be to emphasize the division of the country. 'Sir, it has been stated that the greatest merit of this Bill is to do away with the distinction between Punjabis and Sindhis and Pathans and this and that, but you do not realize that by dividing Pakistan into two you are manifold magnifying that provincialism, by making it a local patriotism for the two regions. Then no longer the cry will be Punjabis and Sindhis but the cry will be Bengalis and non-Bengalis.'[1] Other speakers saw the situation in even more dramatic terms. The essence of the Bill, said Abul Mansur Ahmad, is that

[1] Constituent Assembly of Pakistan, *Debates*, Vol. I, p. 274, August 24, 1955.

the political bosses of West Pakistan 'must be able to talk to the the people of East Bengal in one voice so that they may not use that position of numerical superiority. That is the unfortunate basis for the integration of West Pakistan. The very idea is wrong. If I were left with bringing an integration Bill I would have given a much better Bill which would not have been based on fear for and conspiracy against East Bengal.'[1]

A large part of the suspicion of the Bengalis was engendered by a paper that came to be called 'the document.' This was designed as a plan of strategy for the fulfilment of the unification scheme, and went into some detail about the political measures that would be required. It was said to have been drafted by Daultana, and no denial of his authorship was forthcoming. It was produced in the House by Sardar Abdur Rashid, who as a former Chief Minister had been one of those concerned with putting the plan into operation.[2] 'The document' was not published, but lengthy extracts were read into the record by several members. The following three selections, which serve to indicate its general character, were quoted by the Leader of the Opposition:[3]

> 'One method must be renounced at the very start. Pure force will not do. It would destroy the willing adherence and acceptance of the smaller Provinces which is the only "climate of opinion" in which future nationhood can grow. Besides a "One Unit" thus forced will not outlast the regime which has imposed it. Its dissolution will inevitably become the main slogan of the next elections, it will present an irresistible opportunity to the politicians of East Bengal to revert to the small brother's big brother's role of West disruption, it will destroy the as yet unfixed foundations of the interim "One Unit" government which would require the restraint

---

[1] Constituent Assembly of Pakistan, *Debates*, Vol. I, p. 1423, September 30, 1955.

[2] Rashid had been dismissed from his post as Chief Minister in July. He had largely withdrawn his support for the one-unit plan on the ground that the assurances he had received safeguarding provincial rights were not to be honoured (*Ibid.*, pp. 490 ff., September 5 and 6, 1955).

[3] *Ibid.*, pp. 1455–7, September 30, 1955. The attribution to Mr. Daultana is on p. 1451.

and toleration of cordiality to find its roots. . . . And above all it would for all times isolate Punjab as the Villain of the Piece which tried to force its selfishness down unwilling orphaned throats just crushing it between Bengal domination and a small Province's suspicions and hatred.

'Punjab must be kept quiet. The folly of our friends must be checked. At a later stage Punjab will have to take the lead. At that time I hope an effective, intelligent Punjab leadership will have been put in place both at the Centre and at Lahore.

'In actual fact, however, One Unit will mean more effective power to the people of West Pakistan than they have hitherto enjoyed. The present position is that all real power lies with the Central Government in which Bengal has the dominating share.'

Much of the time of the Assembly was devoted less to discussing the merits of the scheme than the demerits of the method by which it had been brought into operation. Mr. Suhrawardy made a speech, covering twenty-six pages of the official *Debates*, on the subject of 'Khuhroism.' His central point was a personal accusation against the Chief Minister of Sind. 'You struck terror—and I say this with confidence—that you struck terror into the hearts of the Members of Sind Assembly when they came to vote.'[1]

The government had its majority, though it is probable that some of its supporters were less than happy about some aspects of the proceedings. The Opposition did not challenge the general principle of the Bill,[2] though they attempted to delay its acceptance by moving that the Bill be circulated for eliciting public opinion and that it be referred to a Select Committee. On this last motion the Opposition recorded nineteen votes, including three from the Punjab and two from the Frontier.[3] At its final reading only thirteen votes were cast against the Bill, and all but one of these were from Bengal members.[4] Two weeks later, on

[1] Constituent Assembly of Pakistan, *Debates*, Vol. I, p. 647, September 10, 1955.
[2] A division was challenged by a government supporter who then voted with the majority. The vote on the motion to take into consideration was 49 to 1.
[3] *Ibid.*, p. 875, September 17, 1955. [4] *Ibid.*, p. 1472, September 30, 1955.

Pakistan

October 14th, the new Province of West Pakistan began its existence.[1]

The Establishment of West Pakistan Act is not a complicated document. It provides that the new province shall take over the functions of the previous provinces and states. Even though they are included within the province, the central government retains its control over legislation affecting the tribal areas or the Frontier states. Under the Act, Karachi was assigned to West Pakistan, and members were chosen to represent the federal capital in the interim legislature at Lahore. However, the members from Bengal expressed some resentment that a city that had been built up with national tax funds should be handed over as a source of income and prestige to the government of one province. Having thus incorporated Karachi in West Pakistan, the Act proceeded to undo most of the consequences of that incorporation by providing that the administration of the capital should continue to rest with the federal government. The constitution, while not formally removing Karachi from West Pakistan, continued its administration under the direct agency of the federal government. Article 211 provides that the President may provide for its government and administration and that Parliament may make laws for the capital, under the Provincial List. It seems, however, that Karachi is to retain its representation in the provincial Assembly at Lahore.

The internal structure of West Pakistan is that of the familiar provincial pattern with a Governor, cabinet and legislature. The interim legislature was elected by the former provincial Assemblies and electoral colleges for Karachi and Baluchistan. One important feature is the provision that for a period of ten years

[1] The coming into force of the one unit scheme did not bring an end to the criticism of its opponents. For example, a Baluchistan Muslim League conference passed a resolution that, 'by the creation of the One Unit the Government has not only failed to achieve the ultimate aim of unity, propriety [sic] and progress but has increased disunity, backwardness and poverty' (*Dawn*, October 17, 1956). It was rumoured in Lahore that the government might be contemplating the restoration of some degree of autonomy to Sind and the Frontier (*Dawn*, December 31, 1956). The opposition to One Unit of the National Party was a main cause of the downfall of the Khan Sahib ministry in March 1957.

The Federal Structure

the representation of the Punjab is not to exceed 40 per cent of the total membership of the provincial Assembly.

From the point of view of administration, the previous division into nine or more separate units was wasteful and, in the long run, unworkable. As the experience of other countries has shown, it is extraordinarily difficult to arrange the voluntary extinction of units of political power. Probably some degree of coercion had to be applied to bring about a major integration such as has been accomplished in West Pakistan. The result of integration leaves an unusual federal system, with only two provinces balancing each other in a state of precarious equilibrium.

CHAPTER VI

Islam and Politics[1]

THE Western political observer is usually unconscious of how large an extent of his thinking is set against the background of nearly 2,000 years of Christian experience. Most of the liberal democracies would now claim that their political institutions are 'secular' either in name or substance, and that, in the eyes of the state, religion is a matter for the individual or for freely formed associations. But this secular position can be understood only in the light of over 1,600 years of co-existence of Church and State as separate entities, now conflicting, now in close alliance but always distinct. Under such circumstances the incursion of religion into political life means the attempt of the Church (whether Roman, Presbyterian, Calvinist, Sectarian or other) to control and limit the State power. The liberal minds of the eighteenth, nineteenth and twentieth centuries have generally agreed that any such attempt should be resisted in the interest of individual liberty. The sixteenth and seventeenth centuries took a very different view, which would probably give a better understanding of what a Muslim is trying to express when he talks of 'the Sovereignty of God,' an 'ideological state' and an 'Islamic Republic.'

Pakistanis often complain of the lack of sympathy and understanding for their cause in non-Muslim countries both before and after partition. The European or American observer instinctively feels that the concept of a nation and a state whose unity depends almost entirely on religion is an anomaly, and a reactionary anomaly. Religion is not now, if ever it was, the basis

[1] The author has made no attempt to give an authoritative interpretation of the political doctrines of Islam, a task for which he is in no sense fitted. What has been attempted is to investigate the teachings and requirements of Islam as they have appeared to different groups of Pakistanis who have concerned themselves with the problem.

Islam and Politics

of nationhood in the rest of the world. The period in European history of the wars of religion is now regarded as a discreditable and almost unintelligible episode of fanaticism and cruelty. The nation-state and the claim to self-rule are based on territorial, economic, cultural and traditional unity. The Muslims of India advanced their claim to national self-expression upon the identity of religious belief. In the Western mind this conjured up vague (and usually unhistorical) visions of Muslim fanaticism, the holy war, the Mahdi, the conquest of empire by the sword, the forced conversion of the Infidel, and the destruction of temples and idols. By contrast the Indian nationalist leaders (Congress) were talking the language of Gladstone and Woodrow Wilson in their claim to nationhood and self-rule. They were armed with statistics and well provided with arguments drawn from economics, military science, geography and history. Against all these stood Islam. When the time came to choose, the Indian Muslims, by an overwhelming majority, rejected economics and geography and chose Pakistan. It is a choice that many non-Muslims have found very hard to understand.

In the twentieth century, to a person with an education in the Christian tradition, religion and politics are by nature and definition things apart. To a Muslim, Islam embraces both terms. The Founder of Christianity recognized a domain that was Caesar's, and did not concern Himself with matters of political organization. Quite the reverse is true of the Prophet of Islam. He founded a state and concerned Himself intimately and continuously with the details as well as the broad principles of its government.

> 'Islam, therefore, right from the inception of the Medinite period, ceased to be a religion in the secular sense of the word. It became the ideology behind the State, the creed which was to determine the policy and legislation of the new polity. . . . The only parallel for this phenomenon is to be found in the Socialistic state of Soviet Russia, where we find a state based on a particular creed and ideology which guides the policy and legislation of the state.'[1]

[1] Muhammad Mazheruddin Siddiqi, *Islam and Theocracy* (Lahore, 1953), p. 30.

Pakistan

The early Christians had no opportunity to administer a system of civil government. Early Muslims had to fight and to govern if they were to hope for survival. The Prophet and the first four Caliphs were temporal leaders as well as spiritual guides. They were the lieutenants of God upon earth, and their aim was to extend the dominion of those who submitted to His Will. They were, as are all Muslims, devoted to the doctrine of unity (*Tauhid*). This asserts primarily that God is One; and the worst heresy in Islam is the elevation of other beings to equality with God. But the principle of unity can be extended to demonstrate that man's personality is also one, incapable of division into pluralistic attributes. Thus man's acceptance of the path of God must be total and must apply to all aspects of his life.

'Islam is a whole, a single indivisible Reality, in which "dualism" of whatever form has no place. It is not merely a creed; it is nor [*sic*] mere thought, nor mere action. It is the embodiment of the ethical expression of the human being's entire life-activity, both individual and national. It is concerned with every sphere of human existence: it is the Divine Law of Nature which governs the right functioning of the human social organism.'[1]

God's word, revealed through His Prophet, is addressed directly to each individual. God's commands are simple and unmistakable, and require no priest or organized Church to intervene between the Creator and mankind. All men owe obedience to God; all are equal in His sight.

'In Medina, under the Prophet, no dual authority existed. There was no church apart from the state, and no organization, religious or non-religious, distinct from the state organization. The state and the church in Islam were merged into a single indistinguishable unity from the moment when the Prophet of Islam took over control of Medina and that early development finally determined the shape of

---

[1] S. Ghaleb Khan Abbasi and A. de Zayas Abbasi, *The Structure of Islamic Polity, Part I, The One Party System in Islam* (Lahore, 1952), p. 2.

things to come. . . . When the Prophet appointed military commanders, Zakat collectors, or religious preachers, they were appointed as ordinary state employees or civil servants and were parts of the state machinery.'[1]

Leading spokesmen for Pakistan have always been anxious to prove that a state based upon Islam does not need to be, and in fact cannot be, a theocracy in the sense of rule by a priestly class. If theocracy is taken to mean a state governed in accordance with Divine law, then the term is acceptable, but the idea of rule by priests is in direct conflict with Islam. Pakistan's first Prime Minister was determined to emphasize this point: 'Islam does not recognize either priesthood or any sacerdotal authority; and, therefore, the question of a theocracy simply does not arise in Islam.'[2]

The demand for Pakistan, and its realization, are not to be understood unless it is clearly perceived that, to the Muslims of India, Islam was more than a religion in the Western meaning. It was, and is, an outlook upon life that embraced social, political and cultural aspects of human behaviour. Islam has guidance to offer in the production and distribution of wealth, in the maintenance of social services, in international relations, and in the structure of family life, in public finance and the proper position of the hands during prayer. All of these, and much more, are integral parts of Islam, not mere deductions from general moral precepts. Islam therefore speaks as plainly to the statesman or the business-man in his professional capacity as it does to the individual conscience or to the man of religious learning.

> 'Pakistan was founded because the Muslims of this Sub-Continent wanted to build up their lives in accordance with the teaching and traditions of Islam, because they wanted to demonstrate to the world that Islam provides a panacea to the many diseases which have crept into the life of humanity today.'[3]

[1] M. M. Siddiqi, *op. cit.*, p. 31.
[2] Constituent Assembly of Pakistan, *Debates*, Vol. V, p. 3, March 7, 1949, Liaquat Ali Khan. [3] *Ibid.*, p. 2, Liaquat Ali.

Pakistan

In a more narrow sphere it was quite certain that Islam in India served to differentiate the Muslim from the Hindu. It is quite untrue to suppose that all Muslims have an identical outlook upon life. There is radical disagreement within Pakistan on the social and political implications of Islam. Two propositions would, however, secure general acceptance. They are, first, that Muslims are not Hindus, and second that, in some sense all Muslims are (or at least ought to be) brothers. This twin-based consciousness of separate identity is the real basis of Pakistan. The events of the last ten years have strengthened rather than weakened that sense of separateness from the Hindu, whatever symptoms of disunity within Pakistan they may have witnessed.

Of the two propositions the negative has been given first. The consciousness of separate identity is not new, and it would be quite wrong to imagine that Iqbal and Jinnah created the feeling of national identity and common interest. More than eighty years ago Sir William Hunter could write of the Muslims of India not merely as a community but also as 'a race,' and of their exhibiting at intervals 'their old intense feeling of nationality.'[1] The same author could point also to growing separatism among 'the fanatical section.' 'During the last forty years they have separated themselves from the Hindus by differences of dress, of salutations and other exterior distinctions, such as they never deemed necessary in the days of their supremacy.'[2]

The differences between Hindu and Muslim were and are far greater than can be conjured up to the mind of a European or an American by describing them as matters of religion, in the same way that one might talk of differences between Catholics and Protestants or even Jews and Christians. Muslim and Hindu do not eat together, do not visit one another's homes and of course they do not intermarry. (There are exceptions to these prohibitions, especially amongst Western-educated city dwellers, but they continue to represent the experience of most inhabitants of the sub-continent.) It is the full extent of this gap between himself and his Hindu neighbour that was present in the mind of a

[1] W.W. Hunter, *The Indian Musalmans* (Calcutta, 1945, reprinted from 3rd edition, 1876, 1st edition, 1871), pp. 143-4.   [2] *Ibid.*, p. 172.

Muslim when he reflected that the two communities did not form one nation. Consequently the simple independence of India, which was desired so ardently by the Indian nationalist, meant something quite different to the Muslim. Mr. Jinnah expressed his feeling in 1939: 'Therefore, in my judgment ... democracy can only mean Hindu raj all over India. This is a position to which Muslims will never submit.'[1]

Before the beginning of the Pakistan movement these sentiments were almost entirely negative and defensive in their application. It was especially galling for a Muslim to have to live under infidel rule, since the state fills a distinct role in his religious life. Indeed, if the state should prove in the last analysis hostile to Islam, his religion may compel the Muslim to face the unhappy alternative of rebellion or, if that is unlikely to succeed, of emigration to a land of the faithful. The cause of Pakistan offered a chance of putting to positive and constructive employment the political teachings of his religion. The Muslim had viewed the approach of independence with apprehension based on the fear of injustice and discrimination under predominantly Hindu rule, and with dismay, in the belief that the preservation and strengthening of an Islamic way of life would become less feasible than it had been under the British *raj*. The establishment of Pakistan gave him, together with his brothers in the true faith, the chance to make a new start in ordering his social as well as his individual life in accordance with Divine Will.

The Indian Muslim could sense that all that divided him from the Hindu as well as all that impelled him to create a new political organism was centred around Islam. It did not, however, require an essentially religious nature or training in order to desire Pakistan. Indeed, most of the men who led the struggle for the new state were not religious-minded men, and the movement itself was not a religious movement. Its participants were of course Muslims, but they were not religious leaders. On the contrary a large body of orthodox *ulama* (men of religious learning) either held aloof from or actively opposed the struggle for Pakistan.

[1] Jamil-ud-Din Ahmad (ed.), *Some Recent Speeches and Writings of Mr. Jinnah*, Vol. I (5th edition, Lahore, 1952), p. 99.

Pakistan

The head of the *Jamaat-e-Islami*, in a speech shortly before partition, asked: 'Why should we foolishly waste our time in expediting the so-called Muslim national state and fritter away our energies in setting it up, when we know that it will not only be useless for our purpose but will rather prove an obstacle in our path.'[1] (The path toward Islamic revolution.)

The background of the men who organized the campaign was not theology and Islamic law but politics and the common law, not Deoband but Cambridge and the Inns of Court. Mr. Jinnah and his lieutenants such as Liaquat Ali won Pakistan largely in spite of the men of religion. They led a secular campaign to create a state based on a religion. They employed for the most part strictly political and constitutional methods, the ballot box, the submission of memoranda to the Viceroy and prolonged negotiations with their opponents. The resort to 'direct action' was held in reserve until the alternative seemed to be nothing but surrender or violence. By contrast it was the secular Congress, acknowledging the spiritual leadership of Gandhi, which did not hesitate to break the law as a normal technique of agitation.

Many prominent members of the Muslim League, before and after partition, were lax in observing what many orthodox Muslims believed to be the outward signs of their faith; they did not grow beards, many did not offer the five daily prayers, a few drank alcoholic liquor and others allowed their wives and daughters to appear freely in public. In outward appearance these were educated, intelligent and reasonably prosperous members of a middle class, who would have found themselves perfectly at home in Western Europe or America. No one who has met such men and observed them in speech and action could imagine for one moment that they are motivated by religious fanaticism. And yet they chose deliberately the risk and the reality of immense bloodshed in order to establish a state where Muslims could order their lives after their own fashion.

It can hardly be over-emphasized that for such men the Muslim cause, which is inescapably bound up with Islam, em-

[1] Sayyed Abul Ala Maududi, *The Process of Islamic Revolution* (translation), (2nd edition, Lahore, 1955), p. 37.

Islam and Politics

braces nationalism and patriotism as well as the narrower meaning of religion. Acceptance of Islam leads to the assertion that the Muslims are a separate nation. Western political theory is then applied to establish the claim for national self-determination. Muslim nationhood was advanced as an axiom; the case for Pakistan was derived from that axiom, not by citations from the law books of Islam but by the political logic of liberal nationalism.

The character of the Muslim leadership, both before and after partition, presents a real problem in discovering the true place and extent of the influence of Islam in Pakistan. A small group of westernized leaders has been predominant in the political parties[1] and in the central and provincial cabinets. Men of similar outlook are in control of the civil services, the judiciary and the armed forces. To such persons Islam serves to provide a tradition on which national unity and loyalty can be based and a set of general principles of individual, social and political morality. And that would indicate the extent of the impact of the teachings of their religion upon the practical operation of the machinery of government. Such men have never abandoned the all-embracing view of Islam, but they have allowed it to be overlaid by the intellectual approach produced by secular education and training, which makes the general assumption that religion is no concern of the state. Their minds often operate upon two different levels: a level of fundamental principle on which they sincerely accept the authority of Islam and the level of practical reality on which they are guided by facts and figures and legal precedents. 'Talking of an Islamic system and thinking of terms of the Western system is an incongruity which is visible all around us. The spirit soars to the lofty heights reached in Omar's time, but eyes are fastened on the spires of Westminster.'[2] The resulting

---

[1] The Muslim League has always contained some influential spokesmen for a different school. For example Maulana Akram Khan has been twice President of the East Bengal League, Maulana Bhashani was President of the Assam League and Moulvi Tamizuddin Khan became President of the Constituent Assembly. Without doubt, however, in the higher positions lawyers outnumbered *maulanas* by a large majority.

[2] The quotation is from a Foreword by Altaf Husain to Fareed S. Jafri, *The Spirit of Pakistan* (Karachi, 1951).

Pakistan

conflict has been the cause of a great deal of confusion in the attempt to define the meaning of an Islamic state.

In marked contrast are the professional men of religion (often slightingly called 'the mullah element') led by the *ulama*, the men of learning. Like men of religion everywhere, they have tended to be conservative. Many of them, including some of the best known *ulama*, were opposed to the campaign for the establishment of Pakistan, largely on the ground that nationalism and Islam were incompatible.[1]

Such men were early separated from their contemporaries who received Western-style education. They attended the mosque and the *madrassah* to receive instruction in Urdu and Arabic. To exercise their minds they had the Quran, the Hadith and the works of the great doctors of Islamic law. For several generations the orthodox have grown farther apart from the English-speaking intellectual. They have concentrated upon the remote past and been unwilling and unable to come to grips with actuality. Only when, as in the Khilafat Movement, the past seems to call to action, do the orthodox feel inspired to intervene in contemporary conflicts. There are in Pakistan men of religious learning who have attempted to understand the consequences of the development of modern science and modern history, but they are not typical and they have not succeeded in exerting a major influence on the opinions of most of their colleagues.

The mullahs have been immersed in the detailed study of the classic documents of their religion. They have not been trained

[1] The pre-partition views of Maulana Maududi were quite definite: 'Among Indian Muslims today we find two kinds of nationalists: the "Nationalist Muslims," namely those who in spite of their being Muslims believe in "Indian Nationalism and worship it"; and the "Muslim Nationalists": namely those people who are little concerned with Islam and its principles and aims, but are concerned with the individuality and the political and economic interests of that nation which has come to exist by the name of "Muslim" and they are so concerned only because of their accidence of birth in that nation. From the Islamic viewpoint both these types of nationalists are equally misled, for Islam enjoins faith in truth only; it does not permit any kind of nation-worshipping at all' (*Nationalism and India* (translation), 2nd edition, Pathankot, 1947).

Islam and Politics

to formulate general principles at a high level of abstraction. Islamic law is precise and detailed, and its mastery requires patience and considerable learning. The practical content of Islam is, in their view, to be found by searching and pondering the Quran and the records available of the conduct of the Prophet and of his companions and immediate successors. This knowledge and its expansion into the full corpus of established law (*fiqh*) is the special province of the *ulama*. They would be surrendering their claim to respect and authority as well as abandoning their proper task of guiding the community if it were decided that *fiqh* had no practical importance for political life in Pakistan.

The great mass of the people (over 80 per cent illiterate) has no formal education. And yet both politicians and mullahs are aware that fundamentally it will be general popular support that will decide whose interpretation of Islam will prevail. Each group is uneasily aware that its case, when presented in its best logical or theological form, may be either unintelligible or unacceptable to a mass audience. A direct conflict between the two forces would be unlikely to result in any very clear result. It would certainly take a long while and would lead to major internal disunity of which Pakistan has already a sufficient share.

Neither the *ulama* nor the intelligentsia have shown any strong desire for a test of strength. The politicians have won the elections but party politics and vote-getting are a part of their stock-in-trade. The political parties that have openly espoused the cause of religious doctrine—the *Jamaat-e-Islami*, the *Nizam-i-Islam Party* and the *Khilafat-i-Rabbani Party*—have made little headway. Most of the religious leaders have gone with the crowd and lent active or passive support to the Muslim League while that party was dominant. In East Pakistan some of them switched their allegiance to the United Front.

The central and provincial governments have been most anxious to avoid being labelled as anti-Islamic. They have sought to avoid any direct clash with religious movements even at the cost of appearing to be willing to make concessions to any agitation that raises the banner of religion. As in so many other matters, successive governments in Pakistan have preferred to wait until

Pakistan

a decision has been forced upon them rather than to establish a clear policy at the outset.

There can be no better example of this desire to avoid action against any agitation which adopts the guise of religion, than the history of the events culminating in the Punjab disturbances of 1953. The point at issue was the hostility of the orthodox Muslims toward a Muslim sect known as the Ahmadiya. The Ahmadis are believers in the teachings of Mirza Ghulam Ahmad (d. 1908), who claimed to be a prophet as well as to be the promised Messiah. This claim is regarded as heretical by orthodox Muslims who hold to the belief that Muhammad was the last of the prophets. The Ahmadis are reputed to have about 200,000 members in Pakistan, and they include some distinguished and prominent men, the most widely known of whom is Sir Mohammad Zafrullah Khan, at that time the Foreign Minister of Pakistan.

The agitation against the Ahmadis was led by religious leaders, many of whom had previously engaged in politics on the side of the opponents of Pakistan. The early stages of the movement were conducted by members of the Ahrar, a politico-religious group which before 1947 had been an ally of the Congress. Being discredited by partition, these men apparently hoped to return to popular favour by leading a campaign of hatred against a distrusted minority. As the movement progressed it won the support of many of the more reputable *ulama*. The objects of the campaign were to have the Ahmadis declared a non-Muslim minority, the dismissal of Zafrullah Khan and the barring from high public office of all members of the Ahmadiya.[1] The methods employed were the holding of public meetings, especially in mosques, processions, and the passing of impassioned resolutions. This led to the intimidation of numerous Ahmadis, and in a few cases to murder. The leaders of the movement, who included two members and the secretary of the government-sponsored Board of *Talimaat-e-Islamia*[2] attended a meeting in Karachi in January 1953, described as the All-Pakistan Muslim Parties Convention. The following resolutions were among those passed:

[1] Munir Report, p. 127. [2] Ibid., p. 131.

'(1) That since, in view of the attitude of Khwaja Nazimuddin, Prime Minister of Pakistan, there is no hope of the demands in respect of the Mirzais [Ahmadis] being accepted, the All Muslim Parties Convention comes to the conclusion that in the circumstances *rast iqdam* [direct action] has become inevitable to secure acceptance of the demands.

'(3) That since the demand for the removal of Sir Zafrullah Khan, the Mirzai Foreign Minister, has not yet been conceded, the Convention demands the resignation of Khwaja Nazimuddin, so that the Muslims of Pakistan should be able to follow and preserve their religious beliefs and Islamic traditions.'[1]

The Convention also appointed a Council of Action which was to make a last approach to the central government before resorting to other measures.

The governments at the centre and in the Punjab had made no serious attempt to suppress the fast-growing campaign. On the contrary, there were substantial indications of government support or acceptance of the demands. Daultana, the Chief Minister of the Punjab, made it clear that he personally accepted the view that the Ahmadis were non-Muslims, but that this presented a problem for the Constituent Assembly and the central government.[2] This was a clever political move, since it enabled Mr. Daultana to show his sympathy for the basis of the demands while explaining that satisfaction could come only from Karachi. Various agencies and supporters of the Punjab government went much farther than the Chief Minister in their support for the anti-Ahmadiya movement. The Punjab Education Department spent more than Rs. 200,000 in two years in subsidies to newspapers. The papers concerned, says the Munir Report, 'were all actively engaged in this controversy, and went on fanning the agitation even during the days that they were receiving the payments.'[3] In 1951 the Punjab government established a department of Islamiat for purposes of religious education. A board of six *ulama* was set up, four of whose members played a prominent part in the movement and two of these were arrested. The

[1] *Munir Report*, pp. 131, 132. [2] *Ibid.*, pp. 263, 264. [3] *Ibid.*, p. 83.

department employed eighteen persons as lecturers, and of these eleven took a leading role in the agitation and seven were arrested.[1] The Punjab Muslim League was also prominent in its support for the forces of disorder. The police prepared a list of 377 members of the League who were involved in the disturbances.

> 'These gentlemen took part in processions, leading violent mobs, violating orders promulgated under section 144 and collecting funds with a view to financing the movement. Among the persons in this list are presidents, senior vice-presidents, secretaries, treasurers and other office-holders of the various Muslim League organizations in the Province. Four of them were Councillors of the Provincial Muslim League, five were members of the Muslim National Guards, two were Advocates, and one the editor of an Urdu daily.'[2]

The central government, even though its Foreign Minister was under personal attack, was little more resolute. Its policy for several months was described as one of 'indecision, hesitancy and vacillation.'[3] And it has already been noted that the Board of *Talimaat-e-Islamia*, paid out of central funds, was deeply involved in the agitation. It is easy to understand the nature of the government's difficulty. The public at large, the religious leaders and many politicians, were agreed in regarding the doctrine of the Ahmadis as heretical and abhorrent. Nazimuddin was a man of deep religious conviction, and regarded the *ulama* with sincere respect. The Constituent Assembly had also decided that Pakistan was to be a state based upon Islam. It was an awkward moment for the government to declare that religious sentiment must be held in check so that the principles of cabinet government might be followed. The situation was allowed to drift until the agitators faced the government with the choice of abdication or resistance.

The Central Council of Action had couched their demands of January 1953 in the form of an ultimatum. This expired on February 22nd, and 'direct action' was planned to begin on the 27th of that month. In the Punjab more than 55,000 volunteers were enrolled for the campaign.[4] On receipt of the latest alarming

[1] *Munir Report*, pp. 87, 88.
[2] *Ibid.*, pp. 266, 267.
[3] *Ibid.*, p. 283.
[4] *Ibid.*, p. 144.

reports, the central cabinet met at 2 a.m. of the morning of the 27th. The Governor of Sind, the Governor and Chief Minister of the Frontier Province, the Deputy Chief of Staff and police officials were in attendance. It was decided to arrest the leaders of the agitation and to ban certain inflammatory newspapers.[1] But by this time the mob was ready to go into action. Mass demonstrations against the police, the Ahmadis and the government soon interrupted normal life in Lahore and other towns in the Punjab. By March 4th areas of the walled city of Lahore had been taken over by the rioters, and the police had abandoned the pretence of having the situation under control. By midday on March 6th communications had been largely severed and the electricity supply had been partly cut. Civil government had virtually ceased to exist, and Daultana was prepared to capitulate. He issued a statement in Urdu which he later described in the following words:

> 'On the 6th of this month, I appealed on behalf of my Ministry and myself, to the people of the Province to help in the maintenance of law and order.
> 'I assured them that my Government would be prepared to open immediate negotiations with the leaders of the Tahafuz-i-khatm-i-nubuwwat movement, and that my Ministers would place their demands before the Central Government with a recommendation that they should be accepted.'[2]

A few hours later, with the approval of Karachi, the local military commander proclaimed a state of martial law, and order was restored by the army in a matter of six hours. Eleven people were killed and at least forty-nine wounded by the military. Martial law remained in effect in Lahore until May 1953. By this time, as a result of a visit to Lahore by Nazimuddin, Daultana had resigned; and in mid-April Nazimuddin was dismissed by the Governor-General.

The Punjab disturbances and their political consequences illustrate the force and the danger of an upsurge of popular feeling

[1] *Munir Report*, pp. 144, 145.   [2] *Ibid.*, p. 167.

Pakistan

that can be generated by the appropriate mixture of religion and politics. The cry of 'Islam in danger' was a powerful weapon in the struggle for Pakistan. Every contemporary politician is aware of the risk that a too adventurous policy may be greeted with the dangerous words, 'Islam betrayed.'

One major difficulty for the politician is that his Western education has set a barrier between him and the common man. And nowhere is this barrier stronger than in the field of mutual understanding of the significance of religion. The politician is true to Islam after his fashion, but it is not, and cannot be, the fashion of the peasant or the urban worker. It is therefore necessary for the political leader to convince the masses that Islam is compatible with modern political forms and programmes.

In this attempt the politician has come up against the *ulama*. Pakistan is offered two widely different interpretations of Islam, each claimed to be the proper ideological basis for the state. At one extreme the Islam of some of the politicians and administrators comes very close to Western secularism; and the other extreme is represented by the narrow (but able) authoritarianism of Maulana Maududi.[1] Each of these interpretations is, in its own way, conservative or reactionary. The lawyer-administrator-politician looks back toward the firm administration of British rule, and wishes to make sure that religious enthusiasm does not serve to undermine law and order. The *ulama* look back to classical Islam, and are determined that no institution shall survive that is not in accordance with Divine law.

Not unnaturally there has been some friction between the contending groups. Responsible political leaders have had to try to win religious support and, at the same time, to make clear to the non-Muslims and the outside world that they are not moti-

---

[1] It should be made clear that Maududi is not in the normal sense an *alim*. He was not educated to be a professional man of religion, and his first job was as a journalist. In 1941 he founded the *Jamaat-i-Islami*, and he has become one of the most influential leaders of politico-religious thought in Pakistan. As such he may be regarded as the most vigorous opponent of those who toy with the ideas of Western secularism. See Leonard Binder, *Islamic Constitutional Theory and Politics in Pakistan* (Harvard University thesis, 1956), pp. 83 ff.

Islam and Politics

vated by bigotry or intolerance. This has been a difficult path to tread, and the attitude of some religious leaders has been an embarrassment. Liaquat Ali, speaking on the Objectives Resolution, deplored the activities of certain 'so-called Ulamas' who, in fact, misrepresented Islam.[1] At a later stage Sardar Abdur Rab Nishtar found himself obliged to try to correct the impressions spread by 'fanatics of the type who appeared before the Munir Commission.'[2] It became fashionable to attack the 'mullah element,' and slogans of 'Down with Mullaism' were painted on thousands of walls in Karachi. One distinguished man of religious training was moved to make a somewhat bitter reply.

> 'Yes, it is always the fault of the mullahs. If there is water shortage in Karachi, it is the fault of the mullahs; if Muslims fight among themselves, it is again the mullahs who are to blame. In short, whatever goes wrong mullahs are responsible for it.'[3]

The proceedings of the Assembly are not the place to find a comprehensive discussion of the relationship of Islam and politics. Obviously political skill rather than religious insight has been the basis for selecting the members, and the rules of debate and the use of the English language combine to make sure that the Western-educated have the better of the argument. The exponents of religious orthodoxy often are unable, or do not choose, to use English and they cannot do justice to their case within the limits of a parliamentary agenda. Consequently the great debate that has been in progress on the meaning of Islam in the twentieth century has been conducted by groups of men who are largely unaware of what the other side is saying and, even when the words are known, unaware of their meaning. And yet this debate has been of great importance in the efforts to shape the political future of Pakistan.

Virtually all Muslim Pakistanis are in agreement that their state

---

[1] Constituent Assembly of Pakistan, *Debates*, Vol. V, pp. 94–5, March 12, 1949.   [2] *Ibid.*, Vol. XVI, p. 560, September 21, 1954.
[3] *Ibid.*, Vol. XVI, p. 483, September 20, 1954, Maulana Mohammed Akram Khan.

Pakistan

should be based on the tradition and teaching of Islam. But there is room for difference in discovering exactly what are that tradition and teaching, and where they are to be found. First, beyond all doubt, they exist in the Quran, the Word of God which stands now just as it was revealed to the Holy Prophet in the seventh century. The second source whose relevance is not completely unchallenged[1] is the Sunnah, the traditions of the Prophet. Most of the Muslim politicians in Pakistan are committed to the proposition that the Quran and Sunnah must form the unchallengeable basis of an Islamic state. Sardar Abdur Rab Nishtar, speaking of his role in the Basic Principles Committee, declared: 'Of course, when it was proved that a certain thing was in accordance with the Quran and Sunnah I accepted at once. I believe that it is in the interest of Pakistan that its policy should be based on the Quran and Sunnah.'[2]

The Quran is available to all, either in the original and authoritative Arabic or in translation, and it is, when compared for example with the Bible, both short and self-consistent. But the Sunnah is another matter entirely. It was compiled in the two centuries or so after the death of the Prophet by winnowing the vast mass of legend that surrounded his memory. There is still controversy between supporters of various compilations of the traditions (*hadith*), and in each case it is admitted that some traditions are less reliable than others. An edition that is widely accepted contains over 2,700 individual *hadith*. The study and interpretation of these is left to those who have been trained in Arabic and the complex disciplines of Islamic law. Thus to know what the Sunnah has to say on a given point it is necessary to ask the *ulama*; hence the need to associate a committee of learned men with the process of constitution-making.

---

[1] It is not suggested that the Sunnah has no validity, but that it is not essential as a basis for an Islamic state. Thus Begum Shah Nawaz, in discussing the 'repugnancy clause' (see below, pp. 220–1), said: '. . . I would have been much happier if the word "Sunnah" were not there, because I believe the word Quran would have been sufficient' (Constituent Assembly of Pakistan, *Debates*, Vol. XVI, p. 512, September 21, 1954).

[2] *Ibid.*, Vol. XVI, p. 560, September 21, 1954.

Islam and Politics

Further evidence of the Islamic tradition is to be found in the recorded conduct of the companions of the Prophet who could base their actions on personal recollection of his views.

> 'It has been accepted in Islam from the very beginning that interpretations of the Quran and the Sunnah having the unanimous approval of all the Companions ... and the decisions of the Caliphs relating to constitutional and judicial problems accepted by the Companions, should be binding on all and for all time. In other words, such interpretations and such decisions have to be accepted *in toto*, as the consensus of opinion of the Companions on any matter is tantamount to an authoritative exposition of the Law.'[1]

This period (A.D. 622–61) has been constantly in the minds of those who concerned themselves with the nature of an Islamic constitution. For it is the only clearly established period of an Islamic state in practical operation. Later systems of government by Muslims, whether in Arabic or Iraq or Turkey, all contained elements of corruption due to the temptations of temporal power and the desire to establish dynastic rule.

So much respect is paid to the period of the Prophet and the 'Rightly-guided' Caliphs, that there are those who propose that Pakistan should proceed to imitate their example. 'They [the people] expected that the constitution would neither be of the type of Britain nor of America, but would be the same thirteen-centuries-old constitution of ours—the Constitution of Medina.'[2]

Such a view was not accepted by the Basic Principles Committee, but its members had to take notice of its existence. One of the members of that committee has urged a more liberal interpretation of tradition than that of the 'back to Medina' school.

> 'These persons would want us to reproduce a society which no longer exists and a polity which was suited to that society. They would make us believe that all that was done at that time was the

---

[1] Syed Abul Ala Maududi, *Islamic Law and Constitution* (Karachi, 1955), pp. 100–1.
[2] Constituent Assembly of Pakistan, *Debates*, Vol. VIII, p. 72, October 4, 1950, Sardar Shaukat Hyat.

final interpretation of Islam and it is not possible for the human intellect to deviate from it in any detail. . . . If we were told to follow the principles which guided the creators of the Republic after the death of the Prophet, there could have been no difference of opinion with them. But when for every action or institution we are expected to find a precedent, we are being asked to act in a most un-Islamic manner.'[1]

There is one further source of the Islamic tradition and teaching—the Shariat, the corpus of Islamic law. The Shariat starts from the clear injunctions and prohibitions of the Quran and the Sunnah. On this basis, by a process of extension and analogy the men learned in the law have erected a vast superstructure, most of which was complete by the close of the third century of the Muslim era. This 'judge-made law,' being based on immutable principles and being reached by a consensus of the learned, has become for most Muslims as infallible and as rigid as Holy Writ itself.

In Pakistan those who wish to see the creation of a state that will be Islamic without being reactionary suggest, without questioning the divine basis of law, that its interpretation may require revision to accord with modern conditions. In this direction Iqbal gave a clear lead[2] and others have followed. Thus Dr. I. H. Qureshi states with emphasis that: 'It has been recognized in all Muslim countries that in many respects the mutable part of the *Shar* requires considerable overhauling, and the immutable bases need a new interpretation.'[3] This desire for a new interpretation is not intended to be an under-hand method of introducing popular legislative sovereignty. On this point the same writer is quite uncompromising. 'In the West the law is

[1] Ishtiaq Husain Qureshi, *Pakistan, An Islamic Democracy* (Lahore, n.d. but probably 1951), pp. 3-4.
[2] Sir Mohammad Iqbal, *The Reconstruction of Religious Thought in Islam* (reprinted Lahore, 1954, first edition 1930), Chapter VI, 'The Principle of Movement in the Structure of Islam,' especially p. 175 where Iqbal holds (following Karkhi) that on a question of legal interpretation, even the unanimous decision of the Companions of the Prophet would not inescapably bind later generations. [3] Ishtiaq Husain Qureshi, *op. cit.*, p. 21.

the will of the sovereign. In Islamic countries the law is the will of God.'[1]

The debate between proponents of different interpretations of Islam has been related largely to the nature of the constitutional proposals. The first official pronouncement came with the Objectives Resolution, which declared that Pakistan was to be a state:

> 'WHEREIN the Muslims shall be enabled to order their lives in the individual and collective spheres in accord with the teachings and requirements of Islam, as set out in the Holy Quran and the Sunnah.'

Later, in 1953, it was decided that the state should be called 'the Islamic Republic of Pakistan,'[2] and this title was adopted in the 1956 constitution. But this is a matter of a name and an aspiration rather than a decision as to form and content.

The widespread use of the phrase 'an Islamic state' gave rise to the belief that there existed somewhere the means of drawing a clear-cut blue-print of a set of institutions that could be unmistakably shown to derive from Divine law. Mr. A. K. Brohi, who was later to become the Minister in charge of the draft constitution, took issue with this view: 'The problem of constitution-making in Pakistan has become complicated due to the false emotional associations that have been formed, due to what I call a wrong insistence on the slogan, viz. that the constitution of Pakistan would be based on the Islamic law.'[3] This standpoint was vigorously criticized as a betrayal of the ideals of Pakistan. Mr. Brohi issued two rejoinders to his critics to show that he had not intended to advocate a constitution in which Islam played no part.

> '... if there be any clear and direct statement in the Quran as to

[1] Ishtiaq Husain Qureshi, *op. cit.*, p. 19.
[2] Constituent Assembly of Pakistan, *Debates*, Vol. XV, p. 664, November 2, 1953.
[3] *Dawn*, August 24, 1952, 'Thoughts on the Future Constitution of Pakistan.' Mr. Brohi was at that time Advocate-General for Sind.

what our constitution should be like, then of course it has got to be followed. . . .'[1]

'I have never said that I do not want Islamic constitution in this country: all I have said is that having regard to the accepted notion of what constitutional law is, it is not possible to derive from the text of the Quran any clear statement as to the actual content of the constitution of any State.'[2]

If the Quran does not provide an explicit basis for a constitution, it would still be possible to create an Islamic state if Muslims, acting consciously in their capacity as Muslims, establish those institutions which they feel to be good. This would remove the necessity for arguing whether an Islamic state would be democratic or authoritarian, federal or unitary; an Islamic state would be one created by good Muslims since their consciences would be informed and guided by the teachings of Islam.[3]

It is not easy for many Muslims to accept the view that Islam does not provide a precise answer to constitutional questions. For them virtue consists in living in accordance with Divine Will. That Will has expressed itself in concrete and detailed terms and, authoritatively interpreted, can provide specific answers to most personal problems. Most Muslims have been taught to look for ethical guidance, whether social or personal, not in the light of abstract principles but according to the terms of the law. After such training it is hard for them to believe that the law is silent on so important a matter as the formation of a state.

For those who persist in searching for scriptural instructions one initial difficulty arises. The Quran does not speak of a series of Islamic states but of one nation of believers—the *millat*. The Prophet's message was to all mankind, and his authority and that of his immediate successors was binding on all true believers. As long as the caliphate continued in existence, the pretence of the political unity of Islam could be maintained. It was for this reason that the Khilafat movement had aroused so much enthu-

[1] *Dawn*, September 21, 1952.   [2] *Ibid.*, September 7, 1952.
[3] This approach to the problem of the Islamic state is discussed at some length in W. C. Smith, *Pakistan as an Islamic State* (Lahore, dated 1951 but published 1954).

Islam and Politics

siasm among Muslim religious leaders in India. After the end of the caliphate many Muslims have shared the dream of a world union of Muslim peoples.

> '... the Islamic Millat is the grouping together, as an independent, self-governing organism, of all those individual human beings who owe allegiance to Allah and His Divine Law, wheresoever they may be....
>
> 'No matter what Muslim country the Muslim comes from, his nationality is Muslim: he is equally the citizen of every Muslim country.'[1]

In the struggle for Pakistan it was possible to gloss over the fact that there is a major difference between the two following propositions. First, that being a Muslim means being a member of a nation which embraces all other Muslims; and second, that being a Muslim means feeling that the Hindus and Muslims in India form different nations. Some orthodox religious men were not prepared to ignore the difference, and they opposed the Pakistan campaign on the ground that it cut across the larger loyalty. The Indian Independence Act created Pakistan as a territorial state, and the new country's law-makers have proceeded on that basis. But the Islamic attitude toward nationality poses three questions for Pakistan. First, are brother Muslims, some 40,000,000 of whom remained in India, to be treated as foreigners rather than as members of the *millat*? Second, and conversely, are the 10,000,000 non-Muslims remaining in Pakistan full citizens in exactly the same sense as Muslim Pakistanis?[2] Third, what should be Pakistan's relationship with other Muslim states? In each instance the law and usage of nations is in conflict with Islamic sentiment, and consequently no clear and consistent answers have emerged.

Pakistan is a reality; the political organization of the entire *millat* is not. In 1947 it therefore became necessary to begin to devise a constitution for the new state. The hope of a larger

[1] S. Ghaleb Khan Abbasi and A. de Zayas Abbasi, *op. cit.*, pp. 5-6.
[2] This question is considered further in Chapter VI.

Pakistan

Muslim political unity may remain, but for the moment Pakistan has a sufficient task in determining and putting to work a satisfactory scheme for its own government.

There may have been those in high places who intended to establish a secular state in the manner in which the Turks, while remaining Muslims, have separated politics from religion. But the ordinary man felt that the sacrifices he had made in 1947 were for the faith, and consequently that his efforts would have been in vain if Islam were not enshrined in the fabric of the new constitution. The *Munir Report* speaks of the 'ceaseless clamour for Islam and Islamic State that is being heard from all quarters since the establishment of Pakistan.'[1] The Objectives Resolution seemed to give assurance that this clamour would be rewarded, and, as has already been seen, the reception of the Interim Report of the Basic Principles Committee, which contained no specifically Islamic provisions, resulted in its hasty withdrawal and modification.

Liaquat Ali was hopeful that even if the body of the constitution had to be mounted in the chassis of Islam, the vehicle would still go in the direction he had already chosen. Thus he seemed quite sure that Islam was on the side of democracy. 'As a matter of fact it has been recognized by non-Muslims throughout the world that Islam is the only society where there is real democracy.'[2] In this approach he was supported by Maulana Shabbir Ahmad Usmani, a man of widely respected learning whose views were held in high regard by the government.

'The Islamic State is the first political institution in the world which abolished Imperialism, enunciated the principle of referendum and installed a *Caliph* (Head of the State) elected by the people in place of the King.'[3]

The opposite conclusion, however, was reached by the authors of the *Munir Report*, where it is stated: 'That the form of Government in Pakistan, if that form is to comply with the principles of Islam, will not be democratic is conceded by the *ulama*.'[4]

---

[1] P. 231.
[2] Constituent Assembly of Pakistan, *Debates*, Vol. V, p. 96, March 12, 1949.
[3] *Ibid.*, Vol. V, p. 46, March 9, 1949.   [4] *Munir Report*, p. 210.

Islam and Politics

The limit to democracy is to be found in the necessity of obedience to Divine Will. The first clause of the Objectives Resolution read as follows:

> 'WHEREAS sovereignty over the entire Universe belongs to Allah Almighty alone, and the authority which He has delegated to the State of Pakistan through its people for being exercised within the limits prescribed by Him is a sacred trust'. . .

The balance between God, the state and the people is thus nicely poised. Popular sovereignty, in the sense that the majority of the people has the right to shape the nation's institutions and policy in accordance with their personal view without regard to any higher law, cannot exist in an Islamic state. Thus a distinguished MCA talked of 'limited democracy': 'The principles of Islam and the laws of Islam as laid down in the Quran are binding on the State. The people or the State cannot change these principles or these laws.'[1]

It becomes important to discover just how extensive is the area covered by Divine Law. And here arises an acute conflict of testimony. An important *alim*, asked whether in an Islamic state there would be any place for a law-making institution, replied:

> 'Our law is complete and merely requires interpretation by those who are experts in it. According to my belief no question can arise the law relating to which cannot be discovered from the Quran or the *hadith*.[2]

Sardar Abdur Rab Nishtar, after 1951 perhaps the leading member of the Basic Principles Committee, disagreed. Speaking of the validity of man-made law, he said:

> 'Any law which is against Quran, of course, will be void, but any law which deals with that sphere of life which has been left to the

---
[1] Constituent Assembly of Pakistan, *Debates*, Vol. V, March 12, 1949, Dr. Omar Hyat Malik.
[2] *Munir Report*, p. 211, Maulana Abul Hasanat, President, *Jamiat-ul-Ulama-i-Pakistan*.

Pakistan

discretion of the people by the Quran, and such matter covers 95 per cent of affairs will not be void.'[1]

If the Maulana's point of view is to be accepted, the need for a legislature virtually disappears. It seems certain that there was no such organ under the first four Caliphs. Law was established after consultation with learned men and experts in various fields. An attempt was made to discover and apply a pre-existing law rather than to make a new one. When a case arose that was not covered by established law, the learned men made their own interpretation (*ijtihad*) as to how the basic principles of Islam should be applied. When the doctors of the law reached a substantial measure of agreement (*ijma:* consensus), the law was held to be infallibly and irrevocably established.[2] In the words of a leading contemporary *alim*: '*Ijma* decisions therefore, based as they are on the Quran and/or *Sunna*, attain almost as much sanctity as the Revealed Commandments.'[3]

If new law is to be found by the process of consensus, it becomes important to know who is entitled to participate in that process. The relevant *hadith* refers to the 'community,' but historically speaking, those concerned have been the jurists.

> 'For the sake of argument, it is true that *ijma* would not be technically complete in any problem, if the majority of the Community explicitly opposed the *ijma* of the jurists. But such an eventuality has never occurred throughout the history of Islam and is virtually

[1] Constituent Assembly of Pakistan, *Debates*, Vol. XVI, p. 328, August 24, 1954.

[2] The doctrine of *ijma* (consensus) is based upon the *hadith*, 'My Community will never unite in error.' From this it follows that, once the community has reached unity, the correctness of their decision is established for all time. Surah IV: 115 also promises damnation to the man who rejects guidance and 'follows other than the way of the believers.'

The issue of the immutability of *ijma*, which is of great importance in understanding the religious approach to the constitution, is discussed at some length in Kemal A. Faruki, *Ijma and the Gate of Ijtihad* (Karachi, 1954).

[3] Maulana Mufti Mohammed Shafi, *Mufti-e-Azam-e-Pakistan*, a member of the Board of *Talimaat-e-Islamia* and formerly Mufti, *Dar-ul-Ulum*, Deoband. The quotation is to be found *ibid.*, pp. 9–10.

impossible because *ijma* is a technical Islamic legal process for which the Muslim community would naturally rely on those qualified and competent in this sphere.'[1]

Such a line of reasoning carries the implication that an Islamic legislature would be a law-finding rather than a law-making body. Consequently its members would have to be something more than supporters of a political programme or representatives of a group interest.

> 'An essential qualification required of the members of the National Legislature is that they must be *'faqih,'* i.e. they must possess a fully adequate knowledge, *and practical experience* of the application of Quranic Law and its attendant sciences.'[2]

A non-Muslim is willing to accept the assurance that there is no priesthood in Islam, but the idea that law-making (whether by creation or interpretation) is to be confined to the practitioners of Islamic law would seem to approach very close to theocracy. This fear is shared by many Muslims, including most of the group of professional politicians. Such men were not prepared to surrender the final power of establishing law to the *ulama*. They agreed almost unanimously that Pakistan should have a legislature in the Western sense.

> 'The legal sovereign shall be Muslim law; but its definition shall be in the hands of a legislature representing the people which will, by deliberation and discussion, decide how to apply the principles of Islam to the needs of the community in varying circumstances.'[3]

The Constituent Assembly therefore proposed to set up a Parliament which would be representative of the nation as a whole.

Since, by common consent, the ultimate legal sovereign is Divine Law, many thought it unwise to leave complete authority

[1] *Ibid.*, pp. 11, 12. The words are again those of Maulana Mufti Mohammed Shafi.
[2] S. Ghaleb Khan Abbasi and A. de Zayas Abbasi, *op. cit.*, p. 50.
[3] I. H. Qureshi, *op. cit.*, p. 26.

Pakistan

with a legislature containing non-Muslims as well as (in all probability) a majority which would know little or nothing of that law. Consequently, in response to considerable pressure, the Report of the Basic Principles Committee (1952) contained a proposal that no law passed by any legislature in Pakistan should be valid if it were repugnant to the Holy Quran and the Sunnah.

The method proposed for passing upon alleged repugnancy was somewhat unusual. Any Bill that was challenged on this ground in the national Legislature was to be forwarded by the Head of the State to a Board, constituted by him, consisting of 'not more than five persons well versed in Islamic Laws.' If the members of the Board were to disagree, the Head of State might make his own decisions as to giving his assent to the measure. If the Board found unanimously against a Bill or any of its provisions, the Legislature would be given a chance to reconsider. If the Legislature re-passed the Bill by a majority of the members present and voting, provided that this included the majority of the Muslim members present and voting, then the measure would become law. Thus the consensus of the community was to be allowed to override the consensus of the jurists, although the non-Muslims were not to be permitted to be instrumental in securing the acceptance of an impugned Bill. The potential complications and difficulties of such an arrangement require little comment. A somewhat similar provision in the constitution of Iran had been condemned by Iqbal as a 'dangerous arrangement.'[1] Much would have depended upon the choice of persons to serve on the Board. But any conflict between a political majority and an Islamic court would have been likely to lead to an ugly political situation.

When the report of the Basic Principles Committee was under discussion in the Assembly, the 'repugnancy clause' was substantially amended. Any law of a Pakistan Legislature which is in conflict with the Quran and the Sunnah was again declared to be invalid. But the later provision was that the Supreme Court alone should have jurisdiction in such a case.[2] Any objection on

[1] Sir Mohammed Iqbal, *op. cit.*, pp. 175–6.
[2] Basic Principles Committee, *Report* (as adopted), para. 6.

the ground of repugnancy to Islam was to be filed within three months of the giving of assent to a Bill. Furthermore, it was provided that, for a period of at least twenty-five years, the repugnancy sections should not apply to 'fiscal and monetary measures, laws relating to banking, insurance, provident funds, loans and other matters affecting the existing economic, financial and credit system.'[1]

The clauses relating to repugnancy were accorded a good deal of publicity both within Pakistan and elsewhere. In their later form they are less far-reaching than might appear at first sight. In the first place they applied only to future laws. Existing laws, whatever their nature, would have continued to be valid unless the legislature decided on repeal or modification. Secondly, the doctrine of repugnancy was to be applied by a court consisting of lawyers trained in the tradition of the Anglo-Saxon common law. Such a court might well have included non-Muslim judges. In any event the judges were directed to determine repugnancy to the Quran and the Sunnah and, unless they so chose, they would not have been obliged to consider themselves bound by existing Islamic case-law. By the time of the meeting of the second Constituent Assembly there had been some third thoughts on the matter. Article 198 of the constitution provides that no law shall be enacted that is contrary to the injunctions of Islam, but this clause is left to the good faith of the Legislatures to enforce. However, within one year of the adoption of the constitution, the President is to appoint a commission to recommend measures for bringing existing laws into conformity with the requirements of Islam and to compile in legislative form those injunctions that can be given statutory effect. The commission is to report within five years of its appointment. It is explicitly provided that Article 198 shall not affect the personal laws of non-Muslims or their status as citizens.

Even if an orthodox Muslim be led to concede that an Islamic state may have a legislature in the Western sense, it does not follow that it should be constituted on parliamentary lines. Most Islamic scholars are agreed that the Western system of elections

[1] *Report*, para. 10(1).

Pakistan

has grave defects in that it allows the unworthy and the office-seeker to be chosen rather than the man of proven character and selflessness. Several writers have therefore proposed schemes of election which are claimed to overcome these defects. One suggestion is that there should be a dual basis of election, belief and function; thus there would be one House representing creeds and another representing occupational groups.

> 'For those who state that they are Muslims first, the constituency in which they should vote for representatives to a house of belief is best expressed by the mosque in which they say their Friday prayers. Here in the company of those who believe like him and whom he knows personally through weekly association, a Muslim should choose the best, the most *al-amin*, from amongst the congregation.[1]'

The basis for the non-Muslim would be comparable, with separate electorates for Hindus, Christians, Communists and those whose primary loyalty is to 'secular nationalism.' The delegates chosen by these primary groups would then constitute electoral colleges for the selection of higher representative bodies. Another suggestion is that the electors, whose duty it is to choose only the most pious and trustworthy of their fellows, should be held responsible for the conduct of their representative. Thus if they choose badly they 'must be taken to account for their faulty judgment in the choice of their representative.'[2] Such an error might lead to deprivation for a period of the right to be represented.

If the electors have indeed chosen the most pious and trustworthy it is difficult for an Opposition candidate to assert that he regards himself as better qualified. The very immodesty of the proposition would demonstrate his unsuitability. In Islam, politics must be regarded as a striving to find the one right answer that is in perfect accord with God's Will, rather than a conflict of sectional interests or a struggle for the enjoyment of office.

[1] Kemal A. Faruki, *Islamic Constitution* (Karachi, 1952), p. 57.
[2] S. Ghaleb Khan Abbasi and A. de Zayas Abbasi, *op. cit.*, p. 54.

Islam and Politics

'In Islam, party-politics are an impossibility, there being only *one party*, *the body of Muslims*, to which each and every adult Muslim belongs as a matter of right, whose ideology is the Divine Law of Nature, and whose existence is governed and directed by the sober, ineluctable truth of Reality.'[1]

Stated so bluntly this doctrine is not acceptable to the large majority of those who have been active in Pakistan's political life. But traces of its influence can be discerned at every meeting of the Muslim League, and lie behind every appeal for the political unity of all Muslims. Most Pakistanis believe fundamentally that if only men of sufficient vision and integrity could be found, the need for organized opposition would disappear.

The divergence of opinion about the possibilities of establishing and altering law was perhaps the most important theoretical issue confronting the Muslim framers of the new constitution. But more attention, at least in political circles, was focused on the office of Head of the State. From the beginning Islam as a political system has placed one man at the head of the state organization. In the very early years he was elevated by a form of election, but since the Caliph was virtually irremovable (except by violence) it constituted elective monarchy rather than democracy. Soon the element of election was superseded by hereditary succession. Thus the weight of Islamic tradition is on the side of the concentration of authority in the hands of one man (though that authority is, at least in theory, limited by the law as interpreted by the juriconsults, and by the injunction to govern by consultation). Many orthodox Muslims, whose political education had perhaps begun with the Khilafat Movement, wished to see executive power centred around the person of the Head of the State.

'The responsibility for the administration of the State shall primarily vest in the Head of the State, although he may delegate any part of his power to any individual or body.'[2]

[1] S. Ghaleb Khan Abbasi and A. de Zayas Abbasi, *op. cit.*, p. 36.
[2] *Report of the Sub-Committee to Examine the Suggestions Received on the Interim Report of the Basic Principles Committee*, p. 44. The committee was dis-

Pakistan

The Board of *Talimaat-e-Islamia* had definite opinions on the qualifications and duties of the Head of the State.[1] He should be 'the trustee of the interests of the Millat, the symbol and manifestation of its power and authority and its executive organ in all walks of the State.' He is to be chosen by the Muslims who should 'elect the wisest and most God-fearing person from amongst themselves as their head. . . .' The Head of the State should be male, of sound mind, not blind, dumb nor totally deaf and have completed forty lunar years of age. He should be a man of erudition and learning in the terms of Shariat, and a person of 'poise and composure and . . . able to control his humours.' It is preferable that he should be chosen for an indefinite period, but he may be removed if he ceases to fulfil any of the essential conditions of office. He should govern in consultation with one or more councils, and he is to consider himself responsible to the people. He should lead Friday and Id prayers in the capital and should arrange for the teaching of Islam both at home and among the infidel.

The answer of the political leaders to these suggestions was to explain, with apparent success,[2] that the provisions of the Basic Principles Committee Report regarding the President and his cabinet were quite compatible with the position recommended by the *ulama*. The Basic Principles Committee, however, spent much time in discussing whether Muslims alone or all members of the future Legislature might participate in the election of the President. Finally, it was agreed that all might vote but that only a Muslim would be eligible for the office, and a clause to this effect was incorporated in the constitution.

The insistence that only a Muslim might be Head of the State could have only symbolic meaning within the context of the

cussing the views of the Board of *Talimaat-e-Islamia* and also a pamphlet described as 'The Fundamental Principles of an Islamic State formulated at a gathering of *Ulama* of various Muslim schools of thought under the presidentship of Allama Syed Sulaiman Nadvi Sahib.' The quotation is apparently from this pamphlet.

[1] These views are quoted in *Report of the Sub-Committee on Federal and Provincial Constitutions and Division of Powers*, pp. 57–70, from which these extracts are taken.   [2] See p. 95.

constitution, for the system adopted is that of parliamentary or cabinet government in which the reality of power is intended to rest with the Prime Minister, his colleagues and the legislature. The Law Minister made this quite clear:

> '... it is a mistake to call him the Head of the State. He is only there for "*Nam ke waste*"! He is there for ceremonial purposes.... His position is that of a figurehead, as much and as little as that of the King in England. He has no power at all.'[1]

This is the attitude of a lawyer and a parliamentarian. But the ordinary Muslim finds it easier to understand a system which presents him with a single dynamic character as the personification of his country. The political tradition of Mr. Jinnah, the Great Leader, and the Islamic tradition of the Caliphs unite in support of the desire for a Head of the State endowed with real power.[2]

The struggle for Pakistan was led by men of politics rather than by men of religion. The achievement of their purpose in 1947 presented them with the problem of the role of Islam in the structure of the new state. This, however, was overshadowed by the need for political stability. Most political leaders and the 'modernists' among the men of religion want to see a new flexibility in the social and political thinking of Islam. But to pursue this issue before the new constitution had been brought into operation would have been to invite confusion and internal conflict. The politicians therefore wished at least to preserve a façade of harmony on religious matters until the state should be more firmly established. The orthodox *ulama*, on the other hand, have not felt strong enough, nor sufficiently united, and they have lacked the knowledge of the techniques of effective political action to enable them to take the offensive on behalf of a rigorous return to classical standards. This common wish to avoid dispute during years of national crisis has resulted in a lack of clear-

---

[1] Constituent Assembly of Pakistan, *Debates*, Vol. XV, p. 369, October 23, 1953, Mr. A. K. Brohi.

[2] For a further discussion of the powers of the President see above, pp. 148–52.

Pakistan

thinking and the unhappy suspicion by both sides that much is to be lost by a direct assertion of principle. The Punjab disturbances of 1953 provided a painful reminder of the possible consequences of an open split between the authorities and the mullahs.

Much of the debate concerning the Islamic state has been an argument between those who are talking about a moral imperative and those who are discussing the state of contemporary political affairs. The moralists are certain that they are right, and that their opponents are not merely misguided but heretical, and traitors to the true purpose of the creation of Pakistan. 'Pakistan was established solely for the sake of demonstrating the efficacy of the Islamic way of life.'[1] If this be true the state must firmly dedicate itself to moral and religious ends.

> '... the main objects of an Islamic State are to enforce and implement with all the resources of its organized power that reformatory programme which Islam has given for the betterment of mankind. ... Its distinction lies in the fact that it has to encourage and popularize those good practices which Islam desires humanity to adopt; and to discourage, eradicate and crush with full force all those evils from which Islam aims to purge mankind.'[2]

The politicians did not disagree with this approach, but they failed to see its immediate relevance. In the preamble to the constitution, following the Objectives Resolution, there appears a declaration of submission to the will of Allah. 'WHEREAS sovereignty over the entire Universe belongs to Allah Almighty alone, and the authority to be exercised by the people of Pakistan within the limits prescribed by Him is a sacred trust.' Other sections of the preamble and of the Directive Principles of State Policy also constitute pledges of adherence to the moral and religious precepts of Islam. In order that the future policy of the state shall be more truly in line with Islam, the constitution

[1] Khurshid Ahmad, Introduction to, Syed Abul Ala Maududi, *Islamic Law and Constitution* (Karachi, 1955), p. 1.
[2] Syed Abul Ala Maududi, *ibid.*, p. 128.

includes an article providing for the establishment of 'an organization for Islamic research and instruction in advanced studies to assist in the reconstruction of Muslim society on a truly Islamic basis.' But, of proposals having immediate political or administrative significance, there are only two which have a distinct Islamic connotation. They are the clause relating to repugnancy and codification of Islamic law and the clause restricting the office of President to believers in Islam.

It is hard for a moral reformer to make concessions where his principles are concerned, but it must not be assumed that none of the men of religion were aware of the gap between contemporary society and the true Islamic society, or that they under-estimated the difficulty of establishing a working Islamic state. Maulana Maududi, for example, is prepared to accept the subordination of the executive to the majority decisions of the legislature, since it is not likely that a Caliph or a consultative council of the moral calibre of those of Medina can now be found in Pakistan.[1] Pakistan has suffered infidel rule for so long that its moral, social and economic life has been led far from the true path. 'It is, therefore, inevitable that the required reform should be gradual and the changes in the laws should be effected in such a manner as to balance favourably the change in the moral, educational, social, cultural and political life of the nation.'[2]

In the matter of the new constitution, the mutual forbearance of the *ulama* and the politicians seems to have been rewarded. Both the final version of the Basic Principles Report and the 1956 constitution were accepted without widespread opposition from Muslim groups concerning the Islamic provisions. The East Pakistan Muslim League passed a resolution regretting that the repugnancy clause was not to be enforceable in the courts.[3] This criticism was more than countered by the attitude of the Awami League. Mr. Suhrawardy asserted that his party wanted true Islam in the government and policies of Pakistan, but that the existing state of affairs was so far from Islamic that the title should not be included in the name of the state. 'I say that you are deluding the

[1] Syed Abul Ala Maududi, *Islamic Law and Constitution* (Karachi, 1955), p. 127.   [2] *Ibid.*, p. 52.   [3] *Dawn*, January 29, 1956.

Pakistan

people here by calling this an Islamic state.'[1] He argued that it was quite unnecessary to provide in the constitution that the President was required to be a Muslim since 86 per cent of the electorate would be composed of Muslim voters.

The new constitution has something to offer to both sides; it gives grounds to the orthodox traditionalist that his cause might be advanced, while there is nothing in the Islamic clauses to cause a liberal democrat to feel that Pakistan is incapable of becoming the kind of state he wishes to see.

The constitution does little to settle the fundamental issue of the desirable role of Islam in a modern state. Nor would its adoption serve to bridge what one writer has called the 'wide gulf between the *ulama* of the orthodox schools and the intelligentsia.'[2] This gulf is of particular importance in Pakistan. For this is a nation which claims to form an 'ideological' state, but where there is no agreement on the meaning and application of that ideology. While this disagreement lasts it must continue to lead to confusion and division which the new state can ill afford. The debate may be carried on between the *ulama* and the intelligentsia, but in its political implications it is a struggle for the mind and imagination of the people. Of its consequences for the mind of the ordinary man, the authors of the *Munir Report* write with deep conviction:

> '[The Musalman] finds himself in a state of helplessness, waiting for someone to come and help him out of this morass of uncertainty and confusion. And he will go on waiting like this without anything happening. Nothing but a bold re-orientation of Islam to separate the vital from the lifeless can preserve it as a World Idea and convert the Musalman into a citizen of the present and the future world from the archaic incongruity that he is today. . . .
>
> 'It is this lack of bold and clear thinking, the inability to understand and take decisions which has brought about in Pakistan a

---

[1] Constituent Assembly of Pakistan, *Debates*, Vol. I, p. 2248, January 31, 1956. The Awami League joined the non-Muslims in casting twenty-two votes in the Assembly against the adoption of the name 'Islamic Republic,' *Dawn*, February 22, 1956.   [2] I. H. Qureshi, *op. cit.*, p. 23.

confusion which will persist and repeatedly create situations of the kind we have been inquiring into until our leaders have clear conception of the goal and of the means to reach it.'[1]

Pakistan has enjoyed independent existence for more than nine years. During this period there has been a great deal of discussion of the significance of the requirements of Islam for the new state. Comparatively little attention has been paid to the less spectacular task of acting within the framework of the prevailing constitution to bring laws and policies into conformity with those requirements.[2] For example, there can be no doubt that the consumption of alcohol is explicitly forbidden for Muslims. The constitution provides, as a Directive Principle, that 'the State shall endeavour to . . . prevent the consumption of alcoholic liquor otherwise than for medicinal and, in the case of non-Muslims, religious purposes.' This is a declaration of intention, but the fact remains that neither the central government in Karachi nor the provincial governments have enforced a policy of complete and general prohibition and a major brewery has continued to be a flourishing enterprise in West Pakistan.

Western observers often wonder whether much of the talk of the importance of Islam is to be taken seriously. They mix with officials of the government, politicians, journalists, business-men and officers of the armed forces. And such men, wearing Western clothes and speaking excellent English, do not seem to talk much about religion. And if that awkward subject should arise, in conversation at the bar of a big hotel in Karachi or Lahore, it is likely to be dismissed with a smile: 'The Islamic state? all humbug, my dear fellow.' And the foreigner could convince himself that such views were more widely held by taking note of the thousands of Karachi walls which bore the statement in 1954-55, neatly

[1] P. 232.
[2] A Laws Commission was set up in 1951 under Justice A. S. Mohammad Akram to advise on the legal changes necessary to bring existing law into conformity with the Objectives Resolution. Consideration of its report was overshadowed by the constitution debates and the crisis of 1954-55.

Pakistan

stencilled in Urdu and English: 'Slogans of Islamic State a Political Stunt.'

But it would be rash indeed to draw the conclusion that Islam is of little importance, or that it matters only to the illiterate. The Western-educated are a very small minority in Pakistan. They have for the most part acquired two sets of values. One they derive from their traditional faith; the other has been acquired, often at second-hand, from the English middle-classes. Very few have been able to accomplish a successful synthesis. The Pakistani educated in the Western tradition is apt to slip from one intellectual basis to the other according to the company he keeps and the problem he faces. But he has seldom arrived at the total abandonment of the Islamic tradition which often dominates his emotions, while the Western standards are intellectually accepted rather than deeply felt. The very creation of Pakistan is evidence of this duality, for this religious-nation-state is the supreme product of the Muslim intellectual.

No Muslim public figure has ventured to suggest that Pakistan should discard Islam as the basis of its policy.[1] It has been unanimously conceded that if the Quran has clear guidance to offer on any matter, then that guidance must be followed. It may be argued that this position is, in some cases, a device to appease the *ulama* and the illiterate mass of the people. Even if this were true (which is not established) it would show the judgment of a cynical politician about the political realities of his country. Even if there are those who have ceased to believe in Islam as a living force they still find it necessary to present their proposals behind an Islamic screen if they are to have any influence with the nation-at-large.

Liberal democracy in the West has established a code of public morality of its own, derived from its own experience. This is largely secular in character, though influenced by Christianity. But in Pakistan the only basis for social morality is Islam. This *can* be a democratic morality, but it *must* be believed to be Islamic.

---

[1] General Iskandar Mirza is perhaps an exception. After a press interview it was reported that 'the General held the personal view that religion and politics could be separated and they should be' (*Dawn*, October 31, 1954).

'It is ultimately the innermost convictions of a people which shape its life. For us Muslims,' writes Dr. Qureshi, 'no morality exists which does not find its ultimate sanction in Islam. . . . To ask an overwhelmingly Muslim people to discard its innermost convictions in framing its constitution is to ask it to commit suicide.'[1]

[1] *Op. cit.*, p. 5.

CHAPTER VII

The Minorities

THE demand for the independent state of Pakistan was based on the theory that Muslims and Hindus could not successfully live side-by-side in a single political organism. Yet any division of the sub-continent, unless accompanied by mass human migration on a scale never before witnessed, would have left vast numbers of non-Muslims within the borders of the Muslim homeland. The tragic events of partition and its aftermath of violence removed most of the non-Muslims from the (West) Punjab but left nearly 10,000,000 in East Pakistan.

TABLE I
RELIGIOUS DISTRIBUTION OF MINORITIES BY UNITS[1]

Unit	Caste Hindu 000	Sched. Caste 000	Christian 000	Other 000	Total 000	Percentage Total Pop.
East Pakistan	4,187	5,052	107	359	9,705	23·2
Punjab	2	19	401	–	422	2·2
Sind	134	320	2	1	457	9·9
N.-W.F.P.	1	2	4	–	7	0·1
Bahawalpur	1	11	2	–	14	0·8
Khairpur	7	3	–	–	10	3·1
Baluchistan	12	1	4	–	17	1·5
Karachi	5	13	21	6	45	4·0
Total West Pakistan	162	369	434	7	972	2·9
Total	4,349	5,421	541	366	10,677	14·1

Of the entire population, about fourteen in every hundred are non-Muslim, of whom thirteen are Hindu.

[1] The table is derived from *Census of Pakistan*, 1951, Table 6. The item for North-West Frontier Province includes states and tribal areas, and that for Baluchistan includes states. The figures for 'Other' includes 319(000) Buddhists and 30(000) designated 'Tribal' in East Bengal, and 5(000) Parsis in Karachi.

The Minorities

Before 1947 those who had argued for Pakistan had claimed the right to speak in the name of the 100,000,000 members of the Muslim nation. That 'nation' was now divided, and the larger fraction found itself sharing a state with a substantial number of Hindus. Pakistan was the Muslim homeland; what place could it offer to its non-Muslim citizens?

With the history of Western Europe in mind, it is easy to maintain that in a modern democratic state all citizens should be equal without regard to colour, creed or race. But in Pakistan the history of more than one generation had emphasized the incompatibility of Muslim and Hindu. Partition, with its consequent bloodshed and hardship, had appeared to confirm the two-nation theory and had sharpened the passion behind it to a new edge of bitterness. Communal strife and hatred darkened the early days of the new state of Pakistan. The *Quaid-i-Azam* was quite certain that one of the most urgent and important tasks that lay before him and his people would be the establishment of communal harmony and mutual trust. Pakistan was to be one nation, to which all citizens might be proud to owe loyalty.

'Now, I think we should keep that in front of us as our ideal and you will find that in the course of time Hindus would cease to be Hindus and Muslims would cease to be Muslims, not in the religious sense, because that is the personal faith of each individual, but in the political sense as citizens of the State.'[1]

Mr. Jinnah's words have been repeated on numberless occasions during the ensuing ten years. But it must be remembered that they were delivered to the first session of the Constituent Assembly, four days before independence, at a time when Sind and the Punjab depended heavily upon non-Muslims for commercial and technical services, and before pain and death had left their deepest scars. Subsequent events did not cause Mr. Jinnah to retreat in any way from his declared intention to make Pakistan a state founded on complete religious tolerance, and where religion should play no part in matters of politics

[1] Constituent Assembly of Pakistan, *Debates*, Vol. I, p. 20, August 11, 1947.

and administration. But hatred of Sikhs and Hindus and fear of the new India made it hard for the liberal view to gain acceptance. And it was explicitly rejected by many of the *ulama*. The Munir Commission, having quoted at considerable length Mr. Jinnah's speech on national unity, asked witnesses for their comments.

> 'We asked the *ulama* whether this conception of a State was acceptable to them and every one of them replied in an unhesitating negative. . . . None of the *ulama* can tolerate a State which is based on nationalism and all that it implies: with them *millat* and all that it connotes can alone be the determining factor in State activity.'[1]

Some of the persons who gave evidence before the Munir Commission have been rightly described as fanatics. But on the issue of Muslims and minorities their general insistence that an Islamic state would deny power at the highest level to non-Muslims is supported by all serious students of Islam. Maulana Shabbir Ahmad Usmani, whose views were quoted frequently and with approval by members of the government, made this matter clear in a speech in the Assembly which was later reproduced with favourable comment by the Board of *Talimaat-e-Islamia*.

> 'The Islamic State means a State which is run on the exalted and excellent principles of Islam. It is evident that a State which is founded on some principles, be it religious or secular (like the U.S.S.R.), can be run only by those who believe in those principles. The services of such persons as do not subscribe to those ideas may be utilized in the administrative machinery of the State but they cannot be entrusted with the responsibility of framing the general policy of the State or dealing with matters vital to its safety and integrity.'[2]

It must not be concluded that the teachings of Islam serve merely to deprive non-Muslims of certain democratic rights and privileges. Muslims are strictly enjoined to tolerate and to protect

[1] *Munir Report*, p. 203.
[2] Constituent Assembly of Pakistan, *Debates*, Vol. V, p. 45, March 9, 1949.

non-Muslims and to allow them to continue to practise their religion provided they undertake no activities inimical to the welfare of the State and the *millat*.

> 'Unto each nation have We given sacred rites which they are to perform; so let them not dispute with thee of the matter, but summon thou unto thy Lord. Lo! thou indeed followest right guidance.
>
> 'And if they wrangle with thee, say: Allah is best aware of what ye do.
>
> 'Allah will judge between you on the Day of Resurrection concerning that wherein ye used to differ.'[1]

Islam, by long tradition, recognizes and protects conquered tribes of non-Muslims and also non-Muslim groups of native inhabitants who enter into an agreement with Muslim rulers. But in either case their status is that of privileged resident aliens rather than that of equal citizens. An Islamic state is governed according to Divine Law, and a great part of the task of government consists in the interpretation of such law; how, then, can a non-believer be allowed to interpret the law? and how, in a senior position, can he be trusted to execute it with understanding and faithfulness?

The position of the *ulama* is outwardly strange, but it is based upon an inner, if somewhat peculiar, logic. Before partition many of them opposed Pakistan because nationalism was incompatible with Islam. Pakistan was for them too narrow an aim since it would not include all Muslims, not even all the Muslims of India. Now that Pakistan is in existence they are trying to narrow the effective composition of the state to exclude all but the body of true believers. They have accepted Pakistan, but only as the outward form of the sovereignty of God. They wish to establish loyalty to the one true God through the state of Pakistan, and this would leave no place for those who are willing to admit only the lesser loyalty which ends with the state and the nation.

It has been little easier for the Western-educated to adjust

[1] Surah XXII, 67–9 (Pickthall).

themselves to a new concept of nationality. The belief in the unity of the world-wide community of Muslims is derived from the religion of Islam. The two-nation theory, however, is essentially a modification of the Western political theory of the right of national self-determination. As a political movement, the 100,000,000 Muslims of India asserted their nationhood and demanded an independent state. Before 1947 this idea of a state had no specific boundaries. Pakistan was in no sense the product of sentiments of Punjabi or Bengali separatism. The Muslim homeland was an area, any viable territory, which could support the majority of true believers. It requires a prodigious mental effort to accept the transformation that occurred on August 14, 1947, when a Muslim comrade in the struggle for Pakistan became a foreigner because he lived in Lucknow, while a Hindu Congressman living in Dacca became a loyal fellow-citizen. The effort was, in many cases, too great, and some of the intellectuals found means of evading it. A former Cabinet minister and a university professor had this to say:

> 'We [Muslim and Hindu] possess common nationality which is a legal concept but we are not the same nation which is a sociological concept. We are *not* one nation and yet we are citizens of the same State. . . .
> 'Pakistan exists only on that basis—that Muslims are a separate nation—and on no other basis.'[1]

To deny the basic 'sociological' differences between Muslim and Hindu is tantamount to denying the necessity of partition. But it is possible to argue that an 86 per cent majority is sufficient to determine for all time that Pakistan is a predominantly Muslim country and that the threat of Hindu domination has been for ever removed. It may be urged that the struggle for national self-determination is over and that for national consolidation has begun. However, no one would pretend that the 'consolidation' of 10,000,000 Hindus is likely to prove simple.

[1] Constituent Assembly of Pakistan, *Debates*, Vol. XV, p. 540, Dr. Mahmud Husain.

The Minorities

Unfortunately the problem of the place of the minorities is overshadowed by the tension that has existed between Pakistan and India. The leaders of the Indian National Congress accepted partition with reluctance; many Hindu extremists would have fought rather than concede Pakistan, and some of them still talk of a campaign of re-unification. The more virulent anti-Muslims domiciled in Pakistani territory fled to India, and their sufferings as refugees have added to their bitterness and hostility. As with other groups of political exiles, they jealously preserve the memories of real or fancied injustice and oppression, and they give full publicity to the difficulties of those who stayed behind.

Those Hindus who did remain, principally in East Bengal, showed their willingness to accept the new state of Pakistan. But it would be impossible to pretend that they welcomed the events of 1947. They found themselves separated from friends and relatives and cut off from major centres of commerce and education. Those in West Pakistan witnessed and suffered several months of killing and looting and endured total uncertainty as to the safety of their persons and their possessions. In East Bengal, where with rare exceptions communal violence since partition has been avoided, the Hindus could not help but wonder whether it was to be their turn next. And everywhere they have had to bear a constant burden of suspicion and obloquy. All the sins, real and imagined, of the Indian government have been levelled at the Hindus of Pakistan.

The Pakistan government on several occasions has believed that war with India was quite close. Government and people have been aware of hostile propaganda coming across the border. Within Pakistan, Muslim extremists have called for a holy war to capture Delhi and to re-establish Muslim rule in a solid belt across northern India.[1] While such tension exists, any government

[1] There is a tendency in Pakistan, even in circles not normally regarded as fanatical, to indulge in militaristic day-dreams. Thus a *Dawn* editorial (March 28, 1955) declared: 'By way of educating the ignorant, and merely as an academic point, we may say that if Bharat did indeed "invade" East Pakistan, the Pakistani flag might be flying atop the Lok Sabha building in New Delhi before the "invading" forces had negotiated many of the rivers and marshes of our Eastern Wing.'

Pakistan

has to ask itself whether it can rely upon the loyalty of all sections of the country. If war should break out, is it not possible that some Hindus would feel tempted to aid invading forces composed of Hindu troops?

Responsible spokesmen for the Hindus have asserted unequivocally that they accepted all the obligations of citizenship of Pakistan.[1] But it was not to be expected that the Hindu would be able to share all the emotions of his Muslim compatriots. He had been told before partition that Pakistan was to be a state for Muslims, and there was no reason why a Hindu should have wished to see it come into existence. The Muslim League which had fought for and was to rule Pakistan had found no place for Hindus among its members. The Congress, on the other hand, had claimed the political allegiance of most Hindus, and its leaders were regarded with reverence and affection. Those who were politically active had worked earnestly for a free united India only to find, in a moment of near triumph, that they were to be condemned to the status of a despised and suspect minority. Not surprisingly many preferred to leave their homes and sources of livelihood and migrate to India, where they had friends and could find a more congenial atmosphere. Often a family would be divided, with some members staying in Pakistan to look after property or to continue in business or professional life. This, of course, attracted increased suspicion from their Muslim neighbours, for, in a country where family responsibilities are taken more seriously than in the West, it seemed to confirm the existence of divided or alien sympathies. The professional patriots of Pakistan have at times demanded denunciations of India and Indian policies as a proof of loyalty to Pakistan, and the Hindus have incurred further suspicion because they have been unwilling to impute the worst motives and the most sinister intentions to

[1] Seth Sukhdev, presiding over the Sind Hindu Conference in 1948, described the resolve of those of his community who had decided to remain in Pakistan: 'With this faith [in democracy] in our hearts we determined to stick to our Homeland, loyal to the new State, and work for Democracy and Democratic Institutions in Pakistan.' Quoted in Sarat C. V. Narasimham, *The Other Side* (Karachi, 1955), p. 18.

their neighbour. In this sense their sympathies are divided since they find it hard to look upon India as a real or potential enemy. But this is not to say that the Hindus are partisans of India against the cause of Pakistan. They have nothing to gain and everything to lose from such an attitude. Tension between the two countries makes the position of the minorities more difficult and more precarious. And if war should break out, whatever its final outcome, the Hindus would face the prospect of annihilation within the first few weeks. The hopes for prosperity and progress of the Hindu community thus depend largely upon the establishment of close and friendly relations between India and Pakistan.

One of the most distressing features of political life in Pakistan has been the continuing refusal to take the Hindus at their word and to treat them as other than a potential fifth column. This is not the result of official government policy, but is part of a campaign of rancour in which some ministers have at times joined, and which the government has seldom attempted to combat. It has been met and further provoked by extreme accusations of discrimination and persecution brought by the Hindus.

Any Hindu speaker found it very difficult to make a speech in either the Constituent Assembly or the East Bengal Legislative Assembly dealing with Indo-Pakistan relations or the loyalty of the minority community without encountering hostile and ironic interruptions. The following is a fair sample:

'D. N. Dutta (Hindu): Most of the minority members did not want division of India but they are in Pakistan now. They have accepted Pakistan. . . .
'Syed Shamsur Rahman (Muslim): With mental reservations.'[1]

Alternatively Muslim members would lecture the Hindus on their duties and warn them that they were under suspicion.

'Sir, my Honourable friend opposite knows how the enemies of Pakistan utilized them [Hindus] in their own interests by paying

[1] Constituent Assembly (Legislature), *Debates*, 1954, Vol. I, p. 1408, July 3, 1954.

abundant money for the purpose. (*Interruptions.*) He knows how the people living near the Hoogly river [i.e. Calcutta] were responsible for bringing about the results which they desired to the detriment of Pakistan.'[1]

Many comparable examples can be found in the debates of the East Bengal Assembly. One will here suffice.

'If they [the Hindu Opposition] want to criticize the Government on constructive lines, Government would always be prepared to welcome them, but I would like to tell them through you, Sir, that any opposition on destructive lines can never be tolerated. . . . None should be allowed to misuse the privilege given to him by converting the floor of this august House into a platform for the enemies of Pakistan.'[2]

In undivided India the Muslims were the minority community, and they conducted a long campaign for the establishment and protection of a special political status. The Congress, composed predominantly of Hindus, represented the majority and wished to minimize any measure setting special boundaries between one group and another. In Pakistan the numerical position is reversed, and the Hindus are the minority. But the ideas of the League and the Congress concerning the political status of different communities have not changed. The Muslim League has insisted upon the maintenance of special political barriers, while the Congress has urged their abolition.

The institutional form of this protection of minorities was the provision of separate electorates by communities. In this respect all elections in Pakistan until 1954 were in accordance with the scheme established by the Government of India Act. This was, of course, designed primarily to protect the Muslim minority of undivided India. But after 1947 the terminology was not changed

---

[1] Constituent Assembly of Pakistan, *Debates*, Vol. XVI, p. 245, July 27, 1954, Abdul Hamid. The member was speaking of the United Front victory and the subsequent riots in East Bengal.

[2] East Bengal Legislative Assembly, *Official Report*, Vol. IV, pp. 154-5, November 18, 1949, Mayeenuddin Ahmed Chowdhury.

The Minorities

and the separate electorates were provided for the Muslims while the Hindu (plus any unclassified minorities) seats were described as 'General.'[1] The first Constituent Assembly decided that this method should be carried over to the proposed constitution, with categories for Muslims, Caste Hindus, Scheduled Castes, Christians, Buddhists and Parsis.[2]

The Muslim League argument for this system of separate electorates was that it was in the interests of the minorities themselves. Discussing the forthcoming elections in Sind, Mr. Khuhro warned: 'Without reservation not a single Hindu will be returned to the Assembly.' Professor R. K. Chakraverty replied: 'We want to go out of existence; that will do good to the country.'[3] A prominent Sind leader argued the same point before a gathering of his fellow Hindus in 1948.

> 'A staunch democrat would not ask for any political safeguards as against the majority. We should, therefore, demand joint electorates without even as much as reservation of seats. It may be that for a long time Hindus may be out of the legislatures, out of the Local Self-Government Bodies, such as Municipalities and Local Boards. But in the long run things will adjust themselves, and political parties will be formed on political issues, and as political consciousness grows, more and more progressive political and social values will prevail. If as a result, Hindus in Sind are out of Legislatures for some time, the price is worth the experiment.'[4]

[1] The relevant sections of the Government of India Act (Sixth Schedule) were changed by the Government of India (Third Amendment) Act, 1952, and the new provisions governed the East Bengal elections of 1954. The principal change in the system of separate electorates was to make the Scheduled Castes of East Bengal into a separate electorate instead of providing them with certain reserved seats to be filled by the vote of the 'General' electors.

The amending Act was described by Mr. B. K. Dutta: '... the Bill turns the Legislature into a religious fair with Muslims, Christians, Buddhists and members of two newly created religions. Their names are "General" and "Scheduled".' (Constituent Assembly of Pakistan, *Debates*, Vol. XI, p. 65, April 15, 1952.)

[2] Basic Principles Committee *Report* (as adopted), S.50 and Schedule II.
[3] Constituent Assembly of Pakistan, *Debates*, Vol. IX, p. 17, April 11, 1951.
[4] Seth Sukhdev, quoted in Sarat C. V. Narasimham, *op. cit.*, p. 19.

Pakistan

The Muslim League and the government were not convinced by the arguments of the Hindus. The official position was that the Hindu spokesmen did not know their own interests, and needed to be protected in spite of themselves. The Law Minister tried to combat the idea that separate electorates were imposed because the Muslim majority did not wish to mix with non-believers. 'In principle, of course,' said Mr. Brohi, 'if the minorities want to merge we are willing to accept them and embrace them.'[1] Toward the end of the life of the first Constituent Assembly, and after the East Bengal elections had confirmed the popular mandate of many of the Hindu leaders, a final attempt was made to convince the majority that the demands of the minority were widely and strongly supported.

> 'We want to be united with you. We want that there should be one electoral roll for both the Hindus and Muslims. This will accelerate the growth of a nation, *i.e.* the growth of Pakistan.'[2]

The last-quoted speaker was at that time an independent member who had led a pro-United Front group of minority candidates in the Bengal election. But the leader of the Congress party was no less emphatic in his stand against separate electorates.

> 'In my dictionary there is no such word as "majority" or "minority." I do not consider myself as a member of the minority community or this or that community; I consider myself as one of the seven crores [70,000,000] of Pakistanis. I do not want any special rights. I do not want any privileges. I do not want reservation of seats in the Legislature. I say frame the same laws for me which affect everything equally.'[3]

It is not altogether easy to understand the insistence, in the face of these urgent pleas, of the Muslim majority. Undoubtedly the orthodox religious tradition that Muslims and non-Muslims may live at peace within a single state but can never be merged

---

[1] Constituent Assembly of Pakistan, *Debates*, Vol. XV, p. 367, October 23, 1953. [2] *Ibid.*, Vol. XVI, p. 267, August 11, 1954, D. N. Dutta.
[3] *Ibid.*, Vol. XVI, p. 292, August 24, 1954, Shri Sris Chandra Chattopadhyaya.

into one community has a bearing on the majority attitude. Islam enjoins toleration but frowns on fraternity.[1]

Of greater importance has been the transfer to independent Pakistan of pre-partition ideas and stock arguments. In undivided India the separate electorate was to the Muslim a safeguard against Hindu domination through the use of a 'brute majority' of votes. Muslim Leaguers had fought for forty years to achieve and defend this precious shield. They had done their best to extend similar protection to the Scheduled Castes and other minorities. Thus the belief that separate electorates are the best guarantee of the rights of minorities had become deeply ingrained in the minds of a generation of Muslim politicians. Consequently it seemed surprising to many Muslims that what they had desired so ardently should be rejected with equal fervour by the Hindus when the positions were reversed. They had held that the Congress attitude was part of a sinister design to establish Hindu hegemony. When the Pakistan National Congress declined to abandon this stand further Muslim suspicions were aroused. Perhaps, it was suggested, the present members of the central and provincial Assemblies did not truly represent their constituents and were opposing the majority for the sake of raising an outcry. Or, on an even more sinister plane, perhaps they were putting up a smoke screen behind which the Indian government could deprive the Muslim minority in India of its safeguards.

Such suspicions do not deserve to be taken seriously. The Hindu position is quite understandable, and has been repeatedly advanced. It is that while their political representatives are forced to be nothing but spokesmen for a minority interest they will lack effective political influence. As stated by Mr. D. N. Dutta: 'This party [Congress] is treated with contempt, and it deserves that because, Sir, we have not got the potentiality of being converted into a majority party unless there is one common electorate.'[2]

---

[1] Thus Surah V, 51 runs: 'O ye who believe! Take not the Jews and Christians for friends. They are friends one to another. He among you who taketh them for friends is (one) of them' (Pickthall).

[2] Constituent Assembly of Pakistan, *Debates*, Vol. XI, p. 74, April 15, 1952.

Pakistan

Under the separate electorate system a Hindu politician finds himself forced to address himself to an all-Hindu electorate. The major issues before the country may be economic or international, but it will be of little use for the Hindu to discuss policies in such areas, since the real battle for control of the government will be fought out by Muslims. A candidate is compelled to campaign on communal issues, since he has little to gain by appealing to interests which unite the communities or which cut across communal lines. And often the simplest way to unite his own community will be to attack the other. In this manner communal hostilities are likely to play a prominent and bitter part in every election, dividing the Muslim from the Hindu and the Scheduled Castes from both.

Supporters of the Muslim League may have concluded that there are certain advantages for their party in the system of separate electorates. Most Muslim politicians, especially before the 1954 election in East Bengal, felt that the League, having triumphed over its rivals in achieving Pakistan, would be assured of a long monopoly of office in the new state. The Hindus might be expected to be in opposition; separate electorates might serve to keep them isolated, and further, to divide the Caste Hindus from the Scheduled Castes. Moreover, any group of dissident Muslims could make common cause with the Hindu Opposition only at the risk of being branded as traitors to the *millat*.

Since the Hindu community was located mainly in Bengal it was in the interest of those who opposed Bengali influence to keep apart the members of the two communities so that they should not make common cause on matters affecting the east–west struggle.

> 'Since constitution-making has acquired a serious tempo, the leaders from that province (Muslim Leaguers as well as others) have advanced the claims of majority. They do not seem to attach any weight to the fact that the Bengal majority is made up of the Hindu element, whose influence should not be permitted to jeopardize the Islamic basis of Pakistan. If this claim were accepted, it would be tantamount to a recognition of a combined Hindu–Muslim domination over the rest.'[1]

[1] *The Times of Karachi*, August 25, 1954, editorial.

The Minorities

According to this line of argument the Bengal majority is not genuine since it requires Hindu participation.

The Muslim League itself would find it difficult to open its ranks to non-Muslims since both its history and its programme mark it as the organ of the Muslim nation.[1] And yet, with joint electorates any political party would have to appeal to Hindus as well as Muslims. In East Bengal, with separate electorates, non-Muslims would have less than one-quarter of the total seats; with a joint electorate the votes of the minorities might determine the outcome in a far higher proportion of seats, even though the number of members returned from the minority communities might be smaller. It is probable that a large majority of Hindu votes would be cast in favour of candidates promising increased autonomy for East Bengal and closer economic and political ties with West Bengal. And for historical reasons as well as these aspects of policy, the effect of the change to a joint electorate would be the worsening of the prospects of the Muslim League.[2]

Within the province of East Bengal, general Muslim opinion does not appear to be strongly opposed to the establishment of common electoral rolls. As long as the constitution ordains separate rolls the emergence of an effective joint political party is unlikely. But in 1954 candidates were entered under the designation 'Minorities United Front,'[3] and ten of these were

[1] The refusal of the League to accept non-Muslim members combined with the view of many of its supporters that Pakistan and the League are equivalent terms, made it very hard for a Hindu to produce a satisfactory gesture of political loyalty. A Hindu party in support of the Muslim League is a contradiction in terms, and any Hindu group was therefore compelled to be if not in opposition, at least separate from, the ruling party. Professor Raj Kumar Chakraverty moved a resolution in the Constituent Assembly regretting the continued existence of communal parties and suggesting that the League might be re-formed on a wider basis as the Pakistan League. The motion was withdrawn without a division. (Constituent Assembly (Legislature), *Debates*, 1949, Vol. I, pp. 109 ff., February 22, 1949.)

[2] It may be asked whether, after the results of the 1954 election, the League's prospects in East Bengal could possibly become worse. The policy on separate electorates, however, is of long standing and the League has not yet faced up to the revision of its policy and its organization that is necessary if it is to regain any influence in that province.   [3] *Dawn*, April 5, 1954.

Pakistan

successful. In addition the Ganatantri Dal had been formed on the basis of joint membership and candidates under its banner contested both Muslim and non-Muslim seats. Immediately after the election the provincial Awami League took steps to open its ranks to non-Muslims and affirmed its support for the principle of joint electorates. This action was confirmed by the Council of the provincial Awami League by an overwhelming majority.[1]

The Hindus have deeply resented the Muslim efforts to keep them politically apart. But they feel even more strongly about what they regard as the attempt to split their community in two. The Scheduled Castes (otherwise low caste, out-caste or depressed classes) represent a major social problem within Hinduism. The Government of India Act gave them special protection by reserving for members of their community a number of seats in the legislatures. This was not the same as the creation of a separate electorate since members of the Scheduled Castes voted separately at a primary election to choose not more than four candidates; at the final election all 'General' voters were permitted to participate.[2]

The Muslim League, even in pre-partition days, had maintained that the Congress truly represented only the Caste Hindus. In tactical moves to weaken and discredit the Congress, the League, while preserving its own exclusively communal basis, made gestures of friendship and protection toward the Scheduled Castes. Thus, as a counter to Congress insistence on naming a nationalist Muslim to a seat in the 1946 interim government, the League included a Scheduled Caste Hindu as one of its five nominees.[3] This policy was continued after partition, and the same member of the Scheduled Castes was chosen as the first person to preside over the Constituent Assembly. Mr. J. N. Mandal then became a member of the central cabinet as Minister for Law and Labour. Unfortunately for the government, after three years of office, Mr. Mandal removed himself to Calcutta

[1] *Dawn*, October 23, 1955. The vote was 600 to 5.
[2] *Government of India Act*, 1935, Fifth Schedule, SS. 4, 6.
[3] E. W. R. Lumby, *The Transfer of Power in India* (London, 1954), p. 119.

The Minorities

without bothering to resign either as a minister or as an MCA.[1] The Muslim League government of East Bengal also for some time contained a member of the Scheduled Castes. After the restoration of the United Front ministry in 1955 and the re-organization of the central government, members of the minorities were included in both cabinets.

In the electoral arrangements for East Bengal under the electoral law of 1952 (and in the Basic Principles Committee Report), it was laid down that the Scheduled Castes should be treated as a separate community, with its own seats and its own lists of voters. Since the Scheduled Castes comprise about 55 per cent of the Hindu community, this has the effect of splitting the principal minority in two. This division serves to focus attention upon the inferior position of the Scheduled Castes *vis-à-vis* the caste Hindus and to render less likely the concentration of attention upon issues which unite both sections of Hindus against the Muslim majority. Further, it prevents the Scheduled Castes from looking for leadership to members of the better educated and politically more vigorous group of caste Hindus.

The official explanation for the establishment of a separate electorate for the Scheduled Castes is that it will enable the less-privileged to attain full political and social maturity which has been denied them during two thousand years of caste oppression. It was also contended that such a safeguard was desired by the people of the Scheduled Castes themselves. There is some evidence in support of this latter argument.[2] Of the four private Scheduled Caste MCA's in the first Assembly, two were described as Muslim League Associates and functioned for most purposes as members of the government party.[3] Thus at one stage the

[1] Mandal's defection was the subject of a statement by the Prime Minister and a discussion in the Assembly (Constituent Assembly (Legislature), *Debates*, 1950, Vol. II, pp. 652 ff., October 14, 1950).

[2] Thus the Secretary of the All-Pakistan Scheduled Castes Federation was reported to have made a strong attack on joint electorates in November 1955. He described separate electorates as 'the corner-stone of the country' (*Dawn*, November 9, 1955).

[3] They were Akshay Kumar Das and Dhananjoy Roy, while Birat Chandra Mandal and Prem Hari Barma were members of the Congress.

government could claim the support of three out of five Scheduled Caste members. The defection of Mr. Mandal has, however, already been related. It would seem also that the remaining two supporters of the government were not anxious to be recorded as being in favour of the separate electorate.[1] Scheduled Caste support for the Muslim League in East Bengal rested on an equally doubtful basis. It was alleged that certain Scheduled Caste politicians, including Mr. D. N. Barori (who became a provincial minister), had changed their views on receipt of government jobs.[2]

The main political organ of the Scheduled Castes is the East Bengal Scheduled Castes Federation. In 1949 the Working Committee of this party passed a unanimous resolution demanding a joint electorate but with reservation of seats for the Scheduled Castes.[3] Three years later the East Bengal Minorities Conference (of whose five hundred delegates three hundred came from the Scheduled Castes), passed the following resolution: 'Separate representation on communal basis is anti-nation and antithesis of democracy which is the essence of freedom.'[4] The Conference, however, recommended that seats should be reserved for the Scheduled Castes for a period of ten years. The issue of separate electorates was, of course, discussed during the election of 1954. In the result, not one of D. N. Barori's group favouring separate electorates was returned,[5] and the Scheduled Castes Federation gained twenty-seven out of a possible thirty-eight seats.[6]

For nine years the discussion of the question of joint or separate electorates dragged on in that curious and unhappy manner that has characterized so much constitutional debate in Pakistan. It

[1] When the Congress group walked out of the Constituent Assembly as a protest against the discriminatory character of the new constitution, Messrs. Das and Roy followed them out of the Chamber (*Debates*, Vol. XV, p. 658, November 2, 1953, and *Dawn*, November 3, 1953).

[2] Constituent Assembly of Pakistan, *Debates*, Vol. XV, p. 169, October 14, 1953.

[3] Sarat C. V. Narasimham, *op. cit.*, p. 72.   [4] Quoted *ibid.*, p. 74.

[5] Constituent Assembly of Pakistan, *Debates*, Vol. XVI, p. 540, September 21, 1954. The statement is made by Mr. D. N. Dutta.

[6] *Dawn*, April 5, 1954.

The Minorities

has seemed to be the deliberate policy of many groups and individuals to refuse to stand up and be counted. The way seemed always to be left open for a change of policy if the political situation of the day required it. The arguments used on the electorate issue were unconvincing; only the caste Hindus took one position and stuck to it. Some Muslim Leaguers said they favoured separate electorates because the minorities wanted them; others that joint electorates would mark a betrayal of the ideology of Pakistan. The Awami League declared in favour of joint electorates though several prominent members left the organization on that score. The United Front contained a section that was pledged to joint electorates and a section that was pledged to resist them to the last. The Republican Party was nominally open to non-Muslims, and was led by a man who had formerly believed that all the inhabitants of the sub-continent of India could be members of one nation. Yet the bulk of the party's members were just out of the Muslim League and retained their former beliefs.

It is not surprising that the second Constituent Assembly decided to defer a decision on the issue. During the debate several representatives of the minorities asked for joint electorates either with or without reservation of seats. Besides the Hindu members of the Congress they included two ministers (A. K. Das (Scheduled Caste) and K. K. Dutta), and a Christian (Peter Paul Gomez). However, the constitution provides that, 'after ascertaining the views of the Provincial Assemblies and taking them into consideration,' Parliament may pass an Act to determine whether joint or separate electorates shall be adopted. This transferred the matter to the provincial arena. The discussion in the provincial Assemblies was no more satisfactory than it had been in the Constituent Assembly.

The West Pakistan Assembly was the first to deal with the issue. The Assembly had ten non-Muslim seats, but unlike those of East Pakistan, they were not further divided into Scheduled Caste, Christian and caste Hindu. These seats had been filled by the votes of the members of the former provincial Assemblies voting by districts. Thus the minority representatives had been picked by

Pakistan

the predominantly Muslim members of those legislatures. It is therefore not certain that they formed a fair reflection of the opinion of the minority communities. It was stated by one of them that all ten were in favour of the system of joint electorates but with reservation of seats for non-Muslims.[1] This statement, however, does not appear to have been confirmed by subsequent events.

The proceedings in the Assembly were opened by the Law Minister, who moved a resolution in favour of separate electorates. The Chief Minister, who was known privately to favour joint electorates, then moved an amendment. This was to the effect that separate electorates should be adopted 'in view of the demand of the minorities in West Pakistan to have separate electorates.'[2] This drew a bitter attack from a Muslim League member who said that to support separate electorates on the grounds that this was what the minorities wanted was to demolish the two-nation theory.[3] This line of argument, which the Hindus not unnaturally find intolerable, insists that the minorities must be isolated in order to prove that the Muslims are truly a separate nation. The Hindus had always opposed the system, and after they had addressed a memorandum to the Chief Minister, he agreed to withdraw his amendment.[4] A Christian spokesman then strongly supported separate electorates, saying that 'Christians living in Pakistan had identified themselves with their Muslim compatriots to the fullest extent. Whatever suits the Muslims in Pakistan suits the Christians as well, and they will co-operate with the Muslims in every respect.'[5] The only speakers against the motion were one Hindu, one independent member and the leaders of the Sind Awami Mahaz (G. M. Syed and Pir Ilahi Bakhsh). After four days' debate the matter was put to the vote, and the resolution in favour of separate electorates was

[1] Letter from Madhavji Dharsibhai in *Civil and Military Gazette*, June 5, 1956.   [2] *Dawn*, August 2, 1956.
[3] *Ibid*. The speaker was Mian Manzoor-i-Hassan.
[4] *Ibid*., August 3, 1956.
[5] *Ibid*., August 4, 1956. The speaker was Joshua Fazal Din; the quotation is indirect.

carried by 129 to 10. Two minority members, Hindus, were on the losing side. The Republicans and Muslim Leaguers voted in favour or abstained. Since the total membership of the Assembly was 310, a large proportion of the MCA's either abstained or thought it prudent not to attend the session. Shortly after this vote the Assembly adjourned without proceeding with a substantial programme of official business.[1]

The Republican ministry could not have secured a majority if it had not adopted separate electorates. However, at the end of September the Republican Party held a convention to adopt a constitution and approve a manifesto. The party's stand remained obscure, though Dr. Khan Sahib, in a later speech, tried to clarify it. He is reported to have said 'that he had personally all along been in favour of joint electorate since he considered it to be the *sine qua non* for the national solidarity which should be the prime consideration of each and every patriot.' Further, the Republicans believed in the one-nation theory, and their manifesto 'clearly lays down that territorial nationalism in a Muslim State supplements and does not negate the concept of Millat.' Khan Sahib 'advised his Party men to tell the people that electorate had nothing to do with religion.'[2] These statements raised the interesting question of the difference between them and the policy adopted in the Provincial and National Assemblies. When the discrepancy was pointed out to Dr. Khan Sahib, he produced a remarkable argument. 'Replying to a question he said the policy and the manifesto of a political party had an unquestionable supremacy over the decision taken in a legislature.' But he left room for manœuvre, since 'he reiterated his earlier statements that he would always respect the public opinion even if it meant acceptance of separate electorates.'[3]

At the beginning of October the East Pakistan Assembly turned its attention to the electorate issue. The debate, which lasted for eight hours, produced what were called 'uproarious scenes.'[4] A motion for separate electorates was put to the vote and declared

[1] *Dawn*, August 7, 1956.
[2] *Ibid.*, October 31, 1956. All the quotations are of indirect speech.
[3] *Ibid.*
[4] *Ibid.*, October 3, 1956.

Pakistan

lost. The Chief Minister's motion for joint electorate was then carried on division by a vote of 159 to 1. The Opposition, showing the customary reluctance to be recorded on the losing side, declined to vote, though some eighty-four members were observed remaining in their places.[1]

The Speaker permitted no amendments to be moved, and this resulted in protests and a walk-out by certain Scheduled Caste members led by A. K. Das (a former central Minister of State, who had recently joined the Republican Party).[2] These Scheduled Caste members had wished to press their demand for joint electorate with reservation of seats for their community for a limited period.

One week later, meeting for the first time in Dacca, the National Assembly considered the Electorate Bill. The atmosphere of hectic uncertainty that has accompanied most major controversies in Pakistan was marked on this occasion. On the first day of the session the Republican leaders were summoned to a conference at the residence of the President. Later in the day the Coalition Party was told that it had been decided not to adopt a joint electorate for the whole country, but to allow each province to be accorded the system of its choice.[3] The Bill was printed and distributed on the same night and presented to the Assembly on the following day. After two days of heated debate, the Bill was passed by a final vote of 48 to 19.[4]

The Prime Minister, H. S. Suhrawardy, introduced the Bill and also closed the debate. He said:

'The two-nation theory was advanced by the Muslims as justification for the partition of India and the creation of a state made up of

[1] *Dawn*, October 2, 1956. [2] *Ibid*.
[3] *Ibid*., October 10, 1956. When passed, the *Electorate Act*, 1956 (XXXVI/1956) provided in four short clauses that for national and provincial elections, East Pakistan should have a joint electorate and West Pakistan separate electorates. The *Electorate (Amendment) Act*, 1957, established joint electorates for both East and West Pakistan. (*Dawn*, April 25, 1957.) The key vote was 36 : 14.
[4] *Ibid*., October 12, 1956. On two amendments the Opposition registered as many as 21 votes.

geographically contiguous units where the Muslims were numerically in a majority.

'Once that state was created the two-nation theory lost its force even for the Muslims. . . .

'There is, then, a radical difference between the conception of the Millat-i-Islam which transcends geographical boundaries, and the conception of a Pakistani nation or "Quom" . . . which has boundaries and has a peculiar entity which differentiates it from other nations.'[1]

The remainder of the debate was confused. A member of the United Front said that his party was for separate electorates but that he could not agree.[2] A Republican announced that he had resigned from his party rather than accept a joint electorate.[3] Mr. C. E. Gibbon affirmed that the Christians had always wanted separate electorates.

The note of fear and suspicion of the Hindus was to be found in many speeches advocating separate electorates. Mr. I. I. Chundrigar, the leader of the Muslim League, stated that there were three reasons for the Hindu rejection of separate electorates.

'First reason was historical. In undivided India they had pressed for joint electorate and now in Bharati Constitution the Muslims demand for separate electorate had been denied. The Hindus here, therefore, felt embarrassed in asking for separate electorates.

'The second reason, he said, was that joint electorate would provide them with the ground to divide one section of Muslims against the other. Both the sections would have to depend on their support.

'Third reason was that it might ultimately create disruption and ill-will.'[4]

Such a speech makes it evident that, more than nine years after partition, the old prejudice remains: Hindus are to be regarded as disloyal to Pakistan. The Prime Minister was not prepared to accept this implication. 'You tell me today what signs have they

[1] *Dawn*, October 11, 1956. [2] *Ibid.*, October 12, 1956, Lutfur Rahman.
[3] *Ibid.*, Sayed Ahmad Nawaz Shah Gardezi.
[4] *Ibid.*, October 13, 1956 (indirect quotation).

shown of loyalty to Pakistan? My answer is clear. What have you done for them to get their loyalty? In what way have you shown them that you treat them in the same manner in which you have treated the Muslims?'[1]

All the minority groups in Pakistan had a more general ground for uneasiness arising from the decision to bring into being an Islamic state. The Hindus had listened hopefully to the words of Mr. Jinnah and they found no cause for alarm in the Interim Report of the Basic Principles Committee. But later developments of the proposed constitution showed the addition of more and more Islamic provisions. It seemed that the very proclamation of an Islamic Republic would place them in a position of permanent inferiority. Hindus opposition to all references to the official status of Islam was continuous. It began with the discussion of the Objectives Resolution, when eighteen amendments were moved by Hindu members seeking to establish the secular and neutral position of the state.[2] On any issue that united Muslim against Hindu there could be no doubt of the outcome, and all protests were brushed aside. In November 1953 the Congress Party reached the conclusion that it was accomplishing no useful purpose by continuing to be present in the Constituent Assembly while the constitution was under discussion, since effective decisions were being taken elsewhere and the views of the Hindus were, in any event, certain to be disregarded. Mr. Chattopadhyaya, the leader of the Congress, made a statement on behalf of his party. He complained that League party decisions were being brought hastily before the Assembly without due warning, and were then voted through without adequate discussion. He cited seven causes of Hindu dissatisfaction. First, the two-nation theory divided Pakistan perpetually into superior and inferior communities. Second, the clause in the proposed constitution relating to the invalidation of laws repugnant to the Quran and the Sunnah would not spare even the personal laws of non-Muslims. Third, the doctrines of Islam were to be officially taught by agencies of the state. Fourth, the name of the country was to

[1] *Dawn*, October 13, 1956.
[2] Constituent Assembly of Pakistan, *Debates*, Vol. V, March 12, 1949.

be an Islamic Republic. Fifth, the office of Head of State was not to be open to a non-Muslim. Sixth, the minorities were to be isolated by means of separate electorates. Seventh, the method of arriving at decisions in the House was 'undemocratic and definitely prejudicial to the interests of the minority.'[1] At the conclusion of this speech the members of the Congress Party left the Chamber followed by Akshay Kumar Das and Sri Dhananjoy Roy. With one or two exceptions they did not return to the Assembly for discussions on the Basic Principles Report until the final debate on the adoption of the report as a whole.

The first speaker from the Opposition in that debate was Professor Raj Kumar Chakraverty.

> 'Mr. President, Sir, in November last, the members of the Congress Assembly Party walked out from this House in protest against the very unfair and undemocratic Constitution that was being foisted upon us by the brute majority of the members of this House. . . .
>
> 'We have come here today at this final stage of the adoption of the B.P.C. Report, not because we have withdrawn our objections to this undemocratic Constitution, but because we want to lodge our protest all the more strongly and emphatically and we say that we are no party to this Constitution; we know we have not been able to change a comma or semi-colon, nor shall we [be] able to change a second comma or semi-colon in this Constitution that the majority party will foist upon this country. But we shall have this satisfaction on this day when the fate of Pakistan and that of the people is being decided that we record our protest.'[2]

The last vote to be taken in the First Constituent Assembly was on the motion: 'That the Report of the Basic Principles Committee, as amended, be adopted.' Twenty-nine members, all Muslims, voted in favour; eleven members, all Hindus (but including the four Scheduled Caste members), voted against.[3]

These were the speeches and grievances of a political opposi-

---

[1] Constituent Assembly of Pakistan, *Debates*, Vol. XV, p. 658, November 2, 1953.   [2] *Ibid.*, Vol. XVI, pp. 504, 505, September 21, 1954.
[3] *Ibid.*, p. 571.

tion. The Hindus knew that, owing to their status as a permanent minority, they could not hope to win their case by the democratic means of manœuvring for the support of wide sections of the electorate. Their language was perhaps more vivid and their cries more piteous in that they were appealing to the conscience of the majority within Pakistan and trying to attract the attention of opinion beyond the boundaries of their own country.

The majority was aware of the real need to assure substantial rights to the minorities, both as individual citizens and as groups. Accordingly, one of the first actions of the Constituent Assembly was to establish a Committee on Fundamental Rights of Citizens and on Matters Relating to Minorities.[1] Many of the proposals of this committee, which after discussion and some amendment were accepted by the Assembly, related to the rights of the individual, applicable equally to members of majority and minority communities. The provisions of the 1956 constitution incorporated many of the approved recommendations of the earlier drafts.

Some of the safeguards for the minorities were embodied in the Directive Principles of State Policy. This chapter of the constitution is intended to stand as a declaration of general intention, and its provisions are not enforceable in the courts. But these directive principles make it clear that Islam is to be the official religion of the state, which is charged with a positive duty to uphold and propagate its teachings. Other religions are to be permitted to continue without interference. Thus it is declared that 'Steps shall be taken to enable the Muslims of Pakistan individually and collectively to order their lives in accordance with the Holy Quran and Sunnah.' On the other hand, 'The State shall safeguard the legitimate rights and interests of the minorities, including their due representation in the Federal and Provincial Services.'

The constitution recognizes a special obligation toward the less privileged groups in the country. Article 205 provides: 'The

[1] This committee was set up before partition, on the motion of Liaquat Ali Khan, and included Mr. Jinnah as a member (Constituent Assembly of Pakistan, *Debates*, Vol. I, p. 35, August 12, 1947).

The Minorities

Federal and Provincial Governments shall promote, with special care, the educational and economic interests of the Scheduled Castes and backward classes in Pakistan, and shall protect them from social injustice and exploitation.' Machinery is to be established by the President to ensure that this clause is given effect. With the full consent of the Hindu members, Article 21 was included as a fundamental right: 'Untouchability is abolished, and its practice in any form is forbidden and shall be declared by law to be an offence.'

In addition to these constitutional guarantees there have been Ministers for Minority Affairs in the Central and East Bengal cabinets. These appointments were made as a result of the agreement reached between the Prime Ministers of India and Pakistan in April 1950. The Fundamental Rights Committee Report included a recommendation that such ministers should be provided for in the constitution. However, this provision did not find a place in the final constitution. The central ministership of Minority Affairs was normally held in conjunction with other portfolios, and no special funds were appropriated for that function.

There is in the constitution, as a Fundamental Right, an article that offers protection to cultural minorities. 'Any section of citizens having a distinct language, script or culture shall have the right to preserve the same.' This appears to be more a declaration of principle than an enforceable provision.

The most significant guarantees of rights of religious minorities are provided as Fundamental Rights, and are therefore capable of being enforced by the courts.

Article 18 reads:

'Subject to law, public order and morality—
(a) every citizen has the right to profess, practise and propagate any religion; and
(b) every religious denomination and every sect thereof has the right to establish, maintain and manage its religious institutions.'

As a protection of the religious practices of the minorities this provision seems almost meaningless. To give a guarantee to a

Pakistan

minority 'subject to law, public order and morality' means that the majority may do what it pleases if it is prepared to write its prejudices into law. The history of the American Bill of Rights has shown that it is precisely against law, that religious rights of unpopular minorities need protection.

Other sections of the Fundamental Rights serve to protect the educational status of the minorities. No state-owned or aided school shall deny admission to any person solely on the ground of race, religion, caste or place of birth. No one shall be compelled to take part in any religious instruction or ceremony of a religion other than his own. Every religious community may establish schools for members of its own faith. Further, there shall be no discrimination in granting tax exemption to any religious institution. Finally, no person shall be compelled to pay any tax for the propagation or maintenance of any religion other than his own.

The provisions of the new constitution indicate the prevailing attitude toward minorities in Pakistan. Such provisions are intended to form a general framework within which public policy will operate. The contemporary well-being of the minorities has depended upon the laws in force from 1947 to the present, and upon the willingness of the administration and the people at large to deal fairly and generously with their non-Muslim compatriots. The ill-will of a local police constable or of a clerk in a permit-issuing agency may be a greater instrument of oppression than any attitude of the provincial or central government. This, however, is an area in which sure conclusions are hard to reach. Many Hindus have grievances in Pakistan and many have endured hardship; but many Muslims have equal grievances and have suffered also. Can it be established that in the former case the hardships are directly related to membership of a different religion? The Hindu answer is usually 'Yes'; the official answer almost invariably 'No.' Before examining some of the evidence, it is perhaps worth advancing the hypothesis that, while the central and provincial governments have made sincere efforts to avoid inflicting injustice upon the minorities, certain policies have borne more heavily in operation upon the non-Muslims.

The Minorities

During the debate on the Objectives Resolution, the leader of the Opposition painted a grim picture of the plight of those he called 'my people.'

> 'The officers have opted out, the influential people have left, the economic conditions are appalling, starvation is widespread, women are going naked, people are sinking without trade, without occupation. The administration is ruthlessly reactionary, a steam-roller has been set in motion against the culture, language and script of the people.'[1]

Many of the complaints of the Hindus are concerned with the discriminatory administration of general laws and the extra-legal actions of local officials. The following are some of the grievances mentioned in a debate in the East Bengal Legislative Assembly: the seizure of weapons from Hindus, thus leaving them defenceless against robbery or riot; the exaction of large contributions to the *Quaid-i-Azam* Relief Fund; arbitrary arrest and detention of Hindus on security grounds; and the discriminatory requisitioning of Hindu property for public purposes.[2]

Many Hindus have complained that virtually no members of their community hold high administrative office either at the centre or in East Bengal, and that new appointments have not been given to Hindus. At first sight this grievance appears particularly serious in view of the large proportion of senior administrative appointments held by Hindus before partition, especially in Bengal. However, the official reply is convincing. It is that, at the time of partition, the Hindu civil servants as a body chose to serve India rather than Pakistan. Mr. Liaquat Ali Khan argued that this showed, not Pakistani hostility to the Hindus, but a desire on their part to weaken Pakistan.[3] As far as new appointments are concerned, vacancies in the Central Superior Services are open on equal terms to Muslims and non-

---

[1] Constituent Assembly of Pakistan, *Debates*, Vol. V, p. 94, March 12, 1949.
[2] East Bengal Legislative Assembly, *Official Report*, Vol. III, pp. 41 ff., March 23, 1949.
[3] Constituent Assembly of Pakistan, *Debates*, Vol. V, p. 97, March 12, 1949.

Pakistan

Muslims, and a special quota of posts is reserved for qualified members of the Scheduled Castes. But the Hindus do not enter the competition for these appointments.[1] East Bengal has gone farther than the centre in trying to attract non-Muslims into the public service; 23 per cent of vacancies in the provincial and subordinate services are reserved for qualified non-Muslims. The lack of success of this policy was discussed by the Chief Minister, who cited figures of candidates and appointments, and stated:

> 'So, Sir, the main difficulty is that the young men belonging to the minority communities have gone to West Bengal. They are prosecuting their studies in the Colleges and Universities there. They do not appear in examinations and whatever number appear, when offered appointments, decline to accept the offer.'[2]

One undoubted hardship borne by the Hindus has been the working of the evacuee property laws. When, in 1947-48, millions of people fled from one Dominion to the other, they were forced to leave behind most of their property that could not be carried. This applied especially to the land and buildings that had provided the livelihood and the shelter for a large proportion of the refugees. Relations between India and Pakistan being far from cordial, and free movement between them being quite impossible, the settlement of the claims arising out of that migration has proved long and difficult. Each government, arguing that it was simply retaliating against measures already taken by the other, took control of evacuee property and began to use it as the basis for resettlement and compensation for the refugees who had entered its territory.

A great deal of Hindu property is owned by the family rather than by the individual, and the legal determination of shares of individual ownership is a most complex process. Thus if a joint

[1] In 1953, 385 candidates appeared for the Central Superior Services Examination; 2 were Christians, 1 Hindu and 1 Scheduled Caste. Pakistan Public Service Commission, *Report on the Central Superior Services Examination* (1953), Part III.

[2] East Bengal Legislative Assembly, *Official Report*, Vol. X, March 17, 1953, Mr. Nurul Amin.

The Minorities

family has some members in East Bengal and others in Calcutta, it is not easy to decide whether the property in East Bengal falls into the category of 'evacuee property,' and hence becomes subject to government control. Naturally the family wishes to retain possession and the right to dispose of it at will. The government of Pakistan has been equally anxious to make sure that Indian-owned property is not converted into liquid form and smuggled out of the country. Government officials have therefore been tempted, once their suspicions were aroused, to take possession first and to argue the case afterwards. It is probable that some non-Muslims remained in Pakistan only with the intention of disposing of their assets and then removing themselves and the proceeds over the border. To prevent this the law established a category of the 'intending evacuee' whose property was taken under official supervision.

A very high proportion of the commercial and more wealthy families of Hindus in East Bengal had both relatives and financial connections before 1947 in areas which fell outside the boundaries of Pakistan. In view of the uncertainty and tension prevailing in the sub-continent, it was not surprising that many of them wished to safeguard some of their resources in institutions likely to continue under the control of their co-religionists. In any event, Calcutta was the major financial and commercial centre for undivided Bengal. And yet, after August 1947, it was regarded almost as a sign of disloyalty to have transferred money from Dacca to Calcutta in June or July of that year. On the other hand, it was of legitimate and vital concern to the new government of Pakistan to ensure that a sudden flight of capital did not further damage the already weak state of the economy. The result of this conflict has been that some Hindus have attempted to evade the government's controls, while those very controls have pressed harshly upon many innocent members of the minority community.

Another blow to the economic interests of the Hindus in East Bengal has been the programme of land reform carried out by the East Bengal government. Many of the large *zamindars* (landholders) were Hindus, and the application of this scheme has had the effect of diminishing the relative economic power of that community. The poorer Hindu cultivators, however, are as likely to benefit as their Muslim neighbours if the land reform is properly carried through.

More sinister, from the Hindu point of view, is the belief that pressure has been brought to bear on employers to reduce the proportion of non-Muslim workers. That there is some ground for this suspicion is confirmed by the following extract from the minutes of the Working Committee of the Provincial Muslim League of East Bengal:

'The Working Committee notes with resentment the policy of the Tea gardens, Commercial firms, in employing non-Muslims, by by-passing and neglecting the claims of Muslim applicants. . . . This Committee also requests the Government to issue necessary directions to the companies and firms.'[1]

It would be wrong to suggest that the minorities in Pakistan are living in a state of terror or active oppression. Apart from the outbreak of communal violence in East Bengal in 1950,[2] there has been little cause for physical fear since the dark days of 1947-48. But the minorities as a group have lacked political influence, and Pakistan is a country in which such influence is of great importance. They have felt their position to be at best the equivalent of the Muslim who is excluded from official favours, and at worst they have been regarded as actual or potential traitors. The majority insistence on the creation of an Islamic state has forced the non-Muslims to the view that the state is not neutral in matters of religion, and that when an issue arises involving a conflict between Islam and another religion, the state power will be used against the minority. Pakistan is to be an ideological state, and the minorities, by definition, do not accept that ideology.

The Christian and the Parsi are not suspect to the same degree

[1] *Minutes*, dated September 28, 1949.
[2] An official statement on the causes and nature of these riots is to be found in East Bengal Legislative Assembly, *Official Report*, Vol. IV, pp. 181 ff., March 10, 1950.

The Minorities

as the Hindu, since their political connection with India is less close. But the smaller minorities are not part of the Islamic *millat*. They are licensed infidels who may go their own way provided they do not seek to oppose or undermine the ideology that is the basis of Pakistan. In undivided India these groups had always been minorities and never hoped to be otherwise. Perhaps, if partition had not taken place, they would have been happier in a country that was more clearly multi-religious and openly committed to secularism in politics. Probably their commercial prospects would have been brighter in a larger and more diverse economy. But those who have remained have freely decided to live in Pakistan and their loyalty is not questioned.

The sole representative of the non-Hindu minorities in the first Constituent Assembly was Mr. P. D. Bhandara, a Parsi.[1] The Parsi community has usually avoided taking a stand in political affairs, but some of its members must have been surprised at the ardour of Mr. Bhandara's support for the Islamic state.

> '... it is my fervent prayer on behalf of the minorities that the future Constitution of Pakistan will be Islamic not only in name, but also in actual practice. For by a truly Islamic constitution, on the corroboration of History, the minorities have much to gain and little to lose.
>
> 'Our country is not adaptable to the Western democracy; nor have we the capacity or the means for the luxuries of a constitution of the Western pattern. What we need is an unadulterated, unmixed Islamic Constitution.'[2]

Other members of the Christian and Parsi communities may be less eager to embrace their minority status, but many would agree that their best hopes for the future lie in the security of unobtrusiveness, and acquiescence in the dominant ideology of the state.

The device of 'lying low' cannot be adopted so simply by the

[1] Mr. Bhandara was elected in 1952, replacing B. L. Rallia Ram, a Christian (*Gazette of Pakistan*, January 11, 1952).

[2] Constituent Assembly of Pakistan, *Debates*, Vol. XVI, p. 310, August 31, 1954.

largest of the minorities—the Hindus of East Bengal. Early in 1955 there were reports (mainly from India) that Hindus were leaving the province by the hundred thousand. The Indian Prime Minister suggested that the cause was perhaps deteriorating economic conditions in that area. The Pakistan explanation was that sources in West Bengal were offering cash grants to refugee cultivators, and that these were especially attractive to the poorer members of the Scheduled Castes.[1] It was not denied that migration on a substantial scale was taking place. However, for many years there has been considerable movement from the villages to the large towns. The largest city in Bengal has been, and still is, Calcutta. If employment opportunities exist, and wages and prices seem favourable, the peasant Hindu may be tempted to seek his living in the big city from purely economic motives, and no feeling of loyalty to Karachi is likely to deter him. Similarly, if he believes that he will get land or money by moving to West Bengal or Bihar, the existence of a recently drawn political boundary is not likely to stand in his way. In the spring of 1956 a conference of senior officials of the governments of East and West Bengal was held to try to diminish the rate of exodus.[2] The Indian government agreed to take action to avoid giving overt encouragement to Hindus who might be considering migration. But according to Press reports the movement continued.[3]

The outlook for the Hindu educated classes is, on the whole, more depressing than that for the cultivator. Formerly they dominated the professions of law and medicine, and substantially controlled much of the commerce of eastern Bengal, as well as occupying a large proportion of jobs under the government. Many of the doctors and lawyers and merchants remained after partition, though most of the civil servants departed. But the new generation is looking to India for its future. Calcutta offers a greater variety and a higher level of educational institution than

[1] *The Times of Karachi*, March 28, 1955.
[2] *Pakistan News* (London), May 19, 1956.
[3] *Dawn*, July 25, 1956, quoting a report from the Indian Ministry of Rehabilitation, says that the average monthly refugee migration from Pakistan rose from 10,000 in 1954 to 20,000 in 1955 and 33,000 in 1956.

is available in East Bengal. And the education offered is certain to be more congenial to the cultural and religious outlook of a Hindu. When it comes to making a career in Pakistan, there is the constant fear, not always justified but always present, that, either now or in the future, the interests of the Hindus will suffer on account of religious prejudice.

In general, the Hindu community in East Bengal is likely to diminish in size, in wealth and in talent. The speed and inconvenience of this process will be determined not so much by relations between Hindu and Muslim in East Bengal, but by wider factors. If Pakistan can achieve political stability and is able to find a means of living in friendship with India, then many of the fears of the Hindus will diminish. But if Indo-Pakistan relations continue tense, the Hindu minority will assuredly suffer.

CHAPTER VIII

The Citizen and the State

IN spite of the violence that accompanied the birth of Pakistan, the new state began its life with a glorious vision of the possibilities of the development of a Muslim homeland, free for the first time in centuries from the double domination of British and Hindus. The *Quaid-i-Azam's* message on the first anniversary of independence reflected this optimism. 'Nature has given you everything; you have got unlimited resources. The foundations of your State have been laid, and it is now for you to build, and build as quickly and as well as you can. So, go ahead and I wish you God Speed.'[1]

The belief was widespread that the creation of Pakistan would lead to an era of freedom, justice and prosperity. The political theory of the semi-educated in Muslim India had been centred largely on the concept of exploitation. India as a whole had been exploited by the British; expel the British and the drain on Indian wealth would cease and the Indian national income would show an immediate and substantial rise. Within India the Hindus had exploited the Muslims; create Pakistan and the flow of wealth would be diverted from Hindu to Muslim hands. When independence had been achieved but was not followed by a dramatic rise in living standards, it became necessary to find a new villain. This was easy for East Pakistan; West Pakistan had simply adopted the exploiter's role lately abandoned by the British and the Hindus. In West Pakistan the reaction was more complex, and led to a feeling of general frustration as well as specific complaints against corrupt and inefficient leaders, landlords, civil servants, and the continuing machinations of Indian and Western imperialism.

[1] *Quaid-i-Azam Speaks* (Karachi, n.d.), p. 250.

Unfortunately it was obvious that living standards had not risen in the first nine years of independence. A senior official of the central government reached the following conclusions: 'It is ... probable that the per capita income after 1954–55 would be less than what it was about seven years ago. Inequalities in income have increased. A smaller national income, relatively to the size of the population, more unequally distributed than before, implies that the living standards of the masses of the people which were already very low, have deteriorated still further.'[1] At the bottom of the scale come the property-less refugees who have somehow survived as beggars and casual labourers in and around the larger cities of West Pakistan for a period of ten years. The cultivators of East Pakistan and the landless tenants of the west are little more prosperous. Both wings of Pakistan have suffered from a series of natural calamities, floods being the most serious, which have in turn led to food shortages. An atmosphere of permanent crisis in both the urban and rural economy has been broken only by the commodity price boom of the Korean war and the bumper food crops of 1953–54.

These serious domestic weaknesses have bred disillusion among all levels of the public. The situation has not been improved by the relative lack of success of the nation's foreign policy. Pakistan has not won Kashmir, and has not been able to persuade the rest of the world that pressure should be brought to bear upon India to produce a satisfactory solution. It is probable that no action by the government of Pakistan could have brought the desired result, but the prestige of the country has undoubtedly suffered from the failure to achieve its foremost objective.

To these and other causes of dissatisfaction the normal reaction has been to blame Government. Government in Pakistan has been regarded as a vague, monolithic and omnicompetent organ, which can give or withhold at will. This is, in many ways, the legacy of British rule. Paternalism was the keynote of the administration. Instruments of self-government were liable to turn into

[1] M. L. Qureshi (Chief Economist, Planning Board, Government of Pakistan), *Address delivered at the Conference of the Pakistan Economic Association*, Peshawar, 1955, p. 11.

instruments of sedition and, consequently, they needed supervision and control. The major political struggle of the generation before 1947 was for independence; and that struggle required the subordination of local issues to the national effort. The District Officer was the man who had real power at the local level, and he was the representative at first of the British *raj* and then of the central or provincial government. Democracy elsewhere has often originated in the efforts of local authorities to resist pressure from above. No local authority in Pakistan has been able to stand up to its provincial or central superiors. Large numbers of local councils in West Pakistan have been in a state of suspension for periods of ten years or more. In East Pakistan the local Boards have had a much more successful record, but their powers have declined since partition in relation to those of the province.

It must be admitted that the record of some of the local bodies has not been such as to inspire confidence. In the period before 1947 they were used as agents for national political parties; since independence they have lent themselves to political intrigue designed to bolster or reduce the influence of some provincial politician. In West Pakistan the man-in-the-street has taken little interest in the doings of his local authority unless a particular action, or lack of it, affects his own welfare; certainly he has not learned to regard local elections as a means of asserting democratic control over an important agency of government. In East Pakistan the greater political maturity of the voter is substantially due to the working of a genuine if limited system of popularly-chosen local Boards.

To the ordinary man Government truly begins with the provincial administration and its local representative. It is at this level that the machinery of law and order, of taxation, of flood control and irrigation and of famine relief, begins to operate. While Government, the bureaucratic apparatus, functions impersonally, the character of the provincial ministry can make a real impression on the popular imagination. It is as though the machine and its operator could be distinguished. Government makes a decision that is unwelcome; it is still possible to appeal against that decision before the Commissioner or a minister. The machine is inhuman, but its working is tempered by the humanity of its directors. Provincial and central ministers frequently proceed on tour, hearing complaints against the administration of government and the conduct of its agents. These are accompanied by requests for redress of grievances that often have no direct connection with the government. A ministerial visit becomes a progress in state attended by local politicians, officials and petitioners.[1] This is a method which maintains some personal contact between Government and the governed in a paternal system. But it is not a substitute for a structure in which government at all levels is effectively controlled by the electorate.

There has been little reason for the voter in Pakistan to develop the feeling that he was master of the central or provincial government. The central government was somewhat dubiously responsible to the Constituent Assembly or the National Assembly. But, in more than nine years, there were no direct elections of those Assemblies. In the same period each province conducted one direct election. The nature of the elections in West Pakistan has already been described; in East Pakistan the election was followed by Governor's rule for one year and then by a period in which the Assembly was not permitted to transact business. The majority of voters have thus enjoyed one opportunity to

[1] Dr. Khan Sahib was in high popular regard in his capacity as a protector of the poor. As Chief Minister of West Pakistan he set aside two afternoons a week on which the public might present their petitions. If the matter seemed appropriate he would then take personal action. The following quotation reveals much about the working of Government in Pakistan.

'Dr. Khan Sahib, West Pakistan Chief Minister, is proceeding to Kamoke, Gujranwala District, on Sunday to look into the allegations against the Secretary of the local Municipal Committee, made by a Lady Health Visitor who was dismissed from service recently.

'The Lady Health Visitor called on Dr. Khan Sahib on Friday to narrate a lengthy story about the alleged irregularities being committed in the Municipal Committee by the Secretary.

'The Chief Minister has directed the Commissioner and the Deputy Commissioner to be present during his stay at Kamoke.

'Another inquiry to be made by the Chief Minister at Kamoke relates to an abduction case. The husband of the abducted wife complained to the Chief Minister that his wife was forcibly taken away from him and was being kept by certain persons against her wishes' (*Pakistan Times*, June 30, 1956).

Pakistan

cast a vote, and that experience has not given them a sense of popular sovereignty.

The working of the political system has not served as a means of civic education for the public. The discussion of issues has usually been subordinated to the struggle for office and prestige. Political parties have been organized from the top downward, and their local organizations have tended to come to life only when the party leaders had to arrange a demonstration of support or protest. The programmes of the parties have meant nothing to the ordinary man. The single, clear and intelligible issue presented by the parties has been that of autonomy for East Bengal. The fight for Pakistan before 1947 was so much more simple and dramatic than anything that has been a source of political debate since independence.

However, the ordinary man is aware of his country's independence and he takes pride in it. It is a source of satisfaction to hear the name 'Pakistan,' and to have an Air Force and a Navy and an Army. A sovereign independent republic can claim equality with all other nations in the eyes of the world. The foreign rulers have gone; Muslim Pakistanis sit in positions of power, authority and prestige. Every Pakistani is a nationalist at heart, and there are few who regret the passing of the old order.

The fulfilment of nationalist ambition has not been accompanied by a general increase in material prosperity. Neither has it witnessed 'a new birth of freedom under law.' A major criticism of British rule in India was that it was incapable of providing a satisfactory means of political self-expression for Indians. At a certain stage the decision had to be taken to make the ultimate concession, to transfer power, or to apply repressive measures. In view of the latter need, the state was armed with a wide range of powers to curtail the scope of political activity. If law and order were to be maintained and the minimum processes of government to continue, some such powers were essential. But their use was bound to be resented.

With independence it was hoped that the need for Pakistanis to have arbitrary powers over the political activities of their fellow citizens might have disappeared or, at least, diminished.

The Citizen and the State

In fact the first nine years have been marked by continuing political crisis. Consequently the use of drastic powers has been frequent and extensive.

There is always the danger that political agitation may develop into civil commotion and riot. Any government must be armed with powers to take action if this should happen. The main instrument for this purpose in Pakistan has been Section 144 of the Code of Criminal Procedure. This provides that a magistrate, in order to prevent a riot, may issue an order directing any person to refrain from specified acts, such, for example, as making a political speech. An order under Section 144 may forbid the holding of public meetings or processions in a specified area. Such an order may remain in force for two months, but the provincial government may extend its period of operation. The magistrates are civil servants and, in their law and order duties, they fall under the direction of the Home Departments of the provincial governments. It has been possible for a magistrate to prevent the holding of public meetings for months at a time. One MCA complained that the Punjab had been free of Section 144 for only nine months in two and a half years.[1] It has also been possible to reach the decision that the speech of an Opposition leader is more likely to lead to a riot than that of a minister.

Other sections of the criminal law restrict what may be said or written in the course of political debate. Thus a person who 'brings or attempts to bring into hatred or contempt, or excites or attempts to excite, disaffection towards the Government established by law in the provinces . . .' commits an offence punishable by a maximum sentence of transportation for life.[2] Another offence bears the heading: 'Condemnation of the creation of the State, and advocacy of abolition of its sovereignty.'[3] This is punishable by not more than ten years' rigorous imprisonment.

[1] Constituent Assembly of Pakistan, *Debates*, Vol. I, p. 629, September 9, 1955, Mian Iftikharuddin.
[2] *Pakistan Penal Code*, S.124A. Charges under this section were brought against Khan Abdul Ghaffar Khan in connection with his opposition to the amalgamation of the provinces of West Pakistan (*Pakistan Times*, June 18, 1956).
[3] *Ibid.*, S.123A.

Pakistan

In an illiterate society the public meeting is an important means of arousing political interest. But the newspaper also plays a significant role since its contents are passed on orally to those who cannot read. The press in Pakistan has often been wildly irresponsible. There are many newspapers whose standards of accuracy and fairness would be accepted in any country, but there are others which do not hesitate to resort to libel and incitement to violence. These are apt to be small, vernacular papers with a very restricted investment in property or corporate reputation. They arise overnight and disappear as readily. The main structure of press laws was enacted under British rule to deal with incitements to violence and the deliberate disregard of law.[1] The law provides that newspaper publishers and keepers of printing presses may be required to give security deposits which are liable to forfeiture without a judicial trial. It is forbidden to sell, distribute or publish unauthorized newspapers. It is also an offence to 'encourage or incite any person to interfere with the administration of the law or with the maintenance of law and order.' Under the Security of Pakistan Act[2] the government may ban a paper for a considerable period or order pre-censorship to be imposed. A maximum penalty of three years' imprisonment may be awarded for breaches of this statute. The Press laws constitute a perpetual reminder to publishers and editors to exercise caution in their professions. The provisions of these Acts have been brought to bear upon newspapers found by the government to be unruly. In 1949, in the federal capital alone, the central government banned four papers for periods ranging from three months to one year and ordered pre-censorship over three papers for periods up to three months. The minister concerned explained: 'Action was taken because the papers in question were indulging in writings prejudicial to the interests and stability of the State. In all cases the Press Consultative Committee, consisting of the representatives of the Press, was consulted and its advice followed.'[3]

[1] The principal law is *The Indian Press (Emergency Powers) Act*, 1931, as amended.   [2] Act XXXV/1952.
[3] Constituent Assembly (Legislature), *Debates*, 1950, Vol. I, p. 671, April 6, 1950.

The Citizen and the State

The most serious concern for the preservation of civil liberty in Pakistan arises from the laws governing preventive detention. Such laws have a long history in the sub-continent.[1] The Bengal State Prisoners Regulation (Regulation III of 1818) is still in force throughout Pakistan. It provides for detention for 'reasons of state' connected with foreign affairs, the tranquillity of princely states and the protection of British territory from internal commotion. Circumstances, says the preamble to the original Regulation, '. . . occasionally render it necessary to place under personal restraint individuals against whom there may not be sufficient ground to institute any judicial proceeding, or when such proceeding may not be adapted to the nature of the case, or may for other reasons be unadvisable or improper.' Detention was to be ordered only by the Governor-General in Council and was to be reviewed every six months. Khan Abdul Ghaffar Khan, in whose interest many of the less usual aspects of the laws of repression have been explored, served a period of detention under this Regulation.

Under the Government of India Act, until 1952, the federal legislative power in Pakistan extended to making provision for preventive detention 'for reasons of State connected with defence or external affairs,' while the provincial power could apply 'for reasons connected with the maintenance of public order.' This position was changed in 1952, and the power to legislate in connection with the maintenance of public order or the maintenance of supplies and services essential to the community was added to the Concurrent List.[2] The constitution of 1956 reverted to the position as it was before 1952 except that the federal power may now be used 'for reasons connected with defence, foreign affairs, or the security of Pakistan.'

The federal legislature exercised its powers by passing the Security of Pakistan Act, 1952, which superseded two previous central ordinances issued under the authority of the Governor-

[1] For a general discussion of the law of preventive detention, see Mohammad Iqbal, *Law of Preventive Detention in England, India and Pakistan* (Lahore, 1955).
[2] *Government of India (Second Amendment) Act*, 1952.

Pakistan

General. The Act was to be valid for three years, but this was later extended.[1] The central government was given power to detain any individual 'with a view to preventing him from acting in any manner prejudicial to the defence or the security of Pakistan ... or ... the maintenance of public order....' Within one month the person detained was to be informed of the grounds for his detention, but the government was able to withhold 'facts which it considers to be against the public interest to disclose.' The *détenu* might then make a written representation against the order requiring his detention. Within three months from the issue of an order, the case had to be laid before an Advisory Board which consisted of two persons, qualified to be High Court Judges, appointed by the government. The Board was entitled to consider the evidence placed before it and to call for additional materials, but it was not permitted to hear oral evidence by the *détenu* or his counsel or witnesses on his behalf. On receipt of the report of the Advisory Board the government was to 'pass such order thereon as appears to the Central Government just and proper.' However, the government was to review all cases every six months.

Under the Security Act the government was also able to take action against a political party or other organization believed to be acting in a manner prejudicial to the security of Pakistan or the maintenance of public order. Powers under the criminal law are also available to ban an 'unlawful association.' Political parties which have been prohibited include the Communist Party and the Red Shirts.[2]

Powers of preventive detention in the interest of public order

---

[1] *Security of Pakistan (Amendment) Act*, 1956. This established April 30, 1957, as the termination for the Act's validity. A further extension for twelve months was made by Presidential Ordinance in 1957. (*Gazette of Pakistan*, Extraordinary, April 27, 1957.) It should be noted that many of the powers of the Security Act are extensions of the provisions of the wartime *Restriction and Detention Ordinance*, 1944 (III/1944).

[2] The Red Shirts are an organization which opposed the establishment of Pakistan and has since urged the creation of an autonomous state for the Pushto-speaking areas. The ban on this party was originally imposed under the North-West Frontier Public Safety Act, but in 1956 it was declared unlawful under the Criminal Law Amendment Act, 1908 (*Dawn*, July 8, 1956).

lay within the competence of the provincial authorities. Each of these produced its own public safety law.[1] In most cases these were promulgated by the provincial Governors either as ordinances or as Governors' Acts under Section 92A. They provided that provincial authorities, which often meant the District Magistrate or District Superintendent of Police, might arrest and detain any individual without warrant or conviction. In some of the safety laws a maximum period of detention was fixed, but in others there was no limit except a requirement for regular review of each case by the government. Some of the laws required reference of cases of prolonged detention to a judicial reviewing authority, although any findings made were not binding on the government; others made no provision for review.

Laws relating to sedition and subversion invariably use words that cannot be reconciled with the principles of unadulterated political liberty. Those governing 'incitement to disaffection' in England or 'conspiracy to advocate the forcible overthrow of the government' in the United States have been widely criticized for the inroads they made on the liberty of the citizen. But any state must be armed with power to defend itself against certain types of inimical political activity. The test of such powers must lie in the extent of their employment and the safeguards that surround their use.

The effect of a repressive law depends in part on the belief that the government has powers that it will not hesitate to use, should the occasion arise. Thus a threat may be as effective as an actual arrest, and will lead to less awkward questions in the press or the legislature. In practice there have been quite enough arrests to convince the most sceptical that the power of preventive detention is a reality. The central government, which does not have the primary responsibility for the preservation of law and order, has used its powers with restraint. In September 1950 it was reported that thirty-eight persons were detained;[2] by 1951 the total had fallen to sixteen.[3] In West Pakistan, from August

[1] Mohammed Iqbal lists twelve provincial safety laws issued from 1946-50, op. cit., p. 260.
[2] Constituent Assembly (Legislature), *Debates*, 1950, Vol. II, p. 20, September 30, 1950). [3] *Ibid.*, 1951, Vol. I, p. 403, March 26, 1951.

Pakistan

1947 to December 1955, the total number of persons arrested and detained under the laws of the various provinces was 909.[1] It is in East Pakistan that the laws of repression have been used most widely. The climax was reached when General Iskandar Mirza assumed power as Governor after the dismissal of the United Front ministry. An official announcement in October 1954 reported that, out of 1,466 persons arrested under the East Bengal Public Safety Ordinance, 957 had by that date been released. It was added that 'The persons arrested include not only subversive political workers but also other anti-social elements such as smugglers, black-marketeers, etc.'[2] Another, though smaller, wave of arrests was instituted after the return to power of the United Front government. A large section of the Dacca police had gone on strike, and 125 persons were detained as a move against any attempt to create disturbances.[3] Arrests on such a scale seem to indicate that persons were detained in groups rather than because of evidence that as individuals they presented a threat to public order. Inevitably it took several months to sift the evidence and to release those who appeared to offer no major menace to peace and good government. The complacent tone of the Governor's attitude cannot be regarded as altogether reassuring. 'Some statements have appeared in the press criticizing the policy of the Government in regard to the arrests suggesting that a number of innocent persons have also been taken into custody. As I said earlier, every case of detention is being carefully reviewed by the Government. As a result of such examination till today 726 persons have been released.'[4]

[1] *Dawn*, August 5, 1956.

[2] The figures were given in a Press Note. The comment quoted seems also to have come from the official announcement but it may have originated with the APP despatch (*Ibid.*, October 11, 1954).

[3] *Ibid.*, December 3, 1955. Those arrested included two MCAs and several MLAs. A Committee of Privileges of the Constituent Assembly found that a serious breach of privilege had occurred in connection with the arrest of its members (Constituent Assembly of Pakistan, *Debates*, Vol. I, pp. 2107 ff., January 26, 1956.)

[4] Broadcast by General Iskandar Mirza on August 9, 1954. Text in *Dawn*, August 10, 1954.

The Citizen and the State

The existence and use of the safety laws have been under continuous criticism since their inception. A sign of their unpopularity has been the unwillingness of the provincial Assemblies to approve such measures. Most of the repressive laws were issued as ordinances or promulgated as Governor's Acts for this reason. One of the Twenty-One Points of the election manifesto of the United Front was a demand for the repeal of the safety laws and the release of all political prisoners. On two occasions the United Front ministry announced the release of all *détenus*, though further arrests were made later. At one stage the central government intervened to instruct the provincial authorities neither to release certain political prisoners nor to repeal the detention laws.[1] Soon after the Ataur Rahman ministry had come to power, the provincial Safety Act was repealed without opposition.[2] The government of West Pakistan at first showed itself similarly anxious to put an end to arbitrary powers of arrest and detention,[3] but it also encountered the reluctance of the central authorities to dismantle the structure of preventive measures. A little later Dr. Khan Sahib himself seemed to have come to value their provisions. According to a press report, 'he said there is nothing wrong with the Safety Laws, only what mattered was its [*sic*] use. In his opinion the use of the Safety Act against the supporters of separate electorates would be quite justified if they did not mend their behaviour.'[4]

Much of the hostility against the safety laws was directed toward alleged abuse of their provisions. The government had ample scope for detaining an individual under cover of one or another of a variety of laws. The safety laws were unpopular, and had been denounced by many political leaders. Consequently some other provision would be tried first; if this were successfully challenged in the courts, the authorities would transfer the detention from one Act to another. This made a mockery of the role of the courts in preserving the liberty of the citizen. On occasion warrants for re-arrest were issued because it seemed likely that the courts would grant bail or admit a *habeas corpus*

[1] *Pakistan Times*, 18, 26, June 1956. [2] *Dawn*, September 21, 1956.
[3] *Pakistan Times*, June 29, 1956. [4] *Dawn*, October 31, 1956.

Pakistan

petition.[1] Thus a man whose release had been ordered by a court might find himself re-arrested on the court steps on substantially the same grounds. In one case (Hamesh Gul) where a man had been arrested three times under different provisions and finally tried for political offences under the Frontier Crimes Regulation,[2] the court had this to say: 'The proceedings under the Frontier Crimes Regulation therefore are offensive and obnoxious to all sense of justice and fair play in any advanced country.'

The central government was always strongly influenced by the opinions of the civil service and the police. Several prominent cabinet ministers had had previous experience in government employment under British rule; very few of them had been imprisoned for indefinite periods for reasons of state. The central government, many of whose members had not had to face the experience of direct popular election, was always more remote from local political activity than were the provincial cabinets. But, apart from this, the centre was conscious that it bore the ultimate responsibility for the prevention of chaos and the continued functioning of government throughout the country. Liaquat Ali, as Prime Minister, had no doubt that it was his duty to place the security of the state before all other considerations: '... we have not detained one single individual because of our political differences with that person, and so there has been no misuse or abuse of power.... I want to tell this House that if in the interest of the safety of Pakistan it is necessary to detain not 16 but 16,000, I shall not hesitate to do so. The safety and integrity of Pakistan comes first, the liberty of individuals comes after.'[3]

---

[1] For two such cases see *Pakistan Times*, November 30, 1954 (case of Hamesh Gul) and *Dawn*, July 9, 1955 (case of Sajjad Zaheer).

[2] *The Frontier Crimes Regulation* (III/1901) was intended to deal with offences committed in tribal areas and the procedure was in accordance with tribal usage. One of the issues referred in this case to the tribal court was the following: 'Are the accused guilty of attempting to bring into hatred and contempt and to incite disaffection towards Pakistan Government established in law by spoken and written words?' The sentence imposed for this offence was seven years' rigorous imprisonment (*Pakistan Times*, November 30, 1954).

[3] Constituent Assembly (Legislature), *Debates*, 1951, Vol. I, p. 406.

The Citizen and the State

The centre had been compelled to intervene with the imposition of martial law in the Punjab and had felt it necessary to impose Governor's rule on East Bengal. The government had also to face the challenge of the Rawalpindi Conspiracy, in which the Chief of Staff of the army and other senior officers had planned to overthrow the government.[1] No senior administrator could forget that from 1942 a great deal of political activity had taken the form of extreme violence. Under such circumstances a small dose of prevention, even though repugnant to the liberal conscience, may well ward off far greater dangers to life and liberty. In the hands of a skilful demagogue a crowd can become a riotous mob. At a time of tension, when political passions are running high, a strong case can be made for the banning of meetings and the temporary restraint of political agitators. The danger

[1] An air of mystery still surrounds some aspects of the conspiracy. Detection of the plot was announced by the government in March 1951. The Prime Minister made a statement in the Assembly: 'They planned . . . to resort to force with the support of Communist and revolutionary elements, making use of such members of the armed forces as they could tamper with. . . . The country was to be brought under a military dictatorship, when the existing authorities, both civil and military, had been eliminated. The Government was thereafter to be patterned on the Communist model, but under military domination. For this purpose economic and constitution-making missions were to be invited from a certain foreign country' (Constituent Assembly (Legislature), *Debates*, 1951, Vol. I, p. 34, March 21, 1951).

The Assembly then passed the *Rawalpindi Conspiracy (Special Tribunal) Act*, 1951, which established a special court to try the case *in camera*. Any sentence might be imposed and there was to be no appeal. Fourteen of the accused were found guilty and sentences ranging up to twelve years' imprisonment were imposed after a trial which lasted for eighteen months (*Dawn*, January 6, 1953).

In spite of the serious nature of the accusations there was a good deal of sympathy for the accused and considerable opposition was shown when the Assembly was asked to validate the Special Tribunal Act which had become invalid as a consequence of Tamizuddin's Case. The Act was validated but only after the government had announced that none of the convicted men would be returned to prison (Constituent Assembly of Pakistan, *Debates*, Vol. I, p. 1475, October 1, 1955).

One reason for the popularity of the conspirators was a widespread belief that the primary aim of the plot was the military conquest of Kashmir. Conclusive evidence for this theory has not been made public.

is that security officials are always ready to scent danger and to suggest that the time for preventive action has arrived. Without rigorous safeguards this kind of attitude can easily be used to create a police tyranny or a system of political oppression.

The Government of India Act had not included a Bill of Rights. The first step toward framing a constitution taken by the Constituent Assembly was to set up a committee on fundamental rights. Part II of the constitution bears the heading 'Fundamental Rights' and contains twenty articles. One of these articles provides that any person who is arrested shall be produced before a magistrate within twenty-four hours, informed of the charges against him and allowed to be defended by a lawyer of his own choice. However, these safeguards do not apply to anyone detained under a law authorizing preventive detention. No *détenu* is to be held for more than three months unless an Advisory Board has reported that there is 'sufficient cause' for continued detention. The Advisory Boards are appointed by the Chief Justice of Pakistan and the Chief Justices of the provincial High Courts.[1] There is no requirement that the *détenu* shall have the right to scrutinize and question the validity of the evidence that has led to his detention, though he must be informed of the grounds on which the detention order has been made, and given a chance to make a representation against the order. Even with the safeguards under the constitution, it is still possible for a person to be held for three months entirely at the discretion of the executive and there is no limit to the number of separate occasions on which a man may be arrested and detained. However, the requirement of judicial scrutiny and approval for continuous detention for longer than three months represents a major improvement over the previous situation.

Article 5 declares that 'All citizens are equal before law and are entitled to equal protection of law'; and further, that 'No person shall be deprived of life or liberty save in accordance with

[1] Advisory Boards under Article 7 were constituted soon after the constitution came into operation. The Central Board approved the continued detention of forty-one persons while the Board in East Pakistan ordered the release of ten persons (*Pakistan Times*, June 23 and 24, 1956).

law.' The liberty of the individual often needs protection against unjust law. This is not provided by the constitution unless the courts develop some equivalent of the American concept of 'due process of law.' In the Federal Court cases arising out of the dissolution of the first Constituent Assembly, the judicial capacity for expanding the scope of judicial review was clearly demonstrated. It may be that the Supreme Court will study further at the school of John Marshall in interpreting the new constitution.

The constitution guarantees freedom of speech and expression. This right is subject to 'any reasonable restrictions imposed by law in the interest of the security of Pakistan, friendly relations with foreign States, public order, decency or morality, or in relation to contempt of court, defamation or incitement to an offence.' The draftsmen of the constitution were attempting to make an instrument that would be legally as complete as possible. They therefore avoided the simple language of the American Bill of Rights upholding freedom of speech and of the press, and strove to foresee all legitimate grounds for limiting absolute freedom of expression. As a result, it will require the most courageous effort of the courts if this fundamental right is to be a solid foundation for free speech. The courts have one word to work with: the word 'reasonable.' This word, qualifying 'restrictions imposed by law,' in this, and three similar articles, was not present in the draft presented to the Assembly in January 1956. It was inserted during the passage of the constitution[1] to meet the apprehension expressed by many members that without it the safeguards might prove meaningless. It does give to the courts the power to inquire whether any restriction imposed by law is reasonable in the light of its stated purpose. On the other hand, the list of permissible grounds for restriction remains as a formidable obstacle to the realization of a full measure of free speech.

Other sections of the constitution proclaim the right to assemble peacefully and without arms and to form associations or unions. In each case the exercise of the right is subject to reasonable legal

---

[1] Constituent Assembly of Pakistan, *Debates*, Vol. I, February 13, 1956.

restrictions. Slavery is totally prohibited, and all forms of forced labour are forbidden except for compulsory national service.

It has already been shown that life and liberty are protected by the constitution. The safeguards for property operate only within strict limits. 'No person shall be deprived of his property save in accordance with law.' Property may be taken for public purposes by a law which provides for compensation, and fixes the amount and specifies the principles on which the compensation is to be paid. There is no guarantee that the compensation shall be equivalent in value to the property acquired. Further, nothing in Article 15 affects the validity of any existing law or the acquisition of any property which is classed as evacuee property.

There is no reason why Pakistan should have adopted the view of the sanctity of property that was held by the United States or England in the nineteenth century. In fact, Pakistan is committed by its constitution to the ideals of the welfare state. Several of the Directive Principles envisage a substantial degree of public control over national resources and of public provision of benefits for the ordinary citizen. The state is to endeavour to remove illiteracy and institute free and compulsory education as soon as possible. It is also to try to raise the standard of living of the common man by 'preventing the concentration of wealth and means of production and distribution in the hands of a few to the detriment of the interest of the common man. . . .' Public policy is to be directed toward the provision of jobs for all, with reasonable facilities for rest and leisure. A scheme of social security is envisaged, and the state is to seek to provide the 'basic necessities of life, such as food, clothing, housing, education and medical relief,' for all those who are unable to earn their own living. These are all noble ideals; one can only wish that Pakistan were a little nearer the possibility of their fulfilment.

It would be misleading to leave a discussion of the citizen and the state at this point. The consideration of civil liberties has concentrated upon those areas in which freedom seems to be in danger. But the place of free speech in the United States could not be learned entirely from reading the proceedings of the McCarthy committee; nor would justice be done to the liberty of the subject in England by concentrating upon the story of Defence Regulation 18B. These are the battlefronts of civil liberty, and it is necessary to see how the struggle goes, and where the lines are drawn. But the existence of a challenge to liberty should not be permitted to obscure the reality of a free society. And Pakistan is a free society in spite of the limitations that have been described. Major political opposition is operating freely at the centre and in the provinces. Anyone may attack the Prime Minister or the cabinet on grounds of personal capacity or political activity. Political criticism is free to the point of slander, and the ordinary citizen does not walk in fear of the secret police if he should dare to think ill of the administration. The press is vigorous and is demonstrably in a position to seek to undermine the political support of the party in power. There is a real public opinion which actively, if not very effectively, resents the imposition of limitations on freedom of expression and personal liberty. Civil liberties in Pakistan are not enjoyed to the full extent that prevails in other less troubled democracies, but Pakistan is far from being a police state.

CHAPTER IX

The Public Services

THE government of British India was a bureaucracy—one of the most remarkable and successful bureaucracies developed in any country. It was honest, devoted, energetic within reason and, on the whole, efficient. It was created to fit the special needs of British rule in India. A small group of British officials was to retain ultimate authority in their hands in order that the supremacy of final control from London might not be challenged. Before World War I the system was not tempered by any element of responsibility to an Indian assembly or electorate. Even after the Acts of 1919 and 1935, the central government was not brought under the control of an elected legislature and, in the provinces, the prerogatives of the Services were protected by statutory provisions and the special powers of the Governors. Moreover, every province was aware that Governor's rule, that is a return to non-responsible bureaucracy, was at all times a possible alternative to cabinet government.

At the same time as the introduction of limited responsible government the process of indianization of the services was intensified. A small but growing percentage of the posts in the superior Services had been allocated to Indians during the last quarter of the nineteenth century.[1] This was now to be carried to the point where it was contemplated that at least half of the senior positions would be filled by Indians. These Indians pledged their loyalty to the British Crown and to the maintenance of British rule in India, and many of them became, in appearance and outlook, more British than Indian.

Under these circumstances it might have been imagined that lasting and deep hostility to the Services would have taken root in the minds of those who were fighting for independence, and that one of the first consequences of self-rule would have been

[1] By 1915, 5 per cent of the Indian Civil Service was composed of Indians (Sir Edward Blunt, *The I.C.S.* (London, 1937), p. 52).

The Public Services

the replacement of individual civil servants and a radical change in the system. Nothing of the kind has happened in either Pakistan or India. On the contrary, the former hirelings of the alien rulers who had sent obstreperous politicians to gaol in 1939-46, became loyal and valued servants of the state, fully capable of sending obstreperous politicians to gaol in 1947-56. And the general administrative system and the special constitutional safeguards for civil servants have been carried into the new constitution.

In Pakistan the administrative system inherited from undivided India has been changed only to the minimum extent necessary to meet the strain of partition and to assume some of the new functions resulting from the development policies adopted by the new state. The essence of the system has not been touched and has been warmly defended. This is hardly surprising in view of the fact that many of the leading holders of political office have had previous careers largely or wholly in government service; Ghulam Mohammad, Chaudhri Mohamad Ali, Amjad Ali and Iskandar Mirza are examples. The last-named gave his view of the respective position of politicians and civil servants when he was Minister of the Interior. 'You cannot have the old British system of administration [and] at the same time allow politicians to meddle with the civil service. In the British system the District Magistrate was the king-pin of administration. His authority was unquestioned. We have to restore that.'[1]

The 'British system' had ruled India for more than a century, and was understood by all levels of Indian society. Every peasant knew where the administrative machine came into direct contact with the soil. Above the village officials and those in the subdivisions, the higher administration began. Nearest at hand stood the District Magistrate (primarily an administrative not a judicial officer, called in some places Collector or Deputy Commissioner). Beyond the District Magistrate, and to be seen only at rare intervals, came the Commissioner, followed by the Governor of the province, the Viceroy and the King-Emperor. The upper reaches of the hierarchy were surrounded in the imagination of the ryot by clouds of remote splendour. The whole imposing

[1] *Dawn*, October 31, 1954.

Pakistan

structure was called Government. The District Magistrate was Government on two legs; he represented all aspects of the administration, justice, taxes, social services, land settlement, famine relief.[1] He spent much of his time riding from one village to another, watching over the lives of his 'subjects' and seeing that government orders were executed in all parts of his District. The belief that the District Officer should get out and see the people is still accepted in Pakistan. A ruling in 1955 lays down that: 'Every officer should spend at least ten nights in a month away from his Headquarters and submit a tour note to his immediate superior officer.'[2]

Most of the important posts at all levels were held by members of the Indian Civil Service. These posts included those of Governors of most of the provinces, members of the Viceroy's Executive Council, Federal Court and High Court judges as well as the top secretariat positions in the centre and the provinces, and the majority of Commissioners, District Magistrates and Sessions Judges. There is a tendency to think of a bureaucracy as a large number of persons sitting in offices at the national or provincial capitals. This was never true of the I.C.S. The total number of 'civilians' serving in the secretariat of India and all the provincial secretariats in 1939 was 218, and the total strength of the I.C.S. for that year (including 194 appointments on the judicial side) was 1,299.[3]

The remarkably small size of the I.C.S. provides the key to much of the pattern and methods of administration. Before 1920 most of the officers were Europeans, and it was therefore obvious and simple to draw a sharp line between them and the lesser grades of public servant. By 1939 over 40 per cent of the I.C.S. was composed of Indians,[4] but these had been assimilated by education and training to the pattern of their British colleagues.

---

[1] A recent analysis of the role of the district officer is given in Akhtar Hassan Aslam, *The Deputy Commissioner* (Panjab University thesis dated September 30, 1953).

[2] *Report of the Council for Administration of West Pakistan*, p. 9.

[3] Philip Woodruff, *The Men Who Ruled India: II. The Guardians* (London, 1954), App. B.   [4] *Ibid.* The figure was 540 out of 1,299.

The Public Services

Whether European or Indian, the young recruit to the I.C.S. was bound to feel that he belonged to a small elite group of 'guardians' —the 'steel framework' upon which the integrity of the state depended.

These men entered the Service at an early age, and all looked upon it as a life career. They were immediately given considerable responsibilities, and they were told to get on with their jobs without waiting for precise orders from above. The young civilian learned his job many miles from the provincial or national capital. Training began in the districts, and the new official soon found himself with a subdivision to look after or even temporary charge of a district. Since a district might contain as many as 4,000,000 inhabitants, the responsibility involved was considerable.

This system of government was largely negative in outlook. Its primary function was the preservation of peace and order. If public tranquillity were preserved and the revenue collected, the peasants might be left to lead their lives according to the fashion of the past two thousand years. It is not for those who live in more fortunate countries to underestimate the vital importance of a system that effectively preserves law and order. No district officer could forget how close to anarchy lay the communities under his supervision. He had to be continuously aware that his action within a matter of minutes might make the difference between a display of bad temper and a serious riot involving scores of lives and homes.

In the longer established democracies, the preservation of law and order is a basic assumption of government rather than a duty requiring continuous vigilance. But the first few weeks of Pakistan's existence saw the new state almost submerged in a torrent of violence and anarchy. It was therefore natural that the nation's leader should have drawn attention to the paramount task of administration. 'You will no doubt agree with me that the first duty of a government is to maintain law and order, so that the life, property and religious beliefs of its subjects are fully protected by the State.'[1] The civil authorities bore the strain of

[1] Constituent Assembly of Pakistan, *Debates*, Vol. I, p. 18, August 11, 1947, M. A. Jinnah.

Pakistan

those weeks of disorder, and much of the credit for the successful establishment of the new state is their due.

Between 1919 and 1939, parallel with the introduction of increasing responsible government in the provinces, the importance of social service and development work had been growing. But these were years of peace, and 1939 found elected governments in office in the provinces and an atmosphere of genuine if limited co-operation between government and the parties. The ensuing eight years saw a regression to a more primitive level on which law and order (and the war effort) were once more paramount. Development had to be regarded as a luxury to be fitted in when other more pressing duties permitted.

What has been said so far relates mainly to the closing years of British rule. But the structure and methods of the administration in Pakistan form a direct continuation of the traditions of British India. An official recruiting pamphlet announces with assurance: 'The Civil Service of Pakistan is the successor in Pakistan of the Indian Civil Service, which was the most distinguished Civil Service in the world.'[1]

When the public services were divided in 1947 Pakistan was in an extremely poor position. The national capital, New Delhi, fell to India, and so did the capital city of Bengal. Civil servants whose homes were in those cities faced a major upheaval if they decided to migrate to Pakistan. India assumed authority over six major provinces whose territory remained undivided and whose governments maintained relatively smooth operations. Pakistan contained two unpartitioned provinces, Sind and the North-West Frontier Province, each of which was small and neither of which had a full independent cadre of senior civil servants. The impact of physical dislocation was therefore much more serious in Pakistan. Most of the normal requirements of government for buildings, office equipment and records were lacking. In New Delhi, while there was considerable initial confusion, it could at least be known that a ministry existed at a definite place and had a telephone number and an officer in charge. In Karachi no such essential minimum could be guaranteed. Government had

[1] *Careers in the Pakistan Central Superior Services* (Karachi, 1954), p. 3.

The Public Services

to be improvised by men sitting on packing-cases, writing notes to each other in pencil.

The population of Pakistan was nearly one-quarter that of India. But the proportion of the public service that chose to serve Pakistan was far less than this. Muslims had taken less readily than the Hindus to Western education, and hence to the higher branches of the government services. It was stated in the Constituent Assembly that only eighty-two members of the I.C.S. and Indian Political Service came to Pakistan.[1] The proportion of top-ranking officers was even less. Mr. Gurmani described the situation: 'Sir, your Central Government was set up literally from scratch. At that time [1947] Pakistan inherited only one Muslim officer of the rank of a Secretary to the Central Government, and you had not even half a dozen officers of the seniority and experience of Joint Secretaries to the Central Government.'[2]

In some of the inferior grades the position was reversed and the new government was faced with responsibility for maintaining a large surplus of employees who, in response to the urging of their patriotism, had abandoned their homes to serve the Muslim homeland. The surplus was especially great in the Commercial Departments, the Railways and Posts and Telegraphs.[3]

Because Pakistan was short of trained senior civil servants, the new government showed itself eager to employ British members of the old I.C.S. and other services. Of twenty-seven Secretaries and Joint Secretaries in 1950, seven were listed as 'non-Pakistani.'[4] Several of these senior officials were still serving, more than nine years after independence. It was particularly noticeable that the first two officers to take charge of the Establishment Division (concerned with the personnel administration

---

[1] Constituent Assembly of Pakistan, *Debates*, Vol. I, p. 2104, January 26, 1956, Hamidul Huq Chowdhury.

[2] Constituent Assembly (Legislature), *Debates*, 1953, Vol. II, p. 733, October 1, 1953.

[3] *Ibid.*, 1948, Vol. I, p. 147, March 2, 1948, Ghulam Mohammad.

[4] *Ibid.*, 1949, Vol. II, p. 465, January 12, 1950, Liaquat Ali Khan and 1950, Vol. I, p. 309, March 23, 1950, Ghulam Mohammad.

Pakistan

of the central government) were in this category. At the end of 1952 a total of 214 civilian non-Pakistani officers was employed, 109 of whom were connected with the defence services. Of 105 in civil agencies, 75 were British.[1]

The government decided to create a successor to the I.C.S., and this was called the Civil Service of Pakistan (C.S.P.). To fill the senior vacancies, in the early years more than one hundred officers were recruited for the General Administrative Reserve. These older men were offered appointment for a limited number of years, and it was intended that they should make way for members of the C.S.P. when these became available. This latter service is recruited and organized on substantially the same lines as the I.C.S. Some fifteen or twenty appointments a year are made to the C.S.P.; candidates must be from 21 to 23 years old and graduates of a recognized University. The selection is by competitive written examination and oral interview.[2] The written examination is of the kind familiar to graduates of English universities. There are compulsory papers in English, General Knowledge and an English essay. In addition there is a wide range of optional subjects.[3] The results of the examination serve to establish an order of merit, but this is not necessarily conclusive in determining the offer of appointment. Some twelve central superior services, all of them of a non-technical nature, recruit their members through the same examination.[4] It is generally understood that the C.S.P. and the Foreign Service are entitled to the better-qualified candidates, but the personal choice of the

[1] Constituent Assembly (Legislature), *Debates*, 1952, Vol. II, p. 205, November 15, 1952, Khwaja Nazimuddin.

[2] For details of the rules and methods of selection see Pakistan Public Service Commission, *Report on the Central Superior Services Examination, 1953* (Karachi, 1954).

[3] On reading some of the questions one might wonder whether British rule had ceased. For example: 'Estimate the greatness of Warren Hastings by a reference to his initial difficulties and subsequent dangers'; and 'Give an account of the suppression of social evils and cruel rites during the rule of the East India Company' (*Ibid.*, Part II).

[4] The superior services include the C.S.P., the Pakistan Foreign Service, the Pakistan Police, the Postal Service and the Income Tax Service.

candidate and other factors may be taken into account in making appointments.

In order to secure fair distribution of government servants between the various regions of the country, quotas are established for each province. The first 20 per cent of vacancies are filled on the basis of merit alone; the remaining 80 per cent are required to be divided equally between East and West Pakistan. Provided that qualified candidates are available, 6 per cent of the vacancies are reserved for members of the Scheduled Castes. The purpose of this scheme of provincial quotas is to ensure that the parts of the country which are less favoured in higher education shall have a reasonable share of superior appointments. Only two of the eighty-two I.C.S. and Political Service officers were from East Bengal, and that province has long maintained that it was entitled to special treatment to establish parity. A pledge is included in the constitution, 'to achieve parity in the representation of East Pakistan and West Pakistan in all other [non-defence] spheres of Federal administration.'

Recruits are appointed to the Civil Service of Pakistan on probation, which usually lasts two years. They undergo a period of training for nine months at the Civil Service Academy at Lahore. Among other subjects they are required to study Urdu or Bengali, whichever is not the language of their home province. After this they proceed to East Pakistan for practical training at provincial headquarters and in the districts. Finally, they are sent to another country of the Commonwealth, usually the United Kingdom, to obtain experience of democratic administration under different conditions. For five years the C.S.P. officer is then posted to one province, after which he must serve for at least three years in the other wing of the country. After ten years the C.S.P. officer will thus have had practical experience in both East and West Pakistan and at both district and provincial levels, with perhaps a term with the central government. It is deliberate policy that the members of this service should not become permanent desk officers sitting in Karachi. Appointments in the central secretariat are limited to terms of three to five years, after which the officer must return to provincial or district service.

Pakistan

When the system works successfully, it means that the C.S.P. is provided with officers who are, in the widest sense, general administrators capable of turning their hands to any task of government that may arise. On the other hand, it means also that the senior policy advisers of the central and provincial governments seldom become really expert in any one line of public policy.

The C.S.P. departs in one respect from the practice of its predecessor. A member of the I.C.S. was assigned to the cadre of one province, and he would normally leave that province only to serve at the centre. In Pakistan there is one central cadre and, in the interest of strengthening national unity, it is intended that transfers between the provinces shall take place regularly.

The Civil Service of Pakistan is the pivotal service around which all other administrative groups, central, provincial and local, are organized. Its recruitment and general pattern are under the control of the central government, although while serving in a province, an officer may be posted and promoted by the provincial government. The fundamental structure of the service is laid down in Rules promulgated by the central government.[1] These rules establish certain specified posts as belonging to the cadre of the C.S.P. In 1954 there were 519 such posts in the total authorized strength. Of these, 49 appointments in the provinces were reserved for persons promoted from the provincial services; this left 470 posts to be filled by members of the C.S.P. Junior posts, intended primarily for the training of young officers, accounted for 134 positions, leaving 336 appointments of or above the rank of District Magistrate, 80 of which were with the central government. This is a very small group to control the administration of a nation of 80,000,000 citizens. In practice it was smaller than the cadre establishment would indicate, for the C.S.P. was conducting its recruitment slowly and on a long-term basis, and it had not filled all the vacancies to which it was entitled.

The Civil Service of Pakistan occupied most of the senior

[1] *Civil Service of Pakistan (Composition and Cadre) Rules.* These are issued from time to time by the Establishment Division of the Cabinet Secretariat. For the Rules issued in 1954 see *Gazette of Pakistan,* June 18, 1954.

positions in the central and provincial secretariats. Alongside and beneath that service worked the provincial services, and the lesser services of the central government. Twenty-five per cent of the superior posts under the provincial governments were reserved for persons promoted from the provincial services and, when C.S.P. officers were not available, this proportion was exceeded.[1] Thus a career in a provincial service could lead to an appointment as Secretary in charge of a department of a provincial government.

The organization of both the provincial and central governments is similar. Each consists of a secretariat and a number of attached departments. The difference between the two was defined by the government of West Pakistan. 'A clear distinction should be made between the functions of the Secretariat and those of the Attached Departments. It should be the responsibility of the Secretariat to formulate policy, while it should be the responsibility of the Attached Departments to implement that policy.'[2] The distinction in practice is never so sharply drawn.

Each province is divided into Divisions, each under the control of a Commissioner. There are three Commissioners in East Pakistan, where their role has not been regarded as much more important than that of transmitting orders and information from the provincial government to the Districts. In West Pakistan the scheme for integration provided ten Divisional Commissioners and gave them substantial powers. 'The Commissioner is the pivot of the Administration. He shall be in charge of administration in general within his Division, and shall ensure that the policies of the Provincial Government are properly implemented.'[3] He is to keep a special watch on matters affecting law and order, and he is responsible for the discipline of the government servants under his authority. He is to superintend and control the revenue administration and to co-ordinate the development activities within his area. Immediately below the

[1] In 1956, of fifty Deputy Commissioners in West Pakistan, twenty-three were members of the Provincial Civil Service.
[2] Letter from Chief Secretary, West Pakistan, No. 21/55/Integration, dated October 16, 1955.   [3] *Ibid.*

Pakistan

Divisions are the Districts which have long been the main unit of all aspects of administrative activity. Each District has a District Magistrate or Deputy Commissioner, and the majority of these are members of the C.S.P. There are fifty Districts in West Pakistan and seventeen in East Pakistan, where areas are smaller though population is greater.

The public services are provided with certain constitutional guarantees of fair treatment.[1] These are modelled after the provisions of the Government of India Act, which were designed to protect the British appointed civil servant against the possible hostility of an Indian cabinet or legislature. No disciplinary action may be taken against a public servant 'by an authority subordinate to that by which he was appointed.' In other words, a member of a central service, even though serving in a province, cannot be punished by the provincial authorities. In any disciplinary case the civil servant must be given a chance to defend himself and is entitled to at least one appeal against any adverse finding.

The constitution also established the Federal and Provincial Public Service Commissions. These are appointed by the President or the Governor, acting in his discretion. A majority of the members of each commission must be 'persons who have held office in the service of Pakistan for not less than fifteen years.' The term of office of members is five years, but they may not be dismissed except under restrictions similar to those for the removal of a judge. The primary duty of the Public Service Commissions is to conduct the examinations for recruitment to the services. They are also to be consulted by the governments on matters of personnel policy and on individual disciplinary cases. The central and provincial governments are not required to accept the advice of the Public Service Commissions, but the annual reports of the Commissions are to contain references to any instance in which advice was rejected or consultation did not take place.[2]

[1] Part X of the constitution, headed 'The Services of Pakistan.'
[2] *The Fourth Report of the Pakistan Public Service Commission*, 1952, p. 12, refers to five instances of disagreement between the Commission and the government.

The Public Services

It would be wrong to suppose that the public services in Pakistan have been regarded as beyond criticism. The most serious ground for complaint is that the administration is not sufficiently prepared, in either organization or outlook, for the change in emphasis from law and order functions to development activities, required by the establishment of an independent and progressive state.

'... with the attainment of independence and the shift in emphasis in government policies from regulating the life of the community to positive actions for promoting its welfare, the system has become outdated and seriously inadequate. So far as law and order, administration of justice and collection of revenues—responsibilities which continue to vest in the Government as the irreducible minimum of administration—are concerned, the system continues to serve the country reasonably well. The efficiency of the system within this essential field invests it with a factitious appearance of adequacy for all purposes, including the new and supremely important task of planned development. This, on the one hand, creates a psychological atmosphere of complacence unfavourable to reform, and, on the other, increases the inertia of the system, its power of resisting change.'[1]

The C.S.P. has been criticized for continuing the tradition of the I.C.S. and regarding itself as an elite minority, separated from and superior to the lesser services which share the work of administration. Now that all services are manned by Pakistanis there seems to be much less reason for making a sharp cleavage between one service of highest power and prestige and those whose tasks are only slightly less important. In particular the technical services feel that in modern civilization they deserve to enjoy higher pay and status and closer participation in the formation of government policy. The Planning Board found that the division of the general administrative services into watertight compartments, 'encourages class-consciousness and mutual

[1] Government of Pakistan, Planning Board, *The First Five Year Plan, 1955–60*, Vol. I, p. 99.

jealousies, [and] creates conflicts in many common areas of administration. . . .' The present system is resented also by the provincial services which find themselves in a position of general inferiority.[1] Provincial politicians have some reservations about a system which provides them with top advisers who may shortly be transferred to Karachi.

The Civil Service of Pakistan has been attacked for its tendency to assume an autocratic manner. Its members have been conscious of the fact that, if responsible government breaks down, they will take over full powers. The political life of a politician has not been long in Pakistan; whereas the senior civil servant has had a much better chance of lengthy enjoyment of power and prestige. Under these circumstances the civil servants have been at least the equals of cabinet ministers, and their education and experience of administration has often rendered them their superiors. This is a state of affairs that can find a final remedy only when cabinet government has been successfully established at the centre and in the provinces.

There has been a distinct decline in the efficiency of the public service since partition. This was inevitable since Pakistan inherited so small a proportion of the more experienced officers of undivided India. The new governments had to be hastily improvised and some unsuitable appointments were inevitable. The confused political situation and the many changes in ministerial direction did nothing to make the task of efficient administration more easy. The government of British India developed its administrative system in the latter half of the nineteenth century, and the changes during the last forty years of British rule amounted to modifications rather than a drastic reformation. The first job was to keep existing institutions functioning smoothly; innovations could be considered at length and without undue enthusiasm. The secretariat relied upon well-established procedures, subjecting each new proposal to the scrutiny of the whole hierarchy from lower division clerk to Secretary to government.

[1] It was reported that the Punjab Provincial Civil Service (Executive Branch) Association had asked that the C.S.P. be restricted to central agencies (*Pakistan Times*, June 29, 1956).

The Public Services

This system was inherited by Pakistan.[1] There have been constant complaints of excessive delay in the execution of accepted policy and in the consideration of new proposals. It has been suggested that the machinery of financial control lacks imagination. 'Like a man in a rowboat, it charts its future course mainly by selecting a stationary point in the past and rowing backward toward the objective it seeks to attain.'[2]

Even more damaging to the reputation of the public service have been allegations of corruption. This has taken two forms, political and criminal. The political influence of government servants is very great. An illiterate voter is ready to believe that he should do whatever he is told by government. And the powers of a District Magistrate can either aid or hinder the candidacy of a politician. Consequently political pressure has been at work to persuade or compel government servants to intervene in party politics. The official has often found it difficult to resist such pressure; the result might well be his transfer to a 'penal' station. The Council for Administration of West Pakistan showed its awareness of this danger. It recommended that: 'Tenures for most of the appointments should be fixed and transfers before the expiry of tenure should be rare. Transfers should not be made as a matter of punishment.'[3]

Many civil servants found themselves in a position of considerable power. They could influence the commercial fortunes of private individuals by granting licences, awarding contracts or allotting refugee property. Owing to the shortage of staff such officials often operated without effective supervision or control. The government was fully aware of the dangers. Special pro-

---

[1] There have been several inquiries into the administrative system in Pakistan. Among the more helpful are *The Report of the Administrative Enquiry Committee* (1953) and Rowland Egger, *The Improvement of Public Administration in Pakistan* (1953). In 1956 it was announced that a committee of six Secretaries had been established to 'examine the impact of the Constitution on the functions and structure of the Central Government, particularly with reference to the distribution of powers as between the Centre and the Provinces and recommend changes necessary in the organization of the Federal Government as a result thereof' (*Pakistan Times*, June 21, 1956).

[2] Rowland Egger, *op. cit.*, p. 33.   [3] *Op. cit.*, p. 10.

Pakistan

visions for dealing with such cases were made by the Prevention of Corruption Act, 1947,[1] and the following year the Special Police Establishment was brought into being. A member of the cabinet explained the purpose of this body: 'The functions of the Special Police Establishment are to investigate and bring up for trial cases of bribery and corruption involving transactions with the Central and Provincial Governments.'[2] In five years more than 5,000 corruption cases were registered, though less than one in ten of these appears to have resulted in conviction.[3] East Bengal established a Special Anti-Corruption Department which in 1948 filed 6,160 cases and secured 2,388 convictions; these were in addition to 5,485 cases recorded in the ordinary police courts.[4] Of course it cannot be assumed that a government servant was a guilty party in each case, but the vast numbers serve to indicate that corruption was widespread.

A further step in the drive against corruption was taken with the Civil Services (Prevention of Corruption) Rules promulgated by the central government in 1953. Under these Rules an officer is to be presumed guilty of corruption if he has 'a general and persistent reputation of being corrupt,' and he or his dependents are in possession of property for which he cannot account or he has assumed a style of living above his visible means.[5]

Any criticism of the public services in Pakistan must be set against one paramount fact; the machinery of government has continued to function through ten years of extraordinary difficulty. This has been due almost entirely to the work of the services, for the quality of the political leadership has been neither high nor vigorous. The public has become inured to the idea that the politicians are corrupt, but it can still be incensed by the

[1] Act II/1947 (pre-partition).
[2] Constituent Assembly (Legislature), *Debates*, 1948, Vol. I, p. 320, March 8, 1948, Fazlur Rahman.
[3] The figures were: Cases, 5,345; convictions, 358; departmental punishment, 224. *Ibid.*, 1953, Vol. II, p. 732, October 1, 1953, M. A. Gurmani.
[4] East Bengal Legislative Assembly, *Official Report*, Vol. III, March 23, 1949, Nurul Amin.
[5] Constituent Assembly (Legislature), *Debates*, 1953, Vol. II, p. 204, September 24, 1953, Mohamad Ali.

revelation of the betrayal of trust by a civil servant. The general attitude was well summed up in the report of the Planning Board: 'While we do not dispute the view that the standards of integrity and efficiency have shown deterioration in recent years, we nevertheless think that the structure and system of public administration inherited from British rule has served the nation well.'[1]

In Pakistan the judiciary is to be regarded as a part of the civil service. In his duties as District Magistrate, the C.S.P. officer exercises both criminal and revenue jurisdiction, but the main part of his duties lies in the field of administration. However, after a period of service he may ask to be transferred to the Judicial Branch. More than fifty judicial appointments, including those as judges of the High Courts and as District and Sessions judges, are included in the total cadre of the Civil Service of Pakistan. The Judicial Branch is recruited in equal proportions from C.S.P. officers, who have already acquired administrative experience, and the Bar.[2] The constitution requires that, to be qualified for appointment to a High Court, a person must have been an advocate for at least ten years, or a member of the C.S.P. for the same period who has served as a District Judge for at least three years. Appointment is made by the President after consultation with the Chief Justice, the provincial government and the provincial Chief Justice. To qualify for the Supreme Court, five years' service on a High Court or fifteen years as an advocate is the minimum requisite.

The fact that many of the judges in Pakistan are members of the C.S.P. and have had experience as administrative officials means that the courts have a substantial degree of sympathy for the needs of government. But, once a judge is appointed he is guaranteed security of tenure. A judge of a High Court may be removed only with the concurrence of the Supreme Court; and a Supreme Court judge may be removed only by a resolution supported by two-thirds of the members of the National Assembly.

There has been a long-standing demand that the judiciary should be made completely independent of the executive. A Directive Principle of the constitution provides that 'The State

[1] *Op. cit.*, p. 127.   [2] *Pakistan 1954–1955* (Karachi, 1955), p. 9.

shall separate the Judiciary from the Executive as soon as practicable.' This is not primarily aimed at terminating the recruitment of civil service judges. The judiciary has been held in high regard in Pakistan and has been compared favourably with the other services. 'If on our country's tenth Independence Day unqualified homage is to be offered to anyone, then undoubtedly the country's judges have amply qualified for that honour.'[1] Much of the credit for re-establishing Pakistan on the road to democracy is rightly given to the Federal Court, which showed no hesitation in questioning the validity of arbitrary actions on the part of the government.

The demand for judicial separation applies to the combination of judicial and executive functions in the hands of the District Magistrate. At present the District Magistrate is often responsible for making rules, enforcing them, and punishing their violation. A scheme for the partial separation of these functions was put into operation in the Punjab in 1954. Each district was assigned an Additional District Magistrate to handle judicial functions. He hears appeal from lesser magistrates and deals with original cases under the Pakistan Penal Code.

If a country is to achieve stability, the government of the day must be able to count on the loyalty of the armed forces. Muslim troops had always formed a large proportion of the Indian Army, and, although there was some initial disorganization, Pakistan began its existence with a powerful and well-disciplined army. The Navy and the Air Force have had to be built up from much smaller nuclei. The armed forces have steadily refrained from taking an active part in politics, though it is clear that they have had little patience with some of the political manœuvring for power. When the nation was faced with the crisis of 1954, the army Commander-in-Chief, General Ayub Khan, entered the cabinet as Defence Minister. This was to show the people and the outside world that the forces were behind the government. Apart from this gesture General Ayub took no open political stand, and as soon as the second Constituent Assembly began to function he returned to his purely military duties.

[1] *Dawn*, August 14, 1956, editorial.

The Public Services

The officer grades of the civil and military services form the strongest bulwark of national stability. They constitute a distinct and clearly recognizable group. Those in the more senior positions were trained under British rule and have learned to place a high value on discipline and order. They are the products of a similar education, and they were largely dissociated from the active political struggle that preceded independence. The politicians have spent nine years in tearing each other to pieces. When responsible government broke down the civil service took over, with the armed forces ready to lend their assistance if required. The periods of direct bureaucratic rule have been in many ways those of most efficient government. There are large numbers of people in Pakistan who would not be dismayed at the thought of a lengthy period of government by soldiers and civil servants. A former provincial cabinet minister expressed his feeling in this manner: 'Every Pakistani soldier is a true patriot; he has great respect and deep love for his motherland, and is determined to sacrifice his all, even his life, in defending it. I have complete confidence in our Forces, and it is my heart's desire that they should take charge of the administration.'[1] And one of the Karachi newspapers laid down an order of priority for the government to follow: '... we do believe that in our own situation the first call on the Government is to stabilize the country; democratizing it can only be a secondary objective.... We are sure that if democracy clashes with the objective of stability, the people will rather prefer some other system.'[2]

It seems that, if the civil and military services had wished to take over the functions of government, nothing could have stopped them. But their attitude has been that they will support any political regime that can demonstrate its capacity to govern. It is unlikely that they would do much to insist upon democracy, but they will do nothing to overthrow it.

[1] Constituent Assembly of Pakistan, *Debates*, Vol. I, p. 272, August 24, 1955, Mian Jaffar Shah. The speaker was, however, not so enthusiastic about possible rule by the civil service, 'the erstwhile agents of British Imperialism.'
[2] *The Times of Karachi*, April 28, 1955, editorial.

CHAPTER X

Pakistan and the World

A PEOPLE struggling for self-government is apt to see the rest of the world merely as a background to its own immediate endeavours. The Irish, the Poles, the Jews in Palestine, the Greek Cypriots have, each in their turn, contended passionately that nothing mattered except national independence. For them, the other nations of the world, large or small, fell into three categories: friends, enemies and the irrelevant. Friends are those who give enthusiastic support to the national cause, by word or deed, and irrespective of the motive for that support; enemies are those who side with the oppressor. 'If the Hindus give us Pakistan and freedom,' said Firoz Khan Noon,[1] 'then the Hindus are our best friends. If the British give it to us, then the British are our best friends. But if neither will give it to us, then Russia is our best friend.'

Such was the mood of Pakistan on the eve of independence. But the division of the world into friend and foe did not prove quite as simple as expected. The Congress Party had finally agreed to the creation of Pakistan, but there were many in India who regarded their neighbour with suspicion and even outright hatred. Britain had departed from the sub-continent, but there were indications that, if it came to a choice, she would prefer to be friends with India rather than with Pakistan. Lord Mountbatten remained as Governor-General of India, and was a personal friend of Nehru; Sir Cyril Radcliffe had decided upon the fatal boundary line which gave most of the Gurdaspur district (and access to Kashmir) to India.[2] The United States had favoured

[1] Cited in A. B. Rajput, *The Muslim League Yesterday and Today* (Lahore, 1948), p. 109.
[2] Many Pakistanis regard the Punjab boundary line as an act of deliberate malice on the part of the chairman of the boundary commission and the Viceroy. See Lord Birdwood, *Two Nations and Kashmir* (London, 1956), p. 75.

Pakistan and the World

independence for India and Pakistan, but knew and sympathized much more with the land of Gandhi and Nehru than with that of Jinnah. Pakistan was a new and unfamiliar state, basing its claim to nationhood not on the familiar appeal against the iniquities of rule by British colonialists, but on the distinction between Muslim and non-Muslim. Russia was an enemy of the empires of Western Europe, but had shown no enthusiasm for Pakistan as a separate unit in the sub-continent. The natural friends of Pakistan might have been expected to be found in the Muslim world. But Egypt and Indonesia had their own independence to fight for, and had no time to spare much thought for Pakistan. Turkey was not inclined to respond to an appeal to Islamic solidarity, and Afghanistan, the nearest Muslim neighbour, had claims to make on Pakistan territory and was the only nation to vote against the admission of Pakistan to the United Nations.

In the first appraisal of her position among the community of self-governing nations, Pakistan could find no single country which could be counted as an unfailing friend and ally willing to lend aid and comfort in time of need. Many observers preferred to reserve judgment, waiting to see what kind of a state this was going to be and whether it was strong enough to survive and be vigorous.

Those who had fought for Pakistan had struggled to compel recognition that the Muslims of India were a separate nation and should have a territorial state. The inevitable first object of foreign policy had to be to show the world that Pakistan was a reality and was capable of maintaining its independence. The main obstacle to the creation of Pakistan had been the Congress desire for a united India; after August 1947 it was necessary to convince the same Congress, now installed as the government of the Indian Dominion, that Pakistan was here to stay.

There can be no doubt that India began her independent existence in a much better position to command the respect and interest of the outside world. The name of India was known to everyone, whereas Pakistan was an unfamilar and possibly unstable complication on the political map of Asia. India was the largest democratic nation in the world. Her influence was likely

Pakistan

to be much greater if she was accepted as the leading spokesman for free Asia. The creation of Pakistan had been a challenge to the idea of a free united India, which had been the dream of the Indian National Congress. The existence of a disgruntled Pakistan, ever ready to resent any suggestion of Indian pre-eminence, was a constant irritation to India's assumption of moral leadership in international affairs.

From the point of view of Pakistan, the only basis for proper relations was the acceptance of exact equality between the two Dominions (republics). Mr. Jinnah had never agreed to any constitutional formula which would have denoted a lesser status for the Muslim League. India contained two nations: one sovereign nation is the equal of any other sovereign nation. This was the creed of the founders of Pakistan, and they had no intention of diminishing their claims when the major victory had been won.

It follows that issues of prestige have played a predominant part in Pakistan's relations with India. Many political leaders and most of the articulate section of the population have reacted with emotional intensity to any suggestion of Indian superiority in any field. This was probably the inevitable consequence of the years before partition. But the degree of passion has been heightened by the feeling, largely justified, that on every matter on which the real interests of the two nations have come into conflict, India has contrived to emerge victorious.

In August 1947 it was not clear where the territorial boundaries of Pakistan would lie. The Radcliffe award was not announced until the eve of partition, and left considerable areas of uncertainty. But the principal cause of doubt arose from the position of the princely states. It had been agreed that the ruler of each state would be free to decide to join one or other of the new Dominions. Between the decision in June to divide the sub-continent and the date of independence, most of the states decided to join India. Bahawalpur, Khairpur and the states of Baluchistan and the North-West Frontier joined Pakistan. The future of three other states—Junagadh, Kashmir and Hyderabad—caused great trouble between the two countries.

Junagadh lies on the Kathiawar peninsula and had no great claim to importance. Its ruler was a Muslim, while most of his subjects were Hindu. The ruler announced his accession to Pakistan even though there is no land connection between the state and the territory of Pakistan. An uprising broke out against the ruler and Indian troops moved in to restore order. After a plebiscite, the state was admitted to the Indian union. Pakistan has refused to recognize the validity of this action and has regarded it as a violation of her territory.

The dispute over Kashmir[1] has been far more serious, and remains the principal and most virulent source of hostility between the two countries. To Pakistan the issue is quite simple. The state of Jammu and Kashmir is inhabited by a population that is predominantly Muslim (77 per cent in 1941). Its ruler, the maharajah, was a Hindu prince, and his court and administration favoured the Hindus in composition and outlook. For Pakistanis, the broad principle of partition was that Muslim majority areas should go to Pakistan, the remainder to be included in India. The determining factor in British India was the wish of the people of the area concerned. Thus in the North-West Frontier Province and in the Sylhet district of Assam a plebiscite was held, resulting in each case in the inclusion of the area in Pakistan. The British Parliament considered that it lacked authority to compel the princely states to adopt a similar procedure. British paramountcy was held to lapse from August 15, 1947, and the ruler of each state was left free to decide whether to accede to India or Pakistan. The rulers were advised to consider the influence of geography, economics and the composition of the population.

Kashmir was the only state which could seriously contemplate a threefold choice—accession to India or Pakistan or independence. It had common frontiers with both Dominions and with foreign powers, and if friendly relations with both Dominions had been possible, it might have sustained economic independence. There were strong reasons why the maharajah was unwilling to

[1] Detailed accounts of the Kashmir dispute may be found in Lord Birdwood, *op. cit.*, J. Korbel, *Danger in Kashmir* (Princeton, 1954) and M. Brecher, *The Struggle for Kashmir* (Toronto, 1953).

accede unconditionally to either India or Pakistan. The Dogra regime had not been supported by either of the two major political forces, the National Conference (pro-India), or the Muslim Conference (pro-Pakistan). A Hindu court dominating a Muslim people was unlikely to find favour with Pakistan. The forces aligned with the Indian National Congress, led by Sheikh Abdullah, were democratic and socialist and bitterly opposed to all forms of autocracy.

In these circumstances the maharajah hesitated. He proposed to both governments a 'standstill' agreement, by which facilities enjoyed by Kashmir before August 1947 should be temporarily continued. But by this time the state was showing signs of disintegration. As independence approached, partisans on both sides began to prepare for the use of violence. News of savage destruction was received from the Punjab, and refugees spread their tales of murder and looting. An anti-Muslim movement in the state 'was initiated with all the appearance of a systematic persecution.'[1] An armed revolt of Muslims was under way in Poonch. In October the Muslim rebels were joined by tribesmen from the North-West Frontier. The government of Pakistan has denied repeatedly that it was responsible for organizing the tribal invasion. But it seems clear that many local officials lent their assistance. The maharajah's forces were unable to defend Srinagar against this latest onslaught, and an appeal was sent to New Delhi for military aid. The Indian government insisted that this could be provided only after the formal accession of Kashmir to India. Accession was offered by the maharajah on October 26th and accepted by the Indian government the following day. The Indian army then took over and established military control of the greater part of Jammu and the Vale of Kashmir.

Neither the tribesmen nor the Muslim Kashmiri rebels (now called the forces of Azad Kashmir) could meet the organized power of Indian regular troops. In order to prevent the total conquest of Azad Kashmir, Pakistani troops were moved into the state in 1948 and came into direct conflict with the Indian army. The fighting was ended by a cease fire which took effect on

[1] Birdwood, *op. cit.*, p. 49.

Pakistan and the World

January 1, 1949. The cease fire line left the main centres of population in Indian hands, though a strip of territory along the western border and the thinly peopled north-west were retained by Pakistan.

A year before this the dispute had been laid before the United Nations. To India the issue was a simple act of aggression by Pakistan. Kashmir had acceded to India. The presence of Pakistani irregulars (tribesmen) and armed forces was therefore a violation of Indian soil. Thus no solution would be possible until Pakistani forces had been withdrawn.

To Pakistan the situation appears in a quite different light. The maharajah's authority had been virtually set aside by the majority of his subjects. 'The Maharajah himself fled and found sanctuary in Jammu. His writ had ceased to be supreme in the major part of the state. He was thus in no position to barter away the future of the state through an Instrument of Accession.' 'If anything, here was an act of naked Indian aggression against a defenceless people, committed under cover of a fraudulent and invalid instrument of accession, surreptitiously obtained from a Hindu ruler who had lost the confidence and support of his people and whose writ had no longer any force within the State.'[1]

The United Nations spent much time in attempting to find a solution. The Security Council, the United Nations Commission for India and Pakistan, General A. G. L. McNaughton, Sir Owen Dixon and Dr. Frank Graham were all involved in the effort to mediate. The principal objective was to bring about a plebiscite in which the Kashmiris could freely decide their own future. The principle of a plebiscite had been accepted by both sides. Lord Mountbatten's letter accepting the accession of Kashmir had contained the words: 'In consistence with their policy that in the case of any State where the issue of accession has been the subject of dispute, the question of accession should be decided in accordance with the wishes of the people of the State, it is my Government's wish that, as soon as law and order have been restored in Kashmir

[1] Government of Pakistan, *Foreign Relations* (Karachi, 1956), p. 12 (extracts from speech of Prime Minister Mohamad Ali in the National Assembly, March 31, 1956).

and its soil cleared of the invader, the questions of the State's accession should be settled by a reference to the people.'[1]

No agreement could be reached on the withdrawal of armed forces by both sides and other conditions for a free expression of choice. Successive mediators were compelled to announce their failure, and direct meetings and correspondence between the Prime Ministers of the two countries brought a solution no nearer. In the meanwhile a Constituent Assembly had been elected in Indian Kashmir. The elections were not contested by any organized opposition, and they were in no way an opportunity for a decision on the issue of accession. The Assembly declared the final adherence of the state to India and adopted a state constitution on this basis.[2] Economic and political ties with New Delhi were also strengthened. However, not even the most enthusiastic Indian supporter could pretend that all was well with the political state of Kashmir. The maharajah had served his purpose and had been speedily deposed. More serious was the arrest and imprisonment of the only substantial political leader in Kashmir, Sheikh Abdullah, who had led the National Conference and had been Chief Minister from 1948–54.[3] New state elections took place in early 1957, but advocacy of accession to Pakistan was not permitted.[4]

The general policy of India seems to be to improve the economic condition of the state while keeping tight control over political activity. The promise to let Kashmiris decide for themselves has never been disavowed, but the Indian government has hedged it round with so many conditions and reservations that its fulfilment is most unlikely. Pakistan's view of India's policy has been given by Chaudhri Mohamad Ali.

'In defence of his refusal to allow the people of Kashmir to decide their own future by means of a plebiscite, the Indian Prime Minister

[1] Text given in Birdwood, *op. cit.*, p. 214.
[2] *Pakistan News* (London), November 24, 1956, gives the Pakistan answer to the declaration of irrevocable accession.
[3] Birdwood, *op. cit.*, ch. 13 *passim*.
[4] A. M. Rosenthal, 'The Clouds Over Kashmir', *The New York Times Magazine*, May 5, 1957.

has talked of the prosperity of that part of Kashmir which the Indian Army holds in its steel grip. Here you have an argument in the best colonial tradition and it is interesting that the Indian Prime Minister, who claims to be uncompromisingly opposed to colonialism, should put it forward. While he holds Kashmir by force with the help of some 100,000 Indian soldiers, backed by the State Militia and the notorious "Peace Brigade" and detains numerous fighters for freedom in the State prisons, the Indian Prime Minister talks of the blessings of Indian rule. The people of Kashmir want freedom. He offers them instead bread, bread at the point of the bayonet.'[1]

Opinion in Pakistan is uniformly and implacably determined that Kashmiris must be allowed to choose to join their fellow Muslims. Pakistanis do not doubt that a fair plebiscite would yield a decision in their favour. They cite Indian reluctance to organize a vote or any genuinely free elections as an indication of hypocrisy in the Indian claim of popular support. Feeling in West Pakistan, ten years after partition, was still at fever heat. In the east wing, though the degree of passion was less, the sense of injustice was universal. It is impossible to foresee a state of mind in Pakistan that would permit truly friendly relations with India unless the greater part of Kashmir is permitted, if its people so choose, to join Pakistan. No public figure in West Pakistan would feel that his life was safe if he declared in public that he was willing to accept as inevitable the incorporation of Kashmir in India.

This is, perhaps, primarily an issue of prestige. It is intolerable to Pakistan that a Muslim majority area should be prevented from joining the other Muslim majority areas of the sub-continent. To suggest that Kashmiri Muslims might be better off in a secular, democratic India is to question the whole validity of the two-nation theory on which Pakistan is based. It is hardly surprising that many Pakistanis are stirred to fury by the attitude revealed in the following questions: 'Whatever the people of the Kashmir Valley may decide (and they have *not* stated that they are anxious to join Pakistan) does liberal opinion seriously think that India—

[1] Government of Pakistan, *op. cit.*, p. 19 (speech of Mohamad Ali, March 31, 1956).

stabler, more democratic, more progressive in her political and economic ideas—would be a worse choice than Pakistan, which is theocratic, unstable, retrograde and now helplessly dependent upon foreign aid? Will Kashmir's accession to Pakistan, which will leave India with a permanent sense of injury, be a gain for democracy and freedom?'[1]

Apart from prestige, Kashmir is important to Pakistan from the point of view of defence. The natural communications of the region follow the river valleys; the Jhelum flowing down from Srinagar toward Rawalpindi and the Chenab down through Jammu in the direction of Sialkot. Until 1956, when the Banihal tunnel was completed, there was no all-weather road between Srinagar and Indian soil. Pakistan forces in Kashmir would not pose a serious threat to Indian security; Indian forces in control of the state would, however, outflank the main defended positions of the Punjab. Further, the control of the upper reaches of two of the Punjab rivers would enable great devastation to be inflicted on the agriculture of West Pakistan without resort to military action.

The third princely state whose disposal gave rise to bad feeling between India and Pakistan was Hyderabad. Here the position of Kashmir was, in part, reversed. A Muslim prince ruled a Hindu people, many of whom resented his authority. Once again the ruler asked for a standstill agreement, and this was endangered by the outbreak of widespread disturbances within the state. Finally, Indian troops engaged in a police action to restore order and remained to supervise the incorporation of the state into India. It would have been a geographical and political impossibility for Hyderabad to have joined Pakistan, and this was fully realized by Mr. Jinnah. But Hyderabad had been a centre of Muslim culture and influence, and its forcible engulfment by India produced regret and resentment in Pakistan. And it seemed unfair to many that India should be able to march into Hyderabad and Junagadh to save the people from misrule by an unpopular prince while preventing Pakistan from taking comparable action

[1] *The Round Table*, Vol. XLV, 1954-55, p. 72 (Indian correspondent). This comment is typical of much Indian liberal opinion.

in Kashmir. Insult was added to injury by Indian insistence that her conduct was governed at all times by high moral principles.

The quarrel over the states has been the most bitter and persistent of the causes of friction between India and Pakistan. But there have been many other differences. The necessity of a hurried division of the assets of British India—funds, stores, weapons, records, rolling stock—was bound to cause ill-feeling. Most of these assets were located in Indian territory. It was necessary to hand over a fair proportion in order that the state of Pakistan might begin to function. Obviously, in the tense conditions of July to December 1947, there was a strong temptation to delay the transfer of items of value and to deliver only the less desirable materials. Hope that certain common services might be maintained in 1947-48 had to be largely abandoned in the face of the virtual separation of the two countries by miles of ravaged villages and flaming towns. However, agreement was reached on the allocation of income tax receipts, the payment of pensions and the division of the Post Office Savings Banks, but the vital transfer of a share of the monetary reserves was held up by India for several months.[1]

A much more prolonged controversy between the two countries involved evacuee property. Vast assets were left behind by the refugees who fled before the violence of 1947-48. Each government felt that its first concern must be to put to use the land, buildings, and commercial and industrial property, rather than let them stand idle, while legal title was established. The migration was on such a scale that millions of claims were involved which could never have been precisely checked and settled. Much resentment has been generated by the policies adopted by the two governments to re-distribute this evacuee property.

Under British rule the Punjab was developed in many ways as a model province. Its rural economy depended on the waters of the six rivers—Indus, Jhelum, Chenab, Ravi, Beas and Sutlej. This upper Indus basin was developed as a single unit with an immense network of irrigation canals. Partition cut across natural

[1] *The Round Table*, Vol. XXXVIII, 1947-48, p. 593.

Pakistan

geographical boundaries and left the headwaters of all the rivers outside Pakistan, although the major portion of the irrigated land fell within the West Punjab. It thus became possible for India to interfere seriously with the flow of vital water to the Punjab and Bahawalpur. The eastern rivers (Ravi, Beas and Sutlej) run for substantial distances through Indian territory. The Jhelum and Chenab lie partly in Indian Kashmir. Although there are limits to the profitable use that India could make of these latter, as an act of hostility it would be possible to deny or disrupt their use by Pakistan. A grim warning of such an eventuality occurred in 1948, when the flow of the Ravi was diverted for a month for no apparent reason except malice on the part of the Indian authorities.[1]

In 1951 the World Bank intervened as a mediator in this dispute, and a report was submitted three years later. It was proposed to allocate the eastern three rivers to India and the western three to Pakistan. Major technical objections were raised by Pakistan, which also accused India of violating a pledge not to divert more water pending the outcome of negotiations.[2]

One further cause of friction between India and Pakistan deserves mention. In 1949 the pound sterling was devalued and the currencies of most of the rest of the non-dollar world followed suit. The Pakistan rupee was, however, maintained at its existing level. The Indian government refused to recognize the validity of this decision, and direct trade between the two countries came almost to a standstill. The Pakistan economy was able to survive largely owing to the increase in export prices caused by the Korean war. Pakistanis took great pride in being able to maintain the formal value of their rupee, and were highly incensed at this further example of Indian intransigence. The Pakistan rupee was devalued in its turn in 1955.

At the end of this unhappy catalogue (which could be substantially enlarged), it might seem unnecessary to ask whether

---

[1] For a more detailed account of the canal waters dispute see 'Dividing the Waters,' *The Round Table*, Vol. XLV, 1954-55, pp. 250-258, and David E. Lilienthal, 'Another "Korea" in the Making,' *Colliers*, August 4, 1951.

[2] *The Round Table*, Vol. XLV, 1954-55, p. 246.

Pakistan and the World

Pakistan regards India as friend or foe. And yet the answer 'foe' would be a mis-statement. War between India and Pakistan cannot be regarded as unthinkable, but if it came it would have many of the characteristics of a civil war. It is not possible for the military commanders to forget that they were trained together, and may have fought side by side on other battlefields. Nor can the politicians and civil servants ignore the days when they worked together before partition. And the educated Indian and Pakistani have much in common beside the shared memories of an earlier period. They are, for example, the products of the same educational system. There are some ties that bind some Indians and some Pakistanis more closely to each other than to other groups of fellow citizens. Thus Bengali culture is a powerful link that cuts across the national boundary.

The Pakistani is constantly comparing himself to his Indian counterpart, and is quick to deny and resent any suggestion of inferiority. He has a passionate determination to be recognized as a full equal by the rest of the world, and especially by the Indian. He knows that India is larger, wealthier, and in many ways more advanced. But he will accept no explanation of this that seems to imply superior skill or determination on the part of the Indian.

Pakistan wants to justify herself before her powerful neighbour, to prove that the concept of Pakistan was right and that a stable, progressive Muslim state can be brought into operation. The quarrels between the two often retain the flavour of disagreements between bitter political opponents within a single state. It would be quite wrong to suggest that the feeling of Pakistanis toward India is one of simple hatred. Their attitude is rather one of intense rivalry to the point of bitter jealousy. In this rivalry they feel that India started with most of the material advantages, and yet has insisted on changing the rules whenever a decision seemed likely to go against her. One clear, indisputable political victory for Pakistan would do a great deal toward the reduction of tension on that side of the border.

Relations with India have been the main preoccupation of the foreign policy of Pakistan. When assessing the attitude of other states, the primary question is likely to be: Are they prepared to help us over Kashmir? One area from which support might have been expected is the Muslim world. Pakistan was founded to advance the cause of Muslims. Other Muslims might have been expected to be sympathetic, even enthusiastic. But this assumed that other Muslim states would take the same view of the relation between religion and nationality. In fact the political upsurge elsewhere was based largely on territorial and racial nationalism, anti-Western, anti-white. Religion played a part in this, but it was a lesser part than colour, language and a political theory of violent opposition to 'colonialism' and 'exploitation.' For many Muslims elsewhere it has been more important to align Asians and Africans against the colonial powers than to defend Muslim causes against non-Muslims. The Congress argument that specifically Muslim demands hampered national independence found wide acceptance in other Asian and Middle Eastern countries.

Once partition was accomplished many of the other Muslim states were reluctant to make a choice between friendship for India or Pakistan. If a choice had to be made, India, as more powerful, more stable and more influential, was likely to have the advantage. The leaders of the national movements in Egypt, Syria or Indonesia have not been men who have stressed the role of religion. In some instances they have been opposed by the orthodox and supported by the secularists. The political role of Islam was predominantly conservative or reactionary. In any event, in an all-Muslim country there could be no counterpart to the struggle between Hindu and Muslim.

The belief in the essential unity of purpose and outlook in the Muslim world has been an illusion that has been much cherished in Pakistan. It is only fair to add that professional diplomats and successive foreign ministers have been aware of its limitations,[1] but the vociferous opinion of newspapers and politicians has required that it be paraded for public admiration

[1] Thus the Foreign Minister (Firoz Khan Noon) urged his fellow countrymen to place 'Pak-Islamism' ahead of 'Pan-Islamism' (*Dawn*, October 22, 1956). The enthusiasm for Muslim unity usually increased in proportion to the distance of the speaker from public office.

at regular intervals. As late as November 1956 the President of the Muslim League was reported to have 'suggested that the Muslim countries should form a united Muslim world bloc for their security and survival.'[1]

By this time many Pakistanis had become aware that other Muslim states were not willing to reciprocate Pakistan's gestures of Muslim amity. The essential unity of the Muslim peoples was not questioned, but criticism was directed against selfish leaders who placed other considerations ahead of Islam. Since it was assumed that any other Muslim state ought to be a firm friend of Pakistan, a sign of indifference or hostility was taken as an unwarranted betrayal. Thus the King of Saudi-Arabia was criticized for his failure to share Pakistan's view of the treatment of the Muslim minority in India.[2] It was this feeling of betrayal that led to the passionate resentment shown against President Nasser when he rebuffed the offer of support during the invasion of Suez.

'It will thus be seen that Nasser's hatred of Pakistan and love for Bharat and its Nehru is an attitude of mind not warranted by facts but conditioned by insensate bias and blind prejudice the source of which might well be examined by psychiatrists. It is nevertheless a matter of deep regret that in the veins of this turbulent egotist not the blood of Islam should seem to flow but the turbid waters of the Nile. Nasser will never be our friend; he will never think in terms of Islam except when it suits his own interest.'[3]

The search for Muslim solidarity led to a number of definite policies. The first of these has been a general attempt to bring Muslim governments closer together. The first Muslim International Economic Conference was held in Karachi in 1950, and was presented with a major presidential address by Ghulam Mohammad.[4] The same organization met in Karachi again for

[1] *Dawn*, November 11, 1956, Sardar Abdur Rab Nishtar.
[2] *Ibid.*, September 27 and October 6, 1956, editorials entitled 'Vain Expectations' and 'Our Misguided Brothers.'
[3] *Ibid.*, December 1, 1956, editorial, 'So This is Nasser!'
[4] *The Round Table*, Vol. XL, 1949–50, p. 166.

Pakistan

its third conference in 1954, when Zafrullah Khan presided.[1] A more ambitious plan for a permanent consultative organization of Muslim states had to be abandoned because of the reluctance of some of the invited governments.[2] Contact with heads of state and Prime Ministers of Muslim countries was maintained by means of frequent visits. Official visits to Pakistan in a short period of years were made by the Shah of Iran, the kings of Jordan, Iraq and Saudi-Arabia and the Presidents of Turkey, Egypt, Indonesia and Syria. The President of Pakistan in turn visited Afghanistan, Turkey, Iraq, Iran and Saudi-Arabia. Contact with other leading Muslims was also established through meetings at the time of the *hajj* (pilgrimage to Mecca). Government encouragement was given to various non-official organizations designed to foster closer ties between Muslim states and peoples.

In the United Nations the influence of Pakistan was normally on the side of any Muslim cause. Support has constantly been given to the Arab side in the Palestine dispute. 'I would like to make it clear,' said Mr. Suhrawardy, 'that Pakistan has never recognized Israel, and my policy definitely is that we shall not recognize Israel under any circumstances.'[3] Pakistan has been strongly in favour of independence for Sudan, Libya, Tunisia, Morocco and Malaya. The government also supported the Indonesian struggle for independence and, according to the Foreign Minister: 'On the Irian issue, both inside and outside the United Nations, we have given full support to Indonesia.'[4] The government was less single-minded in its attitude toward the Anglo-Iranian dispute and the opening stages of the Suez crisis. But public demonstrations throughout the country indicated a very loud degree of sympathy for the cause of fellow Muslims.

The desire of Pakistan for Muslim solidarity has always faced a problem in connection with her nearest Muslim neighbour,

---

[1] *Pakistan News* (London), May 8, 1954.
[2] *The Round Table*, Vol. XLII, 1951–52, pp. 258–9.
[3] *Pakistan News* (London), November 24, 1956, quoting a press statement of November 14, 1956.
[4] Government of Pakistan, *op. cit.*, pp. 46–7 (speech of Hamidul Huq Chowdhury, March 25, 1956).

Afghanistan.[1] The Afghans had long had claims to a large area on the North-West Frontier inhabited by the Pathans. These claims were allowed to lie dormant while strong British forces were in control, but they were resurrected against the new government of Pakistan. The frontier, the Durand Line, has been recognized since 1893, but large areas on either side have never been brought under complete civil government. The Afghan government has advanced claims to protect the region inhabited by Pushto-speaking people described as Pakhtunistan. They have also incited disaffection among the tribes within the Pakistan border, and have given aid and shelter to such dubious though picturesque figures as the Faqir of Ipi.[2] Relations between the two states got off to a very bad start when Afghanistan cast the only vote opposing the admission of Pakistan to the United Nations. Opinion in Pakistan usually holds that there is every reason for friendship between the peoples of the two countries, but that the autocratic government of Kabul uses charges against Pakistan as a means of diverting the pressure of domestic issues.

The Afghan campaign reached its peak after the decision to amalgamate the units of West Pakistan, thus incorporating the areas claimed by Afghanistan in a much larger political entity. Public demonstrations culminated in attacks on Pakistani diplomatic property in Kabul and Jalalabad and in public insults to the Pakistani flag. After a lengthy wrangle this episode was brought to an end by the ceremonial raising of the flag by officials of the Afghan government.[3] The note of reconciliation was not to last for long. The Afghans had asked the government of Pakistan to begin talks on the One Unit scheme and, after some delay without an affirmative reply from Karachi, the Afghan ambassador was withdrawn. The Pakistan envoy to Kabul was then also summoned home.[4] The following year saw a renewed improvement of relations. The King of Afghanistan had to postpone a visit to Pakistan on grounds of ill-health, but President Mirza went to Kabul and

[1] See Mohammed Ahsen Chaudhri, 'The Relations of Pakistan with Afghanistan,' *Pakistan Horizon*, Vol. VIII, No. 4, December 1955.
[2] *The Round Table*, Vol. XXIX, 1948–49, p. 74.
[3] *Pakistan News* (London), September 24, 1955.   [4] *Ibid.*, October 29, 1955.

Pakistan

was warmly received.[1] At the end of the year the Prime Minister of Afghanistan visited Karachi and had lengthy conversations about Pakhtunistan, which, it was announced, had 'substantially contributed to a better appreciation of the respective views held. . . .'[2]

Unhesitating support for almost every Muslim cause was bound to lead to friction with some of the Western powers. There is a substantial element of popular feeling in Pakistan that responds eagerly to any opportunity for the expression of resentment against the European, especially the British. Pakistan has inherited its share of the emotions of Asian nationalism which regards what it calls Western colonialism as the root of all social and political evil. A Pakistani interpretation of recent history often insists that British policy has been deeply anti-Muslim, and is still aimed at the suppression of the Muslim peoples. This approach is the product of emotion rather than thought, but the intensity of such emotion can be very powerful. The editorial reaction of a leading newspaper to the Anglo-French attack on Egypt provides an illustration.

'It is not our custom to print an editorial on the front page; but when Britain produces a Hitler who throws his own country's honour and all cherished moral, human and international values which it has itself fostered in the past, out of the windows of the Houses of Westminster into the Thames and proceeds to shed innocent Muslim blood to dye red the Nile, opening a new and unbelievable chapter of perfidy and violence in the history of the human race—a little editorial custom is a small thing to disregard for the sake of proclaiming without losing a single day what the people of Pakistan feel. And what we have said, and very much more, are surging in the minds of all our people now.

'They are asking—and we give voice to their questions: Is this not the rise once again of bigoted and perverted Christendom against the world of Islam in alliance with the Jews! Is this not a threat poised against Muslims from the Atlantic to the Pacific?[3]

[1] *Pakistan News* (London), August 25, 1956.
[2] *Ibid.*, December 8, 1956, official communique.
[3] *Dawn*, November 1, 1956. It is only fair to add that the editor had second thoughts about some sections of this editorial, which were printed the following day.

Britain has often filled the role of the nation's foe, especially for those who are ardent in the cause of Muslim solidarity. But the official government attitude has always stressed the value of friendship with Britain. This has been true of the Foreign Ministers drawn from the Muslim League, Krishak Sramik Party or Awami League. Mr. Hamidul Huq Chowdhury reviewed the position in March 1956: 'As regards the Commonwealth countries, we have the friendliest and most cordial relations with the United Kingdom. It was the United Kingdom, as the House will remember, which was the first country to establish diplomatic relations with us. We have worked together in harmony and concord with the United Kingdom and we have both been aware of each other's needs and requirements.'[1]

Immediately before the republican status of Pakistan was proclaimed, the Constituent Assembly debated a resolution maintaining membership in the Commonwealth. The resolution was moved by the Prime Minister (Mohamad Ali) and supported by the Leader of the Opposition (H. S. Suhrawardy), and was carried by an overwhelming majority.[2] This decision cannot be taken as an indication of firmly rooted popular support for the Commonwealth. As soon as the Muslim League was out of office it began to veer to the more hostile view of British policy which has always been adopted by the greater part of non-official opinion. In November 1956 the League Working Committee passed a resolution which included the following paragraph: 'The behaviour of the British government in their dealings with Muslim countries, particularly towards Iran when that country nationalized its oil industry, towards Saudi-Arabia over the Buraimi Oasis dispute, and towards Egypt over the nationalization of the Suez Canal; their attack on Yemen, and last but not the least, their brutal aggression against Egypt in company with France and Israel has convinced the people of Pakistan that its continuance as a member of the Commonwealth

---

[1] Government of Pakistan, *op. cit.*, pp. 32-33 (Hamidul Huq Chowdhury).
[2] *Pakistan News* (London), February 10, 1956. The debate took place on March 2, 1956.

Pakistan

is positively harmful and, therefore, there is a universal demand for withdrawal of Pakistan from the Commonwealth.'[1]

The attitude of Pakistanis to Britain and the West is ambivalent. They are much more intimately aware of Britain than of other countries (except India). The United States they know distantly, and Russia exists as a symbol. But Britain and the British government have been part of the public life of the Indian sub-continent for many generations. Pakistan's independence was related to the internal workings of the British political system. This degree of British power no longer exists, but something of the attitude of mind that it engendered has persisted.

There has been a tendency to regard the Commonwealth as a means of satisfaction of Pakistan's claims against India. The reluctance of other members to allow Commonwealth conferences to be turned into a court of arbitration, has caused some irritation in Pakistan. Liaquat Ali, returning from the Prime Ministers' Conference in 1949, declared: 'Pakistan must not be taken for granted: Pakistan is not a camp follower of the Commonwealth.'[2] Two years later he was still dissatisfied and refused to go to London until assured that opportunity would be provided for discussions on Kashmir.[3]

This preoccupation with affairs close to her own border led Pakistan for many years to regard the larger international tensions as irrelevant. It was felt that the Korean war was remote from Pakistan's real interests, and, although casting a vote to condemn aggression, no military commitment was made.[4] Pakistan was looking for friends and seeking to out-manœuvre potential enemies; Russia was prepared to ignore Pakistan and Pakistan was content to reciprocate.

The wealth and prestige of the United States made them a desirable friend, but American policy under President Truman seemed to attach more importance to an understanding with India. Pakistan was largely unknown and misunderstood in

[1] *Dawn*, November 17, 1956.
[2] Quoted in *The Round Table*, Vol. XXIX, 1948–49, p. 365.
[3] *Ibid.*, Vol. XLI, 1950–51, p. 170.
[4] Mushtaq Ahmad, *The United Nations and Pakistan* (Karachi, 1955), p. 95.

Pakistan and the World

America. To correct some of this ignorance and incomprehension, Liaquat Ali conducted a vigorous speaking tour in the United States and Canada.[1] In 1953 two changes of government took place. In the United States Eisenhower was installed as president, with J. F. Dulles as Secretary of State; in Pakistan Ghulam Mohammad dismissed Nazimuddin and replaced him as Prime Minister by Mohammed Ali, formerly ambassador in Washington. Mr. Dulles wanted pacts. Mr. Mohammed Ali liked Americans. Pakistan wanted money and arms. In 1954 Pakistan signed a Mutual Defence Agreement with the United States,[2] concluded an agreement with Turkey,[3] and became one of the signatories of the Manila Treaty (SEATO).[4] The following year Pakistan adhered to the Iraq-Turkey treaty (Baghdad Pact).[5]

By entering these alliances, Pakistan had effectively committed herself to the side of the West. The Foreign Minister dealt in cutting terms with those who tried to avoid making a choice. 'To me neutralism seems suspiciously like "fencemanship"—the art of sitting on the fence between two worlds hoping that each will help for fear of losing the sitter to the other. History has witnessed the swift and tragic end of such feats of balancing when they are put to the test.'[6] The Prime Minister, at the Bandung Conference, countered Mr. Nehru's *panch shila* with seven principles of his own, including the right of self-defence, exercised singly or collectively.[7]

Pakistan was less tempted than certain other countries by the concept of Asian (or non-white) solidarity. Pakistan was founded on the basis of the vital difference between groups of Asians, and her leaders can perceive much more dangerous potential enemies than the colonial powers of Europe. Pakistan entered a network of alliances, not out of any strong sympathy for the Western

[1] Liaquat Ali Khan, *Pakistan: The Heart of Asia* (Cambridge, Mass., 1951).
[2] *Pakistan News* (London), July 10, 1954. See also J. W. Spain, 'Military Assistance for Pakistan,' *American Political Science Review*, Vol. XLVIII (September 1954), pp. 738–51. [3] *Pakistan News* (London), April 10, 1954.
[4] See Royal Institute of International Affairs, *Collective Defence in South East Asia* (London, 1956). [5] *Pakistan News* (London), October 1, 1955.
[6] Government of Pakistan, *op. cit.*, p. 56 (Hamidul Huq Chowdhury).
[7] Royal Institute of International Affairs, *op. cit.*, p. 109.

powers but because those alliances offered a prospect of advancing her own standing and interests. The SEATO communique of March 1956 reaffirmed Pakistan's western frontier along the Durand Line and urged 'an early settlement of the Kashmir question.'[1] Hamidul Huq commended the alliances to the Assembly with this explanation: 'As far as Pakistan is concerned the most notable achievement of the SEATO is the joint re-affirmation by the Members of our stand on Kashmir and the Durand Line.'[2]

The American alliance has strengthened Pakistan against a possible threat from India. Many Indian leaders have complained that the receipt of American arms constitutes a threat to India, and this has been used as an additional reason for delay in the settlement of the Kashmir dispute. Such a view, though probably held sincerely, cannot be taken seriously in the light of the superior size, resources, armed forces and geographical position of India.

The Baghdad Pact has additional virtues. It is, apart from the United Kingdom, composed of Muslim states Iran, Iraq and Turkey. It provides the basis for a real partnership of common interests, and Turkey and Pakistan have the two most effective armies in the Muslim world. Membership in this pact has worsened relations with Egypt and Syria, but these two countries had never placed much value on the friendship of Pakistan.

The conduct of foreign policy in Pakistan has been mainly in the hands of experts. As in many other matters there is a sharp cleavage between the Western-educated lawyer or administrator and the domestic politician or journalist. The former tends to take a realistic view of the material and political interests of the country; the latter are inclined to react emotionally and to demand dramatic gestures of love or hatred. The ordinary politician and the man in the street have taken little continuing interest in foreign affairs, except with regard to India. Interest has been spasmodic, concentrating on those crises of international affairs that have affected Pakistan or other Muslim states. The

[1] *Collective Defence in South East Asia*, p. 194.
[2] Government of Pakistan, *op. cit.*, p. 56 (Hamidul Huq Chowdhury).

official attitude has been one of caution interspersed with an occasional more vivid declaration for home consumption.

There have been three Ministers of Foreign Affairs and Commonwealth Relations during the first ten years of independence—Chaudhri Zafrullah Khan, Hamidul Huq Chowdhury and Malik Firoz Khan Noon. They are all men of high educational attainments and great ability. Zafrullah was somewhat isolated from the other members of the cabinets in which he served. His personal relations with some of his colleagues were unhappy, and the fact that he is an Ahmadi did not contribute to harmony. But his advocacy before the Security Council concerning Kashmir should have earned him the gratitude of his country.

Foreign affairs have not been conducted exclusively by the Foreign Ministers. Successive Prime Ministers have taken a direct part in relations with other states. The series of Commonwealth conferences has taken the Prime Minister repeatedly to London. Most of the direct contacts between the Pakistani and Indian governments took the form of meetings or letters between Mr. Nehru and his counterpart in Pakistan. The Governor-General (President) has also played an important role. During Ghulam Mohammad's ascendancy it was clear to all that he was the effective maker of policy. He addressed the Indian Prime Minister in the following terms: 'You and I must unravel the tangles which have caused friction between our two countries.'[1] Even after the new constitution had come into force, there were indications that President Mirza was playing an active part. In 1956 he made a series of journeys that involved far more than gestures of courtesy. It was officially announced that the November meeting of the Baghdad Pact powers had taken place 'in the presence of' the President and the King of Iraq.[2]

The conduct of foreign policy was almost entirely a matter for the President, the cabinet and senior civil servants. Parliament was small, infrequently in session and preoccupied with other matters. Most debates on foreign affairs degenerated into denunciations of

[1] Quoted in *The Round Table*, Vol. XLV, 1954–55, p. 177.
[2] *Pakistan News* (London), December 8, 1956.

Pakistan

India or the imperialist powers. The change in the balance of political forces in 1953-56 did little to alter the main lines of policy. Most of the Bengali members of the National Assembly were not completely satisfied with the acceptance of military alliances. Both in the Muslim League and the Republican Party in West Pakistan provincial politics contained many supporters of a neutralist approach to world affairs. But at the centre it proved possible to obtain sufficient support for the policies of the governing group. The most persistent and wide-ranging critic of the policy of successive governments was Mian Iftikharuddin, who took an extreme left-wing position. In so far as there was deep popular feeling in the country it was to the effect that the government was unnecessarily timid in its dealings with India. On other issues the public would have been much happier to do without Western alliances, but most people were prepared to be convinced by the argument that they were necessary to strengthen the nation against India. The American alliance might well have encountered serious hostility, especially in Bengal, if the Indian reaction to it had not been so loud and so hostile.

There can be no doubt that Pakistan's foreign policy has matured in the course of ten years. Its horizon has expanded from its own borders to encompass much of the world. It is still obsessed by Kashmir, but no longer to the virtual exclusion of all other issues. It would, however, be idle to pretend that domestic changes or the possibility of a settlement with India might not bring about a sudden and drastic alteration in Pakistan's world view.

CHAPTER XI

Prospect

THERE are very few successful democracies. Those that seem firmly established have developed their traditions of social and political justice over a period of many generations. It is a truism, but none the less vital, to say that democracy depends on the insistence by public opinion that the holders of power conform to the spirit of the constitution. This will for democracy inevitably takes time to grow and must be rooted deep in the consciousness of the people.

Democracy has usually developed in countries where there is a reasonable degree of material prosperity and where class or sectional divisions are not intense. Further, some security from the prospect of foreign aggression is necessary in order to permit the luxury of active opposition which attempts to frustrate the policies of the government. War, or the imminence of war, always acts to curtail freedom and open opposition becomes next door to treason.

In the light of these considerations it is not surprising that if one asks: 'Has Pakistan established a working democracy?' the answer must be 'Not yet.' Pakistan began its existence under exceptionally unfavourable circumstances. It is a remarkable achievement that the country has fared no worse. Many foreign observers in 1947 had the gravest doubts about the viability of the new state, especially about its capacity for self-government. But the machinery of government has been established and has been tested by a series of crises that might well have caused its disintegration.

In the field of economic development a substantial programme of industrialization has been carried out. The national accounts have been balanced and reserves of foreign exchange have been maintained. New commercial classes have come into existence

Pakistan

and are learning to operate and control businesses that traditionally were in the hands of non-Muslim communities.

Pakistan has faced the problem of the place of an ancient religion in a modern society. The Islamic state has been proclaimed but the fanatics are not in control of the country. There has been no victory for Islamic puritanism.

Major friction has developed between the east and west wings of the country, but the unifying ideal of Pakistan is still cherished among all sections of the people. There has been no irrevocable cleavage and the chances of closer harmony have not vanished.

Pakistan has avoided some of the worse calamities that might have befallen her. But these achievements are negative. It would be idle to pretend that the political prospect gives much cause for satisfaction. The traditions of cabinet government have not been accepted either at the centre or in the provinces. This is the system adopted by the constitution, but most politicians seem totally unwilling to pay more than lip service to its requirements. The political parties have presented a picture of almost unredeemed failure. At no time since the death of Liaquat Ali has a cabinet been in office that seems to have the clear support of the party, the legislature and the electorate.

Public life in Pakistan has suffered from a marked tendency to try to act on two contradictory principles at the same time. The people want the country to be founded on the full measure of the immutable principles of Islam; yet they are willing to abandon none of the advantages of a modern secular state. They want democracy but they also admire an act of strength and rally to support the man who has acted. They want provincial autonomy but are not ready to deny power to the central government. They want a foreign policy that will give automatic support to all Muslim causes; yet they also desire all the benefits of a policy of selective self-interest.

Thinking about public policy began in Pakistan in 1947. It could not have begun earlier. Many of the fundamental policies of other states have been felt instinctively for hundreds of years. History has taught them which interests are vital and which may be regarded as of secondary importance. Pakistan has to grope its way into its own national consciousness to find a measure of agreement on issues that have been solved in other countries for generations.

The tradition of Pakistan is not one of democracy. The struggle for the establishment of the state was one for the rule of Muslim by Muslim. It was not primarily directed to securing self-government *within* a Muslim state. The objection to British or Hindu rule was that it was alien to the religion, culture and tradition of Muslims, and not that it denied to the individual the right to choose his own rulers.

Pakistan has begun its life with a set of public institutions that are, broadly speaking, democratic. They are institutions that became familiar, at least to the politically conscious, during the closing years of British rule. And the principles of responsible government formed part of the education of those who studied British history and government in the universities and colleges of undivided India. However, the legislatures and cabinets of British India were used not for normal democratic government, but to force the British to leave the country or to convince the Hindus that an independent state must be provided for the Muslims. In these causes it was permissible, in the name of nationalism, to use the outward forms of self-government to undermine constituted authority. It was difficult to develop respect and reverence for the institutions that were being exploited to achieve an ulterior purpose. This was one of the areas in which the mind of the educated Muslim operated on two planes. At one level he had an academic and abstract appreciation of the virtues of cabinet government; at the other and more passionate level he had nothing but scorn and hatred for anything that might stand in the way of the achievement of the Muslim homeland. After 1947, when the first exhilaration of victory had begun to wear thin, he was left to discover how the system might be made to work in the interests of efficient and responsible government.

It is hard under any circumstances to transfer a social institution from one environment to another which has a quite different history. If it is to succeed it must put down roots into the new soil and learn how to flourish in a strange climate. It is unlikely

Pakistan

to function in quite the same manner as in the original country. It needs to be brought into alignment with those aspects of the local tradition that are most favourable to its advancement.

In Pakistan democracy has one considerable advantage: it is the only strongly advocated political theory. There are many ideological currents that carry anti-democratic implications, but they have not been presented as the basis of an alternative form of government. Some of the proposals put forward by the men of religion have been impossible to reconcile with democratic practice. But there has been no open clash between the democrats and the mullahs. Most of the latter proclaim that Islam is a democratic system and, in general terms, are prepared to praise the virtues of responsible government. There are many elements of the population which desire radical and swift action to redress their grievances. They form a reservoir of possible adherents of an anti-democratic movement, but no serious totalitarian groups have yet emerged in Pakistan. The Communist Party, even when it functioned legally, made very little headway, and there are no signs of any marked accession of strength in recent years. The forces on the Right (if that term has much meaning in Pakistan) have shown no greater desire to challenge the working of the institutions of representative government. Conservative forces have been successful in capturing control of most of the legislatures and thereby preventing any very radical measures of legislation or administration. But there is no sign that such groups are prepared to resort to unconstitutional means to prevent adoption of major social or economic changes.

The weakness of parliamentary government has been the failure of the elected politicians to make the system work. Ministries have been overthrown by intrigue backed by threats, rather than by real violence. Holders of political office have shown themselves unscrupulous but not totalitarian. And there have been important sections of the community which have exerted pressure to keep the democratic system in operation. The courts have applied the law as they found it, and that law is based on British precedent. The civil service and the army have shown no desire to back any potential dictator. There may be those

Prospect

who have toyed with the idea of suspending the working of parliamentary institutions, but they have produced no leader who seems likely to obtain wide enough support to undertake such a step. If representative government collapses it will be because its legs are not strong enough to sustain its own body.

There are aspects of the popular moral outlook which favour some elements of responsible government. Islam is a system of obedience to law; its teachings can therefore be used to counter any assertion of arbitrary power. The importance of law goes beyond this. The role of the judge is highly honoured in Muslim tradition, and on occasion the judges were able to control and limit the power of the caliphs. The concept of government according to law is therefore capable of uniting the democratic and religious motives in the minds of the people. The Muslim political ideal is one of justice. Justice is to be accorded to all men whether believers or not (although it does not require that non-believers should be given the same status as Muslims in all respects). Islam enjoins the complete equality of all Muslims before both God and man. There is a link between these ideas and the English tradition of government according to law and of equality before the law. It is perhaps significant that respect for law was established in England long before the achievement of political democracy.

It is a mistake to judge the success or failure of government in a country like Pakistan solely or even mainly by its fulfilment of the ideal standards of the Western democracies. There are more fundamental tasks than the operation of representative institutions. Law and order must be preserved; government should be just and incorruptible; and it should be capable of putting national policies into effect. Personal liberty and parliamentary government are not necessarily inseparable, though they are closely related. Above all, it is necessary to remember that popular government does not spring full-grown from the ground. Pakistan, by its constitution, is publicly committed to the operation of democratic institutions. It is too early to say whether those institutions are likely to mature. Democracy has been accepted as an ideal; there is nothing to indicate that it cannot become a reality.

APPENDIX I

THE CONSTITUTION OF THE ISLAMIC REPUBLIC OF PAKISTAN

EXTRACTS AND SUMMARY

PREAMBLE

In the name of Allah, the Beneficent, the Merciful

Whereas sovereignty over the entire Universe belongs to Allah Almighty alone, and the authority to be exercised by the people of Pakistan within the limits prescribed by Him is a sacred trust;

Whereas the Founder of Pakistan, Quaid-i-Azam Mohammad Ali Jinnah, declared that Pakistan would be a democratic State based on Islamic principles of social justice;

And whereas the Constituent Assembly, representing the people of Pakistan, have resolved to frame for the sovereign independent State of Pakistan a constitution;

Wherein the State should exercise its powers and authority through the chosen representatives of the people;

Wherein the principles of democracy, freedom, equality, tolerance and social justice as enunciated by Islam, should be fully observed;

Wherein the Muslims of Pakistan should be enabled individually and collectively to order their lives in accordance with the teachings and requirements of Islam, as set out in the Holy Quran and Sunnah;

Wherein adequate provision should be made for the minorities freely to profess and practise their religion and develop their culture;

Wherein the territories now included in or in accession with Pakistan and such other territories as may hereafter be included in or accede to Pakistan should form a Federation, wherein the Provinces would be autonomous with such limitations on their powers and authority as might be prescribed;

Wherein should be guaranteed fundamental rights including rights such as equality of status and of opportunity, equality before law, freedom of thought, expression, belief, faith, worship, and association, and social, economic, and political justice, subject to law and public morality;

Wherein adequate provision should be made to safeguard the legitimate interests of minorities and backward and depressed classes;

Wherein the independence of the Judiciary should be fully secured;

Wherein the integrity of the territories of the Federation, its independence and all its rights, including its sovereign rights over land, sea and air should be safeguarded;

So that the people of Pakistan may prosper and attain their rightful and honoured place amongst the nations of the world and make their full contribution towards international peace and the progress and happiness of humanity.

PART I THE REPUBLIC AND ITS TERRITORIES

1. (1) Pakistan shall be a Federal Republic to be known as the Islamic Republic of Pakistan. . . .

PART II FUNDAMENTAL RIGHTS

4. Laws inconsistent with the constitution to be void.
5. (1) All citizens are equal before law and are entitled to equal protection of law.
   (2) No person shall be deprived of life or liberty save in accordance with law.
6. Protection against retrospective offences or punishment.
7. Safeguards as to arrest and detention; limits on preventive detention.
8. Every citizen shall have the right to freedom of speech and expression, subject to any reasonable restrictions imposed by law in the interest of the security of Pakistan, friendly relations with foreign States, public order, decency or morality, or in relation to contempt of court, defamation or incitement to an offence.
9. Freedom of assembly.
10. Freedom of association.

Pakistan

11. Freedom of movement and right to hold and dispose of property.

12. Freedom of trade, business or profession.

13. Rights and safeguards respecting religious and educational institutions.

15. (1) No person shall be deprived of his property save in accordance with law.

 Compulsory acquisition only for public purposes and on payment of compensation. Existing laws and some special categories are not affected by these restrictions.

16. Slavery and forced labour prohibited.

18. Subject to law, public order and morality—
(*a*) every citizen has the right to profess, practise and propagate any religion; and
(*b*) every religious denomination and every sect thereof has the right to establish, maintain and manage its religious institutions.

19. Preservation of culture and language.

20. Abolition of untouchability.

22. The Supreme Court to have powers to guarantee fundamental rights.

PART III DIRECTIVE PRINCIPLES OF STATE POLICY

24. The State shall endeavour to strengthen the bonds of unity among Muslim countries, to promote international peace and security, to foster goodwill and friendly relations among all nations, and to encourage the settlement of international disputes by peaceful means.

25. (1) Steps shall be taken to enable the Muslims of Pakistan individually and collectively to order their lives in accordance with the Holy Quran and Sunnah.

27. The State shall safeguard the legitimate rights and interests of the minorities, including their due representation in the Federal and Provincial Services.

28. The State shall endeavour to—
(*b*) remove illiteracy, and provide free and compulsory primary education within the minimum possible period;
(*e*) prevent prostitution, gambling and the taking of injurious drugs; and

(f) prevent the consumption of alcoholic liquor other than for medicinal and, in the case of non-Muslims, religious purposes.

29. The State shall endeavour to—

(a) secure the well-being of the people, irrespective of caste, creed or race, by raising the standard of living of the common man, by preventing the concentration of wealth and means of production and distribution in the hands of a few to the detriment of the interest of the common man, and by ensuring equitable adjustment of rights between employers and employees, and landlords and tenants;

30. The State shall separate the Judiciary from the Executive as soon as practicable.

PART IV THE FEDERATION

Chapter I.—The Federal Government

32. The President. The President to be elected by the members of both the National and Provincial Assemblies. He must be a Muslim and at least 40 years of age.

33. The President holds office for five years and may not serve more than two terms.

35. The President may be removed by impeachment by the National Assembly; a majority of three-quarters of the total membership is required.

36. In the event of a vacancy or disability the Speaker of the National Assembly is to act as President.

37. (1) There shall be a Cabinet of Ministers with the Prime Minister at its head, to aid and advise the President in the exercise of his functions.

(3) The President shall, in his discretion, appoint from amongst the members of the National Assembly a Prime Minister who, in his opinion, is most likely to command the confidence of the majority of the members of the National Assembly.

(5) The Cabinet, together with the Ministers of State, shall be collectively responsible to the National Assembly.

(6) The Prime Minister shall hold office during the pleasure of the President, but the President shall not exercise

Pakistan

his powers under this clause unless he is satisfied that the Prime Minister does not command the confidence of the majority of the members of the National Assembly.

(7) In the exercise of his functions, the President shall act in accordance with the advice of the Cabinet or the appropriate Minister or Minister of State, as the case may be, except in cases where he is empowered by the Constitution to act in his discretion and except as respects the exercise of his powers under clause (6).

42. It shall be the duty of the Prime Minister—

(*a*) to communicate to the President all decisions of the Cabinet relating to the administration of the affairs of the Federation and proposals for legislation.

(*b*) to furnish such information relating to the administration of the affairs of the Federation and proposals for legislation as the President may call for; and

(*c*) if the President so requires, to submit, for the consideration of the Cabinet, any matter on which a decision has been taken by a Minister but which has not been considered by the Cabinet.

Chapter II.—The Parliament of Pakistan

43. There shall be a Parliament of Pakistan consisting of the President and one House, to be known as the National Assembly.

44. The Assembly consists of three hundred members, though for ten years ten additional seats are provided for women.

50. (1) The President may summon, prorogue or dissolve the National Assembly and shall, when summoning the Assembly, fix the time and place of the meeting:

Provided that at least one session of the National Assembly in each year shall be held at Dacca.

(2) Whenever a Prime Minister is appointed, the National Assembly, if, at the time of the appointment, it is not sitting and does not stand dissolved, shall be summoned so as to meet within two months thereafter.

(3) Unless sooner dissolved, the National Assembly shall stand dissolved on the expiration of five years from the date of its first meeting.

The Constitution

51. There shall be at least two sessions of the National Assembly in every year, and six months shall not intervene between the last sitting of the Assembly in one session and its first sitting in the next session.

54–56. Office of Speaker, rules of procedure and privileges of members of the National Assembly.

57. To become law, a Bill requires the assent of the President. The President may withhold assent or return a Bill for reconsideration. In the event of withholding of assent, should the Bill be re-passed by the votes of not less than two-thirds of the members present and voting, the President is required to give his assent.

58. Definition of a Money Bill.

59. Proposals for expenditure may originate only with the government.

60. No tax shall be levied for the purposes of the Federation except by or under the authority of an Act of Parliament.

63. An annual financial statement is to be laid before the Assembly.

64. Certain sums to be charged upon the Federal Consolidated Fund.

69. When the Assembly is not in session, the President shall have power to promulgate ordinances having the force of law. Such ordinances shall be laid before the Assembly and shall cease to operate six weeks after the next meeting of the Assembly or sooner if so resolved by the Assembly.

PART V THE PROVINCES

Chapter I.—The Provincial Government

70. (1) There shall be a Governor for each Province who shall be appointed by the President and shall hold office during the pleasure of the President.

71–75. The provinces have a form of cabinet government similar in all essentials to that provided for the federation.

Chapter II.—The Provincial Legislature

76–102. Each provincial Assembly consists of three hundred members with the temporary reservation of ten additional seats for women. The general provisions governing the Pro-

Pakistan

vincial Assemblies are similar to those for the National Assembly.

79. (1) No person shall at the same time be a member of the National Assembly and of a Provincial Assembly. . . .

103–104. The executive authority of a Province is to apply to Excluded Areas and Special Areas but a degree of control over such areas is reserved to the central government.

PART VI. RELATIONS BETWEEN THE FEDERATION AND THE PROVINCES

Chapter I.—Legislative Powers

106. Parliament shall have exclusive legislative jurisdiction over the subjects enumerated in the Federal List, the Provinces shall have exclusive jurisdiction over the Provincial List and each may pass laws relating to subjects in the Concurrent List (see Schedule V).

107–109. Parliament may legislate on a provincial matter with the consent of the Province. Parliament has power to pass laws to implement any treaty. The residuary power of legislation lies with the Provinces.

110. In the event of a conflict between a valid Act of Parliament and an Act of a Provincial Assembly, the Parliamentary law shall prevail. However, with the previous consent of the federal government, a provincial Act under the Concurrent List may take effect even though it conflict with an Act of Parliament.

Chapter II.—Financial Provisions

112. Property of Federal and Provincial governments to be exempt from taxes.

116. Federal supervision over certain provincial loans.

118. National Finance Commission representing the Federation and the Provinces, to be established every five years. It is to make recommendations concerning the distribution of shared taxes (including income tax, sales tax and export duties), grants-in-aid and public borrowing.

119. Provinces not to restrict inter-provincial trade.

The Constitution

Chapter IV.—Administrative Relations between the Federation and the Provinces

125. Federation to protect the Provinces and to ensure that their government 'is carried on in accordance with the provisions of the Constitution.'

126. Provincial executive authority to carry out provisions of federal law and not to impede federal executive authority. Federal government may issue certain directions to a Province.

132. Parliament may transfer railways to provincial jurisdiction.

PART VIII ELECTIONS

137-138. President, in his discretion, to appoint Election Commission.

140. The Election Commission shall be charged with the duty of—

(a) preparing electoral rolls for elections to the National Assembly and the Provincial Assemblies, and revising such rolls annually; and

(b) organizing and conducting elections to the National Assembly and the Provincial Assemblies.

141. Whenever the National Assembly or a Provincial Assembly is dissolved, a general election for the reconstitution of the Assembly shall be held not later than six months from the date of dissolution;

142. President may constitute a Delimitation Commission to demarcate territorial constituencies.

143. Qualifications of electors; adult suffrage.

145. Parliament, after consulting Provincial Assemblies, to decide on joint or separate electorates.

PART IX THE JUDICIARY

Chapter I.—The Supreme Court

149. (1) The Chief Justice of Pakistan shall be appointed by the President, and the other Judges shall be appointed by the President after consultation with the Chief Justice.

151. A judge may be removed only by the President after an address by the National Assembly, two-thirds of the members concurring.

Pakistan

156. Supreme Court to have original jurisdiction in disputes between the Federation and the Provinces and in certain disputes between the Provinces.

162. President may request an advisory opinion from the Court.

Chapter II.—The High Courts

166. Judges to be appointed by the President after consultation with the Chief Justice, the Governor and the Provincial Chief Justice.

170. High Courts may issue writs of *habeas corpus*, *mandamus*, prohibition, *quo warranto* and *certiorari*.

PART X THE SERVICES OF PAKISTAN

Chapter I.—Services

179–183. Conditions of service and protection against arbitrary treatment.

Chapter II.—Public Service Commissions

186. Public Service Commissions to be appointed by the President and Governors in their discretion.

188. Functions of Public Service Commissions; examinations, disciplinary matters, claims.

PART XI EMERGENCY PROVISIONS

191. (1) If the President is satisfied that a grave emergency exists in which the security or economic life of Pakistan, or any part thereof, is threatened by war or external aggression, or by internal disturbance beyond the power of a Provincial Government to control, he may issue a Proclamation of Emergency . . .

(2) Under such Proclamation, the President may assume the powers of a Provincial Government and Parliament may legislate for a Province.

(6) A Proclamation shall be laid before the National Assembly as soon as conditions make it practicable for the President to summon that Assembly, and if approved by the Assembly, shall remain in force until it is revoked, or if disapproved, shall cease to operate from the date of disapproval.

192. During a national emergency the President may suspend the fundamental rights.

193. If the President, 'is satisfied that a situation has arisen in which the government of the Province cannot be carried on in accordance with the provisions of the Constitution,' he may assume the powers of the Provincial Government. A Proclamation under this Article is valid for two months but may be extended by the National Assembly for a further four months.

194. Under a state of financial emergency the federal government may issue certain directions to a Province.

PART XII GENERAL PROVISIONS

Chapter I.—Islamic Provisions

197. (1) The President shall set up an organization for Islamic research and instruction in advanced studies to assist in the reconstruction of Muslim society on a truly Islamic basis.

198. (1) No law shall be enacted which is repugnant to the Injunctions of Islam as laid down in the Holy Quran and Sunnah ... and existing law shall be brought into conformity with such Injunctions.

(3) The President is to appoint a Commission to advise on the enactment of Islamic law.

Chapter II.—Appointment of Special Councils and Boards

199. The President shall constitute a National Economic Council, representing the Federation and the Provinces. It shall formulate plans which shall 'aim at ensuring that uniform standards are attained in the economic development of all parts of the country.'

Chapter V.—Miscellaneous

211. Parliament shall determine the area of the federal capital, the administration of which shall vest in the President.

214. (1) The State languages of Pakistan shall be Urdu and Bengali:

Provided that for the period of twenty years from the Constitution Day, English shall continue to be used for all

Pakistan

official purposes for which it was used in Pakistan immediately before the Constitution Day . . .

216. The Constitution may be amended by an Act of Parliament, provided that it has been approved by a majority of the total membership of the Assembly and two-thirds of those present and voting. Certain Articles may be amended only with the consent of the Province(s) concerned.

PART XIII TEMPORARY AND TRANSITIONAL PROVISIONS

This Part provides for the conversion of the existing machinery of government into conformity with the Constitution.

First Schedule. Election of President.

1. The Chief Election Commissioner shall hold and conduct any election to the office of President, and shall be the Returning Officer for such election.

2–22. If only two candidates are entered, the election is by simple majority. If no candidate obtains more than half the votes cast, the candidate with the least votes shall be excluded and a second vote held; this process continues until one candidate has obtained a majority.

Fifth Schedule
Federal List

The federal list of legislative powers includes: defence and associated industries; foreign affairs; citizenship and aliens; foreign and inter-provincial trade; currency and banking; stock exchanges; corporations with business in more than one Province; patents and copyright; navigation and shipping; major ports; posts and telecommunications; mineral oil and natural gas; elections to the National and Provincial Assemblies; preventive detention for reasons connected with defence, foreign affairs or security; federal services; privileges and immunities of the President and Governors; federal taxes.

The Constitution

Concurrent List

Civil and criminal law; scientific and industrial research; poisons and drugs; publishing and the Press; labour relations and social security; refugees and evacuee property; economic and social planning; monopolies; iron, steel, coal and minerals; arms and explosives.

Provincial List

Public order; administration of justice; police; preventive detention for public order purposes; prisons; land; corporations within the Province; land revenue; agriculture; local government; water; education; public health; railways; roads and bridges; vehicles; intoxicating liquor; opium; industries; factories; mines and mineral development; trade and commerce within the Province; markets; salt; forests; gambling; fisheries; professions; provincial services; *zakat*; charities; lunacy; *waqfs* and mosques; taxes on agricultural income, succession to agricultural income, succession to agricultural land, land and buildings; stamp duties and excise on drugs and alcohol; luxury taxes; capitation taxes.

APPENDIX II

CENTRAL AND PROVINCIAL GOVERNMENT

Governors-General and President

Aug. 1947	M. A. Jinnah	Sept. 1948
Sept. 1948	Khwajia Nazimuddin	Oct. 1951
Oct. 1951	Ghulam Mohammad	Sept. 1955
Sept. 1955	Iskandar Mirza	

Prime Minister

Aug. 1947	Liaquat Ali Khan	Oct. 1951
Oct. 1951	Khwaja Nazimuddin	April 1953
April 1953	Mohammed Ali	Aug. 1955
Aug. 1955	Chaudhri Mohamad Ali	Sept. 1956
Sept. 1956	H. S. Suhrawardy	

Ministers, Ministers of State and Deputy Ministers

I. I. Chundrigar		Aug 1947–May 1948 and Aug. 1955–Aug. 1956
Ghulam Mohammad		Aug. 1947–Oct. 1951
Sardar Abdur Rab Nishtar		Aug. 1947–Aug. 1949 and Nov. 1951–April 1953
Ghazanfar Ali Khan		Aug. 1947–July 1948
Jogendra Nath Mandal		Aug. 1947–Sept. 1950
Fazlur Rahman		Aug. 1947–April 1953
Muhammad Zafrullah Khan		Dec. 1947–Oct. 1954
Abdus Sattar Pirzada		Dec. 1947–April 1953
Khwaja Shahabuddin		May 1948–Nov. 1951
Mushtaq Ahmad Gurmani		Jan. 1949–Oct. 1949 and April 1950–Oct. 1954
Mahmud Husain	(D/M)	Feb. 1949–Oct. 1950
	(M/S)	Oct. 1950–Nov. 1951 Nov. 1951–April 1953
Sardar Bahadar Khan	(D/M)	Feb. 1949–Sept. 1949 Sept. 1949–Oct. 1954

Central and Provincial Governments

Ishtiaq Husain Qureshi	(D/M)	Feb. 1949–Oct. 1950
	(M/S)	Oct. 1950–Nov. 1951
		Nov. 1951–Oct. 1954
Nazir Ahmad Khan		Sept. 1949–Oct. 1951
A. M. Malik		Sept. 1949–Aug. 1955
Muhammad Nawaz Khan	(D/M)	Sept. 1949–June 1950
Azizuddin Ahmad	(M/S))	April 1951–April 1953
Ghyasuddin Pathan	(D/M	April 1951–Aug. 1952
	(M/S)	Aug. 1952–Oct. 1954
		Oct. 1954–Aug. 1955
Chaudhri Mohamad Ali		Oct. 1951–Sept. 1956
Syed Khalilur Rehman		Aug. 1952–April 1953
A. K. Brohi		April 1953–Oct. 1954
Abdul Qaiyum Khan		April 1953–Oct. 1954
Shoaib Qureshi		April 1953–Oct. 1954
Tafazzal Ali		Dec. 1953–Oct. 1954
Sardar Amir Azam Khan	(M/S)	Dec. 1953–Sept. 1956
		Sept. 1956–
Murtaza Raza Chaudhry		Dec. 1953–Aug. 1955
M. A. H. Ispahani		Oct. 1954–Aug. 1955
Iskandar Mirza		Oct. 1954–Aug. 1955
Mohammad Ayub Khan		Oct. 1954–Aug. 1955
Ghulam Ali Talpur		Oct. 1954–March 1955 and Sept. 1956–
Khan Sahib		Oct. 1954–Oct. 1955
H. I. Rahimtoola		Nov. 1954–Sept. 1956
Syed Abid Hussain		Dec. 1954–Oct. 1955
H. S. Suhrawardy		Dec. 1954–Aug. 1955 (and Prime Minister Sept. 1956)
Mumtaz Ali Khan		Dec. 1954–Aug. 1955
Abu Hussain Sarkar		Jan. 1955–June 1955
A. K. Fazlul Huq		Aug. 1955–Mar. 1956
Kamini Kumar Dutta		Aug. 1955–Sept. 1956
Ali Muhammed Rashdi		Aug. 1955–Aug. 1956
Nurul Huq Chaudhry		Aug. 1955–Sept. 1956
Abdul Latif Biswas		Aug. 1955–Sept. 1956
Lutfur Rahman Khan	(M/S)	Aug. 1955–Sept. 1956

Pakistan

Hamidul Huq Chowdhury	Sept. 1955–Sept. 1956
Akshay Kumar Das	Sept. 1955–Sept. 1956
Syed Amjad Ali	Oct. 1955–
M. R. Kayani	Oct. 1955–Sept. 1956
Abdus Sattar	Mar. 1956–Sept. 1956
Firoz Khan Noon	Sept. 1956–
Abulmansur Ahmad	Sept. 1956–
Muhammad Abdul Khaleque	Sept. 1956–
A. H. Dildar Ahmed	Sept. 1956–
Mian Jaffer Shah	Sept. 1956–
Zahiruddin	Sept. 1956–
Rasa Raj Mondal (M/S)	Sept. 1956–

Governors[1] and Chief Ministers of Provinces[2]

East Pakistan (East Bengal)
Governor

1947–50	Sir Frederick Bourne
1950–53	Malik Firoz Khan Noon
1953–54	Chaudhri Khaliquzzaman
1954	Iskandar Mirza
1956–	A. K. Fazlul Huq

Chief Minister

1947–51	Khwaja Nazimuddin
1951–54	Nurul Amin
1954	A. K. Fazlul Huq
1955–56	Abu Hussain Sarkar
1956–	Ataur Rahman Khan

[1] The names of persons appointed as acting Governor have not been listed. Thus the interval in the governorship of East Bengal between Iskandar Mirza and Fazlul Huq (1954–56) was filled by a series of acting Governors, including Sir Thomas Ellis and Justice Shahabuddin.

[2] The intervals between ministries in East Bengal, Punjab and Sind are attributable to periods of Governor's rule under Section 92A of the Government of India Act.

Central and Provincial Governments

Punjab (West Punjab)

1947–49	Sir Francis Mudie
1949–51	Sardar Abdur Rab Nishtar
1951–53	I. I. Chundrigar
1953–54	Mian Aminuddin
1954	H. I. Rahimtoola
1954–55	Mushtaq Ahmad Gurmani

Chief Minister

1947–49	Khan of Mamdot
1951–53	Mian M. M. Daultana
1953–55	Malik Firoz Khan Noon
1955	Abdul Hamid Khan Dasti

Sind
Governor

1947–48	G. H. Hidayatullah
1948–52	Din Mohammad
1953–54	H. I. Rahimtoola
1954–55	Khan of Mamdot

Chief Minister

1947–48	M. A. Khuhro
1948–49	Pir Ilahi Bakhsh
1949–50	Yussuf Haroon
1950–51	Kazi Fazlullah
1951	M. A. Khuhro
1953–54	Pirzada Abdus Sattar
1954–55	M. A. Khuhro

North-West Frontier Province
Governor

1947–48	Sir George Cunningham
1948–49	Sir Ambrose Dundas
1949–50	Sahibzada Mohammad Kurshid
1950–51	I. I. Chundrigar
1951–54	Khwaja Shahabuddin
1954–55	Qurban Ali

Pakistan

Chief Minister

1947	Dr. Khan Sahib
1947–53	Abdul Qaiyum Khan
1953–55	Sardar Abdur Rashid
1955	Sardar Bahadur Khan

West Pakistan
Governor

1955–57	Mushtaq Ahmad Gurmani

Chief Minister

1955–57	Dr. Khan Sahib

APPENDIX III

SELECT BIBLIOGRAPHY

JAMIL-UD-DIN AHMAD (ed.): *Speeches and Writing of Mr. Jinnah*, Vol. I (5th ed., Lahore, 1952); Vol. II (Lahore, 1947).

MUSHTAQ AHMAD: *The United Nations and Pakistan* (Karachi, 1955).

NAFIS AHMAD: 'The Indo-Pakistan Boundary Disputes Tribunal 1949-50,' *Geographical Review*, 43 (July 1953), pp. 329-37.

A. H. ALBIRUNI (pseud.): *Makers of Pakistan and Modern Muslim India* (Lahore, 1950).

AMANULLAH KHAN: *The Punjab Legislative Assembly* (University of the Panjab, M.A. thesis, 30/9/54).

MUHAMMAD ASAD (Leopold Weiss): 'Islamic Constitution Making,' *Arafat* (Lahore), March, 1948.

AKHTAR HASSAN ASLAM: *The Deputy Commissioner* (University of the Panjab, M.A. thesis, 30/9/53, and revised version 1956).

S. D. BAILEY: *Parliamentary Government in Southern Asia* (London, 1953).

LEONARD BINDER: *Islamic Constitutional Theory and Politics in Pakistan* (Harvard University thesis, 1956).

LORD BIRDWOOD: *A Continent Decides* (London, 1954).

LORD BIRDWOOD: *Two Nations and Kashmir* (London, 1956).

HECTOR BOLITHO: *Jinnah* (London, 1954).

M. BRECHER: *The Struggle for Kashmir* (Toronto, 1953).

A. K. BROHI: *An Adventure in Self-Expression* (Karachi, 1955).

W. N. BROWN: *The United States and India and Pakistan* (Cambridge, Mass., 1953).

G. J. CALDER: 'Constitutional Debates in Pakistan,' *Muslim World*, 46 (January, April and July 1956), pp. 40-60, 144-56, 253-71.

K. CALLARD: 'The Political Stability of Pakistan,' *Pacific Affairs*, Vol. XXIX, pp. 5-20, March 1956.

A. CAMPBELL-JOHNSON: *Mission with Mountbatten* (London, 1951).

Pakistan

H. E. B. CATLEY: 'Indian and Pakistan Relations with the Middle East,' *Asian Review*, 50 (July 1954), pp. 198–209.

MOHAMMED AHSEN CHAUDHRI: 'Pakistan and the Soviet Bloc,' *Pakistan Horizon*, Vol. IX, June 1956.

MOHAMMED AHSEN CHAUDHRI: 'The Relations of Pakistan with Afghanistan,' *Pakistan Horizon*, Vol. VIII, December 1955.

G. W. CHOUDHURY: 'Constitution Making in Pakistan,' *Western Political Quarterly*, December 1955.

G. W. CHOUDHURY: 'The Constitution of Pakistan,' *Pacific Affairs*, Vol. XXIX (September 1956), pp. 243–52.

KINGSLEY DAVIS: *The Population of India and Pakistan* (Princeton, 1951).

KEMAL A. FARUKI: *Ijma and the Gate of Ijtihad* (Karachi, 1954).

KEMAL A. FARUKI: *Islamic Constitution* (Karachi, 1952).

HERBERT FELDMAN: *A Constitution for Pakistan* (Karachi, 1956).

D. S. FRANCK: 'Pakhtunistan—Disputed Disposition of a Tribal Land,' *Middle East Journal*, 6 (Winter, 1952), pp. 49–68.

A. GLEDHILL: 'The Pakistan Constitution,' *Public Law*, Winter, 1956, pp. 350–67.

SIR PERCIVAL GRIFFTHS: *The British Impact on India* (London, 1952).

SIR JOHN HARDING: 'The India and Pakistan Armies of Today,' *Asian Review*, 51 (July 1955), pp. 175–87.

K. SARWAR HASAN: 'The Foreign Policy of Mr. Liaquat Ali Khan,' *Pakistan Horizon*, Vol. IV, December 1956, pp. 181–99.

SIR WILLIAM HUNTER: *The Indian Mussalmans* (Calcutta, 1945, 1st ed., 1871).

MOHAMMAD IQBAL: *Law of Preventive Detention in England, India and Pakistan* (Lahore, 1955).

FAREED S. JAFRI: *The Spirit of Pakistan* (Karachi, 1951).

JAMAAT-I-ISLAMI: *Trial of Maudoodi* (Karachi, 2nd ed., 1954).

JAMAAT-I-ISLAMI: *Statement of Syed Abul Ala Maudoodi before the Punjab Disturbances Court of Inquiry* (Karachi, n.d.).

Select Bibliography

SIR IVOR JENNINGS: *Constitutional Problems in Pakistan* (London, 1957).
SIR IVOR JENNINGS: *The Approach to Self-Government* (London, 1956).
SIR IVOR JENNINGS: 'Crown and Commonwealth in Asia,' *International Affairs*, 32 (April 1956), pp. 137–47.
Quaid-e-Azam Speaks (Karachi, n.d.).
J. KORBEL: *Danger in Kashmir* (Princeton, 1954).
R. D. LAMBERT: 'Religion, Economics and Violence in Bengal,' *Middle East Journal*, July 1950.
LIAQUAT ALI KHAN: *Pakistan: Heart of Asia* (Cambridge, Mass., 1951).
E. W. R. LUMBY: *The Transfer of Power in India* (London, 1954).
S. MARON: 'The Problems of East Pakistan,' *Pacific Affairs*, Vol. XXVIII (June, 1955), pp. 132–44.
E. S. MASON: *Promoting Economic Development: the United States and Southern Asia* (Claremont, Calif., 1955).
SYED ABUL ALA MAUDUDI: *Islamic Law and Constitution* (Karachi, 1955).
SYED ABUL ALA MAUDUDI: *The Process of Islamic Revolution* (Lahore, 2nd ed., 1955).
SYED ABUL ALA MAUDUDI: *The Qadiani Problem* (Karachi, 1953).
SYED ABUL ALA MAUDUDI: *Nationalism and India* (Pathankot, 1947).
TIBOR MENDE: *South-East Asia Between Two Worlds* (New York, 1955).
MUFAKHIR (pseud.): *A Draft Modern Islamic Constitution for Pakistan* (Karachi, 1954).
DILSHAD NAJMUDDIN: *Political Parties in Pakistan* (University of Panjab, M.A. thesis, 1/10/55).
SARET C. V. NARASIMHAN: *The Other Side* (Karachi, 1955).
Pakistan 1955–6 (Karachi, 1956) (also other years).
'The Fundamentals of Pakistan's Foreign Policy,' *Pakistan Horizon*, Vol. IX, March 1956.
'Pakistan: Towards a General Election,' *Round Table* (September 1956), pp. 382–5.

Pakistan

Pakistan, Constituent Assembly (Legislature), Public Accounts Committee, *Report*, 1947-8 (also later annual issues).

Government of Pakistan, Committee on Organization, Structure and Level of Expenditure—*Interim Report 1950; Second Interim Report 1951; Third Report 1953* (known as *Administrative Enquiry Committee Reports*).

Government of Pakistan, *First Five Year Plan* (Vols. 1 and 2), Draft Report (Karachi, 1956).

Government of Pakistan, *Report of the Council for Administration of West Pakistan* (Lahore, 1955).

Government of Pakistan, *Foreign Relations* (Karachi, 1956).

Government of Pakistan, *Administrative Directory of the Government of Pakistan* (1950).

Government of Pakistan, Pakistan Public Service Commission, *Fourth Report 1952* (1955).

Government of Pakistan, Pakistan Public Service Commission, *Report on the Central Superior Services Examination 1953* (also other years).

Government of Pakistan, *Explanatory Memorandum on the Budget of the Government of Pakistan for 1956–57 and Economic Survey for 1955* (also other years).

Government of Pakistan, *The Assassination of Mr. Liaquat Ali Khan: Report of the Commission of Enquiry* (Karachi, 1952).

Government of the Punjab, *Report of the Court of Inquiry to Inquire into the Punjab Disturbances of 1953* (Lahore, 1954) (known as *Munir Report*).

I. H. QURESHI: *Pakistan: An Islamic Democracy* (Lahore, n.d.).

I. H. QURESHI: *The Pakistani Way of Life* (New York, 1956).

I. H. QURESHI: 'Relations Between Great Britain and the Indo-Pakistan Sub-Continent,' *Confluence*, 4 (June 1956), pp. 471–86.

CHOUDHURY RAHMAT ALI: *Pakistan, The Fatherland of the Pak Nation* (3rd ed., Cambridge, 1946).

A. B. RAJPUT: *Muslim League Yesterday and Today* (Lahore, 1948).

M. H. SAIYID: *Mohammad Ali Jinnah* (Lahore, 2nd ed., 1953).

G. M. SAYED: *Struggle for a New Sind* (Karachi, 1949).

KHALID BIN SAYEED: 'The Governor-General of Pakistan,' *Pakistan Horizon*, Vol. VIII, June 1955.

Select Bibliography

KHALID BIN SAYEED: *The Central Government of Pakistan 1947–51* (McGill University thesis, 1956).

W. C. SMITH: 'Hyderabad, A Muslim Tragedy,' *Middle East Journal*, Spring, 1955.

W. C. SMITH: *Modern Islam in India* (London, 1946).

W. C. SMITH: *Pakistan as an Islamic State* (Lahore, 1951).

J. W. SPAIN: 'Military Assistance for Pakistan,' *American Political Science Review*, 48 (September, 1954), pp. 738–51.

J. SPAIN: 'Pakistan's North West Frontier Province,' *Middle East Journal*, January 1954.

SIR PERCIVAL SPEAR: *India, Pakistan and the West* (London, 1949).

IAN STEPHENS: *Horned Moon* (London, 1953).

RICHARD SYMONDS: *The Making of Pakistan* (London, 3rd ed., 1951).

HUGH TINKER: *The Foundations of Local Self-Government in India, Pakistan and Burma* (London, 1954).

L. R. WILLIAMS: 'The Indus Canals Waters Problem,' *Asian Review*, 51 (April 1955), pp. 137–54.

GLOSSARY

Alim	man of (religious) learning
Amir	ruler
Faqih	learned in (Islamic) law
Fiqh	Islamic case law
Hadith	tradition (of the Prophet)
Ijma	consensus
Ijtihad	free inquiry
Khalifa	caliph
Lathi	staff
Maulana	religious title
Millat	community of believers
Mir	nobleman
Mullah	religious functionary
Nam ke waste	nominally
Nawab	nobleman
Panch shila	five principles
Pir	mystic guide
Quaid-i-Azam	Great Leader
Raj	rule, dominion
Shariat	law (Islamic)
Shura	consultation
Sunnah	traditions (of the Prophet)
Talimaat-e-Islamia	teaching of Islam
Ulama	plural of alim
Zakat	alms tithe
Zamindar	landowner

INDEX

Abdur Rashid Khan, *see* Rashid
Abdul Ghaffar Khan, 54, 81, 85, 110, 271 *n.*, 273
Abdul Qaiyum Khan, *see* Qaiyum
Afghanistan, Relations with, 303, 317–18
Ahmadiya, see also Munir Commission, Riots against, 52, 53, 135–36, 204–7
Ataur Rahman Khan, 33, 173 *n.*, 181 *n.*
Awami League, 25, 31–33, 55, 57, 59, 61, 64, 65–72, 73, 114, 120, 227, 249
Ayub Khan, General, 24, 140, 141, 300
Azad Pakistan Party, 55, 74–75, 85, 121

Baghdad Pact, 18, 321–22
Bahadur Khan, Sardar, 26, 62, 63, 128, 136 *n.*, 142 *n.*
Bahawalpur, 155, 184; Representation, 79; Revenue, 185
Baluchistan, 118, 155, 184; States Union, 79, 155
Basic Principles Committee, 90–100, 210, 211, 217, 224; Composition, 90; Report, 86, 139, 148, 179, 182, 216, 220, 227, 255
Bengal, *see also* East Pakistan, 14, 77, 158
Bhashani, Maulana, 68, 201 *n.*
Brohi, A. K., 86, 88, 139, 148, 213–14, 242
Budget, 22, 115

Cabinet, 20–25, 58, 65, 119, 124–54, and Assembly, 86–87, 110, 113
Canal Waters, 16, 21, 311–12
Chattopadhyaya Sris Chandra, 114, 242, 254, 259
Christian(s), 262–64; Representation, 78, 79, 241
Chundrigar, I. I., 25 *n.*, 66, 151, 171, 253
Civil Service, 18, 169–70, 284–301; Minorities in, 259–60
Communist Party, 55, 73–74, 328
Congress, Indian National, 12, 15, 34, 54, 77, 195, 200, 204, 237, 303, 306
Congress, Pakistan National, 54, 55, 60, 64, 65, 84–85, 120–21, 242–43, 254

Constituent Assembly, *see also* National Assembly, 20–21, 23, 48, 77–123, 128, 132, 136, 143, 205–6, 219, 249; Committees, 116 (*see also* Basic Principles, Public Accounts); Composition, 77–83; Dissolution, 24, 146–48; Parties in, 64–68, 74; Sessions, 80
Corruption, 297–99
Court, Federal, 30–31, 128, 143–47, 169, 189, 281; Sind Chief, 142

Dasti, Hamid Khan, 29, 62,128
Daultana, Mian Mumtaz Mohammad 28, 43, 51, 60, 63, 75, 83 *n.*, 103 *n.*, 104, 119, 128, 136, 137, 190, 205, 207
Detention, Preventive, 164, 273–78, 280
Devaluation, 17, 312
Distribution, Federal, 155–93; Finances 165–68; Offices, 134; Powers, 163–65; Seats, 87, 92, 97, 178–80

East Pakistan, 18, 24, 29–30, 31, 68, 155, 158, 159, 160, 172–83, 233, 276; Assembly 251; Dissatisfaction, 92,97, 156–61; Election, 29–30, 56–57, 242, 248; Minorities, 232, 245; Parties, 56–61, 72–73; Revenue, 166–68, 175–77
Elections, 139, 221–22, 269; Constituent Assembly, 77; East Pakistan, 29–30, 56–57, 67, 242, 248; N.-W.F.P., 55; Punjab, 55, 70; Sind, 27; West Pakistan, 67, 192
Electorates, Separate, 78, 240–54; Electorate Act (1956), 252 *n.* (1957), 252 *n.*
Emergency, Powers, 143, 152, 154, 159–62, 169; Proclamation, 141, 143
Evacuee Property, 17, 21, 282, 311; Minorities, 260–61

Fazlul Huq, A. K., 29, 30, 31, 57, 58, 60, 67, 72–73, 83 *n.*, 85, 119, 153, 158, 171
Fazlur Rahman, 23, 110, 111, 119, 136 *n.*, 189
Federalism, *see* Distribution, Federal

Ganatantri Dal, 60, 74, 122
Gazder, M. H., 102, 104, 106, 108, 109–11, 140

353

Pakistan

Ghulam Mohammad, 22, 23, 32, 81, 112, 128, 133-48, 315, 323
Government of India Act (1935), 24, 25, 85, 92, 95, 101-13, 122, 123, 126, 127, 129, 146, 147, 154, 155, 159, 163, 164, 169, 240, 273
Governor-General, *see also* President, 20-23, 27, 32, 109, 118, 127, 188, 207; Assent, 101; Discretion, 104; Powers, 102-13, 129-48, 160, 170
Governor, Provincial, 24, 27, 83, 103, 119, 123, 152-53, 159, 169, 170-72, 207; Powers, 102, 154, 160, 162
Gurmani, Mushtaq Ahmad, 25 n., 29, 32, 62, 119, 136 n., 138, 142 n., 153, 171, 189, 289

Hamidul Huq Chowdhury, 67, 81, 103 n., 174, 319, 321-23
Hindu(s), 11, 12, 15, 54, 99, 110, 157, 198-99, 232-65, and Islam, 89; Representation, 79, 113
Hyderabad, 16, 310

Iftikharuddin, Mian, 75, 110, 117, 121, 324
India, Relations with (*see also* Kashmir, Canal Waters), 15, 16, 17, 155, 265 303-13
Indus, 16, 184, 311-12
Iqbal, Mohammad, 198, 220
Islam, 11, 35, 69, 87, 194-231, and democracy, 125, and minorities, 234-54
Islamic State, 89, 93-96, 202-31, 234-35, 254
Ispahani, M. A. H., 25, 81, 140, 141

Jamaat-I-Islami, 55, 203, 205 n.
Jinnah, Mohammad Ali, 19-21, 26, 27, 34, 36, 100, 126, 131, 159, 182, 198-200, 225, 233, 310
Junagadh, 16, 155 n., 305

Karachi, 27, 118, 155, 167, 173, 177, 184, 185, 192
Kashmir, 16, 21, 305-10, 320
Khairpur, 184; Representation, 79, 155; Revenue, 176, 185
Khan, Liaquat Ali, *see* Liaquat
Khan Sahib, Dr., 25, 26, 32, 62, 65, 75, 119, 142, 189, 250
Khilafat, 34-36, 223

Khuhro, Muhammad Ayub, 27, 43, 50, 55, 62, 63, 75, 81, 83 n., 103 n., 119, 128, 185 n., 188
Krishak Sramik Party, *see also* United Front, 57, 72-73, 153

Lahore, 18; Resolution, 36, 57, 158; Riots, 136, 207
Language, State, 87, 88, 92, 94, 97, 99 n., 180-83
Liaquat Ali Khan, 20, 21, 23, 38-39, 40, 44, 63, 89, 90, 92, 100, 132, 134, 135, 163, 174 n., 181 n., 200, 209, 216, 278, 321

Mamdot, Iftikhar Husain Khan, 28, 43, 51, 55, 63, 68, 81, 83 n., 103 n., 118
Mandal, Jogendra Nath, 81, 84, 246
Maududi, Maulana Abul Ala, 93, 200 n., 202 n., 208, 211 n., 227
Millat, 12, 38, 215, 223, 224, 234-36
Minorities, *see also* Hindu(s), Sikh(s), Christian(s), etc., 100, 119, 232-65
Mirza, Iskandar, 24, 25 n., 30, 32, 100, 104, 111, 119, 134, 140, 141, 142, 152, 160, 171, 230 n., 276, 285, 317, 323
Mohamad Ali, Chaudhri, 31, 45, 65, 67, 119, 134, 136 n., 138, 308, 319
Mohammed Ali, 23, 29, 31, 45, 49, 65, 81, 87, 88, 97, 101, 105, 110, 112, 119, 128, 134, 138-42, 163, 180, 321
Munir Commission, 22 n., 204-7, 209, 216, 228, 234
Muslim Countries, 18, 303, 314-18, 322
Muslim League, 20, 23-25, 27, 29, 33, 34-49, 53-58, 62, 64, 65, 68, 70, 77, 78, 82, 86, 89, 100, 114, 125-26, 161, 200, 223, 241, 245, 249, 257, 319,; Candidates, 47; Council, 39, 40-41, 44, 46, 62; East Pakistan, 227, 262; Organisation, 40-42, 47, 163; Parliamentary Party, 31, 45, 83, 87, 97-99, 106, 110, 112, 120, 136, 187; Punjab, 206; Working Committee, 41, 44, 66

National Assembly, *see also* Constituent Assembly, 149, 150, 153-54
National Party, 76, 192 n.
Nazimuddin, Khwaja, 20, 23, 25 n., 29, 45, 81, 83 n., 101, 109, 110, 127, 128, 133-37, 148, 163, 174 n., 183, 205, 207

354

Index

Nehru, Jawaharlal, 321, 323
Nishtar, Sardar Abdur Rab Khan, 23, 25 *n.*, 46, 62, 81, 93, 136 *n.*, 171, 209, 210, 217, 315
Nizam-i-Islam Party, 57, 61, 72, 203
Noon, Firoz Khan, 13, 25 *n.*, 28, 51, 65, 81, 83 *n.*, 119, 120, 128, 136, 163, 171, 185 *n.*, 302, 314 *n.*, 323
North-West Frontier Province, 14, 18, 26, 68, 155, 184–92; Election, 55, 77, Revenue, 166; States, 79, 155
Nurul Amin, 29, 83 *n.*, 98, 110, 175 *n.*, 177

Objectives Resolution, 89–90, 159, 209, 213, 216, 217, 226, 254
One Unit, *see* West Pakistan—Unification

Pakhtunistan, 317–18
Parsi(s), 262–64; Representation, 79, 241
Pirzada, Abdus Sattar Abdur Rahman, 23, 25 *n.*, 50, 51, 64, 83 *n.*, 103 *n.*, 104, 109, 110, 128, 136 *n.*, 187, 188
Planning Board, 295, 299
President, *see also* Governor-General, 122, 123, 148–54, 169, 224, 225; Assent, 153
PRODA, 81, 102–5, 110, 111, 112, 140, 163, 174
Punjab, 14, 16, 18, 28–29, 68, 155, 160, 179, 184–92; Election, 55, 70; Minorities, 232; Revenue, 164, 176; Riots, 135–36, 137, 204–7, 227
Public Accounts Committee, 116
Public Service Commission, 294

Qadiani, *see* Ahmadiya
Qaiyum Khan, Abdul, 25 *n.*, 26, 82, 128, 139
Quaid-i-Azam, *see* Jinnah
Qureshi, Ishtiaq Husain, 136 *n.*, 177 *n.*, 212–13, 231

Rahimtoola, Habib Ibrahim, 25
Rashid Khan, Sardar Abdur, 26, 63, 68, 128, 163, 187 *n.*, 190
Rawalpindi, 21; Conspiracy, 279
Refugees, 14, 15, 19, 21, 125; East Pakistan, 263–65; Representation, 79

Republican Party, 32, 33, 63–67, 75–76, 244, 251
Repugnancy, 96, 220–21, 227
Rights Fundamental, 154, 280–82; Committee, 256–58, 280

Safety Acts, 271–77; East Pakistan, 73
Sarkar, Abu Hussain, 31, 32, 59, 60, 120
Scheduled Castes, 84; Federation, 60, 64, 65, 120, 122, 248; Representation, 78, 241, 246–48
Shahabuddin, Khwaja, 25 *n.*, 81, 171
Sheikh Abdullah, 308
Sikh(s), 18, 54; Representation, 79
Sind, 14, 18, 26–28, 155, 160, 184–92; Revenue, 167, 176
South-East Asia Treaty, 18, 321–22
Suhrawardy, Husain Shaheed, 25, 29, 31, 32, 59, 60, 65, 68–72, 85, 119, 120, 121, 134, 144, 158, 191, 227, 252–54, 319
Supreme Court, *see* Court—Federal

Talimaat-e-Islamia, 91, 94–96, 204, 206, 224 *n.*, 225, 234
Talpur, Mir Ghulam Ali, 25, 103 *n.*, 141
Tamizuddin Khan, 21, 90, 110, 201 *n.*
Two-Nation Theory, 12, 15, 16, 37 199, 201, 233, 250, 252–53, 304

Ulama, 95, 199, 202, 205, 208–16, 224–28, 234–35
United Front, 24, 29, 31, 33, 57–61, 64–67, 68, 72–73, 74, 119, 120, 160, 161, 187, 203, 247, 249, 253, 277
United Kingdom, Relations with, 319–20
United Progressive Party, 60, 64, 65, 122
United States, Relations with, 17, 113, 138, 302, 320–22

West Pakistan, 16, 31, 159, 179–80; Parties, 61–64; Revenue, 167; Unification, 28, 32, 71, 120, 143, 183–93

Zafrullah Khan, Chaudhri Mohammad, 53, 136 *n.*, 142 *n.*, 204, 205, 316, 323